P9-EMH-704

THE WAR WITHIN
THE UNION
HIGH COMMAND

MODERN WAR STUDIES

Theodore A. Wilson
General Editor

Raymond A. Callahan
J. Garry Clifford
Jacob W. Kipp
Jay Luvaas
Allan R. Millett
Carol Reardon
Dennis Showalter
David R. Stone

Series Editors

THE WAR WITHIN THE UNION HIGH COMMAND

Politics and Generalship during the Civil War

Thomas J. Goss

University Press of Kansas

© 2003 by the University Press of Kansas
All rights reserved

Published by the University Press of Kansas (Lawrence, Kansas 66049), which was organized by the Kansas Board of Regents and is operated and funded by Emporia State University, Fort Hays State University, Kansas State University, Pittsburg State University,
the University of Kansas, and Wichita State University

A Bookspan Book Club Edition

Library of Congress Cataloging-in-Publication Data

Goss, Thomas Joseph, 1964–
    The war within the Union high command : politics and generalship
during the Civil War / Thomas Joseph Goss.
        p. cm. — (Modern war studies)
Includes bibliographical references and index.
    ISBN 0-7006-1263-7 (cloth : alk. paper)
    1. United States—History—Civil War, 1861–1865—Campaigns. 2.
Generals—United States—History—19th century. 3. Command of
troops—History—19th century. 4. United States. Army—History—Civil
War, 1861–1865. 5. United States—Politics and government—1861–1865. 6.
United States—Military policy. 7. Military art and science—United
States—History—19th century. 8. Generals—United States—Biography. I.
Title. II. Series.
    E470.G74 2003
    973.7'41—dc21
                        2003005821

British Library Cataloguing in Publication Data is available.

Printed in the United States of America

10 9 8 7 6 5 4 3 2 1

The paper used in this publication meets the minimum requirements of the American
National Standard for Permanence of Paper for Printed Library Materials Z39.48-1984.

DEDICATED TO MY FATHER AND MOTHER

*who nurtured my curiosity enough while I was young
to aspire to start a project this large,
while instilling in me the discipline to complete it.*

CONTENTS

ACKNOWLEDGMENTS

I wish to thank my doctoral adviser, Dr. Mark Grimsley, for providing intellectual support and patience to a busy, anxious, and at times overly eager graduate student. I am also grateful to Dr. Allan R. Millett and Dr. David Stebenne for being on both my master's and doctoral committees and providing suggestions that greatly improved my final product. I thank Dr. Samuel Watson for enduring the painful process of proofreading my initial prose and Dr. Carol Reardon for helping the formulation of my initial organization.

In retrospect, I recognize the debt I owe to Colonel Cole Kingseed (ret.) for keeping my nose to the grindstone and providing periodic encouragement during my seemingly long years of writing. I also wish to thank Alan Aimone and the research staff at the USMA Archives as well as the staffs of the Library of Congress and the National Archives for enduring and assisting my endless research questions.

I am especially grateful to my wife Andria and two wonderful daughters, without whose toleration and encouragement this project would not have been possible.

INTRODUCTION

In the spring of 1864, Union armies stood poised to start the hoped-for final campaigns against the Confederacy. Yet when Union Major General Henry Wager Halleck contemplated the potential effectiveness of these armies, he was troubled by his lack of confidence in some of the men assigned to command such vast forces. After three years of war and a progression of Union commanders, three of the five army commanders directing these offensives were "political generals" that Halleck and many of his regular army peers held in utter contempt. As chief of staff of the Union army and its former commanding general, Halleck had a harsh judgment of the capability of this type of amateur commander and asserted that "it seems little better than murder to give important commands to men such as [Nathaniel] Banks, [Benjamin] Butler, [John] McClernand, [Franz] Sigel, and Lew Wallace, and yet it seems impossible to prevent it."[1] Halleck's frustration was evidence of the twin strands of a national military heritage that shaped the armies of the Civil War: an embryonic professional spirit in the fledgling American regular army officer corps and a cultural faith in "natural genius" and the perceived ability of every American to master the required military skills to command as a wartime volunteer officer.[2] During the course of the war, this stereotyped division between regular army general officers and political generals developed into an often bitter and partisan relationship that symbolized the friction between these two military traditions.

An interesting historical question arises from Halleck's complaint to William T. Sherman after being appointed Union chief of staff that "it seems impossible to prevent" politically appointed amateurs from gaining significant army commands, even after three long and bloody years of war punctuated with military debacles authored by untrained commanders. Most of the current military literature on the Civil War echoes this sentiment and ignores the amateur generals or interprets the appointment of this entire group of politicians-in-uniform as "simply murder" for the Union cause. The political generals' behavior and contributions to the war effort are often interpreted to be so poor that they create puzzlement about why they were appointed at all and why they were trusted to command troops in battle.[3] This aspect of the Civil War military policy seems decidedly odd by present-day standards. A typical congressman of today would no more believe he had the talent and ability to command a military battalion (much less a division or an entire army) than he would feel qualified to perform medical surgery. Examining the reasons why this selection process yielded so many general officers who lacked any form of military background, men who became caricatured as "political" generals, is one of the objectives of this book.

The very size of the general officer corps reflects the significance of general officer appointments and any perceived stereotypes on all aspects of the Civil War because the selection and actions of these commanders shaped the conduct of the war. The number of Civil War generals would have seemed impossible to the Union commander in chief at the start of the war, for by the surrender at Appomattox the president had appointed 583 general officers. Since the regular army officer corps in 1860 consisted of only 724 line officers, with 4 serving generals and 76 active field grade officers, the sources and selection of the generals who would be waging the war was an essential task for Lincoln.[4] The administration, the public, and the officers themselves tended to divide generals into two groups: professionals and amateurs. Over the course of the war, this division resulted in stereotypes of West Point graduates and political generals that shaped how individual officers were judged by peers and historians.

My goal is to examine the resulting conflict between U.S. Military Academy graduates and political generals during the American Civil War because this clash represented a larger struggle over the very definition of effective generalship and the evolution of professionalism in the U.S. Army officer corps. My growing interest in Civil War generalship and the presence of amateur commanders in the Union high command led me to question what the Lincoln administration actually expected of Union general officers, both individually and collectively, and upon which criteria they would be judged. Consequently, the focus of my research, given the relatively positive historical depiction of "professional" general officers (mostly West Pointers) and the mostly negative historical depiction of "political generals," was the differences between these two types of generals in their selection, their views of the war, and their relationship toward military policy. My main question evolved into what these stereotyped differences said about the nature of generalship during our nation's most bloody conflict.

A View through a Jominian Prism

Because of the intense interest in the war and the celebrated role that key military leaders play in its popular legacy, a constant theme in Civil War military history has been a struggle to examine and judge generalship. Prominent West Pointers have by far attracted the lion's share of attention. Ulysses S. Grant, William T. Sherman, Henry W. Halleck, and even general officers like Ambrose Burnside have multiple biographies. Often the measure for these men is taken as their individual success against opponents or in comparison to other West Pointers who preceded or succeeded them. A second type of Civil War officer, the politically appointed amateur, has also received attention from historians, but by no means in equal proportion and often only in contrast to their West Point peers. The degree of historical attention the regulars enjoy compared to their amateur peers reflects the triumph of the regulars' standard of what was required for successful generalship, and these criteria tend to base each general's historical standing on his record of tactical victories and operational success.

During the decades following the surrender at Appomattox, the legacy of Civil War political generals was recalled with contempt because the voices and norms of the more successful and famous commanders, nearly all West Pointers, dominated the recounting of the war. In books and magazine serials like *Battles and Leaders of the Civil War* (1887–1888), famed military commanders shared their combat experience with the public and popularized the glorious Union victories. The popularity of Ulysses S. Grant's *Personal Memoirs* and William T. Sherman's *Memoirs*, along with the autobiographies of other West Pointers, gave powerful voice to their version of the war. Especially in Grant's and Sherman's cases, these books also helped air the West Pointers' justifications for the harsh treatment given to some of the most prominent amateur commanders and continued the wartime practice of lumping these commanders together in a caricature of military incompetence and political ambition. In this arena and during this period, the reputations of former political generals also fared poorly because their articles and memoirs were not received with the same popular applause as their West Point peers, often because of the clouded endings to many of the amateurs' military careers.[5] In many of these initial firsthand accounts, the interest of the readership focused on the military clashes in the field, as that aspect of the war was the most popular and provided the more heroic elements of the struggle.

Until the advent of "new" military history in the 1960s and 1970s, most Civil War studies either focused on biographies of key figures like Grant, Sherman, or George B. McClellan or tilled the well-plowed fields of strategy and operational art principally because of the consistent popular interest in the conflict's military aspects.[6] Books that examined famous campaigns or sought the "key" to why commanders won and lost became immensely popular. A recent example of these well-received works is Thomas Buell's *The Warrior Generals*, which had a large popular appeal because of its focus on the "Aristocrat" Robert E. Lee, the "Yeoman" Ulysses S. Grant, and other perennial Civil War military favorites.[7] Except for well-worn stories of the Mexican War, these works rarely leave the campaign trail and the battlefield. This tendency has led to a continuance of the poor reputation of nearly all amateur commanders because of the books' nearly exclusive focus on military effectiveness and tactical win-loss records. These criteria have also elevated the stereotypical West Point general to a standing above the amateur generals in preparation, expertise, and tactical ability—with the added generalization of the unsuccessful "professional" commanders like McClellan or Don Carlos Buell, who is deemed to have failed because of individual character flaws. The reason for the perseverance of this Jominian approach to the topic may be the impact of popular interest and the inherent difficulty with wrestling with and conveying the partisan quagmire that was politics in wartime Washington.[8]

Some recent works have tended to be more balanced in addressing the political issues that influenced the military conduct of the war. This "new military history" has been defined as a study of the institutional, cultural, or social aspects of military organizations, with a conscious distancing from the attention previously given to command and operations. This approach "demilitarized" military history and produced studies that went beyond events on the battlefield as causal factors. Written by a new generation of historians, many of whom did not begin as military historians, their differing backgrounds and viewpoints advanced differing interpretations of the character and conduct of the war. Historians such as Bruce Catton and James McPherson, who view the Civil War primarily as a political struggle, necessarily present a different view of political generals.[9] Going beyond the question of simple tactical success, Catton, for example, raised important questions concerning the appointment of political generals.[10] Instead of focusing on the battlefield, these historians evaluated the appointment of popular political figures to military command in light of the effect these appointments had on the war effort as a whole.

In spite of the rise in prominence of political studies of the war, recent popular and academic Civil War history has tended to belittle political generals and has continued to use a Jominian approach to warfare that seems to have military operations occurring in a social and political vacuum. The enormous volume of literature on the military aspects of the Civil War has classified the amateur military commanders into a simple caricature of battlefield incompetence.[11] For example, the prominent study *Why the South Lost the Civil War* sums up Butler's contribution to the war effort by stating that he "became notorious largely for his military incompetence," and T. Harry Williams makes a similar cursory judgment of Massachusetts politician-turned-general Nathaniel Banks in his popular book *Lincoln and His Generals*.[12] Even Bruce Catton labeled the promotion of Banks to major general as "the strange custom of that war," which "entitled" Banks to a prominent military command simply because he was a national political figure.[13] Even recent biographies of McClellan, Grant, and Sherman, while addressing the complex political nature of Civil War generalship, focus primarily on the military aspect of the war and advance the stereotypical critiques of political generals whenever these amateurs interact with their subjects.[14] With critiques such as these, the label "political general" has become a signal for the reader to expect military ineptness on the battlefield, supposedly the primary source of a series of battlefield debacles for both sides.[15]

Though interpretations have changed as to what constituted an effective Civil War general, the stereotype of political generals as inept tacticians, ambitious schemers, and military failures has not evolved to an appreciable extent either for most historians or for much of the popular readership. The political generals' reputation for battlefield defeats is certainly accurate for many in this group, but this orthodox caricature neglects their vital contribution in rallying popular support for the war and convincing the people to join the mass citizen armies as volunteers. The principal cause for this neglected aspect of the war is the near universal acceptance of a definition of generalship based solely on military criteria, a lens rooted in popular beliefs about how the war was won or lost on famous battlefields and by famous generals.[16] The essentially Jominian view of warfare as an enclosed system of battles to force military defeat upon an enemy's armed forces may be a good tool for judging individual tactical ability, but it is deceptive if used to stereotype political generals because it places the burden of victory solely on the battlefield. By definition, a stereotype focuses on common group attributes at the expense of individual characteristics. Although stereotypes as generalizations have value, and the prevailing view of political generals as horrible battlefield leaders contains more than a grain of truth, some are counterproductive by obscuring a more nuanced picture. I believe this to be the case for the group of individuals selected as generals during the Civil War because of the persuasiveness of the "political general" stereotype.

A War within a War

These modern stereotypes of Union generals during the Civil War, and the friction between them, are not a product of modern historians, but in fact are a continuation of contemporary views. The cover of the popular weekly magazine *Vanity Fair* had a very obvious cartoon depiction of this sentiment as early as August 17, 1861. "Ah! Major General McClellan," says a member of Congress interrupting the Union commander, "I have a friend here I wish you to know—Make a capital Brigadier General—First class militia general—splendid politician—carried his county for Old Abe by a big majority. You may have heard of him—General Political Hack," hints the politician, pointing toward a portly uniformed man. "Yes, Sir," replied the professional-looking General McClellan, "Don't want him, Sir, at any price—had enough of that style already." The message behind newspaper coverage like this was not subtle, nor was it only directed at political generals. Although many editors during the first year of the war began to decry the political intrigue that these amateur commanders appeared to inject in the war, the tactical failure of West Point generals soon attracted their scorn, as many newspapers began to label all Military Academy graduates as being too slow and conservative to wage a civil war. In reality, the American Civil War was both a colossal military conflict and a vicious political struggle, intertwined and inseparable, and the derisive caricature of political generals and the harsh criticism of some West Pointers stem from differing understandings of the relationship between these two contests.

In spite of this long and often bloody heritage of embracing "natural leaders" to lead American armies in war, the conclusion of the Civil War marked the end of their prominence in the upper ranks of command. Some popular politicians would serve in uniform during the Spanish-American War in 1898, but the war was planned and conducted at the strategic level by regular officers who started long careers as cadets at the U.S. Military Academy (USMA). By 1917, the thought of a congressman or state governor leading troops in France without any military training or education would have been deemed ludicrous and perhaps even criminal by the American public, but, contrary to many interpretations current today, this same thought in 1860 would have been alien only to a handful of regular officers and advocates of military reform.[17] The source of this fundamental change in American military culture was a long and divisive struggle from 1861 to 1865 between regulars and amateurs over the definition and expectations of generalship. It took a war within a war to effect this shift because it was only through the discrediting of popular amateur commanders that the advocates of a professional officer corps could gain widespread recognition for their position that military expertise came from education and experience.

Just what was a "political general"? I use three basic criteria in answering this question.[18] The first is appointment directly from civilian life to general officer rank and immediate assignment to a command position without previous Civil War service in the lower officer ranks. Although this requirement automatically excludes a large number of volunteer generals who started the war as field grade officers and received their initial commissions for political reasons, these officers, mostly local and state political figures, owed at least some of their advancement to brigadier status to field service as a regimental commander. The second criterion is that a political general had a prewar career dominated by political, not military, service. The third condition, the lack of previous experience as a commissioned officer in the regular army or enough previous wartime military experience to justify appointment to general officer rank on solely military grounds, will again remove from consideration general officers who were appointed for reasons other than political patronage.

The Civil War officers who meet all three criteria are the group most historians consider when mentioning political generals. There are well-known exceptions to these simple criteria, such as Union Major General John C. Frémont, who was previously a commissioned officer in the regular army, and John A. Logan, who began the war as a regimental commander before being appointed as a general officer. Yet, both of these politicians-in-uniform were clearly made general officers and given important commands for political reasons, as demonstrated by the immense level of political pressure exerted on

Lincoln by their influential supporters. In the end, some subjective analysis must be done to present an accurate list of officers who should be considered political generals. To further limit the scope of this study, I concentrated on the members of this group with little or no military experience who were given command of large tactical units or military departments in order to evaluate the true contribution to the war effort these men made while maintaining a manageable number of case studies. The result was a focus on men such as Benjamin Butler, Nathaniel Banks, John McClernand, John Frémont, Franz Sigel, and John A. Logan, who not only met the subjective criteria but also were considered "political generals" by their fellow officers, the Lincoln administration, and contemporary newspapers. Most important, these specific individuals come to mind for modern Civil War readers as typical of this label.

In sharp contrast to these amateurs stood regular officers who either had made the army their career or had substantial combat experience from the Mexican War. To define these protoprofessional officers, I used the inverse criteria for the politically appointed amateurs. General officers during the Civil War who were selected based on their military qualifications for the job had at least one of two experiences in common: being a USMA graduate or service as a career regular with frontier or Mexican War experience. Yet, because of the annual promotion of Military Academy graduates into a very small officer corps, the ranks of the regular officer corps were dominated by West Pointers. Though terms like "regulars" and "professionals" are often used to describe this group, the only clear distinction that can be made to separate these regular officers from their amateur peers is by isolating Military Academy graduates. In contrast to the political generals, these men were chosen for senior positions in the Union army largely because of the diploma they had received from USMA. Therefore, when discussing "regulars" in the high command, I will consider only the graduates of the Military Academy, such as Halleck, Grant, Sherman, McClellan, or Ambrose Burnside, who were labeled as such by their fellow officers and the public. For this study, the key is not in dividing generals into two pools, but in identifying the stereotyped differences between the two groups as well as the expectations of the administration and public opinion of each type of commander.

This struggle between West Point graduates and politicians-in-uniform shaped the foundation of professionalization of the U.S. Army officer corps.[19] For military professionalization of the officer corps to be realized, the fundamental task of officership needed to be mastered: the expertise most concisely expressed in Harold Lasswell's phrase "the management of violence."[20] It is not sufficient for the institution to claim this skill, for the external client must grant professional status before a monopoly on expertise and social responsibility can be realized. The very acceptance of amateur generals by antebellum society provided what may have been the greatest retardant to military professionalization. Therefore, how and when society recognized the specialized expertise yielded to regular officers through education and experience and granted them autonomy in the performance of their trade are critical to this debate. By 1865, many West Pointers had triumphed in the struggle to gain recognition of their individual expertise and effectively ended the American tradition of embracing amateur military commanders. The regulars' views of generalship and the need for professionalization prevailed and have shaped the evolution of American military culture ever since.

Conclusion

My goal for this book is a revision of the historical approach to the examination of generalship, analogous to using a new lens to portray Civil War commanders. However, my intent is not to revise the tactical reputations or rejudge the military effectiveness of commanders like Butler, Banks, Sherman, or Halleck. I agree with much of the criticism of amateur generals' performance but do not believe it warrants painting the entire group with the broad brush of incompetence. I also agree with much of the praise given to Grant, Sherman, and their fellow West Point graduates, yet I do not believe that these men started the war better prepared for the military tasks that awaited field commanders than those they labeled as "amateurs." Accordingly, I do not attempt to judge the comparative military efficiency of individual Union generals; my intent instead is to provoke thought about better methods for evaluating their generalship and their role in the war.

I will also limit my study of Civil War political generals to the North. Although the practice of appointing prominent politicians to general officer rank occurred in both Union and Confederate armies, there was a vast difference in their influence on the two opposing war efforts. When compared to Lincoln's appointments and assignments, Confederate President Jefferson Davis's professional bias in selecting and promoting generals, due to his West Point background, his tenure as secretary of war, and his experience from the Mexican War, lessened the number and impact of political generals in the Confederacy. The Confederate practice of politically motivated appointments shared many roots with that of the Union because of their common political and military culture, but where the Union army evolved into the

U.S. Army, the Confederate army and its general officer corps disappeared at Appomattox. For these reasons, I focus only on the political generals who wore blue, though many conclusions drawn from this group are transferable to their Confederate peers.

This book will reveal how the Lincoln administration had different expectations of appointed general officers, each being given his command with a form of mandate to accomplish tasks that would make Union victory closer or more certain. The president, the public, and fellow military officers viewed these selections through the lens of American military heritage and popular culture, which lumped military leaders into two stereotypes: either "professionals" from West Point or "natural leaders" selected from outside the military. Since the Lincoln administration had different expectations of general officers, each being assigned a specific task based on his background, experiences, and aptitude, I conclude that these expectations should be addressed in judging the commanders' effectiveness: was a general moving the Union war effort closer to eventual political and military victory? Because this was Lincoln's standard, it is the appropriate criterion to judge Union generals regardless of their background and military performance in the field.

Although politically appointed amateur generals and West Point–graduate general officers during the Civil War shared similarities in tactical competence, political involvement, and reliance on patronage, the true relationship between the political and professional officers was a fractious struggle for dominance. The root of this clash was a sharp divergence in their views of the approach required for successful generalship. As will be shown, the different prewar experiences of the two groups led to two views of the problem facing generals: the regulars viewed the war as largely a Jominian military problem requiring a focus on the battlefield to destroy the enemy army and seize strategic points, while the politically adept amateurs viewed the rebellion as a partisan political struggle for power and political allegiance in both the South and in Washington. Although even this generalized dichotomy broke down for many officers, the resulting friction between West Pointers and political generals eroded Northern morale and damaged the war effort. The war was not won until a group of commanders that could be trusted by the Lincoln administration to reconcile these two efforts rose to command the Union armies. These pervasive stereotypes obscure a nuanced picture of Union generalship that reveals that all Union senior commanders were in actuality "political generals" because, to paraphrase Clausewitz, generalship is inherently "a continuation of politics by other means."

CHAPTER ONE

"Military Knowledge or Political Affinity"
The Legacy of a Dual Military Tradition

When the first cannon shot struck Fort Sumter, the federal government in Washington faced a military situation for which it was woefully unprepared. A small regular army manned seacoast fortifications or was scattered across the West guarding the frontier. A significant portion of its officer corps had already joined in the rebellion, thereby removing some of the most promising commanders from an already small group of seasoned senior officers and inexperienced junior officers. Once the states from the upper South joined their confederates in secession, the military task of putting down the rebellion became an enormous challenge because of the vast territory and resources now controlled by the forces seeking to resist the initially small Union army. Though untutored in military matters, the new president understood the need for an armed force to end the rebellion, yet Abraham Lincoln realized at once that he lacked a sufficient pool of trained officers to organize and command a rapidly expanding army. In the colossal task of quelling a rebellion that extended over an area of 733,144 square miles, the Lincoln administration faced a monumental responsibility in raising and guiding an army of the size required to put down the rebellion. Who could the new president dare trust to lead the armies in this crucial challenge?

The heritage of the antebellum officer corps reveals the cultural foundations behind the stereotypes of the amateur political general and the professional career officer that emerged so quickly in the days after the shelling of Fort Sumter. The continual friction between career soldiers and wartime volunteers was a constant theme in the fledgling American military tradition, as was the absence of a national military strategy to dictate the proper function of military force in the young Republic. The wartime practice of appointing popular politicians to military command will be shown to be a common occurrence prior to the Civil War—as were the claims of partisan politics these appointments inspired. The rising number of uniformed military reformers decried this tradition and sought to demonstrate the need for education and experience in the high command, yet these same efforts branded many of the officers as elitists and caused a backlash against this rising military "aristocracy." As the following pages will reveal, these two powerful undercurrents would do much to shape who was appointed to the ranks of Union general officers in 1861.

This legacy of a dual military heritage in the American officer corps, of both career regulars and politically appointed amateurs, bore fruit during the crisis of 1861 by presenting the Lincoln administration with two separate and competing sources for general officer appointments: one basing their qualification for command on experience and expertise, the other relying on "natural genius" and the perceived ability of every American to master the required military skills. American military heritage also appeared to reward popular political figures with a means to improve their political standing during times of war. Lincoln understood the importance of generalship in this vast military undertaking and the effect of the split heritage in the officer corps. "It so happened that very few of our friends had a military education or were of the profession of arms," the president told stalwart Republican politician (and volunteer major general) Carl Schurz. "It would have been a question whether the war should be conducted on military knowledge, or on political affinity."[1]

This statement highlights Lincoln's dilemma; during an insurrection, the government required generals who were both politically astute and dependable concerning the issues involved in the political contest. Yet, the same commanders also needed to possess the strategic vision and tactical ability to bring victory in the military struggle. The task of finding generals who met both of these qualifications was only made harder by the absence of men with proven military command expertise and the limited number of candidates with any military education and experience at all. In selecting general officers for the expanding army, Lincoln's initial attempts to rally support and judge expertise revealed an apparently traditional dilemma between gaining support for the war and military efficiency, a tension caused by factionalism, partisan patrons, and an absence of a clear military policy on the force required to win the war. The result in 1861 was a natural division between officers with military qualifications and popular political figures whose appointment to military command brought political benefits.

A Military Tradition of Amateur Generals

The harnessing of "political generals" during the Civil War was part of a long tradition of amateur military commanders during each of America's wars that dated back to the colonial militia. The roots of the recurrent appointment of these amateur military leaders lay in nineteenth-century American culture. It has become a historical truism that a nation's military is a reflection of its society, and therefore, to understand the origins of the practice of appointing amateur generals, it is necessary to study the politics and popular culture of the times. Two aspects of society prior to the Civil War influenced the policymaking regarding these appointed military leaders: the political culture and the military heritage of nineteenth-century America. These two influences on military policy combined to produce the legacy of political generals and to create an atmosphere in which these amateur commanders not only could command in time of war but also further their political careers by their service.

The most evident characteristic of nineteenth-century American political culture was the pervasive faith in democracy across the growing Republic.[2] Americans firmly believed in their experiment with representative democracy and were determined to make it succeed.[3] This conviction can be seen in the dominance of political parties and in the high voter participation percentages during the antebellum period. At school, local offices, and state governments, Americans became enamored with their use of the ballot and their loyalty to the party system, which peaked during the period of mid-century sectional strife when over 75 percent of eligible voters participated in presidential elections between 1848 and 1872.[4] These political values were also prevalent at the community level with equal levels of voter turnout repeatedly recorded for local and state elections. As Civil War historian Philip Paludan describes, "Practically from cradle to grave Northerners were immersed in a political-constitutional culture that took life in their communities."[5] The dominant strands of the political culture of this immersion during the Civil War period were a product of Jacksonian America and the sectional crisis of the antebellum period.

The major effects of Jacksonian America on political culture were twofold: a populist campaign of antielitism and a growing dominance of partisan patronage in the establishment of the second party system.[6] The rise of this first "self-made man" to the presidency of the nation ushered in an era of popular belief in egalitarianism. Jackson all his life had waged a campaign against the trappings of aristocracy and privilege, and this drive against elitism spread throughout the republic as his popularity grew.[7] A second effect of Jacksonian democracy on the nation was the extension of the party spoils system into all aspects of federal, state, and local government. After Jackson's two terms, the use of governmental patronage increased until it peaked during the Lincoln administration when almost 90 percent of federal positions would change hands after the election of 1860.[8] This introduction of partisan politics into all aspects of appointments would combine with the anti-professional campaign and the popularism to affect the military culture of antebellum America. With a distinct lack of institutional separation of military and civil functions of government and the lack of a professional corporateness in the officer corps, the army could not prevent the antielite and partisan patronage character of the political culture of Jacksonian America from influencing the nation's military culture.[9]

This faith in the ideals of a virtuous citizen-soldier was mirrored by a cultural belief that the best form of military commander in a republic was the example of Cincinnatus, the Roman leader who twice left his farm to save the republic by commanding the army at a time of national crisis. The attractiveness to Americans of the story of Cincinnatus was his willingness after victory to voluntarily return the power and titles lent him and return to the plow. Such virtuous behavior also became part of the American ethos when the founder of the country displayed the same willingness to step down after the revolution and after his second term as president. The heroic George Washington passed into the American lexicon as the perfect general for the armies of a republic. For many Americans, the logical result of such sentiment was a crusade against military professionalism. This ideological and political campaign consisted of significantly more than just ideological rhetoric about the superiority of a militia-based system in a republic.[10] The vehemence and rhetoric of this antiprofessional crusade only increased the regular officers' defensiveness about their professionalism and the value of the Military Academy.

Another aspect of the populist military tradition in America was the use of military service as a stepping-stone in politics. Wartime service by a politician allowed him to display the required patriotism and to gain popular recognition in nearly all the communities in the country. The American search for heroic leadership for political office was seen in the popularity gained by even local political candidates' use of military titles or records of wartime service to add stature to their campaigns. This political use of military service occurred long before the Civil War and was actually present in all of the American campaigns of the nineteenth century. The number of local and regional politicians who could emerge as popular candidates from even a single battle could be astonishing. The Battle of the Thames during the War of 1812, which passed into the American military ethos as the "Bunker Hill" of that war, helped build the future political careers of one president, one vice president, three governors, three lieutenant governors, four senators, and twenty congressmen.[11] With examples such as these, ambitious politicians were quick to understand the potential benefits of military service during a national emergency.

The experience of the Mexican War and the politics of "Mr. Polk's War" were in many ways a dress rehearsal for the use of political generals during the Civil War. President Polk may have appointed a lesser number of political generals than Lincoln later would, but Polk clearly did it for more partisan reasons and for a solely political purpose by appointing Democrats into high command positions. It should come as little surprise that the Jacksonian patronage system was extended into the wartime military leadership considering the fact that Polk's secretary of war was William L. Marcy, the politician who popularized the phrase "To the victors belong the Spoils."[12] During the course of the Mexican War, Polk appointed thirteen volunteer generals to command the expanding army in Texas and Mexico.[13] Their one common characteristic was that all were loyal Democrats with years of service to the party; nine of the thirteen were previous Democratic state legislators and five had been Democratic congressmen. All were politicians whose military service could be counted on to advance their political careers.[14]

However, Polk's appointment of Democrats to fill the provincial positions did not signal the extent of his partisan intervention in the army officer corps, nor were these appointments enough to settle the president's concern with the potential prestige of a military hero in the opposing party. Polk had the precedent of Andrew Jackson's rise to the presidency from the last war to be concerned about, and he therefore viewed his senior generals as rivals for the country's popular appeal and as potential presidential candidates. The president knew that the three senior regular army generals, Scott, Taylor, and Edmund Gaines, were all Whigs, and he may have feared they would recognize and repeat the precedent of William Henry Harrison's successful bid for the White House. As one of Polk's key wartime advisers, Senator Thomas H. Benton of Missouri, later summarized, the Polk administration "wanted a small war, just large enough to require a treaty of peace and not large enough to make military reputations dangerous for the presidency."[15] This episode of political intrigue and ambition during the Mexican War would be repeated in many forms during the upcoming Civil War. The partisan patronage of "Mr. Polk's War" also accurately foreshadowed many of the frustrations Lincoln would experience in his own effort to solidify support for his wartime policies.[16]

The root cause for these military appointments of amateur generals was the political culture of a nation that was at its core a democracy and the most politicized culture on earth, meaning support for the war would have to be cajoled, stumped for, and rallied.[17] Unlike in Europe, vast new armies could not be created by the central government alone because of the lack of a bureaucratic mechanism of control: troops would need recruiting, they would need to be encouraged to reenlist, and if conscription was required, this unpopular policy would have to be sold to a very skeptical populace as a necessity. Even during a vicious civil war, elections still needed to be won and political coalitions held together. These were the causes of political generalship during the Civil War. The expectation was allegiance and the support of followers, and on this standard the political generals would be judged. While these popular politicians-turned-generals filled the officer ranks in wartime, career military officers, more and more a product of West Point, dominated the peacetime officer corps because of the lack of appeal this service had for all except dedicated regulars.

As the nineteenth century passed, the Military Academy and its graduates played a growing role in the officer corps and the antebellum army leadership inside the active regiments by providing an annual supply of new lieutenants into these small hierarchical and insular organizations. Though graduates did not dominate the general officer ranks until the Civil War, the passing years witnessed a growing preponderance of active duty officers sharing this common commissioning source. As early as 1833, Military Academy graduates made up half the officers on active duty, and by 1860 more than three-quarters of all serving officers were products of West Point.[18] Therefore, West Pointers were slowly becoming representative of the leadership of the peacetime army in the eyes of the administration and the public, and this perception made the school a natural source for leaders during the Civil War. To many in and outside the government, graduates from West Point would supplement amateur generals by providing the desired organizational and tactical expertise for the Union army as they had for the nation during the Mexican War.

West Point and the Struggle for Professional Status

In many ways, the antebellum legacy of the U.S. Army officer corps was a quest for civilian recognition of its military expertise and the granting of professional status, which mirrored a similar struggle by many European officer corps. The reaction of many regular officers to repeated wartime debacles involving untrained militia and amateur commanders was disdain for this part of their military heritage and the strong desire to secure a monopoly on military leadership. To gain this control of the nation's military affairs, the political leadership and the society as a whole would have to recognize the officer corps as being responsible for a distinct and important vocation; military leadership would be bestowed upon a corps of officers possessing specialized knowledge and occupational education and experience.[19] But for the antebellum American officer corps, this drive for professional status was a frustrating quest that was unsuccessful prior to the Civil War. The nature of American culture combined with the lack of an effective military education system to continue the acceptance of the "natural genius" of amateur military leaders and deny occupational legitimacy or institutional autonomy to the regular officer corps. While European armies made progress in their search for occupational legitimacy during this period, the American officer corps failed to reach professional status until long after the Civil War ended.

The Prussian army demonstrated one path to how this goal of professional recognition could be achieved by developing the paradigm of a professional officer corps during the mid–nineteenth century.[20] At the heart of the Prussian military system was a formal educational system that produced officers perceived by society to be masters at the art of war. In 1810, Prussia established the famous *Kriegsakademie*, which became the model of a military university for the study of war and warfare. For a long period, the *Kriegsakademie* was the only military school in the world educating officers at the university level and proved to be the focal point for Prussian professionalization.[21] Other reforms in the Prussian officer corps included a wide range of codified regulations on everything from officer selection (often done as early as age eleven) to senior officer access to the kaiser.[22] A result of these efforts in education and officer development was the growth of the concept of officership as a distinct calling requiring a lifelong study, a status that the government and society grew to accept.[23] With entrance and promotion exams for officers, a progressive system of officer education, and the first true general staff entrusted with national strategic planning, the Prussian officer corps by the start of the Wars of German Unification in 1864 was recognized by its government and by most of society as experts in their vocation and became a corporate body entrusted with all matters relating to the military.

One of the main causes for this unrivaled status was the structure of the Prussian government, as, unlike other European powers, only Prussia had the constitutional arrangement that favored the growth of professionalism in the officer ranks.[24] The Prussian military, and the Prussian state, recognized the kaiser as the military supreme commander and the central authority on all military matters, giving officers a focal point for their loyalty and removing the turbulence in military policy that was so common in most other great powers.[25] Only during periods of political unrest was this authority challenged, allowing the army leadership to isolate itself from politics except during the repeated constitutional crises of mid–nineteenth century Prussia. The rise in the status of the Prussian General Staff during this period reflected an increased faith in their monopoly on military expertise.[26] The army commanders and the General Staff conducted both the Seven Weeks' War of 1866 and the Franco-Prussian War of 1870 almost exclusively on their own authority, with political leaders and even the war minister excluded from any contact with the operational aspects of these conflicts.[27]

For the French officer corps, the legacy of the Revolution was a system of officer promotion based on merit and an expectation of military success, providing a foundation for professional growth. The result was an education system focused on developing military expertise. Many of the schools, such as *St Cyr* and *École Polytechnique*, were primarily technical in focus, similar to West Point, and France had nothing comparable to the *Kriegsakademie*.[28] Yet the French did stage annual exercises at the divisional level to introduce new weapons, test new tactics, and give officers a chance to practice their trade and learn recent developments in warfare.[29] The French made an enormous stride forward in officer professionalization when they formalized a Commission of Defense in the 1840s as a strategic planning body responsible to study and coordinate strategy and military policy.[30] This development led to recognition that military officers had specialized expertise not shared with the uneducated as well as to the rise of the officer corps as the authority in military affairs. Similar to the military conditions in Prussia, the French officer corps emerged from this period of reform with the recognition of its occupational expertise and the corporateness that comes from a monopoly of commands.

Yet, when these European military professionals were challenged by political unrest, the breakdown of constitutional authority proved to be divisive in the officer ranks. In reaction to these periods of internal strife, the Prussian and French officer corps often became active in the political struggles that followed. During the nineteenth century, Prussia was involved in a series of constitutional crises, and its military officers repeatedly chose sides with the kaiser against all political challenges, becoming an active force in the political battles.[31] At times the strife rent apart the officer corps itself, as in 1848 when many junior officers took sides against their own high command.[32] In a similar manner, French officers were heavily involved in politics during constitutional crises in 1830 and 1848. As with the Prussians, the French officer corps was not impartial in any of these political struggles and became a political power broker. The French military went so far as to issue commemorative campaign medals in 1851 for the army's role in backing Louis Napoleon's bloody coup d'état.[33] These events revealed the causal link between political stability and professionalism, and that the recognition of a professional officer corps did not necessarily mean the officers were apolitical or divorced from political loyalties. This factor could be especially significant when a national government was in the midst of an insurrection and a civil war.

For American officers, contact with European officers, accounts of developments across the Atlantic, and a sense of frustration at their own career patterns resulted in a quest to gain similar recognition as professionals.[34] One of the earliest American advocates of military professionalism, and one of its staunchest supporters, Professor Dennis Hart Mahan at the U.S. Military Academy (USMA), defined military professionalism as the vocational expertise in employing the tools of war that would raise performance in the officer corps.[35] To Mahan and the officers who were in the forefront of this reform effort, such expertise could not be simply the exercise of natural talent nor could it be solely the result of experience. Mahan believed this expertise had to involve the integration of theory and practice, for only such a combination could truly set the regular army officers apart from their amateur peers.[36] Victory in this quest would dispel the popular belief that any man of good character and strong patriotism could command American troops in time of war and would remove the wartime challenge by political generals. In the eyes of most military reformers, West Point was to play a key role in laying the intellectual framework required for this change by teaching the specialized military knowledge necessary to be an effective officer.

Yet, developing expertise in strategy and tactics was not the focus of an antebellum West Point education because of the Military Academy's leading role in providing the required technical expertise in the engineering and scientific fields to create an infrastructure for the growing republic. West Point excelled in this role for its contribution to cartography, topography, and the civil engineering projects that supported transportation facilities such as ports and railroads. This spectrum of nonmilitary tasks, which made graduates popular with political supporters and advocates of nationalism, also led to a focus at the Military Academy on practical engineering and hard science.[37] The future army, corps, and division commanders received little instruction in military history or gained much practical experience in tactics to prepare for the challenge of command above the company grade level.[38] The focus on engineering and drill provided little preparation even for service on the frontier.

The study of generalship was also lacking at the Military Academy, with the sole sources of exposure to these complex concepts the brief period of instruction from Professor Mahan and individual fascination with the legacy of Napoleon and his conquests, which were held as the epitome of military skill. In the midst of an educational experience dominated by practical engineering and drill, Professor Mahan offered a nine-hour seminar on "The Science of War," which appeared as only a small part of the course on fortifications and military engineering.[39] Yet for the cadets at antebellum West Point, this class was not a foundation for further study but their only formal exposure to the study of military history, and it fell short of inspiring intellectual growth by any measure. The brief course actually could afford very little time spent on the study of military history and fostered no follow-on program for self-study besides the often small Napoleon Club of faculty and cadets that focused on the principles of the Corsican master of war. Mahan deserves credit as the author of one of the first American contributions to the study of war, yet his seminal work, *Outpost*, was more a text on field fortifications and minor tactics than a practical guide on strategy, military policy, or operational art.[40]

The professor did inspire one of his students to continue the development of American military theory, as Mahan's protégé, Henry Wager Halleck, added even more emphasis to this need for professionalism and the science of war. After graduating from West Point in 1839 and touring France in 1845, Halleck published a series of his own lectures as the book *Elements of Military Arts and Science*, which sought to provide guidance for future generals and staff officers by presenting timeless principles from an extensive study of military history.[41] With a focus on conventional warfare and a neglect of the involvement and complexity of politics in war, Halleck's work followed the intellectual path of Jomini and provided little practical guidance on the complex issues concerning the best strategy to win a war dominated by political concerns.[42] For some future commanders who only had the time, ability, or desire for a cursory study of military theory, the sole lessons that might stand out from Halleck's work were the necessity for preparation and organization prior to active operations and the need to focus offensive operations on seizing strategic points as the only path to victory.[43]

Yet, it was this combination of Jomini, Mahan, and Halleck, all under the shadow of the great Napoleon, that greatly influenced most West Pointers by imprinting Jominian language and concepts on their view of the nature of war.[44] Much of this influence was based on informal individual study of the Corsican master, and it was not developed in any formal study of strategy or tactical principles, but instead shaped the view of the nature of war for many Military Academy graduates by forming the very framework of their exposure to military history.[45] Rather than his timeless principles, Jomini and his American followers provided an outlook on war that focused almost exclusively on military matters and on the study of "war on a map" that encouraged a scientific view of warfare as a military contest between two armies while implanting an affinity for control in the conduct of warfare. The result for many future Civil War commanders was an emphasis on conventional battles and the desire to avoid rashness by thorough and timeconsuming preparation. This approach would be antithetical to the political needs of a wartime government and would lead to frustration for the Lincoln administration and a public that waited impatiently for news of victories.

For the majority of officers or retired Military Academy graduates during the antebellum era, there was neither the inclination nor the structured opportunity to study the profession of arms, as this pursuit did not appear necessary on the frontier and was not a consideration in the seniority system for peacetime promotion.[46] Halleck's work and references to Jomini did not alter the basic education for the vast majority of graduates, as many were without any usable background in the historical study of their profession or of the complex issues of strategy and military policy.[47] Even as practical a subject as drill failed to encourage any study after graduation from the Military Academy, as one of West Point's most distinguished graduates demonstrated during the Mexican War. "I had never looked at a copy of tactics from the time of my graduation," Ulysses S. Grant was willing to admit concerning his service in Mexico. "I do not believe that the officers of the regiment ever discovered that I had never studied the tactics that I used."[48]

The majority of officers did not deem this "book learning" necessary until the war tocsins actually sounded. Early in the Civil War, Brigadier General William T. Sherman had warned his officers that they "must now study their books" and specifically recommended the works of Jomini and Mahan because the challenges of command now exceeded their small pool of practical experience and "ignorance of duty must no longer be pleaded."[49] After the war had commenced and the armies were in the field, it was too late to start a military education for many of these officers, as active operations began before their study was started in earnest and practical matters of drill, logistics, and military bureaucracy rapidly filled any available time. Grant's and Sherman's experiences are significant for revealing how the influence of Mahan, Halleck, and Jomini has tended to be exaggerated by historians given the relatively limited exposure cadets had to this instruction while at West Point and the large amount of time that had passed since their classes with Mahan.[50]

This lack of education proved to be not the only obstacle to the quest for military professionalism, as the very nature of American democracy resisted these efforts. Unlike in France or Prussia, military officers had no aristocratic heritage granting a sense of status in society and also had no central unified authority in a constitutional system that relied on divided control of military policy and was infused with partisan political struggles over military affairs. When there is no single institution of governmental authority, professionalization becomes difficult if not impossible due to the absence of a focal point for the officer's loyalty. Under competing authorities or conflicting constitutional ideologies, an officer corps can become divided by split loyalties and political partisanship that overwhelm corporate values.[51] For many officers, the powerful pull of these forces during times of particularly savage political battle over military appointments and policies, not to mention the intensity of a national civil war, would have the same effect in America as they did in Europe; officers would discard efforts to professionalize in order to survive and interpret the requirements of various factional political leaders.

Even the officers who understood the need to professionalize and the requirements to make this reformation faced their own resistance to occupational legitimacy. In this early period, no national consensus emerged to place the social responsibility for national defense on the regular army. As a result of cultural resistance and an ideological attachment to the militia, the army was not seen as the primary means of defense, dooming any significant manpower reform efforts like Secretary of War John C. Calhoun's "expansible army" plan. Nor was the officer corps entrusted with the policy decisions concerning security of the republic owing to a fear of their involvement in national politics, which was based on a legacy that included a valid threat of this involvement by Alexander Hamilton and his New Army.

During the antebellum era, the U.S. Army officer corps also lacked a developed sense of occupational corporateness, the shared sense of organic unity and culture within a profession that would separate all military officers from laymen.[52] The reason behind this lack of self-identification was mostly based on a manpower policy that left little room for careerists while encouraging many lateral and renewed entries. In the antebellum army, the continuous active duty experience of an officer such as Halleck was rare compared to officers like Sherman who left the army only to return in times of war. Halleck's career is also rare in that while in uniform he focused on military service for the most part while the majority of his fellow officers took up pursuits having little use to their careers. A clear example of this trend is the experience of future commanding general W. T. Sherman who studied law, speculated land and goods, and surveyed land for profit, all while serving as an army officer.[53]

Yet many officers had duty assignments and jobs unrelated to combat that would help prepare them for some of the challenges to come. Halleck and Sherman had both served in California during the Mexican War, working on the contentious political issues that surfaced during its seizure by the United States. During the same period, Burnside served on a commission to draw the new border based on the Treaty of Guadalupe Hidalgo. These types of challenges were good preparation for raising and organizing an army, but not for leading it in the field. Many officers also had breaks in service when they pursued political or financial opportunities outside the army. Halleck resigned from the army and managed a bank in California, an experience that honed his administrative expertise and organizational ability. Burnside left the officer corps and became a major general in the Rhode Island militia and ran for Congress in 1857 as a Democrat, developing ties to politicians in his home state.[54] George B. McClellan and many other West Pointers joined railroad companies. These new challenges improved their managerial ability and put their cognizance of discipline and order to good use. In this manner, the Military Academy produced a sort of national managerial class who were ready to organize and lead large businesses like the railroads and had experience at building corporate behavior and enforcing institutional norms.[55] Such activities, however, did little to develop the military expertise that would later be required of these officers when tasked to command corps and entire armies in battle.

But when the mobilization began after the shelling of Sumter, West Pointers did have the advantage of previous military training, and this is what set them apart from the amateur volunteer officers in the eyes of the contemporary public. "The advantage of a West Point training is precisely that of any other professional education," the author of an article titled "Regular and Volunteer Officers" concluded in 1864. "There is nothing in it which any intelligent man cannot learn for himself in a later life; nevertheless, the intelligent man would have fared a good deal better, had he learned it all in advance."[56] As this line of reasoning reveals, West Pointers were not initially sought after because of some desire for a politically neutral instrument to wage war, but as a group of individuals who possessed some experience at the task required. But their level and range of experience should not be equated with a general military expertise, as West Pointers were prepared only for the aspects of officership that they had been performing as junior officers prior to the war. Without any experience or instruction in higher level leadership, these officers were no more prepared for maneuvering corps and divisions in battle than their volunteer peers. This reasoning resulted in an emerging stereotype of Military Academy graduates as officers more than ready to organize and drill new regiments, but nowhere near prepared for command at general officer levels and completely divorced from the political issues that had led to the conflict.

1861: Forming an Army and a Pair of Stereotypes

The outgrowth of this half-century of military experience was a military system woefully unprepared for the trials ahead. On the eve of the Civil War, the War Department presided over a small regular army with only a mixed bag of volunteer militia units for reinforcement and without any system of trained universal militia organizations.[57] For the volunteer militia officers, the heritage of Bunker Hill, New Orleans, and Buena Vista encouraged faith in a natural American military ability and in the availability of a Cincinnatus to lead the citizen-soldiers during wartime. Yet the annual militia encampments, which consisted of socializing, fancy parades, and a small amount of drill a few days each year, did not prepare these officers for the battlefield. Militia generals like Benjamin Butler of Massachusetts and William Keim of Pennsylvania may have believed their leadership at the encampments gave them command experience, but their uniformed Zouaves and minutemen were still untrained and inexperienced "holiday soldiers." However, West Point graduates were themselves often derided by society and were unable to secure professional status and recognition of their own expertise in military matters. The result was the appointment of two types of generals during the Civil War: former regulars and amateur politicians. Each type carried the burden of antebellum traditions and over time became further encumbered with generalizations about their competency and character.

The firing on Fort Sumter opened the floodgates of war mobilization in the Northern states and brought military policy decisions to the forefront in Washington. On April 15, Lincoln called for seventy-five thousand militia

troops to be federalized for ninety days for "the suppression of insurrection."[58] The administration immediately became involved in heated
debates, both in the Congress and with the state governors, concerning
questions of loyalty and patriotism during the formation of the Union army.
The initial explosion of rhetoric at the treachery of the Confederate States
and the resigning Southern officers had a volatile effect on the political
atmosphere in Washington. The aftermath of the resignation of 239 Southern officers was a melee of vehement antiprofessional rhetoric that grew during 1861 and lasted for most of the war.[59] The conduct of the resigning
officers was thought to be the vilest form of treachery in proving to be disloyal to their sworn oaths at a time of national crisis. For many Northern
congressmen in Washington, this flaw in loyalty seemed a product of officer
professionalization. How could the Republic survive if its military leaders
proved to be professional "hired guns," whose allegiance they themselves
determined?

Rhetoric like this flew around the capital and built into a campaign
against professional military officers. In a status report on Northern mobilization, Secretary of War Cameron's July message to the president included
warnings about the "extraordinary treachery displayed, whether its promoting
cause may not be traced to a radical defect in the system of [military] education itself."[60] Lincoln echoed this sentiment in his Fourth of July message to
Congress wherein he railed against the disloyal resignation of officers while
praising the patriotism of the enlisted men, none of whom had "deserted his
flag."[61] This outpouring of antiprofessional rhetoric caused many in Congress
to ask for the closing of West Point and led to many accusations that professional officers such as George McClellan and Irvin McDowell were intentionally failing to pursue tactical victories over the Confederates. Such
generalization about the lack of regular officers' commitment to the Union
cause would plague West Point graduates for the entire war. Many of the same
voices assailing the real and imagined treachery of several professional officers also cried out for a return to the imagined heritage of an army of virtuous citizen-soldiers commanded by popular amateur leaders.

With the enormous increase in the size of the army during the war, President Lincoln had little choice but to commission a large number of inexperienced field grade officers and to appoint some amateur generals. The
process of granting officer commissions became a daunting task for both the
president and the state governors as the army expanded from less than
twenty thousand at the start of hostilities up to its maximum size of nearly a
million men by the end of 1862. This situation provided an opportunity for

politicians who sought to become involved with the war effort. At a time of such national crisis, many political figures looked upon military service as an outlet for their honest patriotism, while others saw time in the military as a system to influence the war effort. The result of this volunteering was that by the fall of 1861, at least seventeen congressmen had joined the Union army, four as brigadiers, ten as regimental colonels, and the other three as officers on either McClellan's or Frémont's staff.[62] For the most ambitious office seekers, the need to join the moral crusade for the Union and to do their part for the nation led to the quest for stars as a political general.

Lincoln did not spurn the majority of these offers of military service. The growth of the army from scattered companies in frontier posts to massed brigades, divisions, and armies left the president and the War Department without a clear choice of who to promote to general officer rank. With no one fully qualified by prior experience for the new huge commands, a risk would have to be taken with any appointments. Why neglect the established reputations of popular political figures in the search to pick military leaders? These men with proven leadership and organizational skills must have appeared just as prepared as regular army officers to handle the anticipated political aspects of military command during a civil war: how to recruit, where to fight, how to treat civilians, how to maintain support for the war, and what to do with slaves, free blacks, and captured property. Lincoln was a good judge of the American character and understood that the appointment of these political generals would bring political support for his policies, boost recruiting from their supporters, and bind the various factions in the North together in a victorious coalition. Yet, how could the Republic be saved if its military fortunes were placed in the hands of these military novices?

During this initial period of uncertainty as to mobilization requirements and wartime strategy, General in Chief Winfield Scott gained the support of Lincoln and Secretary of War Simon Cameron for two critical recommendations concerning the raising of volunteers, each of which would have an impact on Lincoln's selection process for officers and for generals. Scott's experience in the Mexican War, when he had to keep the regulars together to provide a dependable trained force, convinced him to keep the regular army intact and to organize separate regular and volunteer units. During the first six months of the war, he also gained approval to prevent the release of regular army officers to lead volunteer regiments.[63] This unwillingness to dilute the professional officer corps prevented the spread of trained personnel to the rapidly forming units, as Scott's disapproval led to a reluctance among regular officers to accept brevet rank in new volunteer formations because of their fear of losing regular army rank at the war's end. Though the number of regulars who would have been willing to join and train new Union regiments in the absence of this policy was impossible to tell, their presence could have had a significant leavening effect similar to that of their Confederate peers, who had no established regular units in which to concentrate their limited pool of military experience.

General Scott was initially reluctant to let any serving or former regular officers take a volunteer commission, as this would remove them from the core of regular units he expected to be the decisive element, as they had been in the Mexican War. This informal policy had the effect of limiting the availability of West Pointers to the new units that desperately needed them. Consequently, many serving Military Academy graduates remained in junior positions in the regular army until the policy was discontinued, while their peers who had left the service jumped immediately to high rank with a volunteer commission through the patronage of state governors. Yet Scott's policy was not without its defenders. Major General Jacob Cox believed that the absence of regular officers and the appointment or election of prominent local leaders led to a close identification by the soldiers with the political and ideological motivations of a "people's movement" in favor of the Union.[64] With this mandate to provide the expertise in the Union army also came a sense of distrust as well for the regular officers. "Every effort is making to get men from the Regular army into command," wrote prominent German political leader and future volunteer general Gustave Koerner as he echoed a common sentiment about the need for experienced career officers. Yet the antislavery partisan went on to warn that "most of the West Pointers are of very little account. Most all of them are dissipated and tyrannical; and they hate everybody not of their caste."[65]

Besides internalizing the value of discipline and order, the years at West Point and the seasoning of regular army service gave these future Civil War leaders practice with the aspects of military organization and bureaucracy that would help them form the vast armies of volunteers during the coming struggle. This service as cadets, junior officers, and staff officers would prove beneficial to an army of inexperienced volunteers. Many West Pointers had assignments that foreshadowed the bureaucratic challenges they would face during the sectional struggle. For example, as a very junior officer in the artillery, William T. Sherman served as an assistant inspector general in 1844, as a recruiter in 1846, and as an adjutant in California. These assignments, regardless of how brief or how dreary, led to a familiarization with the workings of the army while reinforcing the importance of organizational order and discipline as only the bureaucracy of an army in peacetime can. Such experience also made the availability of these officers very important to the War Department and state governors assembling a vast army.[66]

One of the principal results of Scott's policies and anti–West Point rhetoric was to deny the state governors experienced leaders for their new regiments and to create a gulf between the regular officer corps and the new volunteer officers. The governors would now have to select amateurs to fill the majority of the new officer positions in the volunteer regiments. With the locus of political power still at the state and local levels at the start of the war, the initial War Department decisions ensured that the recruiting of soldiers and the rallying of support would have to take place at these levels. Even with the initial confusion in the War Department, each 1861 troop quota was exceeded by the states. The state-based system of recruitment proved to be effective during the war when compared to the recruiting efforts made at the federal level.[67] As in previous wartime mobilizations, the small size of the peacetime regular army and the bureaucratic weakness of the central government combined to dictate the involvement of state and local politicians directly in the recruitment process. [68]

During this early phase of Union mobilization, Lincoln attempted to utilize the available military experience to lead the army, but like the state governors in their search for qualified field grade officers, the president was forced to turn more and more to non–Military Academy graduates and non-regulars to fill general officer positions. In 1861, Lincoln appointed 126 general officers of which approximately 65 percent were current or former regular officers.[69] However, this percentage would continually decrease as the war progressed until West Pointers represented less than 40 percent of the men wearing Union stars. Lincoln's record on his wartime appointment of 583 generals[70] reveals the large number of amateurs he was forced to appoint:

West Point graduates	217
Nongraduates of West Point	11
Graduates of other military schools	9
Other regular army (and navy) officers	36
State militia officers	40
European émigré officers	20
Others with Mexican War background	62
Inexperienced civilians	188

Congress attempted to limit this explosion in the general officer ranks by legislating that new appointments be tied to the number of new brigades and divisions raised and to available general officer positions without an assigned officer due to sickness or injury.[71] This initial scramble for general officers was improved upon after the early campaigns of 1861 and spring 1862, when Lincoln and the War Department had a much better indication of which officers were competent to wear the stars of a general officer and were able to use performance as a regimental commander as the primary consideration for most promotions to brigadier.

State governors and legislatures provided an enormous source of influence into the administration's general officer appointments and assignments. To form an effective policy coalition, Lincoln required the support of all the Northern state governments, especially after much of the burden for Union mobilization was placed on the states. However, this proved to be no easy task for administration officials, as they discovered that the ideal of states' rights was not confined to the seceding states. The governors repeatedly mentioned two points about officer commissions. The first was requests to the president to appoint various prominent state figures to general officer rank.[72] These requests would be forwarded to the president by way of congressional delegations who would "nominate" general officer candidates and present the list to Lincoln.[73]

The second was more dangerous for the administration because it involved a direct challenge to the president's authority to appoint generals. Many Northern state governments believed they shared this right whenever the volunteer militia was federalized because a section of their state constitutions dictated that militia and volunteer generals would be appointed by the governor or elected by the commissioned officers in their respective brigades. The most vocal challenge was from New York governor Edwin Morgan who used this reasoning on June 4, 1861, to assert his state's right to appoint the general officers who would command the brigades containing the state regiments.[74] Lincoln and the War Department remained adamant on the organizational authority to only accept regiments from the states and on the president's monopoly on the right to commission general officers. To settle many of these states' rights issues and debates, Lincoln often awarded general's stars to popular state figures to defuse disharmony in the war effort. The president occasionally even intervened with the War Department to ensure that each state received a proportional share of the available military patronage positions in order to placate the governors.[75]

Though the political and the military situation seemed dark for the Lincoln administration in the fall of 1861, there were some signs of promise. While the administration and the War Department at times seemed consumed by chaos and overwhelmed by the secessionist challenge, a military mobilization of unprecedented scale and size had occurred, and a Union army of 600,000 troops had been formed. In the middle of October, Secretary of War Cameron wrote the president to present a self-critique on the mobilization that, while overly optimistic, does highlight the accomplishments of the Lincoln administration in the first year of the war. Cameron cited the legacy of Napoleon as a benchmark (and made reference to the writings of Baron Henri Jomini) and contrasted Napoleon's mobilization of 1815, which was praised by Jomini, with what had occurred in the North in 1861.[76] As the Union had started the mobilization with an army of less than sixteen thousand officers and men, the Northern accomplishment exceeded that of Napoleon "without conscription, levies, drafts, or other extraordinary expedients."

Although Secretary Cameron also claimed that the Union military effort was gaining in efficiency and organization at the end of 1861, and that the mobilization was "evidence of the wonderful strength of our institutions," in the area of general officer appointments, the administration ran into a problem for which neither the initial enthusiasm for the war nor antebellum military policy provided a solution.[77] Burdened in some ways by the American military tradition of a dual source for soldiers and leaders, President Lincoln discovered that there existed no pool either of regular officers or prominent civilians who were prepared for the formidable task of organizing, training, and commanding large bodies of troops in time of war. Without the benefit of prewar training conducted at brigade or division level or prior experience commanding these large units in combat, the administration was forced to guess at the potential in junior officers and civilian amateurs to handle these challenges. Many of the tactical and operational failures of the Union army early in the war were products of incorrect assumptions as to candidates' latent talent for general officer level commands.

Conclusion

For the nineteenth-century American officer corps, the real proof that professional status had not been achieved was the very presence of political generals whenever the nation went to war, a result of society's lack of recognition of a monopoly on military expertise by regular officers. Unlike the governments in Prussia or France, American presidents, congressional leaders, and state governors did not see the need to rely solely on trained military experts during times of crisis, even when the very fate of the Republic appeared to rest on the ability to field an effective military force. As much as the regulars tried to prevent the use and prominence of wartime amateur commanders, they could not stop this tradition. In spite of the drive for recognition of military expertise, regular officers prior to the Civil War were still predominantly amateurs because of the absence of a history of professional service, any occupational legitimacy in a hostile political culture, or a system of advanced military education. As a result, the military policy of the United States possessed a dual source of amateurs and regular military leaders, each growing to resent the other whenever military conflict brought them together.

The military challenge facing Lincoln was so great early in the war that he made do with the best candidates available without initially questioning their lack of military education or political expertise. Instead, the president relied on their ability to fulfill a requirement on the road to eventual victory. As the study of selected general officers during the war will reveal, Lincoln selected and managed his senior commanders based on their potential achievements, their apparent strengths, the current status of the war effort, and the political effect of their appointment. In some ways, his appointment of general officers for high command reveals the idea of "mandates" in appointing commanders: selection and promotion made with the expectation of a certain advantage from commissioning a chosen individual and the assignment of a specific task to that individual based on his abilities. Lincoln was very specific with his senior commanders as to what he expected of them, and their assignment to high-level positions was also based on a perceived ability to deliver the mandated accomplishment.

As time would show, this approach naturally led to a strong political influence in general officer appointments and an attempt to match each of the two strands of military tradition with their inherent strengths. Even from the viewpoint of May 1861, the president and his administration knew they had two consistent needs to suppress such a large rebellion. The first was to gain enough recruits and marshal a level of popular support for the war effort to provide the necessary military tools to wage the struggle. The second was military organization to train the army and military expertise to provide the needed tactical victories. These two distinct requirements played to the diverse strengths of the two sources of military commanders. For the embattled president, prominent politicians could provide popular support for mobilization, while career officers provided the organizational skill and tactical expertise. As the next two chapters demonstrate, this simple concept shaped the mandates entrusted to the initial set of Union commanders.

However, these divergent stereotypes during the first months of the war obscured a far more complex picture on the selection of Union generals. The impression gathered from some popular Civil War literature that the Union army was led by a general officer corps consisting of a vast number of West Point graduates and a handful of inept political appointees does not stand up to historical scrutiny. The majority of the general officers on both sides were not career military professionals but were amateurs promoted from the field grade rank, the preponderance of whom were originally elected or appointed commanders of volunteer regiments. Though some volunteer officers justifiably earned the derogatory comments of their peers and subordinates, the ability of most of these amateurs to master regiments, brigades, and divisions was proven during the many campaigns of the war.

Another potential fallacy is the notion that the political generals were amateurs leading armies made up of career officers and trained soldiers. This was not at all the case, as the regular army units in the North were only a minuscule part of the large field armies, and the vast majority of the units were volunteer regiments formed in 1861 and 1862. Nor were Civil War political appointees assigned to command officers with greater military experience. The majority of their subordinate officers at all levels were civilians elected to positions by the men of their units or were amateur officers themselves appointed for political reasons. As one of the designated political generals wrote after the war, "The whole organization of the volunteer force might be said to be political [but] we heard more of 'political generals' than we did of political captains or lieutenants."[78] Although history recounts the successes and failures of the Military Academy graduates who dominated the high command during the war, most studies neglect the fact that many of their subordinate brigade and division commanders were volunteer officers without any benefit of that level of military training.

There may also be too much of a tendency to treat the regular and volunteer officers as distinct entities, one being fully apolitical professionals and the other amateurs with a political umbilical cord linked to their statehouses. While there is a large volume of historical evidence to support the involvement of volunteer officers in politics, too little attention is given to the involvement of West Pointers and career officers in influencing politics and interpreting policy. Both during the antebellum period and during the war, regular army officers cultivated patrons, actively sought political sponsors to support advancement and promotion, lobbied Congress for corporate interests, and made use of the press to influence policy.[79] The careers of the most prominent West Pointers, such as Henry Wager Halleck, Ambrose E.

Burnside, and William T. Sherman, all reveal instances of both the involvement of political patrons in assignments and promotions and announcing positions on policy questions in order to influence decisionmakers and the public. As will soon be shown, the regular officer corps was little different from the volunteers when it came to courting advancement and assignments and clearly was not divorced from politics. As a result, the majority of both regular army and volunteer generals was guilty of political involvement during the course of the Civil War.

But the administration's political radar was not evenly split between these two potential pools of military leaders. With a civil war declared and blood shed, President Lincoln understood that the most pressing military need was manpower, and key to gaining manpower on such a large scale and in so short a time was popular support for the war effort—and for the politically fragile new administration. In the first two months of the war, the top civilian in the War Department and the highest ranking officer in the army made a set of decisions that placed the burden of recruitment on the states and that led directly to the need for politically appointed general officers. This necessity would prove to be a powerful attraction for a group of politicians willing to don a blue uniform and take the field in the service of the Union. Therefore, many of the most prominent initial appointments to high command were popular politicians who laid the foundation of a stereotype of the "political general." As will be seen, President Lincoln understood and embraced this source of potential leadership. The only question for the administration was who should be selected for appointment to general officer and whether the political benefits of such appointment would outweigh the military risks.

CHAPTER TWO

"The Necessity of the Time"
The Need for Political Generals

In the midst of a national capital burdened with the pressures of civil war, a Union general sat with President Abraham Lincoln and received the president's thanks for past service and his compliments for the general's "great activity and skill."[1] When the meeting ended, the Union general, having just been told by Lincoln of his upcoming promotion and the award of another star to his epaulets, emerged from the White House to find a large and enthusiastic crowd that broke into cheers at his appearance. The story of this meeting between the president and the general appeared in nearly every newspaper throughout the North under headlines heralding the general's "brilliant career" and the expectation of his success at taking Richmond.[2]

Although most readers might be convinced at this point that the newspaper accounts described the arrival of either George B. McClellan in 1861 or Ulysses S. Grant during 1864, in fact they heralded the "Brilliant Career" of Massachusetts politician and militia brigadier general Benjamin F. Butler.[3] Butler seemed surprised at his fortune but not overly concerned with his lack of formal military training. Although his desire for the job of military commander may seem easy to fathom, what was far more interesting was the eagerness of the Lincoln administration to appoint him along with a vast number of other political generals. Butler's progression from an inexperienced state militia leader in 1860 to command of a military district and an army by the summer of 1861 mirrored the rapid rise of many amateur generals and raises various questions concerning the ability and advantage of having popular but untrained citizens as senior military leaders.

On this topic, who was selected for this role in the Union war effort and whether such appointments fulfilled the expectations of the Lincoln administration are important issues. The background of men such as Butler, Nathaniel Banks, and John A. Logan is critical in explaining why these particular politicians were recruited by the Lincoln administration and elevated to Union high command with little if any military justification for such an appointment. These same backgrounds also help explain why such a diverse group of politicians could be lumped together under a single stereotype, and why in some aspects this generalization was appropriate. By exploring the actions and impact of Butler, Logan, and others, this chapter will address the question of what exactly these men were asked to deliver.

Lincoln appointed Butler, Banks, Logan, and scores of others as general officers because of the popular support they could rally for the Union cause as well as the political benefits to the war effort coalition of having these prominent politicians openly behind the president. Recalling the president's challenge in 1861, Major General of Volunteers Jacob D. Cox described this effort to enlist prominent politicians: "It must be kept constantly in mind that we had no militia organization that bore any appreciable proportion to the greatness of the country's need, and that at any rate the policy of relying upon volunteering at the beginning was adopted by the government." Therefore, the well-known Ohio politician labeled it a "foregone conclusion" that most of the new volunteer officers must be popular leaders. "Such men might be national leaders or leaders of the county neighborhoods," Cox concluded, "but big or little, they were the necessity of the time."[4] As this politician-turned-general so astutely implied, the call for political generals was the result of the lack of a strong national central government to set policy, as well as the decision to appoint amateur commanders like himself being made not by choice but by necessity.

A Mandate to Rally Support

Benjamin F. Butler, in many ways the epitome of a political general, represented both the positive and negative generalizations of amateur generalship during this era. He was an early hero of the war and, with the prominent role he played in the war effort, became the symbol of political generals for both policymakers and the public.[5] When Butler arrived in Washington in April 1861, President Lincoln was glad to have the support of such a prominent Democrat, who donated his popularity to the Union cause with every newspaper account containing his name and rank and every speech that proclaimed his political support for the administration's policies.[6] Lincoln was willing to risk Butler's lack of military experience to gain the appearance of national unity behind the war effort regardless of pre-war political partisanship. Many prominent politicians entered the army this way. They received general officer's stars with the understood mandate to rally their supporters behind the administration's war effort and to help hold together the fragile political coalition the Lincoln administration required to continue the war. In this way, political generals show how military patronage continued an American military tradition and symbolized the political power sharing required to rally support across the political spectrum.

Butler's background, a mixture of politics and militia service, established both his desire for recognition as a soldier and his belief in his inherent ability to command, an example of the common opinion of the era that military command did not require specialized expertise and was a task any patriotic leading citizen could succeed in if granted the opportunity.[7] The highlight of his militia duty entailed encampments of six to nine days a year with his company, performing basic drill and enjoying the martial pageantry that was at the heart of the volunteer militia movement in New England.[8] This early militia service proved significant in the minds of Butler and many other future political generals because it spawned a degree of self-confidence and a sense that these men understood the art of war and were ready for command.[9] On the eve of the war, Butler expressed great pride in himself as a military expert owing to his limited militia service and boasted of commanding the largest militia encampment ever. To any that would listen, he claimed to have led a larger body of troops than any general except Winfield Scott, all based on five days of drill and parade with his militia brigade in 1860.[10]

The internal workings of the state volunteer units gave Butler and other antebellum militia commanders a skewed view of military administration and command. The way in which these units were formed and their inter-action with state and local government caused antebellum militia units to be dominated by a mixture of local politics and state military policy, often feeding the belief among militia leaders and state governors that military policy was simply an extension of local partisan politics. Butler demonstrated this partisan mixture by using his political clout to gain command of his regiment and the rank of colonel, then marshaled political allies to save his new rank when attacked by a former political foe who became governor of Massachusetts in 1860.[11] Surviving this challenge, he used his political skills to get elected major general of the Massachusetts Volunteers and reveled in upstaging the furious governor.[12] For Butler and other volunteer militia officers, the result of these types of personal and partisan battles created the expectation that patronage and political alliances would play a major role in any effort to protect and promote military careers.

With as much contact as Butler had with military education and his boasted militia service, this experience in no way was preparation enough for the tactical challenges of Civil War generalship. His recognition of the value of military education did not equate with actual study of the topic, and his brief periods of command at encampments did not consist of actual military training or maneuvers other than small unit drill.[13] Yet, while Butler's pre-war military experience gave him little practical preparation for wartime service in the field, it did give him the sense that he was as prepared as any of his peers. In fact, he was correct in this respect, though not for the reasons he predicted. His background in state and national politics, along with his militia service, helped develop the expertise he would use off the battlefield during the Civil War, and it was these abilities the administration sought when they appointed him. Far more important than the pomp and ceremony of the state's annual encampments, Butler was known for his solid legal and political background as well as his demonstrated skills for getting his political plans adopted, his legal policies enacted, and his audience inspired, which made him precisely the kind of leader the administration needed in the early months of the war.

Between the 1860 election and the shelling of Fort Sumter, Butler demonstrated how some candidates for military appointment could catch the eye of the administration. During these critical months, he became a prominent national voice as a supporter of the Lincoln administration, and he had openly expressed Unionist sentiment early in the secession crisis. In January 1861, when he was being labeled one of the "most ultra of Breckinridge's supporters" and the "bitterest of anti-Republicans" by political foes, he had not hesitated to pledge his allegiance to the Union and attack secessionists in public and in the press.[14] Butler started to rally troops to the cause even before the attack on Sumter. As early as February 1861, the Massachusetts militia major general began to marshal and organize troops throughout New England under the ad hoc Department of New England and coordinated with state governors for the military struggle he predicted was imminent.[15] Butler stood out, contrary to some expectations, as one of the first "War Democrats" to rally to the flag.

As with nearly all political generals, Lincoln did not have to work hard to convince the Massachusetts ex-politician to accept his mandate. Butler's confidence and prominence all but guaranteed his personal involvement at high rank in the great conflict that erupted after the shelling of Sumter.

When the news of the attack reached the courtroom in Boston, he was in the middle of a trial when he dramatically departed the court in midsession, announcing to the judge, "I am called to prepare troops to be sent to Washington."[16] Butler reaped the rewards of this emotional drama by the attention his actions drew in public and in the press; no longer was he referred to as merely a state political figure. He linked his fate to the Union cause by adding the title "general" to all correspondence and referring to himself as a militia general. His actions did attract immediate attention as far away as Boston, giving the people of Massachusetts their first political figure to gain prominence after Fort Sumter.[17]

Foreshadowing the future scheming of many political generals, Butler used the political pull and trickery he had mastered in militia service and as a politician to gain his first command. A political acquaintance of the new secretary of war, Butler immediately telegraphed Simon Cameron and Senator Henry Wilson, chairman of the Committee on Military Affairs and suggested, "You have called for a brigade of Massachusetts troops; why not call for a brigadier-general and staff? I have some hope of being detailed."[18] Leaving nothing to chance, he also arranged a loan with a personal friend who was a bank president to pay to deploy the state militia and openly implied to Governor John Andrew that the availability of the money would be dependent on Butler being named the commander.[19] With the success of these plans, he became the leader of the first brigade the state mustered and began his ascent to becoming one of the first heroes of the war.

By the end of May 1861, Butler would go to the White House and receive a direct national commission as a major general of volunteers in the Union army, with his date of rank making him one of the highest-ranking generals of the Civil War. To many, Butler's selection and promotion seemed to be natural, given the powerful legacy of military amateurism and patronage in the country's heritage. One of Lincoln's personal secretaries wrote after the war that "[Butler] was a lawyer by profession, but possessed in an eminent degree the peculiar American quality of ability to adapt himself to any circumstances or duty, with a quick perception to discover and a ready courage to seize opportunities."[20] Lincoln appointed the militia general because of this faith in inherent martial ability and Butler's attractiveness as a supporter. The president made the appointment, according to Secretary Cameron, because he "deemed the interest of the public service to demand the promotion of General Benjamin F. Butler."[21] This interest focused on rallying Democrats to support the administration, and on this task would Butler be judged by the administration.

Another Massachusetts politician received quick recognition and direct appointment as a major general because he offered similar benefits to the administration. Nathaniel Prentiss Banks had risen in Massachusetts politics during the antebellum years to become the state's Republican governor from 1858 to 1860, elected on his stature as a prominent national figure that began with his selection as Speaker of the House in 1856.[22] After he lost his bid for reelection in 1860, Banks still had faith that his prominence in the party and his advocacy of a sectional compromise would gain him favor with the new Republican administration.[23] This distinction, popularity, and potential influence with different segments of the political spectrum made the ex-governor a prime candidate for military service as a political general.

Even more than Butler, Banks lacked any practical military experience that could justify his appointment as a major general. Prior to the war, he had served on the Military Affairs Committee during his first term in Congress, but he had used that post mostly to improve his standing back home by exerting pressure on the management and contracts for the Springfield Armory in his own congressional district. Banks was unwilling to get involved in setting military policy for the antebellum army. While in Congress, he once claimed that he was "not acquainted with details of military matters, and personally [had] no pride in them."[24] As a state governor, Banks officially commanded the state militia and led it on the annual encampments, but he had little impact on its training and did not practice any form of field command. He merely enjoyed the popular pomp and ceremony of these events.[25] These encampments inspired a political acquaintance to judge the military status of the state militia and write Banks that "the Massachusetts militia, I have no doubt, are as good as any other. Certainly their uniforms are quite as brilliant."[26] Banks's background could not have inspired a belief that he was qualified and prepared to command large bodies of troops in the field during wartime based on his low level of military expertise.

Yet the Lincoln administration commissioned Nathaniel Banks as a major general of volunteers on June 5, 1861. He joined Butler and War of 1812 veteran and politician John A. Dix as major generals with a date of rank of May 16. This direct appointment jumped Banks over all regular army officers except General Winfield Scott and over all volunteer officers except George B. McClellan and John C. Frémont (both with dates of rank of May 14). Far from relying solely on Banks's political savvy, the president assigned the ex-governor to a series of major field commands during the Civil War, even after early debacles in the Shenandoah Valley had shown the limits of his tactical ability. This assignment pattern is significant because it reveals how President

Lincoln believed that Banks's status as a prominent military commander in the field and in the news would rally support for the president's policies.

Lincoln understood the political advantage of having such a prominent moderate Republican in a general's uniform and, a supporting newspaper claimed, wanted very much to have Banks join Butler "in the field."[27] This offer of service at the front immediately paid off for the administration. As soon as Banks was selected, he stepped forward to rally followers to stand with the Union and increased his appeals in support of the war effort. Demonstrating the effectiveness of appointing such prominent politicians, Major General Banks received national attention from the start of the war and justified his selection with his ability to harness such attention. "The eminent intelligence, energy, and activity of these distinguished citizens," the *National Intelligencer* informed its readers regarding the commissioning of Banks and fellow politician Robert Schenk of Ohio to general officer rank, "render their appointment signally judicious and fortunate."[28] This would be Banks's main contribution during the war: to use his prominence to gather support for the war effort and the administration's policies.

In the chaotic first months of the war, Lincoln placed great value on Banks's pull with his constituency and on his national prestige. The president must have known that Banks's public statements about his alignment with the administration by themselves could help rally support from moderates, ex-Democrats, and Know-Nothings.[29] Lincoln also appreciated Banks's loyalty and respect for the cause amid the clamorous cries for military patronage during those first months. Grateful for the opportunity to serve a cause in which he believed, Banks continued his support throughout the war and was one of the few prominent generals always willing to perform any tasks requested by Lincoln.[30] This loyalty was one of the main reasons why the amateur general was given one difficult assignment after another until being mustered out of service in early September 1865, one of the last of the Civil War political generals to be released from his commission.

Regardless of his lack of military experience, Banks became very confident in his military abilities and in the transferability of his political skills to the demands of successful generalship. Always a gifted speaker with strong interpersonal skills, he made a smooth transition to military life and inspired others to perform their duty for the cause. Ordering a set of books on military history and theory, the new major general began a crash course on Jomini and on generalship.[31] While he studied his new profession, Banks enjoyed camp life, the uniform of a general officer, the company of his hand-picked staff, and the martial movements of thousands of subordinates. After one of his first attempts to give commands personally and drill one of his divisions in the field, the amateur general wrote his wife confidently of his ability to command. "I felt as if I had been doing it all my life," Banks boasted, "and I think the officers were surprised."[32] He also believed, with good reason based on the reception he received from the president and the administration, that he was a favorite of Lincoln and of senior cabinet members.[33] This mutual confidence in Banks's generalship would result in his willingness to repeatedly take the field and engage in battle with opponents such as Thomas "Stonewall" Jackson and Richard Taylor, Confederate generals who did not share his lack of military education or experience.

However, decisive battlefield victories were not the service Nathaniel Banks was hired to perform. On the contrary, the Massachusetts politician would fulfill his assigned role simply by being in uniform and in the field. His mandate can best be understood as an issue of political supply and demand. As with Butler, Banks's desire for service during the war coincided with a need for his help in rallying Democrats and moderates to the war effort. Although President Lincoln could have appointed him as a more junior commander at either regimental or brigade level, this choice would not get the prominence or attention required to inspire any of the old constituency and might also have been deemed insulting to the prominent politician. Banks, and more importantly his supporters, may have felt slighted by an assignment more in line with his actual capabilities because of the belief that generalship required only traits that were inherent in every American and that the informal rules of patronage demanded a new military role equivalent in prominence to his old political role. The result was a direct commission to major general and a major field assignment for a man completely untrained in military science and thoroughly unprepared for the challenges of combat generalship in a vast civil war.

President Lincoln similarly harnessed the military service of another politician from his home state of Illinois by appointing former Free Soil Democrat and congressman John Alexander Logan to general officer rank. "Black Jack" Logan would develop into one of the finest combat leaders of the war, would be a very effective field officer, and would rise to become one of William T. Sherman's most experienced corps commanders. Like Butler and Banks, Logan's prewar career did little to indicate his potential as an effective general. Inspired by his father, a vocal politician and war Democrat in the Illinois assembly, Logan did serve in the Mexican War, but he did not see combat. Instead he spent the war on garrison duty in New Mexico. The only opponent this veteran fought was disease, and he never saw a single enemy soldier. Upon his return from the war, Logan became a full-time politician, elected to a series of positions of ever-increasing prominence but never having the time or the interest to become involved with the Illinois state militia. When the shelling of Sumter signaled the outbreak of open hostilities, it was not any sense of military experience that made Logan attractive as a potential wartime commander. Rather it was his popularity with a vital constituency, wavering and allegiance-split southern Illinois, often called "Little Egypt." During the spring of 1861, this volatile region was feeding men into Confederate units in neighboring states, posing a danger to the new Republican administration.

With the loyalty of southern Illinois in doubt, Logan was quiet about his allegiance for months after the firing on Fort Sumter and left open the question of which side of the struggle this region and its most prominent resident would take. Many Illinois residents remembered how Logan gained popularity in 1852 as the chief proponent of legislation effectively banning blacks from entering the state, a stand that did not indicate any potential alliance with the new president or his party. Prior to the special session of Congress, Logan made no major speeches or declarations of intent to his constituency. He waited until July to reveal his strong Unionist sentiments. While Congress was still in session, Logan openly showed his loyalty to the Union by marching with the 2d Michigan toward the Bull Run battlefield. The Illinois congressman, dressed in civilian clothes, spent time under fire helping the wounded and rallying stragglers during the skirmishes before the main battle.[34] The experience of battle and his realization of natural bravery and inherent leadership skills inspired Logan to find a place in uniform to support a cause that was gelling in his mind. He returned to Washington the next day and declared his intent to join the Union army even before the end of the Bull Run debacle.[35]

In a dramatic way, Logan helped secure southern Illinois for the Union. He left Washington after the end of the emergency session of Congress, where he supported every measure that provided men and money for the Union cause. Returning to Marion, a town with divided loyalty in the heart of Little Egypt, Logan delivered a speech on August 19 that clearly and publicly stated his views on the political situation. He climbed on a wagon in the town square and expressed his support for Lincoln with inspiring rhetoric, an action that revealed his value to the administration. "The time has come when a man must be for or against his country," Logan announced. "I, for one, shall stand or fall with the Union and shall this day enroll for the war. I want as many of you as will to come with me." Several immediately stepped forward, and Logan repeated his announcements until he had gathered enough men to muster into service the 31st Illinois. His political appeal was reflected by the fact that eight of the ten companies of the regiment were recruited in his congressional district, and, by some accounts, all but twelve men of his regiment were Democrats.[36]

Appointed as the colonel of this new regiment, Logan began a military career that was remarkable in two respects: it proved that an amateur officer could master the challenges of commanding large units in combat, and it demonstrated the impact that one instance of military patronage could have on the war effort. Yet it was not Logan's military potential, Mexican War experience, or even his ability to marshal a new regiment that brought him to the president's attention as a candidate for high command. Rather, "Black Jack" Logan was seen as a political leader who could rally Democrats to the cause. Logan had been described as the "most powerful of the Democrats in Illinois" and a man who could attract to the Union cause "the loyalty of constituents as probably no other Illinois Congressman of his times."[37] This was exactly the task that Lincoln wanted accomplished and the mandate under which he would appoint Logan as a brigadier general in March 1862. Another of the famous sons of Illinois also recognized Logan's potential to hold Little Egypt for the Union. According to Ulysses S. Grant, "As [Logan] went in politics, so his district was sure to go."[38]

Though his natural leadership ability and repeated tactical success drove Logan higher in the chain of command, it was up to the president and the Senate to dictate whether promotions accompanied these successes. Throughout the war, President Lincoln pushed to get him promoted to maintain his allegiance and prominence. While military patrons Grant and Sherman gave Logan larger commands in their armies, this patronage from the president was vital at the time because old political foes in the Senate voted against his nomination for promotion to major general in November 1862. Given the potential benefit of Logan's continued service and prominence in affecting public opinion in southern Illinois, this first setback was only the start of the partisan struggle over his two stars. While Logan headed a division as a brigadier under Major General James McPherson at the start of the drive on Vicksburg, Governor Richard Yates of Illinois was pushing Lincoln to try again to get Logan promoted "in the behalf of the State and a large majority of her loyal people," as this action would gather support for the government's policies from the people of Illinois and many others in the West.[39] The president resubmitted the request and the Senate approved the promotion in March 1863, with his rank backdated to November 1862. Logan would serve the Union for the rest of the war as a volunteer major general and alternated between commanding a corps in the field and stumping in southern Illinois for the administration and its policies.

Logan's appeal for President Lincoln, like that of Butler and Banks, was the congressman's impact on support for the war through public knowledge of his service, his repeated calls for support for the Union cause, and his defense of the administration's policies during a vicious struggle in Washington being waged by a fragile political coalition. The rationale for these appointments was logical given the pervasive nature of patronage in the political culture and, therefore, the mandates given to these commanders directly related to the reason for their appointment. President Lincoln had an expectation that the political advantage of their support, so desperately needed during the first year of the war, would outweigh any lack of military expertise and experience. In this effort, Lincoln's ear was acutely tuned to the Unionist areas of the upper South and to his need for the support of prominent politicians.

The greatest military challenge facing the president in the immediate period after the fall of Fort Sumter was the need for Union control of the border states. Even a layman's look at the strategic situation gave Lincoln the impression that whichever side gained control of the resource-rich and ideologically divided border region could have a decisive advantage in the war. With rebellion dividing families and setting neighbors against each other, the Civil War in the border states in many ways resembled revolutionary warfare as both sides struggled for control. The use by both sides of regular units, militia, partisans, and guerrilla forces in campaigns that often resembled mixed banditry and terrorism made the war in the border states a triangular conflict for control of the region's populace. As depicted by historian John Shy, a triangular struggle takes place when "two armed forces [and the two governments] contend less with each other than for the support and control of the civilian population."[40] This fight for popular support was exactly what was occurring in the border states and western Virginia, east Tennessee, Kansas, and northern Arkansas.

One effective method of gaining control in such a contested region was through alliances with popular local leaders. The concept of using politically appointed military commanders fit perfectly into this category of struggle. Both sides courted border region support by appointing political leaders as military commanders and having these individuals rally support among their former constituencies. Some of the potentially most influential leaders received offers of position and rank from both of the opposing war departments. As late as August 17, 1861, Lincoln even secretly offered a general's commission to future Confederate general Simon Bolivar Buckner of Kentucky if he would remain loyal to the Union.[41] Many prominent politicians from the contested areas used this opportunity to advance their own interests while supporting the side with which they agreed. Fiery Senator James Lane of Kansas offered to raise eight to ten thousand state troops and to organize four thousand Indians and convinced Lincoln that he should direct the war effort in Kansas. If he was given the authority to rally and command this force, he promised to mount an invasion of Texas.[42] Although Lane's Texas expedition was a failure, the troops and support he raised in Kansas proved to be vital contributions to Union success in the neighboring state of Missouri.

The border region produced a large number of the politically appointed military generals in the Union army. These included Kentucky congressman William Ward, who was commissioned as a brigadier and went on to become a respectable brigade and division commander while fighting in Kentucky and Tennessee. Lincoln even appointed a political general from Texas when Unionist and former Texas congressman Andrew Hamilton offered to support the Northern cause. Commissioned as a Union general, Hamilton served as the military governor of the Department of Texas, reestablishing a loyal government in occupied areas of his home state. Along with Cassius Clay of Kentucky, James Craig of Missouri, James Cooper of Maryland, and others, these men brought political experience and skill, along with their military inexperience, into the Union efforts to return federal control to the contested border regions. Although their contributions in rallying Union support are impossible to quantify, these popular leaders were a vital asset to the North every day that their constituents and neighbors knew they were wearing Union stars on their shoulders.

From the start of the war, Lincoln knew the inherent dangers involved in this military patronage and perfectly understood what he wished to avoid in his military policies. He had served in Congress during "Mr. Polk's War" and witnessed firsthand the damage of partisan infighting on military policy-making and strategy. With this in mind, Lincoln wanted to keep the war from becoming a partisan Republican campaign against slavery if he wanted to avoid the sort of antiwar campaigns that had plagued Polk during the Mexican War. The president therefore needed the assistance of the "War Democrats" to maintain support for a collective war for the Union. The title War Democrat was given to the numerous national and state Democratic politicians who supported the Lincoln administration's war effort and favored suppressing the rebellion militarily over peaceful disunion.[43] Early in

the war, the administration attempted to remove partisanship by the formation of a new Union Party of politicians who supported the war and by
appointment of prominent War Democrats to important military commands.[44] Although the former policy failed at the national level due to the
strength of the partisan political parties, the latter bore fruit throughout the
war and greatly increased support for the sometimes fragile administration.

Lincoln also had to satisfy the other end of the political spectrum to maintain the integrity of his own party. The more radical Republicans pushed from
the start for immediate emancipation and additional harsh war measures
against the South.[45] To focus their influence, the radicals in Congress formed
the Joint Committee on the Conduct of the War, which held hearings and
announced public verdicts on various aspects of the war in an effort to pressure Lincoln to support more extreme policies.[46] They also attempted to
influence Lincoln on military appointments and promotions by endorsing fellow supporters such as General John Frémont and opposing conciliatory leaders such as George B. McClellan. It was largely pressure from this group that
drove Lincoln into repeatedly granting commands to Frémont, Ohio, abolitionist Jacob Cox, and even former Democrat Ben Butler, who drew radical
support for his stand against the return of runaway slaves, who he first deemed
"contrabands of war." The pressure from the radicals may have become tire-
some to the administration, but their support remained vital to passing the
legislation needed to fuel the Union war effort. The interest group that these
appointments pleased least was the serving regular army officers.

Butler's clashes with General Scott over strategy during the first months
of the war laid the foundation for a growing mutual aversion by career officers, West Pointers in particular, and the politically appointed amateurs. As
general in chief, Scott opposed the appointment of Butler. This reaction was
not personal, as Scott argued against any use of volunteer generals who
lacked military knowledge and experience. The first clash occurred after
Butler occupied Baltimore with his brigade without orders. Butler stated
afterward that he believed Scott would not have approved because of his
desire to wait for a coordinated advance against points around the capital by
a more organized and better prepared operation.[47] After Butler conducted
numerous independent actions in Maryland without waiting for specific
orders, he was transferred to command Fortress Monroe and the small number of Union troops on the peninsula, most likely due to Scott complaining
enough to the new president. Butler responded by writing the secretary of
war and other political allies to discover the reason for this move and to
defend all the actions taken in Maryland by claiming that they were

designed solely according to Butler's interpretation of the desires of the administration.[48] This direct appeal to political allies would prove to be a precursor of what was to become a common practice by general officers, both regulars and amateurs, during the Civil War.

The first endeavors to lessen the danger of military incompetence by political generals began with early efforts to close the gap between inexperienced and untrained volunteer officers and the regular army officer corps through the process of screening volunteer officers and testing their knowledge of military fundamentals. The frequent military disasters suffered by the Union armies that began with First Bull Run spurred attempted reforms in the officer corps.[49] On February 6, 1862, the War Department issued General Order No. 12, which called for a halt to general officers commissioning civilians to be on their staffs as a means to control the military patronage system and prevent out-and-out cronyism. Defending these actions, the War Department claimed to be "frequently embarrassed by the actions of general officers of the volunteer service."[50] But for all the efforts of career soldiers like Scott and Halleck, early attempts to mandate and test some level of military knowledge for Union officers failed due to the need for political support from untrained but popular political figures and the general shortage of qualified officers for an army increasing so drastically in size.

However, regular officers scored their first victory in the battle to gain recognition for a distinct military expertise when the president agreed in 1862 to establish standard criteria for wartime general officer appointments. With no formal requirements for what it took to be a general prior to 1860, the deluge commenced at the start of the war, with candidates from across the spectrum of military competence. The predictable reaction by regulars such as Scott and McClellan was to push for the recognition of professional status for military officers that inherently valued the education and experience West Pointers had in abundance. This approach required a mechanism to prevent the appointment of politicians like Butler and Banks, who lacked any formal military training.

The result of this pressure was Lincoln's attempt in August 1862 to halt the flood of requests for military patronage appointments. Following Scott's endorsement of the language, Secretary of War Stanton issued General Order No. 111: "Hereafter no appointments of major-generals or brigadier-generals will be given except to officers of the Regular Army for meritorious and distinguished service during the war, or to volunteer officers who, by some successful achievement in the field shall have displayed the military abilities required for the duties of a general officer."[51] This order from the

War Department also called for a formal examination of any candidate for brigadier's stars. But imposing this limited standard was merely a reaction to true incompetence on the part of some of the initial Union officers, who were already in uniform. It also proved to be an ineffective way for regulars to gain a monopoly on commands, as the most prominent amateur generals were already holding commissions and had powerful political allies to silence any calls for their removal.

The political return of these appointments was seen even at the time. Prominent abolitionist Wendell Phillips praised the president's actions by judging that "Butler . . . and a score of such Democrats, by accepting commissions, and flinging their fortunes in with the flag, settled the doubt [as to a war of one party], and saved the Union."[52] With the support of prominent Democrats such as Butler, former Massachusetts governor Nathaniel Banks, Illinois politician John Logan, and numerous others, Lincoln gained the support of many rank-and-file Democrats and raised recruits in Democratic districts. Although the efforts to establish a Union Party eventually failed, the administration was able to maintain enough support at the opposite end of the political spectrum to pass needed mobilization legislation and to raise the armies required to prosecute the war.

Motivating the Home Front for War

Because of their popularity within a geographic region or with a segment of the political spectrum, these military amateurs were appointed as general officers with a mandate to rally support for the administration by appealing to their former political constituency to join them in uniform, conducting local recruiting drives and forming units that they would later take into battle. Collectively, these men filled a capacity they were well prepared for, and many would serve this need until the surrender at Appomattox. Though political generals such as Butler and Banks failed repeatedly to meet expectations on the battlefield and therefore added to the popular generalization about incompetent amateur commanders, nearly all of them did meet the political mandate from the commander in chief by rallying support and gathering recruits for the Union cause. The effectiveness of this coalition-building is apparent in the positive coverage given to local Union Men Rallies throughout the country, where prominent national and local politicians would share the stage with political generals to inspire and harness such a "mass meeting of Union men, without distinction of party."[53]

Although the War Department issued no coordinated plan for wartime recruiting, the mobilization process in the Northern states was similar in many aspects. After each governor received the secretary of war's assignment of the state quota for a call-up of volunteers, he would divide the quota into regional or county shares and task local leaders to gather recruits. Indiana's adjutant general described the events in a typical recruiting effort:

> Upon receipt of a call from the President, the Governor's plan was to issue a proclamation, stating the requisition made for additional troops, and call upon citizens to fill it at once. He always endeavored to get the influential men in every neighborhood enlisted in the work. Meetings were held, patriotic and stirring speeches were made, and regularly commissioned recruiting officers were induced to zealously exert themselves everywhere. . . . These indispensable officers were selected from the men of the district, of influential character, who were especially qualified by energy and capacity for organization, as well as being conspicuous for their local popularity.[54]

State governors like O. P. Morton of Indiana understood that the outcome of the stirring speeches and patriotic outpourings could often depend upon the reputation and the prominence of the speakers.

Therefore, calls from prominent politicians who had joined the ranks and thrown their support behind the Union could have a major influence on the success of recruiting drives. This awareness of his constituency helps explain Morton's selection for his first adjutant general on the day of Lincoln's initial call for seventy-five thousand militia: popular politician, state militia brigadier, and future major general Lew Wallace. Wallace immediately utilized his political experience to harness "influential men" to speed up the first mobilization.[55] Though it is difficult to judge the number of volunteers who were swept up in these drives who would otherwise have avoided enlistment, the recruiting by political generals had an unmistakable impact. As most Civil War regimental histories begin with the election of officers and the mustering of the regiment, it is very difficult to assess the impact of appeals by various political generals. However, those regiments that had contact with political generals after they were mustered in often use the most glowing phrases when describing their speeches and appeals for supporting the cause.[56] Such forums provided the perfect opportunity to use the skills honed through years of political appeals to harness recruits for the war effort.

In a manner similar to state and local antebellum politics, these newly minted military leaders often used political affiliations to form vast pyramids of military patronage. These networks stretched into nearly every town and city, rallying local leaders, often with the promise of military rank, to gather recruits from their friends and supporters. Mass rallies were a staple of such recruiting drives, the natural medium for politicians in uniform to use their oratory skills to collect volunteers. At these gatherings, politicians and leading citizens, many of whom were seeking officer positions in the new units, would give speeches and attempt to tap into the well of patriotism. Local leaders, many of whom would already be in uniform, would echo these calls until one would cry, "Who will come up and sign the roll?"[57] Inspired by the combination of appeals by prominent antebellum politicians and the calls of homespun citizens they knew, men would step forward to enlist, resulting in surges of volunteers. This process was repeated in every state in the North as governors sought to form regiments, brigades, and even divisions without trained officers.[58]

The prestige and attention that politicians such as Wallace could add to a recruiting campaign made this a natural task for most of the Union political generals. In fact, the majority of these political appointees began their military service with a clear understanding with the administration that they would rally their supporters to the colors in exchange for their stars. Lincoln and Cameron were often very open about the deals made for political appointments. In a telling example, Lincoln directed Cameron to answer the previously mentioned offer to raise troops by James Lane of Kansas with the following unequivocal message: "We need the services of such a man out there [in Kansas] at once: that we better appoint him a brigadier-general of volunteers to-day, and send him off with such authority to raise a force . . . as you think will get him into actual work quickest."[59] The administration fully comprehended the potential benefits of such spokesmen for the Union cause and was more than willing to risk the dangers of military inexperience for the known dividends of political support. It is possible to look at specific examples of the impact of just a few political generals at critical periods for recruiting in the Union war effort. On at least two occasions, recruiting drives by these amateur generals provided vital manpower for the campaigns that altered the course of the war.

The first occurred when Butler conducted a recruiting drive in New England in the fall of 1861. After his small but well publicized loss in the skirmish at Big Bethel in June 1861, former regular John Wool replaced him at Fortress Monroe. Seeking another command and another position to help the Union, Butler suggested to Lincoln that his new mission should be to marshal Democratic support for the war. "Get the leading Democrats and they will bring in their rank and file, their clientele, who believe in them and would rally about them," Butler offered to the president. "Give me the authority and money to organize and pay troops with, and I will go to New England and enlist six to ten thousand men." This was exactly the help the president needed and fit perfectly the requirement that Butler and others had been appointed to accomplish. Butler promised Lincoln, "I will have every officer a Democrat . . . and if I succeed, you had better try it in a good many other states."[60] Lincoln saw Butler's offer as an opportunity not only to raise more troops, which was constantly a challenge for the federal government, but also to rally additional Democratic support for the war.[61]

Therefore, on August 17, Butler was given permission to raise additional New England regiments, and Lincoln wired that his request to recruit five thousand volunteers was "cheerfully granted." On September 12, Lincoln formally established the Department of New England with Butler as commander to cement the deal with the Massachusetts politician. During that fall, Butler moved throughout New England convincing prominent Democratic politicians to form their own regiments, recruiting their followers to fill the new units.[62] By chance, the height of Lincoln's frustration with the squabbling in Massachusetts occurred right when Secretary of the Navy Gideon Welles approached the president with a plan to seize New Orleans if the Union army could spare the required troops. General in Chief George McClellan recommended against the expedition because he believed he had no troops to spare, but the president saw an opportunity to solve two problems at once. Therefore in February 1862, Lincoln formally abolished the Department of New England and ordered Butler to prepare his new troops for movement to Ship Island in the Gulf of Mexico. Butler's recruiting drive had filled six new infantry regiments and a new artillery battery, all told a total of approximately six thousand volunteers.[63] In the resulting campaign, these New England regiments recruited and commanded by Butler were instrumental in capturing New Orleans and a large portion of Louisiana.[64]

A second significant recruiting drive occurred in the Northwest and involved Illinois Democrat and political general John McClernand. Lincoln appointed McClernand, along with fellow southern Illinois politician John Logan, to influence public opinion in the border regions of the president's home state. Although McClernand had seen limited service in the Black Hawk War nearly thirty years before, his commission as a Union general was based on his potential influence in a region of questionable loyalty to the Union.[65] As a McClernand biographer concluded, "The real reason for the appointment was the fact that McClernand needed the position to get ahead politically, while Lincoln needed a man of McClernand's political talents to aid the cause of the Union."[66] McClernand quickly accepted the appointment and heeded Lincoln's plea to keep the region "right side up."[67] He started his military service by recruiting a brigade in the counties of southern Illinois for his own command and to rally Union sentiment in that area.

The effect that "leading citizens" like McClernand and Logan had in dissipating Confederate sentiment in southern Illinois and in gathering Union recruits was strong enough to earn the attention of fellow Union generals and partisan Chicago newspapers. Newly commissioned Brigadier Ulysses Grant was also on hand to witness the effect that Logan and McClernand had in southern Illinois. In his memoirs, Grant wrote a long passage concerning the rallying of potential secessionists from the bottom half of the state, giving most of the credit to the two political generals. Grant also praised their recruiting ability and recounted the story of how a pair of patriotic speeches from McClernand and Logan convinced one of his regiments to reenlist almost to the man.[68] One Republican newspaper in Chicago gave credit for the emerging loyalty of the entire region, "for they have labored night and day to instruct their fellow citizens in the true nature of the contest, and to organize their aroused feelings into effective military strength. They have succeeded nobly."[69] The paper went on to describe how loyal volunteers from the recently secessionist southern counties of the state had exceeded the enlistment quotas during the fall of 1861.

During the campaigns of spring and summer 1862, McClernand commanded at brigade and division level under generals Grant and Halleck without working harmoniously with either. This situation signaled the start of a feud between former regulars and political generals in the western theater that would eventually end McClernand's military career and may have kept Logan from rising to command an army. McClernand had earned the ire of Halleck and Grant for his inflated claims in the newspapers for credit in the victory at Shiloh and for slurs against Grant's leadership. In August 1862, Halleck gratefully responded to McClernand's request to return to Illinois and assist Governor Yates in rallying new recruits.[70] McClernand did not pass up this opportunity to continue his drive for advancement and his crusade against Grant and Halleck, as he told a large Chicago crowd that "we want the right man to lead us; a man who will appoint a subordinate officer on account of his merit, and not because he is a graduate of West Point. Neither Caesar nor Cromwell were graduates of West Point."[71] The Illinois general repeatedly issued calls for new volunteers while criticizing the current Union chain of command. Many newspapers printed McClernand's speeches, which raised his popularity with the citizens but ruined any chance of reconciliation with Grant or Halleck.[72]

During this period, McClernand also traveled to Washington to sell Lincoln on a secret plan to open the Mississippi with himself as commander.[73] He proposed a deal that Lincoln found too good to pass up; he agreed to throw his support as a northwestern Democrat behind the war effort and raise a new army of recruits to open the Mississippi if the president would agree to grant him command of the expedition. With the western governors complaining about the failure to unblock the Mississippi, Lincoln agreed.[74] On October 12, 1862, Lincoln secretly ordered McClernand to raise new regiments in Indiana, Illinois, and Iowa to form an army to seize Vicksburg and open the Mississippi.[75] Secretary of War Edwin Stanton expressed the hopes of the administration by telegraphing McClernand that "the local interest and feeling in favor of the Mississippi operations and your personal influence are relied on for the increased force, as the bounty-funds will be exhausted by the previous calls."[76] Recruitment had lagged in Illinois, but McClernand attacked the challenge with enthusiasm and a plan.[77] Lincoln's faith proved well placed, as the Illinois general marshaled forty thousand new troops from Indiana, Illinois, and Iowa by December 16.[78]

His political connections and pull were also used to marshal, equip, and concentrate these new units much faster and more efficiently than the formal War Department organization could have done.[79] Because of the small size of the War Department and the limited number of experienced federal military bureaucrats, the same politicians who dominated the region's antebellum politics controlled much of each state's military infrastructure. Therefore, some of these same politicians could return, wearing a uniform and bearing an officer's commission, and have a major impact on local recruiting. This was something a prominent ex-politician like McClernand could do successfully, using a web of antebellum political contacts to coordinate training camps, arrange transportation, and contract for the vast amount of arms and supplies required.[80] Although McClernand afterward was denied command of the campaign in favor of Grant, the new recruits he helped rally in his own corps and William T. Sherman's corps played a vital role in the eventual capture of Vicksburg and gave Grant the troops needed to break the deadlock in the West.

Constituencies along the political spectrum were not the only elements in Northern society marshaled by the appointment of prominent members to military command. Lincoln also relied on political generals to gather the support of the numerous ethnic minorities in the North. The administration courted pivotal German communities in Pennsylvania, Missouri, and cities with the military appointment of prominent German politicians like Franz Sigel and Carl Schurz. Newspaper accounts overtly expanded these politicians' appeals to ethnic Germans with calls to "Germans of Massachusetts: As you Battled for the 'Faderland,' Battle New for your Adopted Country! Remember Franz Sigel!" or for Germans to go to the "General Recruiting office for Major General Sigel's Corps d'Armee *und die aiten deutch Regiment.*"[81] The quest for ethnic support for the war even stretched to rallying immigrants straight off the boat.[82] Many Irish immigrants flocked to the ranks of the Union army after being called out by General Thomas Meagher and other distinguished Irish officers. Much of this recruiting was done through overt appeals to the Irish minority.[83] German abolitionist Carl Schurz even went so far as to announce to Lincoln's secretary John Hay in April 1861 that he was going to the German communities "to arm his clansmen for the wars."[84] With all these potential volunteers (and voters), Lincoln was willing to give national prestige to these popular ethnic figures by means of military appointments and command opportunities if such action would harness their supporters to the Union cause.

In a political system so steeped in patronage, Lincoln made little attempt to hide the quid pro quo involved with the appointment of men like Schurz, Sigel, and others. Lincoln often wrote openly about how many Irish, German, or other types of recruits he wanted from his potential new generals, while these men made similar promises of specific numbers of volunteers in their petitions for military appointment.[85] The threshold for the president in most cases was the most obvious number: if a popular politician could enlist a new brigade-size unit, that man would get the brigadier position as its commander. Lincoln was also willing to exchange military rank for the promise of pleasing ethnic minorities in uniform. When the relief of the popular Frémont in St. Louis sparked unrest in the German community, Lincoln's first reaction was to appoint Governor Gustave P. Koerner of Illinois as a brigadier general and send him to the Union headquarters there. With this "talented German gentleman" on the scene in uniform, the president wrote Major General Halleck, "you can set everything right with the Germans."[86] As this example shows, Lincoln saw military patronage as the best—and quickest—way to bind recognized ethnic leaders to the administration's cause as well as the surest way to harness their popularity.

The clearest example of the pull of one of these ethnic leaders is the effect that Franz Sigel had on the German community. Sigel was a former Prussian military officer who had gained prominence in the German-American community because of his experience in the European uprisings of 1848 fighting against the Prussian aristocracy. Even before the firing at Sumter, Sigel was active in rallying the ethnic German community to the Union cause. In February 1861, he joined a local Missouri militia regiment as their colonel and used his growing popularity to convince hundreds of Germans to enlist in the Union militia.[87] Sigel sensed the approaching conflict and worked with Missouri Republican and future political general Francis Blair to prepare Missouri by forming Unionist "Wide Awakes" and "Home Guards" to oppose the violent secessionist element in the state.

On May 17, 1861, Sigel was appointed as a volunteer brigadier because Lincoln believed the support of the numerous German communities could be decisive in securing Missouri for the North. Sigel rewarded Lincoln's insight when he then recruited a full division of volunteers in St. Louis, with the majority of regiments consisting of German-Americans. As he fought battles in the West with his "Dutchmen," his standing in the German community continued to rise and his notoriety spread throughout the country as "Sigel Committees" sprang up in the German communities in big cities to encourage recruiting and to lobby Lincoln and the War Department for Sigel's advancement.[88] His contribution to recruiting for the Union cause can be seen in the acceptance of "I fights mit Sigel" as an expression of German willingness to join the army and support the Union.

Prominent politicians also served the Lincoln administration, and therefore the Union war effort, by publicly supporting the president's policies. After being relieved and replaced by Banks in New Orleans in November 1862, Butler made a triumphant return to Washington and to his home town of Lowell, being met everywhere with standing-room-only crowds who were enthusiastic about seeing the Union conqueror who had tamed the largest Confederate city. At each stop, at a time when the administration could be legitimately worried about Butler's loyalty, the hero of New Orleans repaid his appointment to military service with fiery speeches supporting the war, calling for immediate emancipation and instructing the crowds to increase their support for the Union cause.[89] Butler followed this tour by testifying to the Joint Committee on the Conduct of the War where he pleased both the radicals and the president by defending the current reconstruction efforts and calling for the use of black troops. He passed up the implied opportunity to criticize the conduct of the war effort and challenge his relief.[90] By leading the drive toward emancipation and defending the administration's policies, political generals like Butler justified their selection through the repeated use of their oratory and political talents.

Another part of the political generals' mandate was marshaling public opinion and stumping the old constituency for support. "Black Jack" Logan, serving alongside Missouri Republican Francis P. Blair in the western theater, demonstrated the positive effect that could be garnered in maintaining popular support for the war just by continuing his service in uniform and periodically visiting his home state to rally the public. Logan would put a popular spin on the war effort by telling cheering crowds he was helping no political partisans or particular party and appealed to them to help the "common cause" of the Union. After the enactment of the very unpopular Conscription Act, Logan made a swing through his old state. He told all who would listen that the legislation was needed because the army needed more soldiers, and that by supporting the law, they would demonstrate their support for the Illinois soldiers already in the field. After the first few of these rallies, President Lincoln repeatedly requested that Secretary of War Stanton place Logan on leave from his command to return to the stump in Illinois.[91]

Logan's speeches were praised in the Old Northwest for the support they drummed up for the administration. One "war speech," which drew heavy applause and newspaper attention, simply called on "every patriot in the land" to come out, volunteer to be in the Union army, and join the righteous cause. Logan declared he was also for a vigorous prosecution of the war and appealed for support for all the Union policies for the salvation of the government.[92] The fiery speechmaker also would often draw upon his own service to inspire support for the cause. "I have seen the Republican stand by my side and the Democrat and the Abolitionist [in battle] . . . they are all fighting for the same country, the same ground, the same Constitution," Logan would tell cheering crowds. "Quit your quarreling. Be for your government, in spite of what anyone may say."[93] His effect in southern Illinois was such that he was thanked, along with other prominent supporters of the administration who had enlisted, for having "labored night and day to instruct their fellow citizens in the true nature of the contest, and to organize their aroused feelings into effective military strength."[94] This statement best summarizes the effect that the political generals had on their constituents when the combination of talented political orator and appointment as a military officer coincided.

At election times or during periods of political unrest in the North, such as the publication of the Emancipation Proclamation in 1862 and the issuance of the Conscription Act in 1863, Lincoln allowed many political generals to leave their units and stump for the Republican ticket and for the president's policies in their states and among their old constituents. At no time was this support more important than during the elections of 1864, when Banks, Logan, and many other generals were granted leave to rally support for Lincoln's reelection, and the president entrusted the task of maintaining order and calm in the streets of New York City to none other than Benjamin Butler, who promised to prevent any repetition of the draft riots of the year before. As a former Douglas Democrat and self-proclaimed Douglas worshiper, Logan campaigned hard to gather votes for the incumbent. "Mr. Lincoln stands, I say, upon the true Union platform," he would tell large crowds across the Old Northwest, "and, therefore, I am for him."[95] Logan's impact on the campaign, when joined with that of other political generals stumping for Lincoln, would help gather the votes necessary for reelection and help the president gain enough of a victory to provide him with a mandate from the people to pursue his war policies until the end. What all these contributions indicate is the conclusion that these political generals played a vital part, perhaps even a decisive role, in rallying volunteers and support for the Union war effort.

Away from the fields of battle, the political generals made a vital contribution to the war effort by using their political skills for the Union cause. Many also played unique roles in assisting the Union victory, including Maryland Whig James Cooper, who organized many of the Union POW camps, John Dix, who organized and led the suppression of the New York City draft riots, and Carl Schurz, whose oratory rallied German abolitionists to the flag. Many of their contributions, such as Francis Blair's drive to secure Missouri or the endeavors of Polish immigrant Albin Schoepf, who fought in Kentucky (and whose sole qualification for general officer rank appears to have been his service in the antebellum War Department as a clerk), never made it into the history books. Together, these men helped establish much of the popular support for the Union war effort. Doing so, the amateur Union generals played a significant role in enabling the nation to survive the gloomy early years of the war.

Though the reputation of the political generals for battlefield setbacks may be accurate for some of the amateurs like Butler and Banks, this standard caricature neglects the vital contribution of the political generals in rallying popular support of the war. The fact that these politicians in uniform organized new regiments, gave patriotic speeches, and encouraged enlistment is not in doubt. The extensive newspaper coverage given to their "war speeches" and "Union rallies" indicates how widespread this effect was and how influential contemporary newspaper editors believed the political generals to be.[96] In this manner, many of these politicians and prominent civilians fulfilled their mandate and justified their appointment as military leaders during a long and terrible war. However, allowing these amateurs to hold field commands was not without risk, for many of them were much less successful on the battlefields of the Civil War.

Conclusion

In many ways, "the Beast" Ben Butler has come to represent the stereotypical political general. Most traditional studies of the war recount his getting "bottled up" in the Bermuda Hundred, disparage his conduct during the Petersburg Campaign, or belittle his failed attempt to seize Fort Fisher. Yet in his autobiography, simply called *Butler's Book*, General Butler was able to truthfully list "several things . . . which have been done by me although I am supposed to have needed a 'technical military education,'" including the pacification of Baltimore, removing the Confederate threat to besiege Washington in 1861, the seizure of Fort Hatteras, and the capture of New Orleans.[97] Added to these military accomplishments could be the early marshaling of the Massachusetts volunteer militia, the intimidation of the secessionist legislature of Maryland and the seizure of their state seal, the recruitment of six thousand volunteers without bounties or impressment, the enlistment of numerous prominent New England Democrats, the offer of a legal solution to the issue of "contrabands," and the active support of a nationally popular Democrat during Lincoln's reelection campaign. This list indicates the folly of comparing regular army generals and political generals by the criteria of tactical success.

Lincoln's need for the support of prominent men such as Butler, Banks, and Logan was inescapable given the nature of the crisis threatening the Republic. Major general and corps commander Jacob D. Cox, an Ohio politician and former brigadier general of the militia, accurately comprehended the nature of the situation facing the administration during the formation of the nation's first mass army when he wrote:

> In an armed struggle which grew out of a great political contest, it was inevitable that eager political partisans should be among the most active in the new volunteer organizations. They called meetings, addressed the people to arouse their enthusiasm, urged enlistments, and often set the example by enrolling their own names first. . . . It was a foregone conclusion that popular leaders of all grades must largely officer the new

troops. . . . It was the application of an old Yankee story, "If the Lord *will* have a church in Paxton, he must take *sech as ther' be* for deacons." [98]

And if the politically astute Union president wished to have a large number of volunteers for the Union army, it was only natural that popular prominent political figures would receive military commissions to influence their supporters during this period of national crisis.[99] In this instance, the president understood that the use of political figures in the military was both culturally inescapable and politically beneficial. As a result, the popularity and political influence of the Union political generals proved vital in recruiting and rallying support for the Lincoln administration's wartime policies.

The argument could be made that many if not most of these volunteers recruited by political generals would have enlisted anyway given the initial patriotic rallying around the flag during the first year of the war. While there is some element of truth to this assertion as far as raw numbers were concerned, the contribution of political generals was not as important in how many as in who was recruited. The number of recruits enlisted by well-known politicians-in-uniform like Butler and McClernand was dwarfed by the calls for volunteers in the hundreds of thousands. But many of the men gathered by Butler and other political generals were Democrats who had opposed Lincoln's election, and their officers were local Democratic politicians. In a similar manner, ethnic leaders like Sigel tied their own followers to the war effort and indirectly to the administration's policies. The involvement of these prominent politicians also significantly aided the strained Union War Department by utilizing local patronage and know-how to gather, supply, and transport the volunteers to federal muster points.

Lincoln's risks with the appointment of political generals may have paid off in what problems the Union did not have: none of the border states joined the Confederacy, the Democratic Party did not consolidate into an antiwar party, no ethnic minorities failed to join the cause, and the Union armies did not halt their offensives for lack of new volunteers. Although the prevention of these disasters cannot be attributed solely to the involvement of political generals, examples of their wartime accomplishments show their contribution to the eventual Union victory. It is this aspect of the Union political generals that has been the most neglected by military studies of the Civil War. Once these neglected facets of Butler and the other political generals emerge, the historical question of interest changes from How could the Union win with such men in uniform? to Could the Union possibly have won without them? The answer to this question may well be a resounding no that shatters the accepted caricature of the group solely as bungling and inept battlefield commanders. Indeed, they were truly a "necessity of the times" in gathering support for the war.

Yet throughout the war, the military task ahead always seemed daunting. Because the Southerners were willing to use force to resist and had fielded their own army, the administration believed that political defeat for the rebellion rested on tactical victories in the field.[100] Though lacking any formal military training and greatly misjudging the political strength of secession in 1861, Secretary Cameron expressed this link between political and military campaigns that was proven very early in the war. In October 1861, he theorized, "Thus it has been made clearly apparent that in whatever direction the forces of the Union have extended their protection . . . has aided to restore and maintain the authority of the government."[101] The political objective of the Union would therefore require military success, and the achievement of military organization and tactical victories would rest in the hands of the appointed generals. This need would drive the search for military "experts," career officers and West Point graduates who would know what to do because of training and experience. How did the Lincoln administration find and harness such experts?

CHAPTER THREE

"Reducing Chaos to Order"
The Need for Regular Officers

Major General Henry Wager Halleck traveled west by train from Washington in November 1861 and dreaded what he would find at the end of his journey. George B. McClellan, the new commanding general of the entire Union army, had assigned Halleck to what McClellan believed to be the second most critical task currently facing the Union. Halleck was sent west to organize the Union war effort in Missouri and along the Mississippi River. "You have not merely the ordinary duties of a military commander to perform, but the far more difficult task of reducing chaos to order," McClellan had warned him. "I trust to you to maintain thorough organization, discipline, and economy throughout your department."[1] On November 19, the new commander of the Department of the Missouri disembarked at St. Louis with a mandate to impose organization, discipline, and economy on the turmoil and discord that was apparent from as far away as the nation's capital.

To a consummate regular like Halleck, utter chaos indeed prevailed in St. Louis and throughout his vast area of responsibility. The war had been going on for over half a year, yet local troops were still without full uniforms or sufficient arms. Union officers had signed massive contracts for supplies that no one seemed able to find, scattered guerrilla bands were operating all over the state, and in spite of a solid corps of loyal citizens, no army large enough to secure the state for the Union was ready to take the field. One full month would go by before Halleck would order his commanders to wipe out the guerrillas in their areas and get their troops ready to take the offensive against the Confederate army under General Sterling Price, a former congressman and ex-governor of Missouri.[2] This pause in operations, while unpopular with the administration and the Northern public, allowed Halleck to make organizing

51

and training his forces what he and most of his West Point peers deemed to be the Union's highest priority.

To the new administration at the start of the war, Halleck's mission in Missouri was one example of how the main burden for the organization and coordination of the vast military effort fell on the small number of available regular officers. Most politicians in Washington and the state capitals assumed that these West Pointers were all trained for this very challenge, ready to prepare the green volunteers and amateur officers to take the field. Though they did not completely share the belief held by many West Pointers that officership was a distinct skill requiring education and expertise, the president, state governors, and prominent politicians invariably entrusted major field commands to Military Academy graduates like Halleck and valued their experience in military affairs. This inclination was due to a generalized faith that some combination of West Point education, service in the regular army, or combat in Mexico or on the frontier made each of these men ready for leadership positions in the rapidly expanding Union army. Yet, if Lincoln and his cabinet actually believed this stereotype of all West Pointers, why were some West Pointers with little actual experience elevated far above senior career regular officers?

Who was promoted out of the regular officer corps to general's stars during the first year of the war will show how the generalized expectation of expertise guided many of these selections. The background and appointment of famous West Pointers like Halleck, George McClellan, Ambrose Burnside, and William T. Sherman to general officer rank will reveal the convoluted political and military calculations that dictated their promotion. Though each was chosen for a similar mandate, their diverse paths to high command splinter the image of a "stereotypical" West Point graduate in 1861. However, the resulting success of these same West Pointers in the initial task of preparing the Union troops under their command demonstrates the validity of some of their assumed organizational and training skills.

Without a formalized system for evaluating performance or potential, the president and his political allies had no agreed upon standard of generalship, even for the former regular army officers. Raised in a political culture dominated by patronage, Lincoln simply made the best choices based on advice from patrons and supporters in his own cabinet, in Congress, and in the state capitals. For the administration, there was simply no way to judge who was ready for the challenge of handling large units other than personal ties, impressions, and reputations. Therefore, while the importance of drill and organizational ability equaled a need for West Pointers, their individual appointments were not based on any systematic evaluation of seniority or combat experience. Rather, the informal system that led to their selection was dominated by political patronage in combination with expectations of expertise in a manner similar to that by which the military amateurs were chosen.

Equating Experience with Expertise

For the Lincoln administration, one of the first tasks in fielding this immense new army was organization. This challenge was enormous, requiring military officers to instill order since no contemporary civilian organization was large or complex enough to produce the specific managerial skills needed. The War Department bureaucracy was quickly overwhelmed during the frantic first months of the war, and it required the assistance of anyone with experience to provide guidance and direction to the flood of new regiments. It was this task that regulars were assigned first. The West Pointers who had stayed in the service or rejoined the officer corps were prepared to deal with this mission because the challenges involved similar tasks to what the majority had done prior to the war. Their shared Military Academy background gave them a mindset that valued the order and discipline they sought to impose. Antebellum West Point yielded a habit of discipline and military administration, shaped by an education system that imposed "regularity," "structured life," and "organization" as shared memories and values.[3] The products of this shared experience were prepared for the task of "reducing chaos to order."

Although military experience was valued and sought after when appointing these new general officers and in assigning commanders to large new units, who was actually selected had a lot more to do with old-fashioned political patronage than with any systematic consideration of level of experience or of command aptitude. When President Lincoln was searching for his first army commander for the troops around Washington, he selected Major Irvin McDowell (USMA 1838), who was then performing duties as a mustering officer, over many more senior candidates like Edwin "Bull" Sumner or George Gordon Meade who had longer service in the army and who had command experience, though only with small units. McDowell, who in twenty-three years of service as a staff officer had never commanded a unit in the field, was appointed as a brigadier in the regular army on May 14, 1861, as a result of the intervention of Secretary of the Treasury Salmon

Chase.[4] Chase convinced the president that McDowell was perfect for the job of forming a volunteer army and supported the fellow Ohio native even after the disaster at First Bull Run. Because of their access to the president and his need for their support, cabinet secretaries such as Chase often were able to influence general officer appointments simply by presenting the names of candidates to a commander in chief who had few friends in the regular army and little knowledge of the officer corps.

Most officers understood this patronage system and the impact it had on promotion, and some future generals understood how to use this system for their own advancement. A young captain by the name of John Pope demonstrated the personal nature of communications and relationships of the antebellum era when he tried to influence a newly elected president from his home state of Illinois with an appeal for a new assignment. Then Pope, serving as a topographical engineer building lighthouses on the Great Lakes, made a direct appeal to a mutual friend of the president's to be stationed in Washington to be near the new president. In a letter dated April 11, 1861, Pope suggested that "it would be well for Mr Lincoln to have near him some Army friend interested in him personally. . . . I would be gratified therefore if the president would order me to Washington . . . as his aide and military secretary."[5] Pope's letter was not unusual for the antebellum officer corps. Though most officers claimed to disdain politics and politicians, the officer corps had a long history of politicking for promotion and advancement.[6]

Pope himself demonstrated this trend as soon as the first shots were fired at Fort Sumter. Within a week of the declaration of war, the young captain began a letter writing campaign to gain advancement and promotion. This action bore fruit for Pope as it did for many officers during that first month of the war. In response to these appeals, the president wrote to Secretary Cameron on April 26, forwarding with his endorsement a request from the governor of Illinois to have Captain Pope released from federal service to assist in the organization and equipment of the military forces of the state.[7] Pope had not only sent his appeal to Governor Yates but had also sent an offer for his services directly to the president. The end result for this ambitious officer was a nomination as a brigadier of volunteers that was confirmed by the Senate in August 1861.

What the communications and appeals for patronage gained for a junior officer like Pope was raising his name to the administration that was controlling appointments and promotions.[8] This awareness was critical in determining who was selected for positions in the Union high command because of the lack of any formal system of evaluating officer potential and effectiveness prior to the crisis. In an organization that relied almost solely on seniority for peacetime promotions, a new president and cabinet would have no place to turn to for information on potential candidates for generalship—except to those officers known to any of them personally. Therefore, the political strength of the recommending patron was important because only those close to, and important to, the president could present candidates for generalship with the confidence their wishes would be heeded. President Lincoln became personally involved in so many patronage deals that he had to ask Secretary of War Simon Cameron to send his blank nominations to be laid before the Senate. Lincoln made so many appointments to brigadier general that he admitted to the secretary that he had forgotten many of the officers' names.[9] This story of patronage was common for nearly every Union general appointed during the first months of the war, whether politician with little military experience or former regular carrying a diploma from the Military Academy.

Perhaps no officer demonstrated a talent for harnessing patrons during the first months of the war more than George B. McClellan. Soon after the first shots of the war, the governors of the three largest states all sought McClellan's services due to his reputation from service in Mexico, from his selection and travels to Europe with the Delafield Commission, and from his success as a railroad executive. McClellan played each offer against the others, encouraged by some of his fellow officers to hold out for the best deal regarding appointment and assignment.[10] This networking paid off in the end with a direct appointment as a major general of volunteers, a major leap for a man who six years prior had resigned his commission as a captain in the First Cavalry Regiment. As this example shows, regulars were not above using contacts and patrons to advance their careers during the war, a continuation of the antebellum legacy of political involvement for patronage purposes.

McClellan's efforts to get an appointment to high command benefited from both an impressive military vita and a wealth of political contacts. En route to see Governor Andrew Curtain in Pennsylvania, McClellan stopped in Columbus, Ohio, to see Governor William Dennison about plans to defend Cincinnati against the feared invading columns from Kentucky. Within hours of their meeting, Dennison rushed a special bill through the legislature appointing McClellan a major general of volunteers from the state of Ohio.[11] Almost immediately, the new commander began to correspond with General Scott and prominent politicians in Washington about his duties, his supply needs, and his own rank in the regular army. As a result, McClellan received the highest possible advancement on May 14, promoted to major general in the regular army. Only General Scott, whose own commission as a major general was awarded when McClellan was just fourteen years old, now outranked the "Young Napoleon."[12] He owed his new position to the patronage and support of Secretary of the Treasury Chase, a former governor and senator from Ohio, who made him a protégé.[13] McClellan used his backer's patronage for his own advancement and was on his way toward replacing Scott as commanding general of the Union army.

Like McClellan, Henry Halleck's military reputation at the start of the war harnessed the support of his own patron, in the person of Winfield Scott, and made his selection as general officer a logical choice for the Lincoln administration. Yet the appointment to general officer rank of a renowned military theorist such as Halleck, dubbed "Old Brains" by many of his fellow officers in the antebellum officer corps, would still require a nomination from the president and approval by the Senate. With this prerequisite, Halleck joined the ranks of all the candidates for stars in needing someone to suggest his name to the president and to marshal the support of key politicians in Congress. Halleck's patron, however, was in uniform, but General Scott performed the same function as many politicians as he brought the officer's name to the attention of the president. Halleck's experience in writing about strategy and military policy convinced the commanding general to suggest his name to the president, with thoughts of having him take over the highest position in the army.[14] Convincing Lincoln to appoint Halleck was an easy task, as he seemed on paper to be the best qualified of all the loyal candidates to be a successful general.[15]

Halleck was not a novice to politics and political influence, and his route to being appointed a Union general in 1861 followed a common path that involved a network of supporters and a commission in a state militia. He had experienced the complexity and impact of politics while assigned in California during the Mexican War. Though he missed the experience of Scott's grand campaign on Mexico City, he waged a far less conventional campaign supporting federal authority in the California territory and had even served for a period as acting secretary of state. After the war, Halleck remained in the region to help the drive for statehood and used his budding legal talent to assist in the formulation of the state constitution. After resigning from the army in 1854, he began a second career in law and business, becoming very successful at both. He was also involved in forming the California militia, called the Pioneer California Guard, and in 1860 was appointed as a major general in the state militia. Armed with this seemingly vast experience, Halleck was appointed a major general of regulars on August 19, 1861, while still in California and was therefore outranked only by Scott, McClellan, and Frémont. Halleck's appointment reflected the value that the Lincoln administration placed on experience while highlighting the role that patrons played in bringing this experience to the attention of the president.

Though much less distinguished and nearly a decade more junior, Ambrose Burnside seemed to have displayed substantial promise at the start of the war, and he was selected to be a general officer by similar means and for similar reasons. Burnside was an 1847 graduate from the Military Academy as an artillery officer who just missed the Mexican War, arriving in the enemy capital just after it fell to Scott's forces. Part of the occupying garrison, the young lieutenant learned army bureaucracy while serving in various staff assignments and completing additional duties before leaving Mexico for frontier duty. During his tour on the southwestern frontier, Burnside was involved in some skirmishes with the Apaches but spent much of his time learning logistics and staff duties before resigning his commission in 1853 after less than six years of service.[16] The result was not a veteran schooled in warfare, but rather an officer with a basic understanding of how an army maintained and administered itself at the small-unit level.

Burnside's time outside the army also added to developing his organizational and administrative skills. After leaving army service, the young entrepreneur went into business manufacturing a breech-loading rifle he had designed while on the frontier. However, his business failed and went bankrupt after the loss of a promised government contract, and Burnside was forced to turn to a friend from his cadet years, George B. McClellan, for employment. McClellan got him a job with the Illinois Central Railroad, where Burnside served as a company treasurer in Chicago and later New York, and from this experience was exposed to the bureaucracy of a successful large organization. During this period Burnside and McClellan also met a young lawyer assigned to their company named Abraham Lincoln. This chance interaction gave the officers name recognition with the future commander in chief. The employment did not add anything to either officer's military experience but did give these West Pointers and many like them further practice dealing with organizational problems as well as the benefit of exposure to influential politicians and businessmen involved with the railroad.

Burnside also became personally familiar with the game of politics and the workings of patronage. The evidence of these skills was how, within three years of resigning his commission, the young West Point graduate ran for Congress and became a major general in the state militia, both while only thirty-one years old. After he built and managed the Bristol Rifle Works in his home state of Rhode Island, Burnside parleyed his limited military experience into an appointment as a major general in the state volunteer militia on June 26, 1856.[17] Also in 1856, he was appointed to the Military Academy's prestigious Board of Visitors. As these two events reveal, state politicians and militia volunteers valued Burnside's West Point training and military service. He became personally involved in politics that same year when he was nominated and ran as a Democrat for one of the congressional seats for his home state, though he lost badly in the election that fall. This immersion in antebellum politics introduced Burnside to many of the politicians in New England who would alternately hail him and damn him later during the war and provided the path he would follow back into the army to the award of stars for his uniform.

At the start of the war, Burnside was quickly selected for a command and promoted to general officer rank in a manner similar to many other West Pointers, with entry as a senior militia officer and politician patrons providing the mechanism for appointment. On the day that Lincoln issued his call for seventy-five thousand volunteers, William Sprague, the governor of Rhode Island, contacted Burnside in New York. The governor implored him to come back to his home state and assist in forming the first volunteer units. Within days, Burnside was appointed colonel and commander of the First Rhode Island Volunteer Regiment with the support of Rhode Island's governor and state legislature. After frantic mobilization and only rudimentary training, Major Irvin McDowell, nine years senior to the new volunteer colonel from Rhode Island, mustered his unit into federal service on May 2.[18] Upon mobilization, Burnside was appointed as a full colonel in the regular army and jumped in rank over McDowell and many others who had stayed in the service. Aided by petitioning from home state politicians and popular recognition for his role at Bull Run, Burnside was promoted in early August to brigadier general with the unspoken mandate of both forming new units and commanding them successfully in the field.

Immediately following his appointment, Burnside was assigned to train provisional brigades before they were mustered into the recently assembled Army of the Potomac. Considering himself no more than a glorified quartermaster and drillmaster, he disliked this tedious duty, yet this assignment was exactly what his limited military experience had best prepared him for and what was the most needed in the embryonic Union army of 1861.[19] Burnside yearned instead to take the field as a commander, his first time under fire at Bull Run indicating to himself his potential in this area. As a result of these efforts to get an independent command, along with the support of various Rhode Island patrons, he was assigned to recruit and organize an "amphibious corps" and garner victories for the Union along the coast of North Carolina. Burnside's service reflected the twin mandate of preparing troops and leading them into battle that was expected of the many regular army officers selected as general officers during the first year of the war.

His selection reveals the informal and personal nature of general officer appointments and the impact that political connections could have in advancing a candidate for promotion. Burnside, an 1847 graduate who had left the service after only six years, jumped over many other more senior, more experienced, or currently serving officers like Winfield Scott Hancock (USMA 1840), Joseph Hooker (USMA 1837), George Meade (USMA 1835), and William T. Sherman (USMA 1840, with thirteen years of service). This disparity in promotion was due to the influence of patronage, as the officer corps had little control over promotions during the first years of the Civil War. Although political patrons could not appoint—only President Lincoln and the Senate could do that—they influenced who was selected by presenting and supporting their candidates' names while also giving the promise of an added benefit of political support if their patronage requests were filled.

Burnside's rise also demonstrates the pervasiveness of political patronage in the early military appointments in the North. Paralleling many of his peers, Burnside's militia promotion to major general before the war, his return to the army as a colonel, and his nomination for brigadier were all based on political support. In this atmosphere, the political pull of the patron was all-important in planting the candidate's name in the president's ear. With no formal standard to judge military expertise and potential for command, President Lincoln was simply doing his best to gain the benefit of patronage and political support by choosing from the candidates known to be available. And the only way a potential general officer appointee could be known to Lincoln was if someone close to him made the suggestion. Although not all general officer appointments began at the statehouse or in the cabinet, all required a political patron to suggest the candidates' names to a president unschooled in military matters and an administration desperate to rally support.[20]

Unlike many of his peers such as McClellan and Burnside, William Tecumseh Sherman was one of the few regulars not willing to go the route of the militia in order to gain a promotion.[21] At the onset of Union mobilization during the first weeks of the war, Sherman disliked the idea of militia service when it was suggested to him by Frank Blair, the patriarch of the most politically powerful family in Missouri. Sherman vowed if he had to return to service it would be with the regular officers and soldiers he had grown to trust in the antebellum army. "The time will come in this country when Professional Knowledge will be appreciated," Sherman replied to his brother John (both his relative and his patron as a U.S. senator) regarding the offer of a volunteer commission, "and I will bide my time. . . . I cannot and will not get mixed up in this present call."[22] The chaos and lack of discipline that Sherman saw in the streets and bars of St. Louis convinced the young academy graduate that these ill-disciplined volunteers and their amateur officers would not take to regular army standards, nor would they prove reliable and effective in the field.

Sherman tried to avoid the offers promised to a West Pointer with his experience, yet his worries for his family's economic security drove him ever closer to donning his old uniform. On May 6, his foster father, a senator from Ohio, urged Sherman to state what position he wanted so that his political allies could work with General Scott to get it; soon after, the senator met personally with President Lincoln to press Cump's career.[23] This sponsorship soon paid off, and after extensive negotiations and political wrangling Sherman got his wish and was appointed as a colonel in the regular army. Sherman's name was soon published as the commander of the new 13th Infantry Regiment, a unit with regular army organization and lineage, though short of trained regular soldiers and officers.

Although initially slower than some in moving up to the senior officer ranks, William T. Sherman had some of the most dedicated and powerful political patrons of any Union officer. After the death of his father at a young age, Sherman was raised by Ohio senator Thomas Ewing, whose daughter he eventually married. His brother John also went into politics and became a congressman before the start of the war. As a result, Sherman's family was one of the best connected in Washington.[24] The day the shelling started at Sumter, Sherman received a letter from his brother recommending that he refuse the offer of a job as War Department clerk, then a significant civil service position that his political ally and friend Secretary of the Treasury Salmon Chase had suggested. Go into the army during the "present disturbances," John advised. "I know that promotion and every facility for advancement will be cordially extended. . . . You are a favorite in the Army and have great strength in political circles."[25] The benefit these political allies brought was not just support and sponsorship but also introductions and exposure to appointment opportunities. This advantage could be seen in Sherman's case. Though not yet on active duty and relatively junior when compared to many serving officers, Sherman got to see President Lincoln face to face during each visit to Washington.[26] His patrons, and their political allies, helped his career at the start of the conflict and proved an asset throughout the war.

The entire process that led to Sherman's selection as the commander of the 13th Regiment was controlled by patronage. It was a question of getting one's name considered and of getting the president's ear, which was where the final decision would rest and which meant that those with exposure to the president dominated the process. Therefore, cabinet members who saw Lincoln daily and state governors whose support was deemed vital had the most pull. This was why one of the quickest roads to general officer rank went through state militia rank. As Sherman was unwilling to go this route, his disdain for state militias actually slowed down the recognition of his potential. Sherman's stepfather, Thomas Ewing, complained that his pride had worked against gathering the president's support, as it had robbed him of allies. "You would have been apptd Brigadier Genl [sic] in Ohio troops," asserted Cump's most powerful patron, "if anyone had said you would have it—but nobody did."[27] Since Sherman did not receive his stars until after Bull Run, this outcome revealed the advantages that state militia leaders, supported by their governors and congressmen, had when seeking a set of stars.

If political connections of friends and family advanced Sherman's career, political pull from one who wished him ill held him back. When Senator Ewing approached the president to gain his foster son the stars of a general officer, the politically powerful Montgomery Blair and the Blair family from Missouri initially seemed to doom his chances. The new postmaster general was bitter that William Sherman had refused the offer of a job in the War Department and was unwilling to accept a volunteer commission with Missouri state troops that his father had offered. "[Blair] spoke of your refusal to accept the Post which they were all anxious to have you fill," the senator warned Cump and recommended he accept a colonelcy if one was offered, since Blair's opposition all but guaranteed cabinet opposition to a brigadier's stars.[28] As his family patrons assured Sherman that the command of the 13th Infantry Regiment would be his, he understood the influence the Blair family had and their opposition to his advancement. "I know the Blairs do not like my refusal to accept the Chief Clerkship of the War Dept. or the leadership of the Dutch [German-American] militia here," Sherman wrote from St. Louis. "I have made a simple plain tender of my individual services . . . and I would not feel slighted if they were ignored."[29] But between the combination of Sherman's own political allies and his solid if uninspiring performance at First Bull Run, the perceptive soldier was eventually appointed a general officer.

Many observers believed Sherman had great potential to command because of his antebellum experience. He was not unwilling to harness this view. Sherman's service in the Seminole War and in California during the Mexican War, while not judged as heroic or inspired, was nonetheless seen as combat experience, and his return north from New Orleans when Louisiana seceded indicated his loyalty to the cause. McDowell, a new regular army brigadier, had told John Sherman and Thomas Ewing that Sherman could be a brigadier or major general of volunteers if he just asked, based on his thirteen years of service and his West Point background.[30] Sherman understood that some in the administration thought highly of him and sought to harness this support to maximize his standing in the officer corps after he decided to return to service. On May 22, he asked his brother John, "You know that these colonels will rank in the order of their appointment—if you are behind the curtain try and get mine as well up as possible."[31] This wish was fulfilled when Sherman was appointed as a colonel and commander of the new 13th Infantry Regiment. He also fulfilled his potential in the eyes of his political supporters by performing well at First Bull Run.[32] These events demonstrate the pervasive nature of patronage in initial assignments, even for an officer like Sherman who made such strong claims to being apolitical.

The disorganized way this system of general officer selection operated in 1861 was demonstrated by the rapid promotion of generals such as Irwin McDowell and Ambrose Burnside, but was perhaps most clearly visible in a neglected offer of service from Galena, Illinois. In late May 1861, as the scramble to find experienced military officers reached a frantic level, a West Point graduate with fifteen years' seasoning in the regular army and combat experience from the Mexican War offered his services "in such capacity as may be offered."[33] His offer received no reply, and the ascent of Ulysses S. Grant would start as a volunteer colonel in the Illinois state militia rather than as one of the numerous direct appointments to general officer that many of his fellow West Pointers received in 1861. Grant serves as an example of an officer possessing some promise of military expertise who was initially overlooked and not given a prominent command until later in the war because of the disorganized system of general officer nomination and the absence of prewar standards for professionalism. Although Grant did have politically powerful patrons in Congress who would help his career later, none of his supporters had the ear of the president in 1861. In the long run, this situation was beneficial because it allowed Grant to gain experience at lower levels of responsibility that was denied many of those directly appointed to major general.

What these appointments and assignments during the first year of the war showed were the expectations placed upon the regulars—their experience and training would be used to organize, train, and lead the rapidly expanding Union armies. But in practice this selection process was very unbalanced, as only some were chosen and others were ignored. The choices bore little correlation to actual command potential, as Halleck, McClellan, Butler, and Banks were appointed major generals while Phil Sheridan, James McPherson, and other future successful Union generals were still majors and captains. The reason why some Military Academy graduates, and some politically appointed amateurs, were chosen and jumped many ranks while others were not was due largely to patronage. Some future Union commanders still headed regiments or languished on staffs in 1861 simply because they were unknown to the administration and lacked political allies to push for their promotion. Yet, in spite of the haphazard nature of these selections, the appointment of West Pointers and former regulars like Halleck, Burnside, and Sherman brought welcome confidence and discipline to the new organizations.

Preparing an Army for War

The need for systematization and discipline was mirrored in each theater of the war as armies on both sides of the struggle became more conventional formations and sought to resemble the prewar regular army in organization and training. The sectional struggle had outlasted expectations that a single campaign would be decisive and had turned into a massive conventional military contest that would be waged by armies of unprecedented size. This change increased the importance of organization and training, as these elements would be necessary to maintain the vast field armies and to coordinate complex staff operations such as logistics on a scale unparalleled in warfare up to that time. The disorder and confusion of the early battles of the war reinforced this concern. Both sides' performances at Wilson's Creek and First Bull Run revealed the formidable tasks involved in engaging in conventional warfare and the unpreparedness of the mass volunteer armies. In the North, the absence of success in early battles like Bull Run was judged to be the natural result of premature advances by poorly trained commanders and undisciplined troops. Therefore, the new troops and their volunteer officers, many chosen by elections in their units and as green as their soldiers, needed regular army discipline and training in order to develop into combat-effective units.

Some of the most well-known West Point generals of the war got their start helping either their home state or the War Department handle the mustering of manpower. The initial mobilization had led to chaos, as tens of thousands of raw recruits rushed to the colors before any system was constituted to receive and organize them. In Ohio, for example, Governor William Dennison anguished over the magnitude of the task of creating an army from the multitude of raw recruits and the few arms available. Ex-governor Jacob Cox, immediately appointed a brigadier in the state militia though he had never worn a uniform, was called on to help the state with this huge task and related one of the root causes of the frustration. According to the newly commissioned political general, Governor Dennison felt embarrassed with every day that passed because of his staff's lack of military experience and training and sought some adviser upon whom he could "properly throw the details of military work."[34] This mandate led to the appointment of George B. McClellan as a major general due to the belief that he possessed, according to the governor, a "just reputation of military organization, and the promise of the ability to conduct the operations of an army."[35] Fulfilling this mandate started McClellan's career as a general officer in a role he was to perform ably since it matched his military experience and training so well.

Similar tasks were assigned to West Pointers across the North as all the Union armies that took the field started with their recruitment, mustering, organization, and training. Regulars more easily accomplished these critical tasks because the creation of trained and ready volunteer regiments required skills and abilities very similar to handling small units in the frontier garrisons before the war. As one historian of the antebellum officer corps observes, "the bureaucratic mental habits and administrative and logistical abilities officers acquired in the antebellum army proved more easily and more effectively transferable to the Civil War context of mass mobilization and attritional warfare" than any other aspects of their mandate to organize the army and lead it to victory.[36] Nearly all of the West Pointers who would achieve general officer rank during the war were assigned to train and organize troops when they first joined the Union army, each attempting to instill regular army standards and discipline into the vast multitudes of disorderly and unpolished volunteers. Forming an army and a new corps of junior officers out of these mobs would take time, and many of the regular army officers who commanded this effort decried all the work needed before the army would be ready for combat.

The new Union troops at this low level of discipline and training soon took the field out of necessity, inspired by heated rhetoric, political pressure, and a desire to settle the war before their ninety-day enlistments expired. General McDowell, who commanded the Union forces at their first major battle of the war, claimed with good reason that his officers and troops were unprepared, yet he appeared as ready to command as any Union officer at First Bull Run. Even though the size of later Civil War armies would dwarf McDowell's field force at Manassas, the challenge of commanding a group of this size with untrained officers and inexperienced staff was enormous, and no doctrine or organization was in place to facilitate control.[37] Though much attention has been focused on the soldiers' lack of training, what is often overlooked is the equally limited experience and training of the officers corps, in which the impact of the regular army officers was overwhelmed by the sheer number of volunteer field grade and company grade officers.

The resulting debacle at First Bull Run was blamed by many in uniform and in government on this unpreparedness and lack of training. West Pointers, and even many volunteer officers who witnessed the battle, became convinced that the cause of the defeat was the rush to fight a battle before the new regiments were ready and the absence of trained officers to coordinate all the actions required on a modern battlefield. During the retreat, many of the new units dissolved and scattered with no organization or control. After the battle, many officers remarked on this apparent lack of discipline and how the new organizations disintegrated, as the few experienced officers were unable to rally the soldiers.[38] They echoed the disheartened remarks of Sherman, who called the retreat of the volunteers an "ugly stampede." Sherman lamented to his wife how he returned to the capital after Bull Run "carried by the shameless flight of the armed mob we led into Virginia."[39] The poor performance of initial Union engagements furthered the rise of West Pointers like Burnside, Sherman, and Halleck, who were asked to introduce regular army discipline and uniformity.

For some West Pointers, this organizational task started with attracting and mustering volunteers on the home front. Their mandate often resembled and was concurrent with the tasks of political generals, as seen in the recruiting trips of newly appointed Brigadier General Ambrose Burnside. While contributing to the training and organization of the Army of the Potomac, Burnside talked to McClellan and Lincoln about his next assignment. Eager for a larger military role, he proposed the formation of an amphibious division for operations along the coast of the Carolinas.[40] The president warmed to the idea and sent Burnside to New England in September 1861 to recruit men with experience at sea for this specific mission.[41] Burnside was very successful at this new task and met his quota for new regiments even though his recruiting drive occurred at the same time as Butler's similar campaign in New England.[42] Although both men were ultimately successful, their different backgrounds drove two contrasting ways of gathering volunteers.

Burnside's conduct of his recruiting effort differed greatly from Butler's during this period not only in how volunteers were recruited but also in who was mustered into the ranks. While Butler harnessed political allies and appealed to partisan motives, Burnside relied completely on War Department quotas, the state muster systems, and orders to the governors from Secretary Cameron. The former regular did not make any speeches or personal appeals to gather volunteers.[43] Whereas Butler tried to build regiments from scratch (to maximize new commands for patronage), Burnside was more than happy to accept regiments that the states were having no trouble filling; in spite of his plan to recruit volunteers with maritime experience, many regiments lacked any such volunteers. While the actual mustering was occurring, Burnside focused on acquiring the necessary shipping and training camps for his new regiments.

This bureaucratic approach toward gathering new manpower was significant because it revealed the influence of the West Pointers' common background in regulation, discipline, and order. Similar to many regular officers in the first year of the war, Burnside appeared more than happy to avoid the state and local political chaos of recruiting. Indeed, the majority of Military Academy graduates used conservative methods of appealing for new soldiers and relied on existing regulations for guidance. Though not as flamboyant or well-known as many of their amateur peers, the West Pointers were expected to succeed at this task because it harnessed their managerial and organizational skills.[44] Many like Burnside did. However, these efforts were more like mustering than recruiting, and Burnside could not claim to have actually motivated any to join up other than those who had already signed the rolls.[45]

Because the need for men was almost constant, the Lincoln administration was more than willing to task West Pointers to assist in this effort, though not nearly at the same level or with the expectations it held for the numerous ex-politicians in uniform. To the War Department, recruiting was viewed as simply an extension of the West Pointers' mandate to organize and prepare the army for the military struggle. Moving new units, mustering regiments, gathering and distributing arms and equipment, and managing training camps were all vital functions that former regular officers could easily perform. But to actually motivate citizens to sign up was a task for which few West Pointers were suited. The only thing these men could use to inspire recruits was their military reputations. Many, like Burnside in the spring of 1864, found their notoriety more of a liability than an asset with men already reluctant to join the Union cause. A background in hardship and harsh military disciple was far more useful after troops were in the ranks.

Once new regiments were mustered, unschooled volunteer officers turned to Military Academy graduates like Burnside and Sherman to provide training and discipline so desperately needed. In the month before First Bull Run, Sherman faced the formidable task of forming an effective fighting brigade with the raw recruits flooding to the colors. Like many West Point graduates, Sherman understood his role and believed he was prepared for the challenge due to experience with small-unit drill and army bureaucracy. Yet despite this confidence, the appearance of his first brigade shocked him. Even with low expectations of his "rabble," Sherman was stunned at his troops' level of order and discipline, calling them "green as grass."[46] The brigade had not formed until July 11, and Sherman was able to conduct only three drill periods before they marched toward Centreville and their first combat along Bull Run. Some new soldiers had not even fired their rifles prior to their first battle, and some of the officers prepared for this clash by reading Hardee's *Tactics*, trying to learn rudimentary commands just to be able to move their units.

This level of unpreparedness would drive Sherman to constantly train his troops and to relentlessly instruct himself in the art of generalship. To ready his soldiers for their first taste of combat, he organized a system of drills encompassing company through regimental levels. Sherman had never done most of these drills before himself, and he admitted, "I had to learn the tactics from books." "But," he concluded, "I was convinced that we had a long, hard war before us, and made up my mind to begin at the very beginning to prepare for it."[47] The new colonel found this training prior to First Bull Run very difficult, as the shortage of experienced and knowledgeable officers led him to try to drill his entire brigade. Sherman repeatedly conducted drill himself, to the point of going hoarse.[48] Yet, his antebellum military experience suited his first wartime command, as he was tasked to organize and train the new regiments that were added to his regular regiment to form an ad hoc brigade.

Sherman's effectiveness was proven by the fact that his brigade did not disintegrate its first time under fire. After fortune turned against the North at Bull Run, the new Union brigade held together long enough to form the rearguard of its scattered division. Sherman's "steady and handsome withdrawal," Confederate commander P. G. T. Beauregard asserted after the battle, enabled "many to escape."[49] Though in combat for the first time, the new brigade commander had the familiarity with drill and discipline that the tactics required. In spite of the challenges of green officers and raw recruits, Sherman was successful in this role and had one of the more disciplined and organized brigades at the Union's first battle. This apparent mastery of the challenges of organizing and preparing new units for the test of combat, added to the impression of success in his first test of the war, led to Sherman's appointment as a brigadier general on August 7, 1861. These factors also cemented Sherman's mandate from the administration, as after Bull Run he was immediately returned to the duty of organizing new volunteer regiments and instilling some level of discipline and training, a task similar to that given to new brigadiers like Burnside.

This mandate was also given to Brigadier General Robert Anderson, hero of Fort Sumter and an 1825 graduate of West Point, who was selected by President Lincoln to go to Kentucky to form a Union army to secure that critical state.[50] When Anderson sought out officers to help him with this task, Sherman's name quickly surfaced. In August 1861, Sherman met with Anderson and Tennessee senator Andrew Johnson and agreed to go to Kentucky to help organize the defense of the state. His specific mission was to help form the Kentucky Unionists into military units; then, once the state's loyalty was secured, to help lead the new army into Unionist east Tennessee.[51] When Sherman and Anderson met the president on the eve of their assignment to that critical border state, Lincoln granted two of Sherman's requests: he received assurances that he would not be placed in command and that his friend from his cadet days, Brigadier General George Thomas, would be assigned with him. Aware of the chaotic situation in the border state, Sherman did not feel ready for the responsibility of an independent command. "Out of the chaos some order in time must arise," he surmised, "but how or when I cannot tell."[52] However, except for this self-imposed restriction, Sherman was appointed as a new brigadier with the same mandate as Halleck, Burnside, and most other former regulars and West Pointers.

To some regular officers, the effort to organize and train this huge new army could seem overwhelming at times, even for the very confident. Sherman himself was initially successful in Kentucky, but he slowly lost faith in success because of the demands of the organizational effort. When Anderson became sick in the fall of 1861 and no other officer arrived to take his place, Sherman grudgingly assumed command. As General Thomas skirmished with Confederates in the field, Sherman attempted to overcome the chaos of mobilization in a state with divided loyalties. He traveled to see the governors of Illinois and Indiana and pleaded for more troops, but met with more excuses than promises. This herculean task slowly eroded his confidence, and he began to sound repeated alarms in telegraphs to his brother and the War Department about his inability to drive back the Confederates, prompting a visit that triggered his fall.[53]

Sherman's fate as the Union commander in Kentucky demonstrated that some West Pointers failed in this organizational effort. His relief also revealed that newspaper accounts and political calculus strongly impacted the fortunes of Union commanders even prior to any clash of arms. In the middle of October 1861, Secretary of War Cameron visited Sherman's headquarters in Louisville to evaluate both the commander and his command. During this visit, Sherman was very pessimistic about success and told the stunned secretary that over two hundred thousand troops would be required to mount the offensive in Kentucky.[54] This estimate proved to be very accurate, as it was the size of Union forces on the Tennessee front later in the war, but it did not reflect the military or political realities of the fall of 1861 and shocked the administration. After hearing Sherman's opinion, Secretary Cameron referred to his request for more troops and his demeanor as evidence that the Union general had lost his sanity.[55] This reaction prompted Sherman to ask to be relieved because he had lost the confidence of the administration.[56] Sherman's dismissal in Kentucky and Secretary Cameron's shock at his pessimism reflected the administration's growing political sensitivity to the popular impression of success at these tasks. However, the challenges of a divided Kentucky may have been too much pressure for any commander during the turbulent fall of 1861, and it is difficult imagining a political general having greater success at building an army and a military infrastructure for future offensive campaigns in such a tumultuous environment.

In some instances, politically appointed amateur generals played the opposite role and caused chaos in their commands by treating their units as tools for patronage and the unveiling of staunchly partisan policy. John C. Frémont's command in Missouri was perhaps the best example of this behavior during the first six months of the war, as the former presidential candidate and "pathfinder" commanded a headquarters brimming with graft and corruption that produced turmoil within his department. For his staff, Frémont appointed Hungarian and German émigré officers and political allies, who dressed in fancy uniforms but lacked the ability, and often the willingness, to establish any orderly headquarters routine. The Lincoln administration received little but frustration from all the money, men, and supplies committed to what appeared to be a growing fiefdom in St. Louis. The final straw came at the end of August when Frémont issued a proclamation on his own initiative establishing martial law and freeing the slaves of secessionists in the state. This radical proposal directly challenged the policies of the administration and led to a brief period of political crisis in the North and the border states.[57]

What was obvious to Halleck when he took over the command in November 1861 was that the all-embracing disorder was due to Frémont's amateurism and the meddling in his military matters by numerous politicians in Washington. Halleck found nothing but fault with the character and behavior of the previous commander in St. Louis. "The conduct of our troops during Frémont's campaign," the new department commander asserted, "has turned against us many thousands who were formerly Union men."[58] The behavior of untrained and ill-disciplined volunteer and home guard units, when inspired by fiery speeches from radical political leaders, often included indiscriminate violence brought down on both friend and foe alike. According to Halleck, continuing these practices would lose the whole state to the secessionists, as it would destroy the local support needed for the field armies to expel the uniformed Confederates and suppress the paramilitary irregulars who supported them. For these acts, Halleck and many other regulars blamed politically appointed amateur commanders who carried their political activities into the service and had extensive legislative and partisan seasoning without any practical experience in leadership or management. The result was a bureaucratic nightmare of inexperience, incompetence, and corruption that was antithetical to everything that an officer like Halleck had come to value in military service.

To Halleck, what was required to cure the ills of his new command was the introduction of the military discipline and bureaucracy the regular army general valued as essential to maintaining an orderly and successful command. Engaged in a struggle with guerrillas for control of Missouri and with an enemy field army threatening battle, Halleck viewed this organizational effort as his first priority when he took over.[59] The new commander claimed in correspondences with McClellan that the situation was so bad after the "Frémont régime" that it required a military "reformation" in order to organize the military effort and produce an effective field army. To start his reforms, Halleck's main demand on the departing Frémont was a request for "books, records, contracts, telegrams" from his period as commander, calling these papers an "absolute necessity . . . in order to transact the business of this command."[60] The offensives sought by various political figures in Washington would have to wait until the army was prepared, as Halleck's belief in the need for organization was strong enough for him to resist persistent calls to advance with cries of unpreparedness.

Halleck continued to value order and discipline above almost everything else. Upon taking command in Missouri, he almost immediately published a general order remarking on the irregularities and neglect in supplies, organization, and military bureaucracy. Halleck labeled these faults "evils" caused by the neglect of proper procedure by inexperienced field and staff officers.[61] The vast majority of his orders and messages during the first two months of his command in St. Louis related to imposing order and bureaucracy.[62] Halleck repeatedly complained to McClellan and the administration about these severe organizational problems. After only a week in command, he wrote to McClellan claiming that the experience had revealed that "everything here is complete chaos."[63] For an officer who valued organization and bureaucracy, the rancorous partisan warfare in Missouri was akin to military anarchy.

Halleck demanded time to organize, as this quest for order consumed his initial period in command.[64] On the first day of 1862, the president told him to coordinate with Buell in order to remove any obstacles to an offensive. His reaction was typical of the responses Lincoln received from the West Point generals. "I am not ready to co-operate with him," declared Halleck. "Too much haste will ruin everything."[65] To avoid this haste, his preparation stretched through the winter of 1861–1862, as the administration and the public grew increasingly frustrated with the lack of military progress. In response to Lincoln's famed order instructing all the Union armies to go on the offensive on Washington's Birthday, General Halleck told the president he could not take the field, as the Confederate army in his department had a larger number of troops available. In his rebuttal, Halleck complained to Lincoln that "I am in the condition of a carpenter who is required to build a bridge with a dull ax, a broken saw, and rotten timber."

What was needed was time, Halleck explained, because this would allow for sufficient training and organization to stave off defeat on the battlefield. "It is true that I have some good green timber," he continued, referring to the volunteer regiments, "which will answer the purpose as soon as I can get it into shape and season it a little."[66] This investment of time, though politically unpopular and frustrating for the administration, was rewarded when Halleck took the field in the spring of 1862 with an organized group of units under more aggressive fellow West Pointers like Grant and Pope. However, Halleck's inaction furthered the anxiety coming from the capitol over the growing tension between the constant political need for military action and the calls from prominent West Pointers that more training was needed.

Halleck also joined the chorus of repeated requests from all the commanders for more regular officers to assist in the task of organizing and training the new volunteers. Recognizing that West Pointers were needed throughout the new army, Halleck was blunt and repetitious with his appeal for Military Academy graduates. "This, general, is no *army*, but rather a military rabble," he complained to General McClellan. "You are aware I am destitute of regular officers and those of the volunteers are, with some exceptions, entirely ignorant of their duties."[67] Two days later, Halleck again wrote to McClellan that the situation in his command was chaos and that he could not accomplish his assigned tasks without more regular officers. He justified this demand for regular army officers with his belief that they were the only officers "of experience and worthy of confidence" in the vastly expanded army.[68] Sherman would later echo this call for regular officers from his command in Kentucky. He wrote to Governor William Dennison of Ohio about the disciplinary problems in his new regiments and observed that his greatest problem was "worst of all no Capts. or Lieutenants to teach the details."[69] This disorder and lack of discipline were natural dangers with untrained troops led by inexperienced officers, and the obvious solution seemed available in the background that West Pointers shared in military discipline and regulation.

Following the fall of Forts Henry and Donelson, the administration responded rapidly to this organizational "reformation," for Secretary Stanton was impressed at the change that had occurred out West. Halleck had indeed established military order and discipline in his headquarters in St. Louis and among the volunteer regiments. The headquarters managed the affairs of the department with precision and efficiency, ending corrupt contracting and lax record keeping. The brigades and divisions that now took the field were well trained, equipped, and could count on an organized and effective supply system. On February 21, the secretary wired Halleck that "the brilliant results of the energetic action in the West fills the nation with joy."[70] This success occurred in part because Halleck's managerial skill, administrative experience, and quest for order were a perfect match for the requirements of his command and for the organizational mandate he was given with his appointment. The administration rewarded the victorious general in St. Louis by granting many of his requests. Grant, Pope, Buell, and C. F. Smith were each promoted to major general of volunteers, and Halleck's own command was extended to include all Union forces between Knoxville and the Mississippi. Yet, while Halleck credited this success to his organizational efforts, it is far more likely that the administration was simply rewarding the one Union commander showing progress in the field.[71]

Other West Pointers played key organizational roles in supporting the military forces in the field, based not on a perceived readiness for combat, but on their already demonstrated managerial skills. Given the enormous impact that logistics and administration had in this rapidly expanding army, West Pointers with administrative experience like Herman Haupt and Montgomery Meigs would make unique and vital contributions both to forming the army and to the eventual Union victory. Haupt was an 1835 graduate of West Point and had served only three months on active duty before resigning to spend the next twenty-five years building bridges and working for the railroad. Yet during the war, he refused an appointment as a brigadier. Instead Haupt served without rank or pay as the chief of transportation for the U.S. Military Railroads (though he signed all his official messages "brigadier general").

Montgomery Meigs, USMA class of 1836, played an equally important role in the Union war effort without serving in a prominent command in the field. He served during the antebellum years in the prestigious Corps of Engineers in a wide range of civilian enterprises including the Potomac Aqueduct and the Capitol dome and developed a firm utilitarian understanding of complex projects. When the war broke out, Meigs lasted one day as the commander of the 11th Infantry Regiment before he was appointed quartermaster general as a brigadier general.[72] Before the end of the war, he disbursed over $1.5 billion and was so effective in the army's logistics that he would receive a coveted promotion to major general in the regular army for distinguished and meritorious service during the war.[73] Many other Military Academy graduates played similar roles behind the scenes organizing the Union war effort, but in many instances the success of their contributions was based in part on expertise gained outside the army in organizational and managerial skills rather than on the training received at West Point or in the field army.

As the year 1861 drew to a close, Halleck, McClellan, and Burnside were in charge of major commands for fulfilling this organizational dimension of their mission, while Sherman had been relieved for failing to do so. Although these initial efforts did not win the war outright, they did set up the organization and systems for success used by later generals while giving valuable training and experience to unpolished volunteer officers. The overall effect of Halleck, McClellan, Burnside, Sherman, and other West Pointers during the first year of the war was the introduction and integration of organization and military bureaucracy in the huge new armies. This task was a vital necessity if the war was to be won on the field, because it changed the "disorderly mobs" of First Bull Run and Wilson's Creek into the effective combat units of later Union campaigns. In effect, such a change validated the initial views of Winfield Scott and other regulars that the war could not be won until regular army drill and discipline was introduced to the new formations.

Conclusion

As the enormous scope of the mobilization effort created turmoil in military administration throughout the North, West Pointers and former regular officers were sought by the administration and by state governors because of the belief that they had the experience to introduce military order and discipline to this new mass army. The scramble for Military Academy graduates was intense during the first year of the war. One volunteer officer claimed that

> there was a time when the faintest aroma of West Point lent a charm to the most unattractive candidate for a commission. Any governor felt a certain relief in intrusting a regiment to any man who had ever eaten clandestine oysters at Benny Haven's [a tavern outside West Point], or had once heard the whiz of an indian arrow on the frontier, however mediocre might have been all his other claims to confidence. If he failed, the regular army might bear the shame; if he succeeded, to the state-house be the glory.[74]

The need for order and discipline in the newly recruited Union armies was judged so great that the West Pointers' actual level of experience and military knowledge was often ignored in the race to gather any men who expressed a confidence in their ability to do the job. In this mission of organizing and training the new volunteer formations, the Military Academy graduates accomplished the tasks of the first part of the mandate that drove their selection and appointment. The previous training and experience of the regular officers in military drill, organization, and bureaucracy enabled the vast new Union armies to take the field in campaigns of scope and scale unprecedented in American military history.

This success led to the desire for West Pointers to use their training and experience to organize the new regiments, brigades, and divisions. The growing reliance on experience and training was a natural reaction in the chaos of initial mobilization, especially since the number of men deemed to possess seasoning in military matters was so small compared to the needs of the new army. Any man of the volunteer units with time in the regular army, in the Military Academy, or in service in the Mexican War, even as a private soldier, was, as the historian of John Logan's 31st Illinois Volunteer Regiment recounted, "looked upon as an authority on all military subjects."[75] The primary mission of these experienced officers, especially the USMA graduates, would be to make the new volunteers resemble the antebellum regular soldiers they were used to leading.

Though needing the support of political generals and their constituents early in the war, Lincoln did value military education and experience, as demonstrated by his assignment of nearly every major field command to a Military Academy graduate. During 1862 and 1863, the percentage of the Union high command held by West Pointers increased further, yet this change may not have reflected any significant alteration in Lincoln's criteria for generalship other than a growing desire for proven commanders. The increase in the number of West Pointers may have been simply the result of a self-fulfilling cycle, as the initial group of division and corps commanders were heavily weighted toward experienced soldiers who became leading candidates for later command. This dynamic formed a pattern, because West Pointers preferred to have fellow graduates as major subordinate commanders and key staff officers, and these officers gained the field assignments necessary to gather the sought-after combat experience. Some of these preferences led toward professional assistance like that between McClellan and two of his friends from his tour with the engineer company at West Point, William Franklin and Fitz John Porter.[76] Such arrangements meant that these officers had a greater chance of being selected for promotion and advancement by the president.

For a military system with no standard to determine potential and no pattern of advancement except by seniority, it was no surprise that a Military Academy background was valued, its graduates sought after, and its benefits generalized. It was commonly assumed by the national and state leaders who sought out West Point graduates that their experience would equate to military expertise; they would be capable both of forming these new armies and of using the gathered military forces effectively to accomplish the desired goals. What underscored this situation for the Lincoln administration was how so many offers of troops from state authorities were accompanied by requests for regular officers, and West Pointers in particular, to organize and train the recruits and to provide military bureaucratic and organizational expertise.[77] A young John Schofield described this role when he recalled how in the first months of the war he "devoted all the time that could be spared from my mustering duties to instructing the officers in tactics and military administration."[78] Yet, with so few political leaders possessing experience in uniform or having any interaction with the antebellum army, this generalization seemed only natural. The error in many of these assumptions of expertise would not be revealed until the Union forces and their generals were tested on the field of battle.

As the success of this effort to turn a mass of volunteers into fielded Union armies demonstrated, West Point graduates did for the most part deliver on their assumed ability to replicate regular army organization and training. Because this shaping of the raw recruits into hardened soldiers made an important contribution to the Union cause, the contemporary stereotype of West Pointers had value in the selection of Union officers. However, behind the rhetoric about Military Academy graduates' "experience," "demonstrated ability," and "authority on all things military" lurked the shadow of patronage and political partisanship that determined who was selected to high command as well as the strength of their support in wartime Washington. How these men were actually chosen shatters the image that their appointment was under a different system than their amateur peers. Acknowledged military officers like Halleck and McClellan could count on their military reputations to gain attention, but such men were few and far between and still required someone in power in the capital to initiate and support discussion of their appointment.

Yet, it would be a mistake to lump together all general officer appointments as similar, because different qualities were sought in the two types of candidates. West Pointers, unlike candidates for a politically based appointment, were valued for their presumed military expertise. The organizational and training aspects of generalship could be assumed to be part of the job and therefore requirements of any commander regardless of his background. This premise was true in essence; political generals, like their more experienced peers, spent this period of the war wrestling with similar bureaucratic problems during mustering and struggling to prepare their green troops for combat. Such responsibilities were not limited to graduates of West Point, in part because of their small number, which ensured that the vast challenge of forming armies would be spread among all commanders. However, military bureaucratic and organizational expertise was the focus of West Point appointments and was actually assumed to be lacking in most amateur officers. One of the by-products of this emphasis on organization and training was the demand by many former regulars for the time necessary to prepare their units for combat.

The quest for time to organize was in the forefront of Union strategy for former regulars in the high command. Scott's Anaconda Plan warned against a rush to take the field, and McClellan's plan for one grand campaign rested on the concept of extensive preparation. To make the kind of army envisioned in these plans would take time, yet this was an unpopular sentiment in the first year of the war and led to repeated political and public prodding of the Northern military leadership to wage immediate aggressive campaigns against the Confederacy. This impatience was the very hazard that General Scott warned of in his appeal for the Anaconda Plan in early May 1861. He foresaw what he described as "the great danger now pressing upon us—the impatience of our patriotic and loyal friends" that would be politically difficult to resist. "They will urge instant and vigorous action," the commanding general warned one of the newest major generals, "regardless, I fear, of the consequences—that is, unwilling to wait for the slow instruction of [troops]."[79] Although the confusion of First Bull Run seemed to justify this worry, regulars like Halleck, McClellan, Don Carlos Buell, and William Rosecrans would be constantly frustrated in their attempts to gain more time to prepare for campaigns. As will be demonstrated in the following chapters, politics more than military calculations controlled the pace of military operations. Politics also determined what military feats would earn the label of victories.

For politicians in Washington and the Northern public at the home front, organization and training were not in demand. Tangible military successes were. Regardless of the success of political generals at rallying support and of West Pointers at forming an impressive army, this was still a military contest and the Southern armies had to be defeated in the field. The Confederacy had to be forced to accept the return of federal authority or the fighting would go on. This result required tactical victories and the occupation of captured areas, which would be the primary challenge for Union generals during the Civil War. On these battlefield results would be based the comparative value of stereotypical amateur and West Point generals. Were these political generals the bumbling tacticians that history (and their regular army peers) made them out to be?

CHAPTER FOUR

"Applying the Guillotine"
Union Generals and the Test of Battle

On August 30, 1862, Lincoln sat in the telegraph office and kept a vigil for news from yet another battlefield. This experience had become all too common for the Union commander in chief during the spring and summer of 1862 as the fighting between the two opposing armies grew in frequency and scale. Like before most clashes with the Confederates, Lincoln initially was confident of the results that evening as Major General John Pope closed in on the elusive Robert E. Lee's Army of Northern Virginia on the old Bull Run battlefield. Nevertheless, in an often repeated scene, the president's hopes were dashed as the messages came in speaking of yet another Union defeat. "We are whipped again, I am afraid," Lincoln lamented in the White House to his private secretary John Hay. Though plagued with setbacks, even on that night the president longed for another battle with the Southerners, repeating phrases like "we must whip these people now."[1] He would have a long wait. The year would prove very trying for those commanders wearing blue, as tactical setbacks, operational frustration, and strategic stalemate changed the high command into a turnstile for Union generals.[2]

Each clash seemed to spell the end of another commander's turn at the helm because of the demand for a tangible military victory from the home front to the capital and then to army headquarters. Major General Henry W. Halleck, as the new Union commanding general in July 1862, realized this political reality quicker than many of his peers and sent repeated warnings to various commanders. He complained to Major General Horatio Wright in Kentucky that the administration was frustrated in August 1862 with the slow movement of Union armies in Don Carlos Buell's Department of the Ohio. "The government seems determined to apply the guillotine to all unsuccessful generals," Halleck protested. "It seems rather hard to do this when the general is not at fault; but, perhaps, with us now, as in the French Revolution, some harsh measures are required."[3] The liberal use of this "guillotine" in 1862 underscored the fact that the Lincoln administration now employed tactical results as the measure of all commanders.

To some of Lincoln's military officers, the reason for the lack of Union battlefield success was tied directly to the continuing practice of giving important commands to inexperienced ex-politicians. Playing the role of spokesman for this sentiment, Halleck judged the capability of this type of amateur commander harshly and asserted that "it seems little better than murder to give important commands to men such as [Nathaniel] Banks, [Benjamin] Butler, [John] McClernand, [Franz] Sigel, and Lew Wallace."[4] Another West Point graduate went as far as automatically equating Banks's "political education" with military incompetence. "I don't believe in natural-born generals," the graduate asserted, "except where they have had proper military training."[5] These views on the link between tactical defeats and political generals were common among regular officers during the war and continue to be somewhat common today.

Looking through the lens of this stereotype, the fates of the group of Union generals promoted in the spring of 1862, a mix of West Pointers and politically appointed amateurs, reveals how they performed and how the "guillotine" was applied. Few ideas about the American Civil War are as pervasive as the bumbling political general or the tactical battlefield as the true measure of a commander. Yet, rarely are either of these generalizations examined and proven, which begs the question: if Halleck's harsh warnings were justified by the times and heads should roll from all unsuccessful generals, what was the measure of "success" that the Lincoln administration used? The answer to this question challenges both generalizations and proves that battlefield results were as political in nature as all other aspects of the American Civil War.

The early battles of the war such as Big Bethel, First Bull Run, Belmont, and Shiloh demonstrate that nearly all Union commanders were equally unprepared for the challenge of commanding in combat. Regardless of their tactical outcomes, all these engagements were permeated with examples of poor generalship and inept tactical ability on the part of Union generals. Though general officers from both sources shared in these results, as battles grew in scale and scope during 1862, the label of military amateur became more and more associated with the ex-politicians wearing stars on their collars. Yet, an analysis of the major battles of the war reveals that while the record of the political generals blends poorly fought defeats with a smatter-ing of inspired victories, the overall record of the West Point graduates was similarly mixed. Stereotypes regarding tactical ability, both contemporary and present-day, greatly exaggerate the difference in performance between West Pointers and political generals; tactical success was not directly related to the type of a commander. What happened to defeated commanders, how-ever, depended on their background; military victories were the main causal factor for the fortunes of individual West Pointers, while results from the battlefield did not directly determine the fate of their amateur peers.

Amateurs at War

Though military amateurs had proven able to command troops effectively in previous American conflicts, the scale, scope, and organizational complexity of the military effort during the Civil War seemed to dictate a need for expe-rienced regulars as commanders. This formidable task was too much for many of the politicians who jumped directly from militia encampments to com-manding divisions, corps, and, for some, to army level commands. In 1861 and 1862, political generals assigned to important field commands would be leading their units into conventional battles that dwarfed any engagements previously fought by the American military. For this reason, the Lincoln administration sought to place the burden of defeating the main Confederate armies in the hands of experienced regulars.[6] However, in actuality, all Union generals were amateurs in 1861. The level of military expertise required to handle the trials of command on the fields of Shiloh and Second Bull Run only came from a combination of military education, training at command, and practical experience—a background few career officers possessed early in the war. The lack of any of these qualifications doomed the most senior of the amateur generals and many West Point graduates to fail the test of battle.

In spite of these challenges, amateur generals achieved many of the first Union victories of the war while the armies were being formed and trained. These early successes included the unlikely accomplishments of Benjamin Butler. His deeds during the first year created an impressive military vita, as the volunteer major general was the conqueror of defiant Baltimore, the commander who raised the virtual siege of Washington, and the captor of Cape Hatteras. At the end of the first year of the war, the largest Confeder-ate city fell to the Union when New Orleans surrendered to Butler and Admiral David G. Farragut in April 1862. As the consummate political general, Butler is perhaps the best example of this mixed record of tactical performance, as he suffered a long series of minor defeats intermixed with victories that either the Union navy or pure persistence granted him.

Although Butler's military career revealed the problem of commanding without any training or study, this deficit did not alter his confidence that he could overcome the formidable tasks of commanding a vast army in the field.[7] Success in politics and the militia gave him faith that a sharp mind and a "firmness of purpose which . . . [was] shown to have been the best military judgement" could overcome his lack of "technical military education"—in his own opinion.[8] As his depiction of his accomplishments during the Civil War reveals, Butler did not recognize the existence of a distinct military expertise requiring experience or specialized education. This level of self-confidence played well in front of crowds and in partisan newspapers, but only further inspired ridicule when repeatedly proven to be unwarranted on the battlefield. The Massachusetts politician's series of battlefield debacles later in the war did not seem to influence his faith in his own capacity to command an entire Union Department. This distinction may have been caused by a view that separated the traits needed to command an army (natural genius, faith in the cause, and providing political purpose) from the more specialized military skills required to lead men in combat (training in tactics, physical bravery, and providing direction in combat).[9]

Butler's first taste of combat, a small engagement at Big Bethel, Virginia, revealed both his lack of experience and his deep-seated worry about the political, not military, impact of a battle's outcome. In late May and early June 1861, he grew impatient sitting at Fort Monroe and decided to strike at the nearest Confederate stronghold located near a small church called Big Bethel, only a dozen miles away. Butler was going to attack this outpost with a group of his green regiments, placing Massachusetts militia general Ebenezer Pierce in command of the attack, even though he was as inexperienced as his newest troops.[10] Although the offensive was on a very small scale and the conditions seemed promising, Butler was unsuccessful. On June 10, he sent out of Fort Monroe over twenty-five hundred troops under Pierce against roughly half their number of defenders. The resulting operation was a complete failure, with over a quarter of the Union casualties lost when two Northern regiments mistook each other for Confederates and opened fire, which disrupted the attack and instilled chaos in the ranks.[11]

The command arrangement at Big Bethel set a pattern for Butler and many other political generals during the war who attempted to command operations while leaving the tactical execution to subordinates. Though the architect of the attack, Butler did not even direct the troops in the field during the advance but rather sent his senior subordinate as the tactical commander. Revealing something of a double standard, Butler had hoped to give charge of the attack on Big Bethel to one of the few West Point graduates in his command but felt that General Pierce deserved the honor because of his more senior rank. This arrangement would be formalized later in the war as a means of taking advantage of the political appeal of appointing popular politicians as commanders while placing an experienced commander under them to lead the troops in the field. At Big Bethel, as at Drewry's Bluff, in front of Petersburg, and at Fort Fisher, this method of command gave Butler someone else to blame for the failure.

Butler overlooked the effect that a lack of expertise could have when an army commander shared this trait with most of his subordinates. His orders for the attack at Big Bethel were neither clear nor free from rambling details (Butler's order included such guidance as "George Scott to have a shooting iron"), and his intent for the assault was too complex for the green troops and untrained volunteer officers.[12] Given the small number of experienced regular officers available in the expanded Union army, Butler and other senior commanders were forced to conduct operations with few staff officers who were adequately trained to coordinate the various elements of the army. Political generals actually made this problem worse by extending military patronage within their units and attracting more novice officers.[13] Political generals, especially after the growth of a mutual tension with Military Academy graduates during the war, tended to favor appointing officers with whom they had prewar ties or were political allies. This patronage, though understandable as an effort to secure mutual trust and effective teamwork, exacerbated the lack of military experience, which was partially to blame for the absence of success.

The president was under extreme pressure from political allies and the public to produce a victory, and Butler's loss in Virginia did not help him quiet the administration's critics.[14] Butler was blamed for this miscarriage as both sides exaggerated the importance of the skirmish, with some newspapers advocating his recall and dismissal from command.[15] Though heralded as a major Union defeat in the press, Northern losses actually amounted to only eighteen killed, mostly due to the exchange of fire between Union regiments that spoiled the element of surprise. For all Butler's mistakes, the amateurism present at Big Bethel paled in comparison to some of the generalship during the days leading up to First Bull Run that occurred the next month under a group of West Point graduates and regular officers. Regardless of the spin placed on the battle, Butler's first attempt at a tactical engagement had failed, and it attracted enough negative attention that he was relieved of command in August 1861. Yet, this battlefield loss was far from the end of Butler's military career.

During the course of the war, Major General Nathaniel Banks had a bat- tlefield record similar to that of Ben Butler. He started out joined by politi- cal generals John Frémont and Franz Sigel on the humbled side of Jackson's Shenandoah Valley Campaign and ended his first campaign having lost almost all the occupied territory he had inherited when assigned as com- mander of the valley in February 1862.[16] In Banks's first experiences as a commander in combat, the Massachusetts politician was routed at Win- chester and was forced to plead with his retreating troops. "My God, men, don't you love your country?" he was said to have shouted at his fleeing sol- diers. From one came the reply, "Yes, and I am trying to get to it as fast as I can."[17] Sentiments and stories like this were common in Banks's command during the disastrous campaign, as he proved unable to coordinate his forces in the valley. The result was the piecemeal employment of Union units at Winchester and Cedar Mountain, a pattern later repeated by Banks at Port Hudson and on the Red River.[18]

Banks's failures as a commander were not simply the product of charac- ter flaws or a lack of internal fortitude. In fact, the ex-governor was repeat- edly praised for his personal behavior in combat and his ability to inspire his troops. John Pope, his commander, praised the Massachusetts politician's "intrepidity and coolness" at the Battle of Cedar Mountain and stated that Banks had repeatedly exposed himself to fire and was an inspiration to his men during the whole fight.[19] David Strother, a journalist and observer of Banks's efforts while traveling with the Union headquarters throughout the campaign concluded that the reason for failure was Banks's dearth of experi- ence in what to do with his men and resources.[20] With no background in or historical knowledge of military planning and command, Banks simply did not know what to do in tight situations like those at Winchester and Cedar Mountain in the summer of 1862.

The low point of Banks's military career and the least effective period of his generalship in the Shenandoah Valley in 1862 did little to impact his self-confidence. Despite his retreat across the Potomac in May 1862, he refused to recognize his failings and continued to report to the War Depart- ment that his losses had been exaggerated. Banks went so far as to boast to his wife that "whatever may be said of our recent movement [fleeing Win- chester], I can assure you that it is one of the most remarkable that has occurred or will occur during the war." Showing a practiced political ability to put a positive spin on bad news, he went on, "It is miraculous almost that my entire command and its trains should escape without harm the long matured plans of an enemy five times our number."[21] Yet no words could camouflage the fact that Banks's campaign in the valley was a disaster for the Union, or that he himself was responsible for much of the damage. But this poor performance was against Stonewall Jackson at his best, and regulars John Pope and Irwin McDowell soon did no better that summer.

Without any victories to rival Butler's capture of New Orleans, Banks added to the emerging stereotype of incompetent political generals by becoming almost an object of ridicule as a field commander. Most of the regular officers involved in Banks's campaigns preferred to focus their blame for the defeats solely on the Massachusetts politician, for many West Point graduates resented his lack of education and experience. One regular officer went so far as to declare that he "could not help being disgusted at the mismanagement and mistakes of civilians who were in high and responsible positions, placed there by political influence, and who could only lead their armies to disgrace and defeat."[22] Even some volunteer officers who fought with Banks were quick to realize after Cedar Mountain their commander's lack of military skill. George L. Andrews, soon to be Banks's chief of staff in the Department of the Gulf, was especially disappointed after the near victory over Jackson. "The action was totally unnecessary," Andrews wrote his wife soon after the battle, calling Banks's performance "about as great a piece of folly as I have ever witnessed on the part of an incompetent general."[23]

Adding to the negative stereotype of political generals was the perception, which too often was reality, of poor discipline and military appearance among volunteer units under amateur commanders. As a result, stories became rampant of the lack of control and order within some organizations lacking the firm grip of an experienced commander relying on old army discipline. Reporter David Strother commented that the one constant in armies commanded by Banks was poor discipline, which one of the general's biographers blames on inconsistency and irregular discipline in the troops from Banks on down.[24] Yet, such behavior was understandable. Without years of peacetime duty or previous service under fire, many amateur commanders did not place any value on rigid enforcement of regulations. For some ex-politicians, regular army discipline seemed not only overly harsh but also counterproductive in making volunteer soldiers into courageous fighters inspired by the cause. Though this comparative absence of firm control may not have been the direct cause of their tacti-

cal setbacks, it did inspire another avenue for criticism against these amateur commanders.

However, criticism of Banks's conduct in the Shenandoah Valley and at
the siege of Port Hudson often ignored the fact that regulars during these
actions were struggling comparably with combat command. Responsibility
for the unsuccessful assaults at Port Hudson has to be shared with Banks's
key subordinates, who also gave poor performances. Each of his division
commanders during the first attack on May 27, 1863, were West Point graduates, and two out of the three were veterans of the Mexican War. Yet each
waited to be ordered to attack in turn even after hearing the fire from adjacent assaulting units. Most accounts of that first assault agree that the senior
division commander, Thomas W. Sherman, was drunk while leading his unit
and responsible for the lion's share of the casualties. The division commanders' performances for the second assault on June 14 were equally poor, as the
artillery preparations and the massing of units warned the Confederates of
what was coming. Enough was done wrong in planning and executing these
attacks that, as had been true in the valley, Banks cannot shoulder all the
responsibility for the losses, though his inexperience did play a major role.

In spite of this widespread lack of experience and training, some political generals did develop into excellent tactical leaders. For the more victorious amateur commanders, this success in combat was based on an
opportunity to gain the needed expertise through practical experience at
lower ranks prior to facing the complexity and challenges of high-level command. Of this group, John "Black Jack" Logan stands as a prime example.
The former Illinois politician finished the war as one of Sherman's best corps
commanders and a leader who had accomplished nearly all of the tactical
tasks he attempted. Logan's success rested on more than his limited Mexican
War experience or inspirational leadership, as Butler was his match in exposure to the military and Banks's soldiers used very similar language when
describing that general's conduct in battle. Logan was able to master the
coordination of units in battle and the challenges of command and control
because he received practical experience with companies and regiments
before he attempted to maneuver divisions.

Logan's prewar experience offered little preparation for the daunting task
ahead, yet "Black Jack" did have a natural talent for command and a knack
for using his personal bravery to inspire his soldiers. With no exposure to
combat during the Mexican War and no experience in the militia or on the
frontier, Logan's first taste of combat occurred during skirmishes just prior to
the battle of First Bull Run, when the Illinois congressman demonstrated his

personal courage by helping the wounded and rallying troops in his suit and top hat. He received his initiation in the art of command during Grant's raid on the Confederate base at Belmont, Missouri, where he displayed the personal courage and inspirational presence that would become his hallmark. After having his horse shot out from under him in a volley of bullets that also shattered his revolver, Logan led the charge into the enemy camp and kept his green regiment moving forward while in the thick of the fighting.[25] He was praised by both Grant and McClernand for holding his 31st Illinois firm while almost all other units disintegrated during the chaotic retreat that followed the arrival of Confederate reinforcements.[26] The raid at Belmont was depicted as a victory by the administration and started the rise of both Grant and Logan at a time when other Union armies were still organizing and preparing for promised offensives.[27]

Logan's tactical record was in some ways unsurpassed among Union general officers, for he never tasted defeat or was tainted with charges of incompetence. It was this record that led to his rise to command larger and larger units. After Logan was severely wounded at Fort Donelson while halting a Confederate attack, he was promoted to brigadier general of volunteers and commanded a brigade and then a division in Grant's Army of the Tennessee during the Vicksburg Campaign. Grant praised Logan by name in his report on the earlier campaign to crack the Confederate frontier and wrote that he was capable of commanding a brigade in combat. Observing that Logan and fellow officer W. H. L. Wallace were "from civil pursuits," Grant was quick to add, "I have no hesitation in fully endorsing them as every way qualified for the position of brigadier-general, and think they have fully earned the position on the field of battle."[28] Logan's service in the field, interspersed with trips back to Illinois to recruit or stump for the war effort, led to the amateur general commanding a corps during the Atlanta Campaign, where he earned the respect of William T. Sherman. Logan finished the war as one of Sherman's best corps commanders and had his tactical leadership receive endless praise from Grant, Sherman, and the troops under his command.[29]

Yet Logan's appeal to the administration had little to do with his successful performance as a regimental commander. After the battle at Belmont, he journeyed to Washington and was greeted by many old friends and political enemies, all glad to talk to the up-and-coming congressman-turned-soldier. At the White House, President Lincoln was more than happy to meet personally with this regimental commander, using the occasion to talk Illinois politics and expressing the hope that Logan's support would play well

among his old constituents.[30] This meeting reflected the newfound importance of "Black Jack," as he was now called, and reaffirmed his assignment
to rally support for the president whenever the need arose. That this popular political leader was also emerging as a heroic military commander was the
icing on the cake for the administration.

Logan's performance was radically different from that of Butler and Banks
for a multitude of reasons, not the least of which were his natural leadership
and innate courage, though Banks, and to a lesser extent Butler, periodically
displayed these character traits. Logan had one obvious advantage over many
of his more senior peers, both amateur and regular, in that he had an opportunity to accumulate expertise as he rose through the chain of command. He
grew better as a military leader with each passing day and with each battle
and skirmish. He took nearly two years of wartime service to reach major
general and division command, the level of responsibility that Butler and
Banks faced their first time taking the field. General Grant, himself the product of a similar process of moving up the chain of command and fighting at
least one battle at each level, recognized the importance of experience and
its importance to his subordinate. Grant valued practical experience and
went as far while praising Logan's development as to label the Vicksburg
Campaign "a military education . . . which no other school could have
given."[31] It was this opportunity to learn and grow prior to having to coordinate brigades and divisions, artillery, cavalry, and logistics, and a large headquarters that made some of these amateurs successful while others failed.

Throughout the course of the Civil War, the impact that political generals had on the tactical level was both limited and mixed. If major Civil War
battles are identified as those fifty engagements having over ten thousand
combatants on both sides, political generals actually commanded the Union
side in only six: Cedar Mountain, Prairie Grove, Port Hudson, Pleasant Hill,
Drewry's Bluff, and Atlanta.[32] The results were mixed, as the two victories
(James G. Blunt narrowly won at Prairie Grove, Arkansas, and Logan,
replacing the slain James McPherson, soundly defeated the Confederates at
the Battle of Atlanta) were more than matched by Union defeats (Banks at
Cedar Mountain, Port Hudson, and Pleasant Hill, and Butler at Drewry's
Bluff). The conduct of these clashes also covered a spectrum of generalship
that ranged from Logan's inspired conduct outside Atlanta and Banks's bold
attack against Jackson's larger force at Cedar Mountain down to Banks's
futile assaults at Port Hudson and Butler's sluggish maneuvers near Drewry's
Bluff. Though campaigns were affected and opportunities gained or lost
because of these battles, the fate of the Union war effort and the morale of

the nation did not rest upon their outcomes, and none of the losses crippled or sacrificed one of the major Union field armies.

Therefore, the stereotype linking political generals and tactical debacles was not justified for the group as a whole, though it was certainly true for some individuals. Contrary to many historical depictions, the performance of Logan and other effective amateurs reveals that the battlefield record of political generals was a blend of victories and defeats, and that it was possible for an inexperienced politician to develop into a capable commander. In fact, many politically appointed generals did develop into effective corps and division commanders for the North, as such notable generals as James Wadsworth, Alpheus Williams, and Jacob D. Cox demonstrated. On at least one occasion, a political general achieved a vitally important battlefield victory when General Lew Wallace delayed Confederate forces under Jubal Early in their march on Washington at Monocacy River on July 9, 1864. These successful amateur commanders provide a counterbalance to any negative stereotype. The overall record of political generals also appears better when compared objectively to the same type of mixed record produced by former regular officers early in the war.

For all general officers during the first years of the war, the effort to develop tactical ability was complicated by an absence of command doctrine; the Union army had no common understanding of how orders and commands were to be communicated and disseminated.[33] The extensive pyramid of volunteer officers at every level of the army required guidance on operations and logistics in language they understood and often were forced to act without a clear understanding of the commander's intent. The result far too often was extremely slow movements and disjointed unit maneuvers that were the staple of stories from Civil War battlefields. This vital facet of command would prove the bane of many Military Academy graduates who were unable to communicate their intentions, and even effective and talented commanders like Grant and Sherman would have to master the process through experimentation.[34] The lack of a doctrine for command led to an inability to clearly communicate plans both for military commanders and between military officers and political leaders.

One example of how an operation could be complicated by a lack of clarity in the commander's intent was Grant's series of orders for the attack on Belmont in November 1861. Grant's sketchy orders did little to coordinate his regiments because his word choice and articulation of his plans sometimes bore a striking resemblance to Butler's clumsy orders for the attack at Big Bethel.[35] Grant's first action at Belmont revealed the pervasiveness of this amateurism, as many of his officers, including those of high rank, allowed discipline to completely break down and barely escaped in the disorganized retreat that ensued.[36] Although this sharp and indecisive action provided seasoning for both the Union soldiers and their commander, the amateurish nature of the command and control speaks volumes on the level of expertise of Grant, his staff, and the regimental officers involved. For many successful commanders like Grant and Sherman, their ability to communicate orders and coordinate operations would only become effective later in the war, the product of abundant practice. The importance of generalship, and the collective level of officer amateurism, was soon demonstrated on a larger scale on the Tennessee River at Pittsburg Landing, located near a small log church called Shiloh.

In early April 1862, the Battle of Shiloh revealed the growing scope and ferocity of the conventional aspect of the sectional struggle, as well as the consequent increase in unprecedented command and control problems for the novice commanders involved. A two-day conflict of nearly one hundred thousand troops, the battle produced unparalleled casualties on both sides.[37] The Southern onslaught caught the Union divisions unprepared in camp, as commanders discounted reports from the weak Union picket line of massing Confederate force. In the initial melee, though division commanders like John McClernand and Sherman cooperated with each other, there was a lack of cohesion to the defense as General Grant scrambled to stabilize his line and frantically sent for reinforcements.[38] The result for the Union army was that individual units threatened with encirclement often withdrew on their own, opened up the flanks of adjacent units, and thereby forced the entire line back toward the river. It was only the poor initial attack formation, the early commitment of Confederate reserves, and the almost complete loss of coordination on the Southern side that allowed the Union line to hold.

This first major bloodbath of the war revealed limits to the expertise of the Union generals, as the army was surprised by the Confederate attack, adjacent unit commanders could not coordinate their efforts, and, even in victory, the army became so disorganized that there was no effective pursuit. Where the clashes during 1861 had seen regiments and brigades maneuvering, divisions fought at Shiloh, and Civil War battles would further increase in size and complexity the following year. With the expanding scale came greater challenges for general officers. Large-scale maneuvers and the difficulty of controlling units that were no longer in the commander's line of sight overwhelmed many generals who lacked practical experience in conducting military operations under fire. At Shiloh, Grant learned how green his Union troops were and that the majority of his officers were equally unprepared for "hard, determined fighting."[39] It should come as no surprise that many Union commanders were not up to the challenge; what was unexpected was how quickly some would adapt to the formidable task of generalship.

For many Union generals, the chaos of the battlefield at Shiloh was overwhelming, and the simplest command tasks could not be performed. This deficiency was seen plainly in the difficulty that Union units had simply marching to the sound of the guns. Relief for the hard-pressed Union forces was slow in coming because some generals were not up to the task of aggressive tactical leadership.[40] A glaring example was Lew Wallace's division, which, because of misinterpreted orders and the poor navigation of its commander, got lost and missed nearly the entire first day of fighting.[41] Though less than four miles away when the attack began, Wallace spent the day marching and countermarching behind the Union army while Grant sent frantic messengers to search for these vital reinforcements.[42] Don Carlos Buell's approaching army also proved frustrating, for they did not arrive until after nightfall even though the closest division was only five miles away when the Confederates attacked. Alerted in the early morning of the need to move to Shiloh, this lead element of Buell's Army of the Ohio did not start moving for five hours and did not arrive for over eight hours. This delay left Grant's army in a precarious position, pressed upon by a greater number of Confederates, and the situation was made even worse by the collapse of many Union units and the flight of their green commanders. This test of skill occurred in combat fiercer than any endured previously by American officers, and only the late arrival of reinforcing divisions allowed the Union to turn the tide the following day.

How much this trying experience helped prepare Union generals for future actions depended on each officer's reaction to what had occurred. The commanders' response to Shiloh was diverse and signaled a division over how the war should be conducted. For more conservative leaders such as Halleck, McClellan, and Buell, the bloodbath at Shiloh furthered a regard for battle as a precarious and chaotic endeavor, a risky and costly tactical contest that should be avoided if possible. After the battle, Halleck wrote his wife decrying the lack of discipline and the disorganization, claiming that his officers were "utterly incapable of maintaining order" and calling both days at Shiloh "terrible slaughters."[43] Condemning the chaos and risks of battle, Halleck subsequently conducted the Corinth Campaign so conservatively as to avoid such "slaughter." As will be seen in the next chapter, he was proud to conduct a campaign that seized the Confederate city without a battle—a result that pleased few others in the North.

But for others, this battle taught a great deal about how to command and control troops during combat and the need for such savagery to end the secession. Grant, Sherman, and many other commanders believed they had learned deep lessons about generalship, their opponent's resolve, and the conduct of battle during this two-day trial by fire.[44] The sheets of musket fire and canister at Shiloh were murderous, but for many officers who survived, the two days of combat provided a grim lesson in leadership under fire. Officers like Sherman and McClernand emerged from the battle more confident in their units and themselves because of their shared experience. In contrast to more conservative officers like Halleck, Buell, and McClellan, some Union generals were willing to engage in further bloody clashes to destroy Confederate resistance. Expressing this view, Grant later asserted that Shiloh had convinced him of the need for more battles, not fewer, to conquer the Confederate determination demonstrated there.[45] Yet, there would be many more tactical setbacks and poor generalship before final victory was won.

The Army of the Potomac demonstrated these shortcomings all too well at Fredericksburg, where the conduct of the battle included Ambrose Burnside's enigmatic tactical orders, poor execution by his wing and corps commanders, and an inclination toward unsupported frontal attacks by the division commanders, all of which played a part in the attack's failure. Burnside demonstrated he was a novice at this level of responsibility, as the resulting battle at Fredericksburg on December 13, 1862, was an unmitigated disaster for the Union army, with a casualty count that rivaled the recent bloodbath at Antietam. What the entire Union leadership was discovering was that a commander's lack of proficiency could be overcome through instinct and innovation on the spot when warfare was on a much smaller scale, as in the regiment-sized assaults of the Mexican War, but that the absence of practical military expertise could not be quickly overcome during the multicorps operations of 1862.

Although the defeat at Fredericksburg had many architects, the main responsibility must rest with Burnside and his inability to communicate his intent before the battle or coordinate his forces during it. The amateurish nature of his orders to Major General William Franklin and the way in which Burnside's intent for a multicorps envelopment turned into a divisional frontal attack proved the low level of military expertise in the upper ranks of the army, even though all of the generals at division level and above had previously commanded troops in combat. Afterward, a frustrated Burnside blamed the assault's failure on the fog and the delay at laying the bridge, though both of these problems were solved before the attack turned into a debacle.[46] Even after suffering huge casualties and recrossing the river, Burnside actually reported to army headquarters that the plan had promised decisive results and that, "as it was, we came very near success."[47]

Yet, the responsibility for the defeat should not rest solely on Burnside, for his subordinate generals had performed very poorly as well. Although Burnside had dictated the overall plan, he left the actual fighting to his wing and corps commanders, the vast majority of whom were more experienced and had seniority over their commander.[48] As the tactical commander for the main assault on Lee's lines, Franklin was responsible for turning an envisioned corps attack into an assault solely by George Meade's division against Stonewall Jackson's entrenched Confederates, causing its failure and indirectly leading to the tangled heaps of Union dead at the foot of Marye's Heights.[49] Unwilling to admit the operational realities of the winter season and the strength of Lee's position across the river, Burnside refused to abandon his quest for battle and sought a "decisive victory" by crossing the river again, though this time nearly all of his subordinates predicted disaster. In the end they were right, for on January 19, the Army of the Potomac began the infamous "Mud March," which would bring an inglorious end to the campaign season and Burnside's tenure at the head of the army.[50]

In spite of these displays of ineptitude, West Pointers commanded the Union side in nearly every major battle of the war because of the administration's continued hope that they would provide the needed expertise. By looking at the major battles, clear evidence emerges of the domination that Military Academy graduates held over high-level commands. Even with the administration's need for the publicity of having prominent political generals "in the field" against the Confederates, West Point generals were in charge during the vast majority of the major Civil War battles. These regulars commanded on the Union side in forty-four out of the fifty largest battles and led all the main field armies in each theater.[51] On the other hand, the six battles in which political generals held the top position were all smaller engagements such as Cedar Mountain (Banks), Prairie Grove (Blunt), and Drewry's Bluff (Butler). This comparison provides more evidence of the limited impact that political generals had on the actual fighting of the war in spite of their bumbling reputation.

This near monopoly was not based on a complete record of success, since the West Pointers' overall tactical results were mixed and comparable for the first two years of the war with their amateur peers. During the course of the war, Military Academy graduates won just over half the battles in which they commanded, with a large number of these victories occurring after the

summer of 1864. Of the forty-four battles commanded by West Point graduates, the results were twenty-five victories (56 percent), three draws (6 percent), and sixteen defeats (36 percent).[52] Additionally, the questionable
tactical leadership at Butler's Big Bethel skirmish and Banks's notorious
retreat from Cedar Mountain pale in comparison to Pope's conduct at Second Bull Run, Burnside's tactical direction at Fredericksburg, or Joseph
Hooker's leadership at Chancellorsville. By another measure that shows the
mixed legacy of Civil War West Pointers, all the principal defeats for the
Union army (First Bull Run, Seven Days, Second Bull Run, Fredericksburg,
Chancellorsville, Chickamauga, Cold Harbor, and Petersburg) were under
the command of these regular army generals.

As this analysis demonstrates, the stereotypical contrast between West
Pointers and political generals is not a valid dichotomy, since tactical effectiveness was related far more to the experience level of the commander than
to whether that commander attended the Military Academy or had extensive service in the antebellum regular army. Even though many factors con-
tributed to each Union victory, there does appear to be a direct correlation
between the number of previous battles that general had engaged in as a
division, corps, or army commander and his chances for tactical success and
operational results. Although this increase in experience cut both ways as
Confederate commanders also improved, there does seem to be a trend of
heightened effectiveness in using the Union's advantage in resources and
troops.[53] In this measure of expertise, West Pointers did have an advantage,
as the average level of tactical experience for commanders who were Military Academy graduates was nearly four times higher than the corresponding level in their politically appointed peers.[54]

The greater success of West Pointers, especially in the last year of the
war, may simply be linked to a greater chance to practice, and hence a larger
foundation of practical experience. This differential only increased as the
war continued because of the domination of the high command by Military
Academy graduates. Because they were often selected for command positions where active campaigning was likely or imminent, these officers gained
valuable experience. By the spring of 1865, Grant, Sherman, and Sheridan
commanded in the last three major battles, each having previously commanded in almost ten major battles, a vast well of practical experience. By
contrast, the last three political generals to command the Union side in battle (Banks at Pleasant Hill, Butler at Drewry's Bluff, and Logan at Atlanta)
had commanded in only six major battles between them. Consequently, the
most senior political generals like Butler and Banks simply never had a

chance to develop basic combat leadership skills before being asked to command large units.

In short, novice commanders, whether political generals or West Point graduates, were missing a common element that led to their shared frustrations on the battlefield. The foundation for an officer's expertise would ideally rest on the twin pillars of military education and experience at progressively higher ranks far more than on natural talent or innate ability, what in the nineteenth century many would have labeled as "genius."[55] Yet it was the absence of these two pillars that many of the less successful political generals and West Pointers had in common. Without experience or expertise in the very challenging task of wartime generalship, most commanders initially appointed to high command naturally met with repeated tactical failures during their first attempts at combat because they had little time to master their new responsibilities. For some, this weakness threatened their ability to command and their appeal to the administration, as their names became associated with incompetence. Such consequences showed that one of the keys to continued popular support for the war effort was tactical victory, which provided concrete evidence to the public that the war was being won.

Different Generals, Different Standards, Different Fates

Though the "guillotine" seemed to await any Union general deemed unsuccessful on the battlefield, President Lincoln applied this strictly military standard very unevenly. By any objective measure, Military Academy graduates who served as general officers early in the war did not fare much better their first time under fire than the true amateurs. Yet, unlike their politically appointed peers, many West Pointers were sacked when they were unable to deliver victories because this was the expectation of these military experts and the standard upon which they were judged. At the same time, their amateur peers survived after achieving a similar lack of success because they were supporting the Union war effort in a manner unrelated to any battlefield outcomes. The needs of the administration dictated two different standards for West Pointers and political generals because of the difference in their anticipated contributions to the Union cause. Consequently, what decided the promotion or relief of Union generals was neither simple assessments of military effectiveness nor the measure of political impact, but rather how well each individual delivered on his mandate and maintained the impression of Union success.

The negative stereotype of political generals may have been so powerful owing to the contemporary and modern attention given to actions on the battlefield. The reputation of Union generals from tactical clashes like Shiloh resonated throughout the North because for those in government, for officers and soldiers, and for much of the public, the heart of generalship was battle. Battles offered some concrete measurements of military effectiveness: comparative casualties, ground gained, prisoners and colors captured, and so on, which made (and makes) the tactical collisions of the main opposing armies the major milestones of the war and the markers of each side's success. This perception was formed in part by newspapers whose tally of victories and defeats in the field, regardless of how strategically insignificant, shaped popular morale and influenced the Northern faith in eventual victory.

Therefore, a general's fate was often linked directly to impressions of tactical success, and his promotion or relief rested on battlefield performance. However, there was far more to the complex internal, international, and countrywide political struggle over secession, slavery, and states' rights than the periodic clash of armies. At times during the war, the nature of American democracy seemed to be at issue in political battles in Washington, in statehouses throughout the North, and in every city and town in the occupied South. Holding together a fragile coalition of diverse supporters, Lincoln recognized this fundamental truth after the fall of Sumter and viewed the promotion and retention of military commanders through this political lens. Union commanders could not avoid the impact of politics on their fates because it provided the scale upon which their generalships were weighed.

However, general officers from West Point had their fate tied to the battlefield far more than their amateur peers because this military sphere provided their sole mechanism for positively affecting the war effort. Unlike the political generals, the mere retention of these men in command produced no advantage for the administration. The primary reason that they were entrusted with command was the administration's faith, shared with the Northern public, that Military Academy graduates knew their trade and could achieve the desired tactical results. Their appointment was not an end, like that of a Butler or a Banks, but rather a means to a further end of anticipated Union military successes. The confidence in individual commanders was also linked to the morale of the army and the home front because of the prominent role that tactical results played in newspapers and political discourse. Consequently, these regular army officers were often judged failures as general officers when the administration and the public perceived them to have failed on the battlefield. When some prominent West Pointers were found wanting under the harsh standard of maintaining the appearance of advancing the military cause, they were often subsequently relieved because of a loss of trust by either the administration or the public.

A clear example of how Lincoln applied this political calculus in determining the fates of his military commanders is revealed in the story of those generals promoted in the pivotal year of 1862. Judging whose performance and potential matched the administration's need for political support and military success, President Lincoln told the secretary of war in early March 1862 to appoint Irwin McDowell, Ambrose E. Burnside, Don Carlos Buell, John Pope, Samuel R. Curtis, Franz Sigel, John A. McClernand, Charles F. Smith, and Lewis Wallace as major generals of volunteers.[56] The resulting orders from the War Department also dictated the appointment of John A. Logan and a number of others as brigadier generals. The fate of these generals during this portentous year of the war revealed that the dynamic through which generalship was tested and the standard upon which it was judged were focused on political, not military, measures. As a result, the fortunes of routed political generals like Franz Sigel and Nathaniel Banks stood in marked divergence from the fates of defeated regulars like Irwin McDowell and John Pope.

The Military Academy graduate who was under a cloud from First Bull Run proved how decisive a commander's reputation and public support could be in determining his fate. McDowell's active service ended the quickest of any of the generals on the March 1862 promotion list, in part because his reputation was already poor after the Union defeat at First Bull Run. In the summer of 1862, he had been demoted to one of the corps commanders in Pope's ill-fated Army of Virginia, and many believed he played a major role in the Union debacle during the subsequent campaign of Second Bull Run. Many in government blamed McDowell personally for both defeats and said he did not deserve to command Union troops. Some even openly questioned his loyalty. The result was a very ugly court of inquiry, with court-martial charges against McDowell and fellow corps commander Fitz John Porter. Soon after the battle, McDowell requested to be formally relieved of command until he could clear his name of the sensational charges made against him.[57] Though he was eventually exonerated, he was not given another field command until after the end of the war.

McDowell's commander during that campaign suffered a similar fortune, as Pope's meteoric rise in the Union high command ended when his army was swept off the field at Second Bull Run. Lincoln initially had much confidence in the brash, aggressive West Pointer who had captured Island Number Ten on the Mississippi River and who had consistently advised the president that with the right commander, the eastern armies could also drive back the Confederates.[58] Pope's elevation signaled the president's growing fatigue with the conservative ways of McClellan, the West Pointer's focus on strategic maneuvers, and his seeming unwillingness to come to blows with the enemy. In June 1862, Pope was given command of the forces that had so futilely pursued Stonewall Jackson in the Shenandoah, including Banks's and Frémont's corps. After issuing a series of bombastic general orders calling for a harsher treatment of the enemy, Pope took the field with his newly formed Army of Virginia only to be completely outgeneraled by Robert E. Lee at Second Bull Run and defeated by an opponent he handily outnumbered. By the first day of September, Pope's routed troops were sadly plodding back into the fortifications around Washington.

Though Lincoln believed the aggressive young general had potential, the president had to acknowledge that the crushing defeat had shattered Pope's reputation in the army. Pope's reversal had also convinced many in the administration that his boasting was not backed up by enough judgment and talent to make him one of the generals who would win the war. Lincoln may have agreed with Pope that McClellan's failure to support him might have caused the loss at Second Bull Run, but the president relieved Pope on September 5 only five days after the defeat and merged his army into McClellan's Army of the Potomac.[59] When confronted with appeals from an irate Pope, Halleck explained to the soon to be banished general that individual careers had to be sacrificed during these difficult times for the good of the army.[60] This explanation accurately served as the justification for Pope's relief. The president may have had few complaints about his generalship, as, unlike McClellan, the new field commander was at least seeking the enemy on the offensive when he was defeated. But Pope had lost the faith of the army and the administration that he could produce victory against the famed operational wizards in the Army of Northern Virginia.[61]

The result of this single Union loss, the commander's relief and banishment from field command, would be repeated throughout the war, as many West Pointers would see their Civil War commands end with a single battlefield defeat. Most of the worst tactical defeats the Union army suffered are paired with the swift demise of the corresponding commander: First Bull Run (McDowell), Second Bull Run (Pope and McDowell again), Fredericksburg (Burnside), Chancellorsville (Hooker), Chickamauga (William

Rosecrans), and the Petersburg Mine (Burnside again). In all occasions of immediate promotion or relief from command after a battle, as occurred with John Pope, Lincoln's decision directly mirrored his general's success or failure.[62] Yet, scrutiny of the more prominent firings shows that it was often the impression of failure rather than any objective military standard that determined the standing of senior military leaders. This viewpoint reveals another facet of the link between the situation in the field and political calculations in the capital, as the need for popular support for the war drove a tendency to measure the mood of public opinion on questions of the war's conduct. The relationship between perceptions and actions, which will be seen in the next chapter to provide justification for the relief of tactically successful generals like Buell and McClellan, is also apparent in the fortunes of Ulysses S. Grant during the fall of 1862.

Grant suffered a series of setbacks and tactical failures in his first drive on Vicksburg but was able to remain in command due to his recognition of ways to avoid the perception of defeat. After a Confederate raid halted his progress down the conventional overland approaches to the Southern bastion and Sherman's disastrous assault on the Chickasaw Bluffs had been repelled, Grant refused to fall back on his lines of communication and start again. "It was my judgment at the time that to make a backward movement . . . would be interpreted, by many of those yet full of hope for the preservation of the Union, as a defeat," Grant explained, justifying the various schemes and projects to bypass Vicksburg that ensued. Knowing that the incessant rains precluded any land movements until the spring, he concluded during the closing days of 1862 that "it would not do to lie idle all this time."[63] The result was a series of attempts to bypass the city that, while complete failures, did keep up pressure on the garrison, maintained the attention and morale of the troops, and most importantly gave the impression of military action and progress.

The astute commander knew that he might well have ended his military career if he had withdrawn back to the Union supply base at Memphis, as sound military logic and many of his subordinates suggested.[64] Yet, though unsuccessful, Grant maintained the president's support when he persisted in trying to find a way to seize or bypass Vicksburg. Lincoln's trust in his generalship was vital during this dark period for the North, a time when many of Grant's Military Academy peers were relieved and an outcry grew against any commander who failed to actively campaign. While Grant awaited good weather and continued with his engineering projects, Lincoln dealt with a rising tide of complaints about the general's failure to take Vicksburg by affirming his support for any general who was taking the fight to the enemy. For this reason, when Vicksburg fell to Grant's persistent pressure after a campaign that climaxed in a display of brilliant operational art followed by a tenacious siege, the president declared that "Grant is my man, and I am his for the rest of the war."[65] Grant's continuing rise throughout the war bears witness to the traits that the administration sought in its generals: perseverance, aggressiveness, success in the field, and a willingness to accept Lincoln's view of the politics of the war.

For some West Pointers, even tactical success could not save their careers from the harsh impact of political malice, a danger demonstrated most clearly by the fortunes of Samuel Curtis. Promoted to major general for winning the Union victory at Pea Ridge on March 7, 1862, Curtis was rewarded for his tactical ability with an appointment as the commander of the Department of the Missouri in the fall of 1862. However, this success in the field was only potent enough to save him until he became a political liability for the administration. In the spring of 1863, the conservative West Pointer began to have major disagreements with Governor William Gamble of Missouri over military operations and federal policy, as Missouri Unionists became embroiled in what the president described as a "pestilent factional quarrel among themselves."[66] After Curtis became allied with one side and the governor with the other, the clashes began to hurt Union support and standing in the state. Lincoln, in an effort to stop the fray, relieved Curtis in May 1863, claiming that "I felt it my duty to break it up somehow; and as I could not remove Gov. Gamble, I had to remove Gen. Curtis."[67] Banished to the Department of Kansas, then to the Northwest, Curtis would never again have a field command, his military career hindered through political ill will and intrigue.

In sharp contrast to the ax that awaited many West Pointers after their first defeat, the fortunes of Banks, Frémont, and Sigel in the Shenandoah Valley in 1862 show how tactical reverses did not end the careers of political generals. Banks's responsibility for the Union losses at Winchester, Cedar Mountain, and Front Royal, and the outcries against his amateur generalship, would have seemed to guarantee that he would never again command troops in the field. Yet, during the administration's frustrating trials of 1862, the ex-governor from Massachusetts was not relieved. In addition, neither Frémont nor Sigel had their commands finished by the setbacks in Virginia in 1862. Frémont, with a sense of pride and a belief in seniority, refused to serve under General Pope and resigned. Lincoln gladly accepted his resignation to remove the political maverick, but the president gave no indication that he would have removed the military amateur because of his embarrassing losses in the field. Sigel also piled up examples of an absence of tactical ability, yet continued to get larger and more important commands until the summer of 1864. Collectively, few political generals were relieved for all the tactical failures caused by their lack of expertise. But, as will be seen in later chapters, their fates were tied to the political strength of the administration, as most were eventually relieved when their political backing could no longer outweigh the cost of their remaining in the field.

Unlike the fortunes of McDowell and Pope, the administration's support and the popular appeal of Banks and other political generals were not completely damaged by the numerous battlefield setbacks. After the debacles in the Shenandoah Valley against Stonewall Jackson, Banks was still front-page news in many papers, with reporters praising his "gallant service" and how he enjoyed the "unbounded confidence of the people."[68] Both Halleck and the president praised Banks's conduct of the Cedar Mountain fight, calling it a "hard-earned but brilliant success against superior numbers."[69] Though Halleck was probably putting the best face on Banks's failure to block the Confederate advance north, Banks's reaction to Pope's appointment over him illustrates how the Massachusetts politician envisioned his role in the war and why so many in the administration still supported him. "It does not trouble me much," he wrote his wife about serving under the more junior West Pointer, "if it is possible to help on the war by this means I shall be glad."[70] His superiors may have simply believed the amateur general's performance was the best that could be expected from a novice commander who was forced to confront Jackson's famous "foot cavalry" in the Shenandoah.

Banks's fate at the end of the Shenandoah Valley Campaign revealed the administration's toleration of these setbacks, based on its expectation of his political value. After joining his corps with Pope's ill-fated Army of Virginia, Banks was hurt during a Confederate cavalry raid when his horse, struck by a stray shot, fell on him. He was barely able to mount and escape with his staff.[71] Banks recovered in the capital and was assigned to command the Washington defenses during the Second Bull Run and Antietam Campaigns. His next assignment after his defeats in the valley was in fact a promotion, as the end of 1862 found him in command of the Department of the Gulf. This pattern was repeated throughout the war for many political generals, as tactical defeats resulted in reassignment to a new area and a gradual return to field command. As Banks's move to the Gulf demonstrates, the trend was to move the most prominent political generals (whose services could not be discounted or cloistered without a stiff penalty in public support) after a defeat to a position that would not task their tactical ability and to a theater away from where the "decisive battles" of the war were expected to be waged.[72]

Though suffering numerous major defeats during the war, on only one occasion, that of Banks after the Red River Campaign, was a political general relieved from field command because of a defeat.[73] Even after this debacle, Banks continued to have a prominent role in reconstruction efforts in Louisiana and was just denied any major field command. As demonstrated by Butler, Sigel, and Banks, after a tactical disaster a political general either would be left in his current position, shifted to another command, or even moved to a larger command. Though much contemporary and historical attention has been placed upon these amateur commanders in the field and highlights their numerous tactical shortcomings, their assignment patterns demonstrate that political factors outweighed any military criteria in the administration's judgment of their success. For the Lincoln administration, the risks of these tactical setbacks were exceeded by the political support amassed every day these popular figures were in uniform, revealing how political generals and their West Point peers were judged using different standards based on distinct calculations of political gain and military effectiveness.

How differently these two diverse standards were applied can be seen in the fortunes of the group of general officers President Lincoln selected for promotion in March 1862. After a year of nearly continuous military campaigning, all the ex-politicians on that promotion list still had the apex of their military careers ahead of them, even though many had already been labeled tactically inept. March 1863 found John McClernand promoted from divisional command to leading one of the corps in Grant's army driving on Vicksburg. Other political generals prospered as well: Franz Sigel was a corps commander in the Army of the Potomac; Lew Wallace was awaiting his only independent command, which would be at Monocacy River; and John "Black Jack" Logan received his second star during the summer of 1863, advanced to corps commander, and earned the Congressional Medal for Valor at Vicksburg. These men proved that politically appointed amateurs could survive tactical setbacks because such defeats did not immediately damage their long-established pull among their constituents (who in fact often tended to blame the administration for failing to support their favorites). This meant that until a political general's reputation for military service was completely ruined, he could still fulfill the main purpose for which he was appointed and rally support for the Union cause.

Fifty Major Battles of the American Civil War

Year	Major Civil War battles[a]	Date(s)[b]	Union commander[c]	Type[d]	Casualties in thousands (%) Union / Confederate[e]	Union result[f]	No. of previous battles[g]	Result for commander[h]
1861	First Bull Run	July 21	McDowell	USMA	2.7 (10%) / 2.0 (6.0%)	Loss	0	Relieved
1862	Fort Donelson	February 12–16	Grant	USMA	2.8 (10.5%) / 16.6 (79.2%)	Win	1	Promoted
	Pea Ridge	March 7	Curtis	USMA	1.4 (12.3%) / 0.8 (5.7%)	Win	0	Promoted
	Shiloh	April 6–7	Grant	USMA	13.0 (20.8%) / 10.7 (26.5%)	Win	2	No Change
	Williamsburg	May 4–5	McClellan	USMA	2.2 (5.5%) / 1.7 (5.3%)	Loss	1	No Change
	Fair Oaks	May 31	Keyes	USMA	5.0 (12.0%) / 6.1 (14.7%)	Draw	0	No Change
	Mechanicsville	June 26	Porter	USMA	0.4 (2.3%) / 1.5 (9.1%)	Win	0	No Change
	Gaine's Mill	June 27	Porter	USMA	6.8 (20.0%) / 8.8 (15.3%)	Loss	1	No Change
	To Malvern Hill	June 29 – July 1	McClellan	USMA	8.0 (9.6%) / 9.5 (10.9%)	Loss	3	No Change
	Cedar Mountain	*August 9*	*Banks*	*Political General*	*2.4 (29.3%) / 1.3 (8.1%)*	*Loss*	*0*	*No Change*
	Second Bull Run	August 27–30	Pope	USMA	16.1 (21.2%) / 9.2 (19.0%)	Loss	1	Relieved
	South Mountain	September 14	McClellan	USMA	1.8 (6.3%) / 2.7 (15.0%)	Win	4	No Change
	Antietam	September 16–17	McClellan	USMA	12.4 (16.5%) / 13.7 (26.4%)	Win	5	No Change
	Corinth	October 3–4	Rosecrans	USMA	2.5 (11.9%) / 4.2 (19.4)	Win	2	Promoted
	Perryville	October 8	Buell	USMA	4.2 (10.5%) / 3.4 (21.2%)	Win	1	No Change
	Prairie Grove	*December 7*	*Blunt*	*Political General*	*1.3 (3.1%) / 1.3 (1.3%)*	*Win*	*1*	*No Change*
	Fredericksburg	December 11–13	Burnside	USMA	12.7 (11.9%) / 5.3 (7.3%)	Loss	2	Relieved
	Chickasaw Bluffs	December 27–29	Sherman	USMA	1.8 (5.8%) / 0.2 (1.5%)	Loss	1	No Change
	Stones River	December 31 – January 2	Rosecrans	USMA	12.9 (31.2%) / 11.7 (33.8%)	Win	3	No Change
1863	Chancellorsville	May 1–4	Hooker	USMA	16.8 (17.2%) / 12.8 (22.3%)	Loss	6	Relieved
	Champion Hill	May 16	Grant	USMA	2.4 (8.3%) / 3.9 (19.3%)	Win	3	No Change
	Vicksburg	May 22	Grant	USMA	3.2 (7.0%) / 1.0 (4.5%)	Loss	4	No Change
	Port Hudson	*May 27/June 14*	*Banks*	*Political General*	*3.8 (29.1%) / 0.3 (7.2%)*	*Loss*	*1*	*No Change*
	Gettysburg	July 1–3	Meade	USMA	23.0 (26.1%) / 28.1 (36.6%)	Win	4	Promoted
	Chickamauga	September 18–20	Rosecrans	USMA	16.2 (30.0%) / 18.5 (27.8%)	Loss	4	Relieved
	Chattanooga	November 23–25	Grant	USMA	5.8 (10.3%) / 6.7 (14.4%)	Win	5	Promoted
	Mine Run	November 27 – December 1	Meade	USMA	1.7 (2.4%) / 0.7 (1.7%)	Loss	5	No Change

1864							
Pleasant Hill/Sabine	April 9	Banks	Political General	1.4 (10.8%) / 1.5 (10.5%)	*Loss*	2	*Relieved*
Wilderness	May 5–7	Grant	USMA	17.7 (17.3%) / 7.8 (12.7%)	Draw	6	No Change
Spottsylvania	May 10–12	Grant	USMA	10.9 (10.7%) / NA	Draw	7	No Change
Drewry's Bluff	May 12–16	Butler	Political General	4.2 (26.3%) / 2.5 (13.9%)	*Loss*	1	*No Change*
Cold Harbor	June 1–3	Grant	USMA	12.0 (11.1%) / NA	Loss	8	No Change
Petersburg	June 15–18	Grant	USMA	8.2 (12.8%) / 3.0 (7.2%)	Loss	9	No Change
Kenesaw Mountain	June 27	Sherman	USMA	2.1 (12.6%) / 0.4 (2.5%)	Loss	7	No Change
Peach Tree Creek	July 20	Thomas	USMA	1.6 (7.9%) / 2.5 (13.3%)	*Win*	6	No Change
Atlanta	July 22	Logan	Political General	3.7 (12.2%) / 8.0 (21.7%)	*Win*	3	*No Change*
Atlanta/Ezra Church	July 28	Sherman	USMA	0.6 (4.8%) / 4.3 (23.3%)	Win	8	No Change
The Mine	July 30	Burnside	USMA	3.8 (18.3%) / 1.2 (10.3%)	Loss	7	Relieved
Deep Bottom	August 14–19	Hancock	USMA	2.9 (10.4%) / NA	Loss	7	No Change
Weldon Railroad	August 18–21	Warren	USMA	4.5 (22.0%) / 1.6 (10.9%)	Win	5	No Change
Jonesborough	August 31–September 1	Sherman	USMA	1.5 (4.2%) / 4.7 (13.0%)	Win	9	No Change
Winchester	September 19	Sheridan	USMA	5.0 (13.3%) / 3.9 (23.9)	Win	5	No Change
Chaffin's Farm	September 29–30	Warren	USMA	3.3 (16.9%) / 2.6 (24.6%)	Win	6	No Change
Cedar Creek	October 19	Sheridan	USMA	5.7 (18.4%) / 2.9 (15.8%)	Win	6	Promoted
Boydton Plank Road	October 27–28	Grant	USMA	1.8 (4.1%) / NA	Win	10	No Change
Franklin	November 30	Schofield	USMA	2.3 (8.3%) / 6.3 (23.2%)	Win	6	Promoted
Nashville	December 15–16	Thomas	USMA	3.1 (6.1%) / 5.0 (21.5%)	Win	7	Promoted
1865							
Hatcher's Run	February 5–7	Grant	USMA	1.5 (4.4%) / NA	Win	11	No Change
Bentonville	March 19	Sherman	USMA	1.1 (6.8%) / 2.1 (12.5%)	Win	10	No Change
Dinwiddie/Five Forks	March 29–31	Sheridan	USMA	2.8 (6.1%) / NA	Win	8	No Change

Major battles total = 50

USMA
44/50 = 88%

Political Generals
6/50 = 12%

	USMA		Political Generals
Win (W)	25 (56%)	Win (W)	2 (33%)
Draw (D)	3 (6%)	Draw (D)	0 (0%)
Loss (L)	16 (36%)	Loss (L)	4 (67%)

USMA Average = 4.7
Win 5.1
Draw 4.7
Loss 4.1

Political Generals Average = 1.3
Win 2.0
Draw —
Loss 1.0

USMA	W	D	L
Promoted	8	0	0
No Change	18	3	10
Relieved	0	0	6

Political Generals	W	D	L
Promoted	0	0	0
No Change	2	0	3
Relieved	0	0	1

(Continued)

Fifty Major Battles of the American Civil War (*continued*)

a American Civil War battles with over 10,000 troops engaged on both sides; Thomas Livermore, *Numbers and Losses in the Civil War in America, 1861–1865* (Boston: Houghton, Mifflin, 1901), 140–141.

b Date(s) of each battle.

c Union tactical commander during the battle.

d Background of the Union tactical commander (Political General = politically appointed amateur, USMA = Military Academy graduate).

e Casualty ratio: Union/Confederate casualties in thousands (% of forces engaged); Livermore, *Numbers and Losses*, 77–139.

f Operational result of the battle for the Union side (win, loss, or draw); Livermore, *Numbers and Losses*, 75–76.

g Number of previous battles for the Union commander as a division, corps, or army commander.

h The administration's judgment of the results: Fate of the Union tactical commander (promoted, relieved of command, no change).

But for the West Pointers on the same promotion list, the administration's expectation of military expertise and tactical success ensured that the high point of their wartime careers was actually behind them. After a year of war, all the Military Academy graduates on that list had been or soon would be relieved. In each case, relief was linked to military performance (for most, directly to a tactical loss on the battlefield): Irwin McDowell (for Second Bull Run), Ambrose Burnside (for Fredericksburg), John Pope (for Second Bull Run), and Don Carlos Buell (for his failure to actively campaign after Perryville) were either banished to lesser commands or sent home to await a reassignment that would not come for the rest of the war.[74] The only Military Academy graduate whose career would survive the year intact was Samuel Curtis (the victor at Pea Ridge), and his demise was rapidly approaching. As the fate of these officers reveals, a specific standard was used to judge their generalship, and if they were found wanting in tactical ability or no longer gave the impression of future success, President Lincoln was more than willing to use the guillotine.

Conclusion

The numerous promotions, firings, and command changes during 1862 demonstrated that General Halleck's warning was valid: the government was prepared to apply the guillotine to unsuccessful Union generals. The main factor that determined who got the ax was the criteria by which success was judged. As will be seen in the next chapter, President Lincoln appeared to set the simple standard in his orders to his generals and in much of his correspondence within the administration that there be the appearance of tactical success and movement forward. Yet, the fate of the general officers clearly shows that this standard was not evenly applied; while West Point regulars, from whom expertise was expected, were often relieved after a single tactical loss, political generals often survived repeated tactical debacles. This disparity was rooted in the way the president picked general officers because the Lincoln administration had different expectations of individual generals, each given his command with a mandate to accomplish a task that would make Union victory closer or more certain. These mandates became the standard for judging the commander's effectiveness: was he moving the Union war effort closer to eventual political and military victory along the lines expected?

In the midst of a civil war, the decision to promote or fire prominent general officers could not be based solely on political strength or military effectiveness, but also needed to be a political calculation of costs and benefits. President Lincoln had to look beyond the battlefield to the second-order effects of his choices in order to maintain Northern morale and a winning political coalition. The danger to the cause of having a Ben Butler in uniform, even at the cost of Union casualties and skirmishes lost, paled in comparison to the damage a talented and popular politician like Butler could do speaking against the administration across New England. A similar danger could be felt if the president maintained unpopular generals like McDowell and Pope in spite of their potential to learn and develop into successful leaders. Under these conditions, the higher military expectations placed upon many novice West Point commanders damaged their chances for success when compared to the "amateur" political generals, many of whom at worst met the forecast of the administration and the Northern public.

Despite the amateur stereotype, the political generals' impact on the battlefields of the Civil War was in some ways negligible, because there is little evidence that any regular who replaced them would have done better during the first two years of the war. For the most part, the cause of this negative generalization was the prevailing matching of Halleck's "unsuccessful generals" title with newspaper reports of (and historical focus on) battlefield results. The formation of the political generals' unflattering reputation based on battlefield incompetence also triggered campaigns against them by political enemies and by many West Pointers. Their inferred incapacity to command became a target for regulars, for it was this expertise that West Pointers sought to monopolize, and caused resentment whenever the president assigned amateurs to high command based on political factors. Even newspaper accounts depicting a stereotypical political general like Ben Butler could be blatant in labeling them incompetent as a group, though somehow the newspapers never attacked any ex-politicians who shared similar political views with the editorial staff.

Some political generals such as John Logan and Jacob Cox developed into effective tactical commanders because they received the gift of time in which to gain experience and learn the building blocks of combat effectiveness. As with regulars like Grant and Sherman, time and practical grounding gave these novices an opportunity to learn generalship. The positive battlefield records that some of the politically appointed volunteer generals attained were due to the critical experience and growth these men shared at regiment and brigade levels, training and experience that was denied the more senior political generals who received direct commissions to the two-star ranks. Therefore, the negative historical stereotype for political generals could be blamed on their promotion directly to senior level without experience with smaller units. The absence of practical training made it impossible for them to coordinate units and control tactical actions through subordinates. The result was the poor generalship displayed at Big Bethel, Cedar Mountain, and Port Hudson. Yet many regular officers depicted the political generals through this caricature of failure by focusing only on the military campaigns of the war, blaming such battlefield defeats on their lack of formal military training or on derogatory character flaws prevalent in any that would choose politics as a calling.

Considering how unprepared all the Union officers were in April 1861 for major battles like Shiloh, their collective mixed performance was perhaps the best that could be expected. It should come as little surprise that the majority of officers behaved like novices under the extreme challenge of their first command under fire. After the war, Sherman admitted in his memoirs how poorly the Union officers had done at First Bull Run but claimed it was the best these men could do with no unit cohesion, no discipline, and "no real knowledge of war." "It is easy to criticize a battle after it is over," he warned readers, "but all now admit that none others, equally raw in war, could have done better than we did at Bull Run; the lesson of that battle should not be lost on a people like ours."[75] What is important for this book is why such an interpretation is rarely addressed and why one group of Union generals bears a disproportionate level of blame for these early tactical setbacks.

Nevertheless, battlefield successes and winning tactical leaders were critical to the cause because each encounter shaped the military course of the war and set the tone for Union home front morale. For President Lincoln, every clash of armies was a political roll of the dice—and one he had little control of once it started. Therefore, Lincoln needed military leaders he could trust. Those who proved they could deliver stayed, and this message was clearly understood by at least some of the Union generals. When Halleck informed General Wright of the guillotine that awaited unsuccessful Union commanders, he also predicted that "there must be more energy and activity in Kentucky and Tennessee, and the one who first does something brilliant will get the entire command."[76] In this way, the battles of 1862 were very valuable for the Union, as they helped identify future commanders like Grant and Sherman while providing the measure of McClellan and Buell. However, this degree of political calculation was not a consideration that many regular officers viewed as anything other than detested "political meddling."

Many West Pointers alternately blamed this injection of politics into the Union high command on the Lincoln administration and political generals.

In concert with McClellan, Buell, and other former regulars, Major General Halleck spent much of 1862 trying to bring order to the Union war effort and to gain victory in a military contest that appeared to be changing with the political winds in Washington. To Halleck, the reason for the changing nature of the war and the growing frustration with the lack of Union military success was one and the same. "I take it for granted, general, that what has heretofore been done has been the result of political policy rather than military strategy," he complained to George McClellan in January 1862, "and that the want of success on our part is attributable to the politicians rather than to the generals."[77] This sentiment about the negative effect of politics on Union military operations was common for many West Pointers like Halleck, but was it a fair complaint? Did President Lincoln and his politically appointed amateur generals hamper the Union war effort with the "burden" of personal intrigue and unneeded partisan politics?

CHAPTER FIVE

"The Government Demands Action"
The Politics of Generalship

After July 1862, Major General Henry W. Halleck became the Union commanding general and, with some reluctance, the unhappy bearer of political urgency for offensive action to all Union field commanders. Such prodding from the capital became all too common as the year progressed. In November and December, he sent a series of appeals in response to building pressure from the administration for action from William Rosecrans's Army of the Cumberland, which sat in camps outside Nashville. Halleck warned Rosecrans, "The President is very impatient at your long stay in Nashville. . . . Twice I have been asked to designate some one else to command your army. If you remain one more week in Nashville, I cannot prevent your removal." Halleck justified this edict by cautioning his fellow West Pointer that "the Government demands action, and if you cannot respond to that demand some one else will be tried."[1] This prevalent warning repeatedly issued from Washington throughout 1862 was not only an indicator of the president's desire for action but also a signal that the administration was more than willing to manage general officer assignments in order to guide the war effort. To the president, the power to assign commanders, which he alone possessed, was the power to steer Union strategy and impose his views on senior military officers.

When Rosecrans received the final curt warning from Halleck that any further delay in Nashville would surely result in his dismissal, the frustrated field commander replied immediately and complained of the lack of understanding in the capital for what many generals deemed were the military realities in the field. Feeling the whip from Washington, Rosecrans told the sympathetic Union general in chief, "I reply in few but earnest words. I have lost no time. Everything I have done was necessary, absolutely so. . . . any attempt to advance sooner would have increased our difficulty both front and rear."[2] Any impression of an unnecessary delay, he explained, did not take into account the time required to prepare and build up supplies prior to any campaign, a vital preliminary step. To many West Pointers, these military maxims could not be ignored except at a commander's peril, as Rosecrans essentially argued that his army could either advance immediately or produce operational success, but stood little chance of doing both. When these arguments of military effectiveness clashed with the political needs of the administration, friction occurred between former regulars like Rosecrans and politicians—both in and out of uniform.

The heart of the issue was whether this discord was the result of the "political meddling" so often complained of by conservative West Point generals during the first years of the war. Among these military commanders, much of the incessant involvement of politicians in military matters was blamed not only on the partisan politicians in the cabinet but also on the ex-politicians in uniform. By the end of the war, these protests were so common and so prevalent that much of the political involvement of the Lincoln administration, Congress, and political generals that sought to impact the military conduct of the war was generalized in a negative manner. Were these complaints about inappropriate political interference justified? By addressing this question and the interaction between Union commanders and the capital, a better understanding will emerge of the link between politics and military action during the war.

An examination of the major campaigns of 1862 reveals that many Union generals, both regulars and political generals, were infused with personal jealousies, partisanship, and infighting that sometimes damaged the war effort and poisoned the relationship between military leaders and the administration. Like their amateur peers, numerous West Pointers echoed the idea of a second front in the capital but had an entirely different definition of the struggle in Washington from the partisan battles accepted by their amateur peers. Rather than a factional and ideological struggle for political dominance, for these generals the challenge posed by Washington was the never-ending fight to prevent the political interference from tainting and disrupting the military contest. This destructive political intrigue provides powerful evidence that, contrary to some historical stereotypes, many "professional" West Pointers in the Union high command schemed as much as their political general peers and resisted tying military operations to the political needs of the government.

The Conservative "West Point School" and the Burden of Politics

As the spring of 1862 progressed, Lincoln's relationship with the commanders of the main Union armies slowly eroded from a state of mutual respect to frustration on both sides. The president sought military advances that would be evidence of Union movement toward victory; in these he was repeatedly disappointed. The resulting erosion of faith in the initiative and judgment of his West Point generals began to convince many in the cabinet that the Union high command did not understand what would be needed to win the war. A political calculation was made about their willingness to support the administration's needs and their potential to gain triumph in the field. For some general officers such as Don Carlos Buell and George B. McClellan, failures in these areas would lead, despite some operational and tactical successes, to their removal because of their unwillingness to fight the war the administration wanted waged. Due to the constant necessity for evidence of military success in the field, the president was always willing to move, remove, or change the mandates of Union generals in order to push the administration's political needs upon military operations.

Starting early in the war, Lincoln used his power to control the assignment of general officers to influence military operations and inspire commanders toward thinking offensively in order to end the military impasse, especially in Virginia. On January 10, 1862, unwilling to wait for the further recovery of the commanding general from typhoid fever, Lincoln met with McClellan's senior commanders in Washington and implied that the Army of the Potomac had remained idle long enough and had grown large to the point of being unwieldy.[3] After McClellan heard about the meeting and felt threatened by a "conspiracy" against him, he met with the president and his cabinet three days later. Despite prodding, the commanding general refused to discuss his plans for an offensive other than to reveal that he did have a design for a campaign. Waiting for this promised offensive stretched into early March and President Lincoln's frustrations grew.[4] However valid McClellan's plan was, and however necessary the delay to prepare his enormous army for action was, the commanding general did little to foster support for the campaign from an administration that had a bona fide responsibility to both know and approve military operations in order to ensure that they supported political objectives.

Reflecting this sentiment, Lincoln's willingness to allow the Union high command to control the war effort slowly dissipated during 1862, not to return until he had a commanding general who held his complete trust.

Without consulting McClellan or Secretary of War Edwin Stanton, he issued an executive order on March 8, designating Irwin McDowell, Erasmus Keyes, Samuel Heintzelman, Edwin "Bull" Sumner, and Nathaniel Banks as corps commanders.[5] Not by coincidence, Lincoln selected the generals who had opposed McClellan's plan to move the army by sea to avoid the Confederates and who displayed a desire to risk battle against the enemy. Lincoln made these assignments in the Army of the Potomac without yielding to "expert" advice that went against his political instincts and needs.[6] According to discussions in the White House after the meeting, the president claimed to have picked the "fighting generals" who advocated action (while McClellan had sought more time to prepare), his desire for aggressiveness providing the deciding criteria.[7]

The general lack of impressive tactical success in the East resulted in the growth of anti–West Point sentiment, fueled by assertions that the Union high command was dominated by generals who did not know how to fight aggressively and were fighting "with kid gloves on."[8] The war would require harsher measures and more aggressive commanders in order to match the famed Confederate generals and their legions, according to radical Republicans in Washington, and the "conservative element of the West Point school" was unable to deliver on these expectations.[9] To many in the administration, the evidence that proved this perceived weakness in Union generalship was the repeated instances of slow deliberate offensives, the conduct of each justified by military principles with little consideration for political concerns. Halleck's campaign to seize Corinth, Buell's drive on Chattanooga, and McClellan's sluggish movement after Antietam demonstrated to the critics that this type of warfare, and the generalship of these commanders, was incompatible with the needs of the Lincoln administration and the Union cause.

Halleck's Corinth campaign was an example of this conservative style of generalship and the ensuing friction with the administration. After the victory at Shiloh, Halleck joined Grant's Army of the Tennessee and Buell's Army of the Ohio in the field, a force that, with the addition of Pope's victorious troops from Island Number 10, numbered over 100,000 men. Though greatly outnumbering the remnants of Albert Sidney Johnston's defeated army, Halleck acted cautiously, nervous about reportedly larger Confederate forces from the moment he took the field.[10] After arriving at Pittsburg Landing, Halleck complained to his wife that "this army is undisciplined and very much disorganized," and bragged how he "straightened things out" upon his arrival.[11] Preparing his forces for the drive on Corinth, Halleck assembled an impressive concentration of Union military talent and an experienced and aggressive set of subordinates.[12] From this promising gathering of men and resources, Lincoln and the Northern public had high hopes of a decisive campaign.

Yet, the resulting offensive pleased few observers, as nearly the entire Confederate defending army was allowed to escape because the conduct of the advance resembled an eighteenth-century war of maneuver and siege against "strategic points." Halleck's enormous force set off for Corinth on May 3, yet did not enter the city until May 30, even though it was only roughly twenty miles from his start point. The Union army averaged less than a mile a day, as Halleck's conventional strategy and the cautious nature of his textbook Jominian campaign required the troops to halt daily and throw up fieldworks all across their front, while engineers built roads to ensure a secure line of supply. Once he reached the Confederate defensive works on the outskirts of the city, he ordered the massive wings of his army to entrench, with every intention of conducting a formal siege.[13] Therefore, although the Confederates constantly expected a Union onslaught, there was no battle at Corinth.[14] Halleck never launched an assault; instead he boxed in the defenders and was more than content to await a level of preparation not yet achieved when the Confederates evacuated the city on May 30. After a short, half-hearted pursuit, Halleck settled into Corinth and gave no thought to following and destroying the Southern army.[15]

Despite Halleck's contentment, the Union victory pleased few in the administration and generated a firestorm of criticism, focused mostly on his conservative planning and lack of aggressiveness. John "Black Jack" Logan, wearing new stars on his epaulets, was extremely disparaging of Halleck's slow, deliberate advance on Corinth, which he later labeled "the most ludicrous feature of the whole war."[16] Many Northern newspapers likewise decried the escape of the Confederate army and bluntly equated the city's fall with a Union defeat. One editor summed up the frustration with the Union advance by claiming that "General Halleck has thus achieved one of the most barren triumphs of the war," due to the readily apparent contrast between seizing a railroad hub and destroying another Confederate field army in the West.[17] Though not completely pleased, Lincoln deemed the capture of Corinth impressive enough to justify Halleck's advancement to commanding general of the Union army, especially when compared to the productivity of the other field commanders.[18]

While Halleck was promoted for delivering results, Buell's and McClellan's commands ended in the fall of 1862 because of their unwillingness to adjust their military operations to the needs of the administration. Although each of the latter commanders had arguably won his most recent battle when relieved of command, it was the perceived lack of aggressiveness and an unwillingness to fight the war in the way the administration wanted that dictated the fall of these generals. The challenges of being the party in power during midterm elections in the midst of a civil war drove the need for the impression of military success and policy achievement. Therefore, the president was under pressure from his supporters to be seen guiding the Union cause toward victory leading up to the 1862 elections. During these trying days for the administration, Halleck repeatedly warned both McClellan and Buell that the administration and the nation could not afford further delays awaiting the start of the offensives.[19] However, this intense political pressure was poorly understood by or supported by the senior Union generals during the campaigns of 1862.

Though Buell's conservative campaign plan was perhaps militarily justifiable given severe logistical constraints and the difficulty of operating in occupied territory, political demands dictated a different strategy. This pressure was ignored. Halleck had gone as far as confidentially warning Buell during his extremely slow drive on Chattanooga that the administration was so dissatisfied that the commanding general had been asked to recommend Buell's replacement. "Permit me, general," warned Halleck, "to say in all kindness that the government will expect an active campaign by the troops under your command, and that unless that is done the present dissatisfaction is so great your friends here will not be able to prevent a change being ordered."[20] Given his understanding of generalship and his temperament, the cautious, deliberate Buell was unable to adjust to the administration's need for aggressiveness. As a result, though successful at driving back Braxton Bragg's Kentucky Raid, he was then fired for failing to wage an aggressive offensive campaign.

With this perspective, many West Pointers believed the decisions that shaped the war should be based solely on military effectiveness, as such an approach would yield the shortest path to military victory in the field. This criterion of military effectiveness led to clashes with the administration when these generals appeared not to appreciate the political aspects of the struggle, as seen in Lincoln's frustrating quest to secure the many Unionists in eastern Tennessee. From the first months of the war, the president was constantly exerting pressure on his generals to clear the region of Confederates and protect the loyal citizens there who sent the White House appeal after appeal for help. When told by both Halleck and Buell in early 1862 that a more prudent military objective was the railroad junction at Nashville, Lincoln complained that their reasoning was unsound, as eastern Tennessee was filled with loyal people asking for protection, while the Nashville area was not.[21] This practical political logic had no effect on the calculations of the two generals, and it would not be until late in the war that Lincoln overcame the resistance within the Union high command toward campaigning in eastern Tennessee. Faced with uncertain logistical lines of communication, limited transportation networks, and Confederate defensive arrangements, rescuing the pocket of Unionist support was just not seen by many Union generals as the best use of military resources. On this and other issues of military effectiveness versus political needs, West Pointers in the Union high command would repeatedly clash with Lincoln and Congress throughout the war.

Buell's relief and the frustration over the situation in Tennessee demonstrated how many West Pointers earned the scourge of the politicians by not seeming to understand the political dimensions of military operations in the same terms as the administration did. Buell had slowly lost the support of his patrons in the capital through his conservative planning and recurring neglect of the politically vital, but militarily marginal, area of Unionist eastern Tennessee. Lincoln had repeatedly ordered him to move into the region, where many Unionists were crying for protection. Not only did the Army of the Ohio fail to accomplish this important task for the administration, but Buell argued with both the president and Halleck that it could not be done given logistical constraints. This argument proved too much for Lincoln as the fall elections neared, and prominent Republican politicians throughout the Old Northwest demanded Buell's removal.[22] Lincoln could not afford to ignore cries from supporters of the war effort with congressional election prospects looking so dim in the West. Though undefeated in the field, Buell's relief was all but inevitable given the popular political demand for a new commander in Tennessee.

Buell did not seem to have any appreciation for the political factors demanding action, and he relied on purely military justifications for his announcement that his army was going into winter quarters in late October near Nashville. Notified once again of the administration's disapproval, he replied on October 22 with a lengthy list of his reasons why, on military grounds, this action had to be taken and then proceeded to move his army in the direction of the city.[23] This was the final straw for the president, and Buell was dismissed. Lincoln relieved him over the objections of Halleck, who shared the president's frustration with Buell's caution, but felt that this approach to campaigning was sound and that Buell deserved more time to carry out his planned offensives.[24] Lincoln, however, had little faith that Buell's generalship held the key to operational success and could not afford the loss of votes that the general's continued service might cost him. He demonstrated in the firing of Buell and the pressure over eastern Tennessee that military efficiency did not shape the Union war effort by itself, that political factors would and must determine how the war would be waged. These political forces clearly called for action and the impression of success, so when Buell was replaced by William Rosecrans, the new commander had a very short honeymoon with the administration before he too felt the telegraph whip to take the field.

It was this expectation of action that doomed George Brinton McClellan, the most prominent general fired during 1862. Though a sound organizer, McClellan's strategic outlook proved antithetical to the president's because he commanded by the mantra that "it would be exceedingly foolish to give way to impatience and advance before everything was prepared."[25] According to this philosophy, McClellan's immense army was never quite prepared enough to act aggressively, and the resulting caution proved the source of Lincoln's greatest frustration during the war. McClellan's slow movement during the Peninsula Campaign and his "change of base" during the Seven Days' Battles nearly ended his career, but he got a second chance for field command during the Antietam Campaign based on his ability to build and motivate the Army of the Potomac.[26] Although credited with a win at Antietam and the repulse of Lee's invading legions in Maryland, within two months McClellan would join Buell on the inactive list, and for similar reasons.

Lincoln and McClellan's deteriorating relationship during the month after the Battle of Antietam revealed the importance the president placed upon aggressiveness and his unwillingness to tolerate differing definitions of successful generalship. Lincoln had repeatedly asked McClellan to take the field and to advance upon Lee during the long month of October 1862. On October 13, Lincoln wrote to McClellan, and the very first line read, "You remember my speaking to you of what I called your overcautiousness."[27] In the same letter, he challenged McClellan to fight if a favorable opportunity presented itself, or to "try" to beat Lee to Richmond by moving along the inside track down the Blue Ridge Mountains. "I say 'try;' if we never try we shall never succeed," Lincoln pleaded, warning McClellan of an obvious fact that seemed to be forgotten by the Union commander: "We should not so operate as to merely drive [Lee] away. . . . we must beat him somewhere, or fail finally." His motivation for these appeals was simple, because the upcoming congressional elections demanded action and McClellan's inaction had come to represent all that was perceived to be wrong with the current conduct of the war.

Lincoln had finally had enough procrastination from McClellan and concluded that the West Pointer's generalship did not match the needs of a divisive civil war.[28] Judged by purely military criteria, the general appeared an effective Union military commander.[29] His ability to build cohesion and esprit were nearly unmatched, he had gotten closer to Richmond than any Union commander until 1864, and if his views on the war diverged from the administration's, he had arguably almost won his kind of war in June 1862. Though McClellan never pressed for a decisive tactical victory and often appeared to be fighting not to lose, he had defeated Lee at Antietam, a deed few Union generals could claim. Yet, it was his conduct of this battle and its aftermath that provided the evidence to Lincoln that the general had to be relieved since he was unwilling to wage the aggressive movements the administration demanded in order to trap and destroy the Army of Northern Virginia.

Though always short of experienced officers, the Lincoln administration had to consider the effect any change in military leadership would have upon the political atmosphere in the capital and on popular morale (although, as will be seen, both of these priorities changed during the war). When changes did occur, they often were tied more to the political calendar than to events on the battlefield. For example, Lincoln kept on Democratic favorites like Buell and McClellan, despite growing Republican protests, as long as political profit could be had from their prominence in the form of Democratic support for Union party candidates. When the administration decided to dismiss popular leaders such as these, care was taken to minimize the political costs. Although an outcry was raised against these two generals for their conduct during September and early October 1862, Buell was not dismissed until October 24, shortly after the October congressional elections in the Northwest. The ax did not fall on McClellan until November 5, the day after the elections in New York and New Jersey, where he was popular. As much as many prominent officers espoused political neutrality and a distaste for politicians of all types, their fate was inextricably linked to the politicians who guided the war effort.[30]

This complete infusion of political reckoning into military strategy and generalship led to Halleck's increasing bluntness about the need for action until it reached the point in December when he warned Rosecrans that his job rested on an immediate advance. Halleck was exasperated by the political pressure caused by Rosecrans's delay in his planned offensive. As he candidly told the army commander, "The whole cabinet is anxious, inquiring almost daily, 'Why don't he move?' 'Can't you make him move?' 'There must be no delay.' . . . You will thus perceive that there is a pressure for you to advance much greater than you can possibly have imagined."[31] Halleck demonstrated his growing acknowledgment of this political aspect of the war by repeatedly warning Rosecrans in early December that the diplomatic situation in Europe dictated that he must take the offensive to clear Tennessee of Confederates. Halleck pleaded with the field commander that "a victory or the retreat of the enemy before the 10th of this month would have been of more value to us than ten times that success at a later date." A victory would be needed by the middle of December, he explained, so that it would be known during the next meeting of Parliament in London.[32]

In response to the near-constant political pressure demanding "action," Rosecrans echoed many Union officers in appealing for recognition of a distinctly military expertise. "If the government which ordered me here confides in my judgement, it may rely on my continuing to do what I have been trying to—that is, my whole duty," argued the frustrated commander. "If my superiors have lost confidence in me, they had better at once put someone in my place and let the future test the propriety of the change."[33] Rosecrans believed, as did Buell and McClellan, that those vocal politicians in Washington had as little knowledge of the current military situation in the field as they did of military tactics and strategy. To most regular army officers, giving field commanders autonomy from political pressure made military sense. Therefore, the friction with the administration over its inability or unwillingness to do that should be anticipated given the expectation that successful generalship would be based more on political calculations than military effectiveness. From this view, military planning should be left to the military experts.

One of the principal causes of the criticism vented on Union generals throughout the war by the administration, Congress, and much of the public was the failure on the part of these generals to communicate their plans and decisions to a nonmilitary audience that many in uniform felt did not need to know "military details." This communication breakdown stemmed in part from a lack of agreement between military officers and politicians on the proper integration of politics and generalship. A clear example of this discord was the often contentious issue of preparation and training prior to actively campaigning. For trained military officers, to avoid battle until their units were ready was a common conviction based upon the critical time needed for organization and training. Yet, this simple military axiom was usually very poorly explained to politicians and to the public, failing to reduce political pressure and the cries of "on to Richmond."[34] Military commanders repeatedly failed to convey a simple military rationale for their decisions to irate politicians and the impatient public. In turn, many Union generals were unwilling to understand the political motivations behind the administration's pressure for action in areas such as eastern Tennessee, which they considered militarily insignificant and a waste of resources.

Though some of the heated rhetoric in these clashes was fueled by partisan posturing, much of the responsibility for these disagreements over Union strategy could be laid at the feet of regular army generals who did not see it as their duty to sell their rationale to the administration. Military principles and historical precedent may have seemed obvious to those who made the military their profession, but their brief, almost cursory explanations did little to appease politicians who demanded to know why the Union armies were not already in Richmond. A clear example of this lack of communication was McClellan and the logic behind his plan for the Peninsular Campaign. Though the military advantage to operating up the York and James Rivers was clear to the senior Union generals, McClellan failed to clearly convey his plans and their logic to Lincoln and prominent politicians in the capital. As a result, these politicians, who felt responsible to their constituencies for the progress of the war, did not develop any faith in Union generalship, and McClellan did not gain an understanding, and therefore a degree of trust, from his commander in chief.

Lincoln often asked simply for the accomplishment of any tangible results to feed the public's hunger for success, and in this quest he more often than not was disappointed during the first years of the war. Even generals of whom the president had the highest expectations resisted the calls for offensive action. As the department commander in St. Louis, Halleck provided an example of this resistance when he answered the president's January 1862 request to name the date he would advance with a diatribe about how the chaotic state of affairs in Missouri made an offensive impossible. Halleck further increased his commander in chief's frustration by ending the letter with reasons why Buell should not advance in Kentucky. The brazen Union commander defended his failure to advance with a curt lecture to the president on military theory and claimed simply that Buell should not move separately, as Lincoln requested, because military expertise advised against it. "To operate on exterior lines against an enemy occupying central position, will fail, as it has always failed," warned Halleck. "It is condemned by every military authority I have ever read."[35] By failing to explain to the president why these theories were valid and by repeatedly resting his judgment on claims of "expertise," Halleck only provided further ammunition to radical Republicans who viewed the conservative Union military leadership as the main obstacle to victory in the field.

This harsh criticism was made sharper by the near-mythical exploits of Confederate generals. The president was constantly asking his generals to match the conduct of the enemy and met repeatedly with explanations that his commanders could not (or would not) risk this level of aggressiveness and initiative. "Are you not overcautious when you assume you cannot do what the enemy is constantly doing?" Lincoln asked McClellan in the fall of 1862. "Should you not claim to be equal to his prowess and act upon that claim?"[36] Expressing the president's frustrations with this weakness he saw in Union generalship, Halleck informed Buell that "[Lincoln] does not understand why we cannot march as the enemy marches . . . and fight as he fights, unless we admit the inferiority of . . . our generals."[37] Against these charges West Pointers such as Halleck, McClellan, and Buell were unable to defend themselves except to request more time and more troops to finish their organizational and training tasks.

Politicians in the capital did not seek reasons not to attack Confederates, nor did citations of "military authority" assuage them; they solely sought results. Lincoln understood that his own popularity, the health of his political coalition, and public support for the war rested on the perception of success in the field. "My own impression," the president replied to a group of abolitionists complaining about his policies concerning reconstruction of occupied territories, "is that the masses of the country generally are only dissatisfied with our lack of military success. Defeat and failure in the field make everything seem wrong."[38] With this simple sentiment, the president incorporated perceptions of military success and the advancement of political objectives into any decisions involving generalship and general officer appointments. This approach meant that the organizational ability and military experience of West Pointers would only shelter them so long from the demand for action.

McClellan was especially aggravating to the administration and the public with his unwillingness to take the field for an offensive campaign after assembling the greatest concentration of Union troops in his Army of the Potomac. "I ask at the hands of the administration and the country confidence and patience," the general explained to an increasingly impatient commander in chief. "So long as I retain my present position I must claim to be the best judge of the time to strike."[39] This rigid justification for inaction infuriated both the administration and its critics in Congress. To impatient political partisans, such as the radical Republicans on the Joint Committee on the Conduct of the War, this assertion of military expertise to justify inaction was simply fodder for a crusade against conservative generalship. Additional resentment came from the political disdain for military assertions of unpreparedness, which were greatly undermined by the perceived ability of West Pointers in gray to perform operational and tactical miracles while the Union generals appeared lethargic and cautious.

Consequently, in making the decision to replace McClellan at the head of the Army of the Potomac, Lincoln claimed he had tried too long to bore with an augur that was too dull to take hold. When Frank Blair confronted the president, pleading that McClellan not be removed, Lincoln gave a clear and concise description of why the general had been relieved and why the decision was final. "I said I would remove him if he let Lee's army get away from him, and so I must do so," Lincoln explained. "He has got the 'slows,' Mr. Blair."[40] In order to maintain support for the war, Lincoln had to keep up the impression of forward progress and military success, and the fierce resistance of the Confederate field armies convinced him they were the main obstacles to winning the war. As McClellan appeared not to share these views, he had to go. In a similar manner to the political involvement in general officer selection and assignments, the fortunes of Buell and McClellan reveal how Union generals' commands and careers were intrinsically tied to political calculations.[41]

Though initially relying on the system of political patronage for advancement, regular army officers did not recognize the dynamics of this patronage system as a pact involving mutual support and benefit. Many of the West Pointers most prominent during the first years of the war felt that they were selected for high rank and major commands based on their military education and experience. Therefore, these newly promoted generals felt no obligation to be politically flexible on occupation policies and on the issue of how the war should be conducted because they believed that they were recognized as the experts on the use of military force. This lack of understanding was most clearly demonstrated by McClellan's fate; the "Young Napoleon" was so confident of his own expertise that he could not comprehend why he was not completely trusted by the administration to manage military operations. Even some generals, like William T. Sherman, who proved very successful resisted policies they disagreed with, such as the formation of the U.S. Colored Troops, because they felt it was enough that they were winning the military contest.

As they fulfilled their initial role in the war effort, Military Academy graduates did manage to prepare and deliver armies of unprecedented size to the battlefield. But even with superior numbers, these early regular generals were often unable to achieve tactical victory and inspired outcries that a different kind of general was needed. Even Sherman's own brother, Senator John Sherman, differentiated between the two tasks assigned to the former regular army generals. The senator believed that the West Pointers were uniquely prepared for the work of organizing an army, "to discipline, to mold, to form lines and squares, to go through the ordinary discipline and routine of the camp," but that battles should be fought and won by volunteer amateurs trained in the stress of actual combat.[42] Similar outcries were heard in the capital throughout 1862, and Congress was joined by a large segment of the populace in its contempt for West Point's ability to foster expertise in the art of command. General Franz Sigel, a political general, recommended to political allies in Congress that more military academies should be established. This step was needed to "destroy the monopoly of West Point," according to Sigel and his patrons, "to bring even into the regular army a liberal element, counterbalancing thereby the aristocratic and conservative element of the West Point school."[43] It was in this atmosphere of political pressure and faultfinding that Union generals were asked to command.

"Jealousies and Political Intrigue Are Greater Enemies Than Any Open Foe"

In the eyes of some self-proclaimed "apolitical" officers like Halleck, political generals were often credited with, or blamed for, injecting politics into the military conduct of the war. To many West Pointers, the appearance in their armies of a Banks, a Sigel, or a McClernand would involve partisan interests in Congress and the administration in the conduct of operations. If the regulars then received guidance outside the narrow bounds of specifically military operations, such as to divert forces to a Unionist region or to give the political general a more prominent role in the campaign, the fuel would be provided for attacks on amateur commanders in general. Leading the attack, Halleck was the most vocal in making these accusations and played a prominent role in the Union high command, which made him very influential in spreading the consequent distaste for all politicians in uniform.[44]

However, as the "jealousies and political intrigue" of the Fredericksburg Campaign demonstrated, Military Academy graduates conducted their own internal battles within the Union high command that had a negative impact on the war effort.

For many politicians in uniform, clashes over policy and the conduct of the war naturally led to the idea of a second front in the capital as the center of a struggle between various political factions over control of the war effort. As early as August 1861, Butler saw this conflict occurring and already considered the war a partisan contest for control. When relieved of command at Fort Monroe, superseded by the consummate career regular General John Wool, Butler expressed the idea that this was a two-front war, with the war against the Confederates sometimes rivaled in importance by the partisan war in the halls of Washington. "I certainly shall not take any too much from these people," General Butler wrote his wife about his political foes in the capital. "I think that these people propose to make this a partisan war, without any of the efficiencies such a war requires. This move [relieving me] has come from my enemies, and I shall have to fight it out with the people."[45] He was not referring to the Confederates, and he began at once to protest his relief to political allies and the press, more than willing as a consummate politician to take his "fight" to the people. Throughout the war, political generals courted public approval, built a network of supporters in the capital and in the field, used the press to gather acclaim, and employed any political forum to wage a bitter struggle with their political enemies. It mattered little whether these opponents wore a gray uniform, a blue one, or resided in the national government.

In a natural outgrowth of this ambition and their practical political experience, political generals were often bold (or wise) enough to correspond directly with congressmen, members of the cabinet, and even the president himself. Butler proved to be a master at this form of communication. In seeking political allies, the ambitious Massachusetts politician went as far as sending his analysis of the debacle at First Bull Run to the Joint Committee on the Conduct of the War and praised the more powerful members like radical Republican senators Benjamin F. Wade and Zachariah Chandler for the "many expressions of kindness and confidence made by your courtesy."[46] As with many political generals such as Frémont and Blair, Butler was popular with the radicals because he promoted their agenda. From this activity he gained patrons who would push for his advancement by adding the radicals' goals to his own.[47] Butler was not beyond appealing to political allies outside military channels to gain support, which could be seen in an appeal to Senator Henry Wilson in November 1862. "I beg you, as Chairman of the Military Committee, to use your influence to have more troops sent here," he asked, "Mass. Troops especially."[48] This was the very behavior that so bothered former regulars like Halleck, yet their ire only increased when such irregular contact proved to be effective.

Postmaster General Montgomery Blair gave a good example of the benefit of this political engagement as he maintained a constant correspondence with Butler and other generals, discussing policy, military operations, and the partisan feelings in the capital. Blair showed the impact that a direct line to the political leaders could have for political generals when he informed Butler, "I received your letter and dispatch, and contrary to your orders I read both to the President, under injunction of confidence however."[49] Butler was even willing to appeal directly to the president to question his replacement in New Orleans by Banks. His long private letter to Lincoln began with the preamble, "I take the liberty of addressing you, not as Chief Magistrate and Commander-in-Chief, but as a friend and a kind and just man."[50] As in the environment of antebellum politics, these amateur generals searched for political allies and sought to gather support from patrons in the capital, an activity at which they were all experienced.

Consequently, political generals fought the war with one eye on the power struggle in Washington. They kept appraised and often adjusted their policies and oratory based on the rhetoric coming from the capital. Many were not as bold as Butler or Frémont in attempting to shape policy, but most of these politicians in uniform, with years of practice at electoral survival, were flexible in their ideological views and content to reflect the current stance of the administration. When Major General John Dix, who had replaced Butler as the department commander in Fortress Monroe, had to oversee the local elections of December 1862 in Norfolk, he left behind his free-soil past to place the reestablishment of the municipal government over considerations of black suffrage and emancipation. Dix mirrored Lincoln's current feelings on both topics by ordering that only whites who had sworn loyalty to the Union could vote and assured these budding Unionists that all their property would be protected, including their slaves. Although unpopular with the radicals, Dix's stance supported the administration, though his conduct of garrison and occupation duties would become harsher and more extreme as the war progressed, reflecting the changing winds in the White House.[51]

Such behavior, whether seeking to shape policy or following the lead of patrons, was only natural for these ex-politicians given their years in Congress and various state legislatures learning the dynamics of American political culture. The result was not only an understanding of the interrelation of policy and military action during a civil war but also a willingness to be vocal concerning the conduct of both. When addressing the issue of fugitive slaves, Butler concluded one letter to the secretary of war, in which he made numerous suggestions about forming the administration's political position on the issue, with an explanation of his involvement. "Pardon me for addressing the secretary of war directly upon this question," he explained, "as it involves some political considerations as well as propriety of military action."[52] Butler reflected a common feeling among political generals and was not beyond determining that "I shall have to take issue with them," referring to the cabinet, when informed of a policy decision with which he disagreed.[53]

In stark contrast to their regular army peers, the reaction from politicians to this infusion of partisan politics into the conduct of the war was generally positive. Butler repeatedly received praise concerning his conduct from Lincoln's cabinet and Congress, including support from his former political adversaries Salmon Chase and William Seward.[54] The openness of these political networks of patrons and allies actually helped Lincoln shape the war effort by giving him enough information concerning his amateur generals' political beliefs to use patronage to hold on to those he gained benefit from while removing ideological opponents. This propensity was clearly demonstrated in the contrast between Butler's lengthy service and Frémont's early demise. Though often injecting turbulence into Lincoln's management of the war, Butler's accommodation of the administration's goals made him a valuable asset, and the president was willing to tolerate some independence.[55] Nonetheless, there was a limit to the freedom granted to military commanders, as Lincoln's reaction to Frémont's proclamation liberating slaves in his department demonstrated. Lincoln clearly saw a divide between the "purely political" and the range of "military" acts and was willing to use his power to assign generals as a tool to ensure a unity of political effort.[56]

This harnessing of political allies and establishing ties to the capital, though also done by many West Pointers, became inextricably associated with the political generals due to the prevalence of partisan rhetoric and the impact these networks had on military operations. Such political activities helped further the stereotype of the political generals as military amateurs waging the war with one eye on the next election. For many regular army officers, these amateurs were just corrupt politicians who served in uniform solely to inject divisive politics into every aspect of the war effort. For this viewpoint, political generals boldly offered their opinions on military matters with an unwarranted confidence that stemmed from the protection they gained from influential patrons.[57] As with many perceptions, this stereotype did have some basis in fact. The typical political general had little understanding of military issues at the start of the war, often focused on partisan instead of military issues, and certainly fought with one eye on the political situation in the capital. Some political generals like John McClernand fed this generalization by treating their command authority as a political mandate and a direct measure of their personal standing.

This approach to command caused a natural clash with regular army peers, even those as tolerant of amateurs as Ulysses S. Grant. But unlike Halleck, Grant did not automatically discard the entire group of amateur generals, instead evaluating each on his ability to perform his assigned role in the war effort and judging his fate accordingly. Grant's approach to the problem of integrating political generals started very early in the war but grew to fruition during the Vicksburg Campaign, when he first drew the sharp contrast between seasoned amateurs such as John Logan and Francis Blair and an ambitious politician by the name of John McClernand. Grant was more than happy to work with Blair and Logan, even praising "Black Jack" as a natural battlefield leader who knew how and when to follow orders. Grant treated these two ex-politicians as members of the team and often remarked on their deep support for the Union. Yet his first skirmish in the clash between regulars and amateurs occurred during the drive on Vicksburg and resulted in a fractious battle in the army high command and in McClernand's relief.

As a corps commander in Grant's army, McClernand had been a constant thorn in his commander's side. The ex-politician had repeatedly called on political allies for favors, degraded his fellow commanders and Grant in the press, and cried to the president about his promised independent command. After the repulse of the first major assault on Vicksburg, McClernand published an inflammatory and self-congratulatory general order in a Memphis newspaper and insinuated that the attack was defeated because of the failure of Sherman and McPherson to support his initial success. This act was the culmination of a year in which McClernand demonstrated an absence of loyalty to his commanders, of cooperation with peers, and of personal tact. The unauthorized press release was finally a clear enough infraction for Grant to justify the need to fire the popular Illinois general, and McClernand was relieved of command on June 18 for failing to follow the regulation requiring the prior approval of published orders.[58] But political pressure forced Lincoln to return McClernand to field command later that year, despite his damaged reputation, though the president had to move the divisive politician away from Grant to prevent Grant from resigning.[59] McClernand's actions, his fighting of his relief, and his eventual reinstatement all combined to make the Illinois politician the archetype of political intrigue and infighting in the Union high command.

Yet some generals who met this stereotype were West Pointers, inspired by strongly held personal beliefs into waging moral crusades for their cause. Though Butler became to many the stereotypical political general, it was one of his Military Academy–graduate subordinates who provided a stronger example of advancing a radical agenda. During the summer of 1862, Brigadier General John W. Phelps (USMA 1836) waged a public campaign advocating the use of black troops, formed a unit of ex-slaves and free blacks without permission from the War Department, and eventually resigned in protest when he was ordered to only use the unit as manual laborers. In an uncharacteristic move, Butler actually disapproved of Phelps's initial efforts to arm black troops, claiming that, as the department commander, he must stop the effort since his authority entitled him "only [to] carry out the laws of Congress as I understand it."[60] However, after this dispute and its publicity revealed a changing wind on the subject within the administration, Butler revealed his political flexibility by claiming credit for "my experiment of arming the free negroes."[61] Contrary to contemporary stereotyping, Phelps's West Point education did little to dampen his political leanings.[62] He was just one example of West Pointers who allowed personal beliefs to influence policy, yet his behavior was downplayed and viewed as personal rather than professional conduct.

Because of the diverse background of general officers, the patronage involved in their appointments, the conflicting goals of their political supporters, and their ambitious personalities, the leadership of the Union army was permeated with a volatile mix of personality, politics, and schemes for advancement. This tendency was true for former regular officers as well as amateur commanders. The absence of command doctrine and an agreed upon standard for generalship only exacerbated a system of command based on personalities and personal relationships instead of rationalized roles and objective assessment. This dynamic appeared to wax and wane in direct proportion to the armies' proximity to the nation's capital, as illustrated by the turbulence at the head of the Army of the Potomac, the most politicized American army in history and perhaps, in the first years of the war, the most dysfunctional. Although this modus operandi of intrigue and personal jealousy was true from the moment that McClellan assigned the army its name, the Fredericksburg Campaign stands as the clearest example of the mingling of Machiavellian infighting and personalities in the "professional" officers of the Union high command.

Though the political involvement of officers in issues of promotion and advancement had been common in the antebellum army, the stresses and opportunities of wartime increased this dynamic exponentially, peaking during periods of unrest in the officer corps, especially during Major General Ambrose Burnside's tenure at the head of the Army of the Potomac. Under McClellan, partisan factions and scheming had become common in the upper ranks of the Army of the Potomac, driven in part by their commander's friction with the administration and his division of subordinates into sides based on this animosity. The eastern army's first commander had left a legacy of bad blood and conflicting cliques, which his many detractors took to calling "McClellanism," a problem, complained the blunt Bull Sumner, of "a great deal too much croaking."[63] Signaling what might have been the high point of this propensity, Burnside's quest for tactical victory was waged in a highly political atmosphere, and the political conspiring began long before the army crossed the river.

With a new commander at the helm in November 1862, the original plan for Fredericksburg was fundamentally sound, as the operational situation initially appeared promising.[64] If the Army of the Potomac moved rapidly, as Burnside hoped to do, they could be across the river and threaten Richmond, forcing the Confederates to react.[65] Burnside initially did move the army swiftly and arrived at the banks of the Rappahannock on November 17, there to await missing pontoons that were to have allowed the army to cross. By the time he was ready to cross, the Army of Northern Virginia was ready and waiting, entrenched on a series of hills dominating the crossing points of the river. By not striking quickly, and by the delayed arrival of the critical pontoons, Burnside was faced with the task of an opposed river crossing against the tenacious fighters of Lee's army.[66] He was determined to offer Lee battle, because he dared not go into winter quarters without a fight, as this decision had sparked bitter criticism against McClellan from the administration and the newspapers the year before.[67]

The resulting campaign was a disaster, and before long the issue of blame became political fodder for old feuds, both for those in uniform and for politicians. Deciding where to place responsibility for the defeat depended largely on one's partisan interest because of the perceived linkage between the failed campaign and the popular standing of the administration. From the first news of a disaster at Fredericksburg, some in the press began vicious attacks against Burnside and sought to damage the administration's public support and force partisan chances in policy. Democratic newspapers, fueled by opponents of the administration, assailed the army commander for incompetence.[68] Radical Republicans, who approved of Burnside's statements favoring emancipation and his aggressive conduct as a commander, took an opposite approach. The conclusion of the Joint Committee on the Conduct of the War was that Major General William Franklin's conduct of the attack on the Union left was the cause of the defeat at Fredericksburg.[69] Burnside ended much of the debate as to the responsibility for the loss, especially the perceived culpability of the administration, by claiming sole authorship of the fiasco.[70] This admission should have ended the infighting over accountability for the defeat and left the results of the campaign as evidence for the president to use in determining the fate of the army and its commander after they went into winter quarters at Falmouth.

Lincoln had not immediately relieved Burnside after Fredericksburg, for he thought the general could still achieve the desired military success. The president had always been reluctant to fire a faithful subordinate, and he had admired Burnside's modesty and loyalty since the fighting at First Bull Run.[71] Burnside had flaws, most of which he freely admitted; he also had a fighting spirit and was defeated while pressing the enemy exactly as Lincoln had been asking for throughout that long frustrating year.[72] Although there was a severe outcry against the administration, which bore the brunt of the criticism for the failed campaign, and great pressure to make a change in command in the Army of the Potomac, Lincoln resisted the temptation to fire yet another general.[73] If Burnside could learn from his mistakes, the president hoped, he could plan and execute a successful crossing and continue the drive against Lee. This hope was drowned in the Mud March and the scheming of Burnside's subordinates.[74]

The debacle at Fredericksburg, combined with the recent trials of some McClellan supporters, the low confidence in which Burnside was initially held, and the machinations of generals like "Fighting Joe" Hooker, created a command atmosphere so divisive as to impact the campaign itself.[75] This threat was recognized at the time, an awareness that furthered the strain on the new army commander. "Jealousies and political intrigue are greater enemies than any open foe," Burnside's most trusted aide-de-camp claimed. "[Burnside] says they [the Confederates] can be whipped, if he can only rely on his officers."[76] Burnside may have been as guilty as any of this insidious activity, as he had originally accepted a command he felt less than prepared for simply to deny the promotion to his antagonist, Joe Hooker. Burnside's plan for the battle may have included a continuation of such scheming, as he intentionally left Hooker in a position to sit out the fight.[77] This environment had a corrosive effect on the trust between commanders, mirroring the outcome of political relationships between the same commanders, members of Congress, and the administration.

This malignancy in the Union high command in the eastern theater became progressively worse as the post-Fredericksburg recriminations turned vicious, revealing a willingness on the part of many Union generals to use intrigue to save their own reputations and conspire for personal advancement. After being driven back across the river, Burnside wrote the president directly to complain of the lack of support from his general officers and declared to Halleck that he would cross the river again in January on his own responsibility, since he believed he was receiving little constructive support from the administration or his subordinates.[78] Yet, Burnside was not without sin in this respect. On the first day of 1863, he went so far as to write the president "an unreserved statement of my views," boldly stating that neither Secretary of War Stanton nor Halleck had the confidence of the officers and soldiers. Therefore, Burnside concluded, they both should be replaced since they bore some responsibility for the state of the army due to their lack of cooperation and assistance.[79]

This growing political intrigue and escalating jealousies rapidly cost Burnside any chance of continuing in command. On the afternoon of December 30, two of Burnside's subordinate generals, division commander John Newton and brigade commander John Cochrane, went to Washington without his knowledge to convince the administration that he was incompetent and should be replaced. Unable to find any sympathetic congressmen, the two generals eventually went to see Lincoln and complained directly to him about the weaknesses they perceived in their commander and his plan to wage another offensive campaign. Adding to this unscrupulous performance, two of the more senior commanders, William Franklin and William F. Smith, wrote Lincoln directly a week after the disaster at Fredericksburg to blame Burnside and suggest that the army return to campaigning on the peninsula. Showing no confidence in their commander, the two shocked the president by stating openly that "the plan of campaign already commenced will not be successful."[80] Lincoln seethed at all this blatant insubordination and ordered Burnside to Washington to confer on his campaign plan, not knowing that the general was already scheduled to visit the capital to testify in the court-martial of Fitz John Porter for his behavior at Second Bull Run. Although

Lincoln's faith in Burnside's ability to command was being eroded by all the intrigue, the president decided to let the planned campaign commence.

Burnside learned of these appeals behind his back and, in reaction to this open erosion of his position and authority, attempted to regain control over his generals by striking back. On January 23, he published General Order No. 8, which brought Hooker and one of his division commanders up on charges for "unjust and unnecessary criticism of [their] superior officers," dismissed both Newton and Cochrane from the service for going to see the president, and relieved a half dozen other officers including Franklin and Samuel Sturgis, commander of the Sixth Corps.[81] Since the president's trust and faith in Burnside's generalship had moved onto shaky ground, there may have been little chance this action would be approved, but it might have been the only tool for bringing these malignant conflicts into the open. In his own view, Burnside was simply attacking what was a near insurrection among his generals.

Faced with Burnside's claim that he could not continue in command unless General Order No. 8 was enforced, President Lincoln was forced to accept the general's proffered resignation. The president had little choice, since the loss of support for Burnside from the other generals in the Army of the Potomac made further friction inevitable unless a change was made. Burnside appeared to be one of the first to see this inevitability when the lack of confidence from his officers damaged his ability to handle the army. After the humiliating conclusion of the mud march, Burnside concluded that "it does not seem strange that success did not attend my efforts," given the discord and scheming by his subordinates.[82] What led to Burnside's relief was a loss of faith by the administration in his ability to command and to further the Union cause. Even though his reputation was surely damaged by the defeat at Fredericksburg, Burnside's removal was not based so much on poor tactical performance as on the destructive infighting that occurred after the battle was over.[83]

Burnside's reputation was eroded further as his struggle with his subordinates spilled into the press and the halls of Congress, and this fratricidal sparring revealed the level of infighting and backstabbing among many Union generals.[84] Not surprisingly given the growing acrimony, the source of the worst interpretations of the battle was other commanders in the Army of the Potomac. Meanwhile, Burnside appealed to patrons and friends, developing a network of political supporters. Both these alliances would become apparent in April 1863, when the Fredericksburg Campaign became fodder for the Joint Committee on the Conduct of the War. The ensuing inquisition turned into a struggle not only over the responsibility for the defeat but also over some of the basic facts of the battle, such as how much leeway Burnside had granted his grand division commanders in making the assault. Fredericksburg also showed how far, to be effective at this point in the war, general officers had to go to maintain support in the administration, even if such efforts meant appealing directly to the president, congressional patrons, or political allies.[85]

Even the commanding general, the contemporary American epitome of a professional officer, got involved in the infighting. Damaging his own reputation, Halleck became a passive chief of staff when he was needed most after the disaster at Fredericksburg.[86] Much of the damage to the Army of the Potomac came from Halleck's behavior during the campaign, when he often appeared to duck responsibility by forcing Burnside to deal directly with the president without the benefit of advice and support from the more senior commanding general. In his official report, Halleck quickly shifted the entire blame for the debacle onto Burnside. Starting his report with the assertion that "this change of base was not approved by me," Halleck went on to defend himself against any responsibility for the Union setback.[87] By helping to poison the dialogue between the field commanders and the president, Halleck failed in his responsibility to address strategic issues and to use his military expertise to advance the Union cause.[88]

This unprofessional behavior did not end with Burnside's relief or the purging from the Army of the Potomac of Porter, Franklin, and the other perceived members of the McClellan clique. "I much fear that the spirit which you have aided to infuse into the army, of criticizing their commander, withholding confidence from him, will now turn against you," Lincoln warned "Fighting Joe" Hooker. "Neither you, nor Napoleon, if he were alive today, could get any good out of an army, while such a spirit prevails in it."[89] Hooker commanded this army into the spring of 1863 and suffered the same fate as Burnside, reaping a firestorm of intrigue and jealousies that he had helped to sow. A week after the Union defeat at Chancellorsville, Lincoln warned Hooker, "I must tell you I have some painful intimations that some of your corps and division commanders are not giving you their entire confidence. This would be ruinous, if true."[90] As the incidents and anecdotes recounted above reveal, a professional officer corps divorced from partisan politics simply did not exist during the Civil War. The end result of all this scheming was that President Lincoln did not view either type of general, regular or amateur, as military professionals worthy of complete trust and autonomy.

Conclusion

Regardless of the infighting and frustration internal to the Union high command during campaigns like Fredericksburg, regular army generals such as Halleck, Burnside, and Rosecrans drew a sharp perceived behavioral difference between themselves and politicians, both in and out of uniform. This assertion and similar sentiments supported their belief that trained and experienced Union generals, at least the West Pointers, must be trusted to determine when, where, and how their units were to meet the Confederates in battle. In a way, these West Pointers sharply complained about "political meddling" because such pressure most threatened their individual and collective claims to military expertise. On the other hand, political generals were much less likely to complain of partisan and personal intrigue because this behavior was so prevalent in their political pasts. Unlike most regular officers, the degree of political pressure was understandable to political generals like Butler and Banks because they grasped the administration's desperation to maintain Northern morale and faith in the cause.

Pressed from both sides in this controversy, Lincoln vacillated on the dichotomy of political expediency and military practicality, as a result alternately prodding and consoling his field commanders throughout 1862 and 1863 about a sense of operational urgency. After the battle at Fredericksburg, when Burnside was contemplating another assault across the river, Halleck's feedback to the plans had an endorsement from the president stressing Burnside's autonomy in determining the time and place for an offensive. "Be cautious," Lincoln warned Burnside, "and do not understand that the government or the country is driving you."[91] Lincoln repeatedly comforted his commanders with this sentiment, but his actions sent another, more powerful message, as the president had relieved both McClellan and Buell for "the slows." The administration may not have wanted to signal this intent and consistently place political pressure on its military leadership, but this meaning was what Lincoln's field commanders understood, be they Burnside, Halleck, McClellan, Buell, Rosecrans, or a host of their subordinates.[92]

The political pressures for offensive campaigns were fueled in part by a public perception that reduced the war to a simple measure: if the army was advancing or had won recent glory on the battlefield, the war was being won. But to the dismay of the administration, and its detriment in the midterm elections, the opposite dynamic was also true: if there was little to celebrate from the military field, then the war was being poorly managed and lost. Echoing this sentiment, newspaper editors often led the tirade against "McClellan and the host of do-nothing generals who Scott and West Point have put at the head of our armies," who seemed unable to beat the Confederates.[93] Such public outcry led the administration and its radical Republican allies to put pressure on field commanders to deliver military victories. This demand, conveyed to a public who constantly sought any indication of how the Union wind was blowing, reinforced an oversimplified view of the war. Since the Union was judged to be winning whenever its armies were advancing, it should come as little surprise that this standard became the mark of a successful general in the eyes of the administration.

Whether the campaign was praised or damned mirrored a sharp difference in opinion on the value of taking cities versus that of destroying armies and reflected yet another divergence in judgments of the proper aim of Union generalship. While Halleck and other commanders focused on geographic objectives, President Lincoln understood that the enemy armies were more important, because they were the obstacles preventing the capture of cities and the reestablishment of federal authority. This lack of agreement on the very purpose of military campaigns was aggravated by the unwillingness of generals to either adopt the objectives sought by the administration or to convince the political leadership to agree to the validity of their planned operations. Part of the responsibility, however, must rest on the generals who failed to convince their political masters of the military necessity behind their plans and timetables. The resulting dissension only furthered the friction between commanders and politicians, adding to the president's sense of frustration. As a result, Union generalship became inherently intertwined with politics, both in interactions with politicians over the conduct of the war and in personal interpretations of the nature of the war.

Yet, this friction may have been unavoidable given the divergence in how regular commanders like McClellan, Buell, and Halleck, on the one hand, and the president and political generals on the other, viewed the need for and purpose of military campaigns against the Confederacy. The initial resistance of conservative West Point generals to the pressure for action was only natural given their belief that the war would be decided on the battlefield—and therefore decisive clashes must not be rushed into. Although Lincoln knew these tactical battles were rolls of the dice, he also believed they were needed to maintain Northern resolve, keep up the confidence of its soldiers, and increase the areas under federal control. The disagreement over the conduct of the war also drove a wedge between West Pointers and political generals and was somehow connected to the vicious infighting that occurred between the two groups. Why did many individual commanders from each source get stereotyped into caricatures, the zealous, inept political generals and the despotic, impotent West Pointers, both perceived as incapable of winning the war?

CHAPTER SIX

"Political Policy Rather Than Military Strategy"
Diverging Views on Generalship

As the year 1863 began, Union commanding general Major General Henry W. Halleck grew increasingly frustrated with his inability to keep the partisan political struggle from seeping into every aspect of military operations. A vocal critic of political generals, Halleck's attention was drawn to Nathaniel Banks's Department of the Gulf, as the politician from Massachusetts had no training in military operations. Banks also appeared to have little comprehension of the military principles that Halleck valued so much or of the direction in which the West Pointer wanted to steer the war. To Halleck's consternation, Banks viewed his mission in the Gulf in political rather than military terms, as clearly seen in his initial proclamation as department commander. He declared the reestablishment of federal control and the enforcement of federal policy as his primary tasks in the Gulf. His initial pronouncement of his goals therefore stressed reconstruction tasks and made no mention of actually fighting the Confederates or of seizing enemy-held geographic objectives.[1] Banks freely admitted that, as Halleck feared, efforts at policy enforcement and the establishment of local loyal governments in Louisiana had interfered greatly with purely military objectives, but the occupation mission and utilization of field troops for garrison tasks was "a necessary diversion."[2] As these messages revealed, Banks was looking at the situation and the tasks ahead from a different perspective, with a focus on political cause and effect that Halleck would not or could not comprehend.

In response, Halleck concluded that Banks did not understand the military situation. He tried to convince the political general that the war in the lower Mississippi was actually going to be won in battle against the main Confederate force at Vicksburg. "Give but little [attention] to the occupation of the country," Halleck directed Banks. "Troops should garrison no part not absolutely essential to the success of [Grant's] plan of action [against Vicksburg]."[3] The concentration of Union forces became a mantra that Halleck would repeat throughout 1863, especially toward political generals like Banks who continued to espouse political objectives that, according to Halleck, defied "military logic." Halleck seemed surprised that despite repeated injunctions against dispersing his troops for occupation duties, Banks persisted in this very course of action. Both Banks and Halleck appeared to grow more frustrated as 1863 passed, each baffled as to the other's lack of understanding of his view of the strategic priorities in the Gulf. This disagreement over what Union generalship required was not unique to these two personalities, as it reflected the increasing friction between the political generals and the West Pointers based on a mutually perceived, and often actual, deviation in their approaches to the war.

The departmental command system inherently revealed this divergence by emphasizing the choice of priorities for military operations. This combination of active campaigning and occupied territory forced nearly all Union commanders to wrestle with occupation duties and reconstruction efforts, even contentious issues like runaway slaves, contraband merchandise, African-American troops, and the cotton trade. As the war progressed, the conflict seemed to diverge into two distinct contests: a vast clash between field armies, filled with epic battles at Gettysburg, Vicksburg, and Chattanooga, and a vicious political struggle between parties and ideologies for control of the populace both North and South. As the clash between Halleck and Banks revealed, the question of which of these contests was the decisive arena of the American Civil War was the source of most of the fundamental disagreement in the Union high command. Although the previous comparison of selected politically appointed amateurs and West Point graduates revealed an absence of the expected difference in military value to the administration and involvement in political patronage, why did the two types of general officers have a fundamental divergence of opinion on the functions required for successful generalship?

Behind the different approaches and quality of policy interactions were more than just varying levels of political and military experience. In fact, the two dissimilar groups of military commanders approached command differently because many of them had different perceptions of the nature of the war. Their prewar experiences led to two views of the obstacle facing generals in the army: regulars tended to view the war as a military problem requiring a focus on the battlefield, while the politically adept amateurs viewed the rebellion as a partisan political struggle for power both in the South and in Washington. When used as a basis for prevailing criticism, this perceived divergence and the resulting unwillingness to understand the opposing view-point further stereotyped the two strands of Union generalship in the eyes of the Northern public and their elected politicians. More important, this fric-tion over the character of the war was the primary cause of the detrimental struggle between West Pointers and political generals.

The Civil War: A Ruthless Partisan Struggle

Faced with warfare along a thousand-mile front, Union generals became involved in mobilization and occupation policies, including everything from the status of runaway slaves to trade policies within occupied areas, cotton sales, the tax collection authority of local government officials, and issues of sanitation and social services. To deal with this challenge, the War Depart-ment established a system to divide up the mobilization and military efforts along geographic lines, usually with a field army of the same name operating in each area. Department commands were established from the start of the war to unify military effort, and their origin created a foundation of military governance and political control of occupied territory in addition to the ongoing conventional struggle.[4] By assigning each department commander a dual role as a field commander and a kind of military governor, this com-mand system inevitably intertwined military and political roles.[5] All depart-ment commanders were therefore forced to wrestle with issues of occupation policy and reconstruction requiring policymaking and policy interpretation. In this aspect of the department command system, political generals made a significant contribution to the Northern war effort because their antebellum political background was good preparation for the challenge of interpreting and implementing occupation policies.

The partisan struggles so common to American politics prepared men such as Butler and Banks for the challenges of acting as military governors because they had a wealth of previous experience to draw on, and in some instances, the expertise and savvy of these former politicians helped shape the course of the entire war. With a similar background in politics, Lincoln understood these strengths and therefore many political generals were assigned to occupation commands.[6] While numerous West Pointers rotated through department commands in both the eastern and western theaters due to political failings and battlefield defeats, Banks in the Gulf, former New

York congressman John Dix heading the Department of the East, and Ben Butler in Virginia remained in their assignments for long periods and demonstrated the value of having experienced politicians in command of military departments. The varied successes and failures of these political generals reveal how this aspect of generalship—a task beyond the capability of many, if not all, career officers from the regular army, who lacked experience at legislative or gubernatorial functions—could influence the tide of war as significantly as battles won and lost.

Governance in occupied areas was a task that a political general was uniquely qualified to perform, as military service to the Union cause gave protective status against political attacks that a civilian political representative would not have had. Not all Union generals became this immersed in shaping policy, but all commanders were faced with the formidable task of implementing and interpreting directives from above and often of dealing with unique civil-military problems that did not fit the approved response, yet occurred every day during the war. Though not all commanders had department or military division level responsibilities, the units they led were the workforce behind the occupation of conquered territory, and Union officers at all levels implemented these convoluted political agendas on the ground. An example of this involvement can be seen in the wartime service of John Logan. Logan was never promoted above corps level or assigned a purely occupation command, yet units under his control had long periods of occupational duties between their active campaigns, the most challenging being in the occupation of Vicksburg in July 1863.

After the fall of Vicksburg, Logan's corps was left behind by Grant to garrison the newly conquered city. Less than a week after commanding a section of entrenchments and waging a conventional siege of the city, Logan was forced to wrestle with issues of contraband slaves, displaced refugees, and paroled Confederate officers, all in a major municipality that was without social services or a trustworthy government.[7] His lengthy political experience proved to be good preparation for these tasks, and even though his time as "post commander" was short, the former Illinois congressman received praise from all quarters on his administration of Vicksburg.[8] Though Logan's experience garrisoning a restive region of the Confederacy was a common duty for nearly all Union generals at one time during the war, the way the political generals prioritized and envisioned these tasks was fundamentally different from the approach of their peers who graduated from West Point.

Asked to enforce policy on contested and ideologically explosive issues, these politicians in uniform were often more than willing to shape and influence policy rather than simply interpret it because of their history of partisan involvement in antebellum politics. One of the first and most significant examples of this willingness to jump into the political arena of the war was Butler's involvement in the potentially explosive issue of runaway slaves. At the end of May 1861, three fugitive slaves entered the Union lines near Fortress Monroe in Virginia, and a Confederate officer soon came to demand their return. Butler, as the military department commander, refused the request and called the runaway slaves "contrabands of war." In a lengthy letter to Secretary of War Cameron concerning the incident, Butler used his political and legal experience to construct an unusual and influential argument concerning the black fugitives who were entering his lines in larger and larger numbers.[9] These slaves were actually abandoned by their owners because of the war, and therefore, he argued, the local military commander was legally justified to emancipate all the slaves entering his lines and suggested that this logic should be ratified by the administration as Union policy. Secretary Cameron, when presented with a new policy that so eloquently left the legal status of "contrabands" ambiguous, had little choice but to heartily approve.[10] Butler, merging his power as a general officer with his political savvy, had consequently originated a new policy on one of the most divisive issues of the war.

Coming from a sharp legal mind wedded to an ambitious political will, Butler managed to offer a solution that pleased almost all sides in the debate over runaway slaves. Because Lincoln had vowed not to touch the institution of slavery, the ingenuity of Butler's solution offered a way to deny this "property" to the rebellion without alienating conservative allies of the administration. On August 5, 1861, Congress passed the first Confiscation Act, legislating Butler's assertion that all slaves entering Union lines could be emancipated as contrabands of war. This was one of the first steps in transforming the war for union into a war for emancipation, and Butler's raising of the issue (while suggesting a solution attractive to both conservatives and radicals in Congress) was significant in influencing Union policy. When compared to the refusal of professional officers like Halleck, Don Carlos Buell, and George B. McClellan to make determinations or take effective action on political questions regarding occupation, emancipation, and reconstruction, the effect of political generals such as Butler, Banks, and John Frémont is obvious. Butler in particular initiated many of the political debates on issues involving emancipation and reconstruction when he took over the Department of the Gulf after capturing New Orleans in April 1862.[11]

Despite (or perhaps because of) the incessant and tumultuous debates in

Washington, department commanders often received little explicit guidance on issues as complex as reconstruction. Political generals were not alone in lacking guidance, as seen in William T. Sherman's complaint during his stint as the occupation commander in Memphis during the fall of 1862. "No instruction had come or could come to guide me," he complained over the issue of runaway slaves. "I was forced to lay down certain rules for my own guidance."[12] Yet the administration did give noticeably more leeway on these contentious issues to political generals due to its confidence in their ideological leanings based on their record in politics. When asked for guidance on reforming the local government in New Orleans, Secretary of War Edwin Stanton told Butler that he was on his own to determine the best course of action to take. "You have been troubled with no specific instructions from this Department," Stanton revealed, "because of the confidence in your ability to meet the exigencies of your command better upon your own judgement than upon instructions from Washington."[13] On the most contested policy issues, the local commanders were frequently left to their own devices to gauge the mood of the Northern public and interpret what the administration wanted done.

Butler and other political generals were often able to make a strong impact on policy issues because of this absence of clear guidance from the War Department, as the bitter partisan fighting in the capital prevented any form of consensus on the major political arguments of the war. During the "contrabands of war" exchange, the secretary of war wrote to Butler that "the [War] Department is sensible of the embarrassments which must surround Officers conducting Military operations in a state by the laws of which slavery is sanctioned."[14] As the very positive reaction in Lincoln's cabinet indicated, many in the administration recognized the potential power and impact of the departmental commanders, and therefore the importance of matching the ideological leanings of the commander with the political objectives of the government.

Encouraged by Butler's stance, Montgomery Blair wrote to the general after the passing of what he labeled "Butler's fugitive slave law" that he was very pleased to see the former Democratic stalwart joining his position on the issue of slavery. Blair recognized that politicians in uniform were in a strong position to help the government with this sensitive issue, as long as their views were in line with the political leanings of the administration. As Butler was in the group of generals meeting this standard, Blair concluded with the judgment that "my opinion in the Cabinet will be to allow you to use your discretion in this matter."[15] Butler joined other political generals in seeing no "law of war" that prohibited continued involvement of senior military officers in shaping occupation and reconstruction policies to match the shifting political currents in the capital. Their willingness to adapt personal political beliefs to match the perceived needs of the administration revealed to Lincoln the advantage of having experienced politicians in this role. Because of Butler's willingness to wage war in the political arena as was required, both the president and the general were happy to see the ex-politician assigned in New Orleans as the commander of a major department to conduct military operations with very little guidance from the War Department.[16]

As the radical inclinations of Butler, Frémont, and other amateur generals became more obvious, they gathered support in the capital, often from unlikely allies in Congress. After Butler was replaced in the Gulf and rumors surfaced of a McClellan "clique" within the officer corps who disapproved of Lincoln's recent Emancipation Proclamation, Charles Sumner, one of the senior senators in Congress, wrote to Butler that he regretted the decision to remove the popular political general from New Orleans. "Mr. Stanton assured me last evening that had he known your real position with regard to the Proclamation," Sumner informed his former political antagonist, "he would have cut off his right hand before he would have allowed anyone to take your place." The senator then concluded the letter by giving the impression that the president hoped to return Butler to the Gulf and that Lincoln "was anxious to keep you in the public service to gratify you." This prevalent type of correspondence highlights the political partisanship and political motivations for the selection and continued service of many political generals, and the value of their willingness to ideologically ally themselves to the administration.[17]

As one of the administration's strongest political allies in uniform, Massachusetts governor Nathaniel Banks's experience in the Department of the Gulf revealed that the structure of the military department command system, wherein the department commander was both the senior field commander and the military governor, dictated the need for political as well as military skills.[18] After suffering repeated defeats in the Shenandoah, Banks relieved Butler as commander of the Department of the Gulf on December 17, 1862, and then spent much of the rest of the war administering the city of New Orleans and reconstructing occupied Louisiana. Banks had to contend with a restless population, an economic depression, foreign influence and intrigue, questions of slave emancipation, and a Northern demand for resumption of cotton production. As the military governor in a conquered region, he wielded dictatorial powers and was responsible for administering the growing area of occupation while still waging an offensive war against the surrounding Confederacy. As a military commander, Banks seized the Confederate stronghold at Baton Rouge, assisted Grant in clearing the Mississippi by besieging Port Hudson, and established a Union lodgment in Texas.

However, Banks's primary contribution to the war effort may have been in his role as military governor of Louisiana. President Lincoln relied heavily on his political experience to govern occupied Louisiana, evidenced by the enormous scope of the tasks that the president assigned to him in their near constant correspondence.[19] Banks was initially intimidated by the responsibilities expected of a department commander of occupied territory and complained to Halleck in January 1863 about the daunting challenges of the Gulf. "I find . . . on arriving here, an immense military government," Banks described, "embracing every form of civil administration, the assessment of taxes, fines, punishments, charities, trade, regulation of churches, confiscation of estates, and the working of plantations, in addition to the ordinary affairs of a military department."[20] In addition, he had to establish some system of labor for the newly freed slaves in order to get the region's economy moving again. Although there were many valid complaints about Banks as both a military leader and a reconstruction politician, it is hard to imagine that a professional military officer, without Banks's experience in legislation and as the governor of Massachusetts, could have made similar gains toward the return of a loyal civilian government to Louisiana.[21]

Efforts to please all sides on this contentious problem were as challenging for the general as being speaker of a divided House of Representatives or governor of a state in the turbulence of partisan politics. As Banks had mastered both of these formidable tasks before, the challenge of forming an acceptable labor policy was met with his expertise in civil government and politics. Working with local political leaders and using his experience at garnering support, he established a new labor system to replace slavery in the vital area of cotton production, and his solution to the problem pleased the administration.[22] Also during 1863, Banks waged a major campaign along the Red River, captured Port Hudson, cut down on illegal trade with the Confederacy, re-created a political structure for the city of New Orleans, and began the difficult task of rewriting Louisiana's constitution, a list of accomplishments that in Lincoln's eyes more than justified his selection.[23]

In this volatile partisan arena of reconstruction, Banks's accomplishments in Louisiana demonstrated what could be done by political generals using their experience at politics and law, traits few West Pointers valued or could match. Because of Lincoln's faith in Banks's political skills and loyalty to the administration, the political general's command became the testing ground for the president's reconstruction effort. During December 1864 and January 1865, Banks testified before a very hostile Joint Committee on the Conduct of the War and before the Senate on his disastrous Red River campaign and the status of reconstruction in Louisiana. Confronted with opponents of the administration's policies from both ends of the political spectrum, he fought back against diatribes objecting to his efforts to restore a loyal government to the occupied state.[24] Afterward, Lincoln expressed sincere appreciation for this service that Banks had performed for the administration. "I do believe that you, of all men," the president told him, "can best perform the part of advancing the new state government of Louisiana."[25] Being a successful military governor or occupation commander required that constituencies would have to be assuaged, political alliances formed, accomplishments publicized, and public support garnered, all challenges experienced before by those with a history of seeking and holding electoral offices.

With their pasts filled with ideological battles in antebellum politics, it was only natural that the political generals focused on the struggle for political allegiance in the occupied areas of the Confederacy as the main battleground of the war. Butler's view, shared by other ex-politicians, was that the ultimate objective of the war was not to destroy the armed forces of the South, but to reestablish federal authority and political control of the contested areas. With this goal in mind, he informed the newly conquered citizens of New Orleans when he took command that they had nothing to fear if they followed his policies, and that military force would only be used to enforce compliance and protect Unionists who were forming the local government.[26] Politicians like Butler and Banks believed that the war in Louisiana could be won or lost as much in the ballot box as on the battlefield. To the political generals fighting this struggle for dominance in the South, the greatest threat to the reestablishment of a loyal government was therefore not the Confederate field forces, but the vicious partisans and guerrillas who emboldened resistance whenever they struck. In deemphasizing the main Confederate armies, most political generals adopted a belief diametrically opposed by their more conventional Military Academy peers. As a result, one of the primary differences in the two approaches, and one of the areas of greatest conflict, was over the need for occupation troops to enforce Union policy.

To Butler and other political generals, any concentration of troops at the expense of protective garrisons was a mistake because the primary battle of the war was for the allegiance of the populace and their willingness to resume following federal authority. Union military forces needed to hold occupied territories in order to enforce policies, Butler repeatedly wrote to Secretary Stanton from New Orleans in June 1862, emphasizing the need for garrisoning captured areas to win each local struggle for political dominance. "It is nearly useless to go over a country with a few thousand men, hundreds of miles, and distances are reckoned in hundreds of miles," he complained to Stanton, "only to leave it again."[27] In July, Butler warned Halleck that he needed control of more troops to disperse guerrilla forces that were plaguing his occupation efforts. Learning that the force he wanted was being consolidated into Grant's field force, Butler complained that this action was unnecessary and downplayed the threat from the main Confederate army.[28] According to the political generals, it was essential to hold "various points" in order to enforce policy and rally political support in occupied areas, even at the cost of smaller field armies.

Therefore, it was natural for these ex-politicians to press for more occupation troops and to stress the need to gain political control of regions still under Confederate control. The two beliefs went hand in hand: the idea that the Confederate leaders were essentially an opposing political party or ideological faction that had gained control of their followers and the need to utilize any means possible, including military force, to break this sinister bond. This tie would have to be broken for the war to end in each region of the South. In a May 1863 letter to Secretary of State Seward, Banks expressed the viewpoint that his success at extending Union authority was directly related to his number of occupation troops. "Nothing is required but a sufficient force to hold the territory to secure its immediate return to the Union," he assured the secretary.[29] Like nearly all Union commanders, Butler, Banks, John McClernand, and other political generals constantly sought more troops, yet they commonly stressed the need for infantry regiments and cavalry units to secure occupied areas and drive off irregular enemy forces.[30] For these ex-politicians, local garrisons rather than reports of far-off battlefield victories would allow them to dominate local authorities and shape civic behavior to meet their reconstruction goals.

As both Banks and McClernand showed during the Vicksburg Campaign, the War Department's calls for concentrating forces into major field armies could be discounted if opportunities presented themselves to expand Union control into areas of the Confederacy. During the first months of 1863, Halleck and Ulysses S. Grant watched in frustration as Banks's forces moved up the Red River and McClernand took his own troops and Sherman's corps on an assault on the Arkansas Post and even contemplated a drive on Little Rock.[31] These minor campaigns were all waged while Vicksburg still gave the Confederates a hold on the Mississippi. The expansion of Union-controlled areas naturally led to strategic consumption, the loss of available combat strength in Union field armies due to the need to garrison their ever-extending lines of communication. This fundamental military problem drove many school-trained generals to oppose "wasting" troops on minor campaigns and holding noncritical areas. But to political generals, extending lines of communication was ultimately a positive event because it extended political control and introduced opportunities for patronage in local governments and local contracting.

The combination of experience at influencing public policy and a view of the war as a partisan political struggle ensured that political generals in the occupied South were constantly attempting to shape the political landscape around them. Unlike their regular army peers, ex-politicians in uniform tended to get involved in local politics, trying to establish a politically acceptable local government, not just an effective one as was usually the case with many department commanders from West Point. Both Butler and Banks demonstrated this approach in occupied Louisiana by not just dictating civil laws to be implemented, but by actually campaigning for their chosen candidates in local elections, at times even selecting the candidates themselves. This type of engagement led to the appointment of George F. Shepley, a former Maine district attorney and friend of Butler, first as mayor of occupied New Orleans and later as military governor of Louisiana, a choice the president made in June 1862 after a recommendation from Butler. Shepley's military career during the war started with Butler's offer of a commission and a place on his staff and ended with his deep involvement in Louisiana politics. This example highlights the willingness of political generals to extend the use of patronage to any opening, even spreading their subordinates through local governments.[32]

With the war perceived as being waged to gain the allegiance and change the foundation of an entire society, many politicians both in and out of uniform were the first to push for the removal of restraint in the conduct of the war. Echoing the sentiments of many radical Republicans in Congress, political generals such as Butler, Frémont, and Francis Blair would be the first to advocate a war that went beyond combating the organized Confederate armies in the field to a struggle encompassing any in Southern society who resisted the Union. These fierce words stood in stark contrast to the war advocated by some conservative early Union generals, who sought to limit the conflict to one, as McClellan implored, conducted "upon the highest principles known to Christian Civilization."[33] Instead, political generals like Butler early in the war called openly for "prompt severity" in occupied territories as well as the use of military force against the economic and political foundations of the Confederate war effort.[34] Democratic politicians in Washington joined conservative West Pointers like McClellan and Halleck in decrying these appeals and their authors for a radicalization of the war, concerned that, as Lincoln predicted, the war would escalate into a "remorseless revolutionary struggle" for and against slavery.[35]

Yet, as with most aspects of the generalizations about either "type" of general, perception did not completely match reality. In fact, there were examples of prominent political generals advocating the same form of restraint for which radicals in Washington (and in uniform) ridiculed McClellan and Halleck. Banks, while commanding in the Shenandoah in March 1862, issued orders attempting to protect the property of local Virginians from his own soldiers.[36] Nor was even a firebrand like Butler that severe when it came to the treatment of local citizens in the occupied South.[37] In the same vein, there is plenty of evidence that political generals like Banks and Butler did understand the importance of training, achieving tactical victories, and concentrating forces for decisive campaigns. They simply deemed that these were not the tasks for which they had been appointed or for which they would achieve success and recognition. However, it was not the day-to-day actions of these men that appeared so prominently in Northern newspapers; it was their harsh rhetoric and bombastic declarations that shaped their image—both in the Northern public and in the eyes of many of their fellow general officers.

As a result, West Pointers like Halleck and McClellan felt a natural dislike and distrust for political generals during the Civil War, only partially caused by the competition for commands and the threat these amateurs posed to regular officers' control of the war effort. Fueled by the opinion that these politicians did not understand how to wage war, many regular officers wailed at each tactical debacle authored by the amateurs in uniform and told all who would listen about the inability of any but trained regular army officers to bear the responsibility for soldiers' lives in battle. For the regulars, this was the primary means to attempt to limit the role that generals like Butler, Banks, and McClernand played in the war because it mirrored the popular standard of generalship: good commanders won battles. Such attacks did achieve the objective of shaping the stereotype of political generals. The very term "political general" was linked to the image of Butler routed at Big

Bethel or Banks fleeing the Shenandoah, which overshadowed the myriad examples of effective amateur commanders like Logan, Francis Blair, or Alpheus Williams (not to mention numerous successful division and brigade commanders). This criticism of military ineptness, while deserved by some individuals, was undeserved for the entire group and hurt the political generals' ability to garner support and accomplish their mandate from the administration because of the decreased confidence of their subordinates, soldiers, and constituencies on the home front.

Halleck repeatedly offered justifications for this rhetorical warfare against the absence of military experience and expertise among these ex-politicians, but the fundamental reason for the friction ran much deeper than different occupations before the war. Indicating a deep-seated bias between the two types of Union generalship, Halleck's disgust with political generals such as Banks was caused by a divergence between their understandings of the very character of the Civil War and how military force could be used to win it. This divergence in perspective and behavior was not absolute—as all Union generals had views on the proper relationship of political and military campaigns that encompassed both field and garrison operations. However, the *perception* of a split between regulars and political generals proved to be more damaging that any actual difference, as the resulting insight created negative stereotypes of both types of Union generals and poisoned the senior officer ranks with friction and rancor when cooperation was so desperately needed. Yet this use of politics, the press, and patrons to form stereotypes in the administration and in the public eye was not at all a one-sided exchange.

The Civil War: A Conventional Military Contest

The need to administer occupation areas and regional commands dragged West Pointers into a realm they often wanted to avoid. Frustrated at the partisanship inherent in these unconventional roles for military officers, many regulars seemed to conceptually divide the war into separate "spheres," a common theme in numerous letters exchanged between the more senior generals such as Halleck and McClellan. By mentally splitting the struggle into "political strategy" and "military strategy," these commanders could define their generalship in purely military terms and thereby attempt to control the expectations and standards that would be used to judge their performance. This view was rooted in the attractiveness of a distinction between disdained partisan political activity and their responsibility to wage the war solely by conventional means with military victory as the goal. By portraying the war as strictly a military struggle, this perspective neglected political goals and led to an emphasis on the battlefield. Yet, as with the image of political generals, this trait was often more perceived than real in many of the former regulars who painted with a Jominian brush.

Contrary to many contemporary claims, Civil War generals from West Point were not completely inexperienced and unschooled in politics because of a near common involvement in the patronage system in their antebellum careers. Others had more practical experience in politics, such as Halleck who served as the acting secretary of state in California after the Mexican War, where he helped formulate the state's constitution. During the years before the Civil War, Sherman also had exposure to politics while in California, handling land claims, while Burnside worked with government to try to get funding for a rifle he designed and produced. Still others became spectators to the factional infighting surrounding the Mexican War, the Seminole Wars, or the Mormon expedition. Such experience brought contact, and some disdain, for the chaos and partisanship of politics to gentlemen who believed strongly in order and discipline. The result of these shared beliefs could be seen in the Civil War when Halleck, like many of his Military Academy–graduate peers, constantly expressed disgust whenever forced to deal with political issues or wrestle with political generals over occupation policies.[38] Consequently, West Pointers' focus on the battlefield often appeared to drive a contrasting approach toward winning the war, a mindset that sought to isolate the military contest from potentially corrupting political influences.

This distaste for the rough and tumble of American politics often led to problems when these officers were forced to deal with many of the most contested issues of wartime policy. The irony was that during the antebellum period many West Pointers established links with state and federal politicians who would later become their patrons during the early years of the war and push them on the path toward general's stars. However, these career soldiers did not have the practical experience in politics that many of their amateur peers possessed. When the dynamics of the departmental command system and the challenges of occupation duties forced these officers to wrestle with policy interpretation, the administration often suffered, as they made decisions based on purely military judgments instead of political calculations. One of the more painful examples of the trouble caused in political issues for the Lincoln administration by West Point graduates was Burnside's very public clash with a prominent copperhead in May 1863.

While banished to a departmental command in Ohio after the debacle at Fredericksburg, Burnside revealed the lack of political savvy of many regular officers by creating a political firestorm with the arrest of the prominent ex-congressman and copperhead Clement L. Vallandigham. In April 1863, Burnside announced General Order No. 38, which declared that anyone who committed "acts for the benefit of the enemies of our country" would be arrested and charged with treason. Completely surprising the administration, he then reported to Secretary Stanton the May 7 arrest of Vallandigham on charges of speaking sedition. Burnside also warned the administration about the resulting unrest in Dayton and the surrounding counties caused by the arrest.[39] He defended his decision to arrest the politician with the rationalization that, as the military commander in Ohio, he had a duty to maintain the army and avoid any slowdown in recruiting. Civilians who were criticizing his actions, according to Burnside, just did not understand the army and therefore did not understand the threat that Vallandigham represented to good order and discipline.[40] When informed of Lincoln's plan to exile the ex-congressman to the Confederacy, Burnside told Stanton that this action was not the original "legal" sentence from a "valid" military court and that sending the Ohio copperhead south would be government interference, weakening his authority in his department.[41]

In the course of two months, one of the senior and most experienced Union generals had thus created unrest in one of the most loyal Midwest states and caused a tempest of anger in the national press. The majority of newspapers of every sector of the political spectrum decried the "tyrannical" use of military tribunals in a secure Northern state. Lincoln reacted to the crisis by informing Burnside of the dangers of his bold act and by stating how the entire cabinet regretted that it had happened. The president also downplayed the political embarrassment over the act with characteristic words of encouragement to the general.[42] Burnside's lack of sensitivity to political realities did little to support the administration's standing in his Department of Ohio, and when the next month he ordered the suppression of the antiwar *Chicago Times*, the president immediately overruled him. Lincoln and much of his cabinet made a similar appeal for political awareness the following month, when General John Schofield began to close copperhead newspapers and arrest Democratic editors in St. Louis.[43]

Even a general as politically astute as Ulysses S. Grant could create political problems for the Lincoln administration because of a lack of appreciation for the political impact of military orders. During 1862, Grant grew frustrated with the illegal cotton trade within his department and sought to eliminate the distraction from military operations by issuing orders to control such commerce.[44] He and his subordinates associated the more disreputable trading practices with some very prominent Jewish speculators, which caused Grant in December 1862 to issue a general order that "the Jews, as a class . . . are hereby expelled from the Department."[45] The result was a firestorm of protest in much of the North over the accusations of dishonesty and disloyalty contained in the order and a stream of questions from prominent congressmen about the administration's stand on this issue. Lincoln quickly rescinded the order, as it addressed a whole class of people, "some of whom are fighting in our ranks."[46] With these and comparable actions, West Point generals did little to help Lincoln hold together his fragile political coalition during the trying year of 1863.

The clumsy intervention by senior military officers into the political arena was only natural given how nearly all field commands involved either occupation duties in the South or direct interaction with state and regional politicians in the North. This function of generalship, scorned by some regulars as a drag on military operations, was unavoidable, as even Halleck had discovered during his efforts to organize the military effort in Missouri. While trying to focus on a deteriorating military situation, Halleck got bogged down with political issues and the complexity of the war, and was forced to deal with constant patronage appeals, individual criminal cases, and endless contracts for arms, equipment, and supplies.[47] As a department commander, the consummate regular also had to deal constantly with state governors about recruiting new regiments, providing logistics, and gathering support for campaign plans. This interaction with policy issues was not restricted to the top echelon of command, as nearly all field commanders became occupation region or area administrators between campaigns as the Union armies consolidated their gains.

Regulars, very similar to their amateur peers, noticed the absence of clear directions from above. Yet, when given the option, many tried to avoid making a policy stand and maintained their focus on military operations.[48] While commanding in occupied Memphis, Sherman complained of this policy vacuum, stating that "neither Congress nor the President has made any clear, well-defined rules touching the negro slaves, and the different generals had issued orders according to their own political sentiments." Understanding his mission as the "maintenance of order, peace, and quiet within the jurisdiction of Memphis," he was allowed to impose his own view of policy and the proper role of civil-military relations on the local population. Yet, this occupation duty did not appear to a self-defined field commander like Sherman to be the decisive aspect of the war. Therefore, he mirrored many of his peers by commanding with an eye on military effectiveness, securing lines of communication, and preparing for the next campaign—even when these priorities clashed with the wishes of local Unionist leaders.[49]

As a result, the coarse and blunt battlefield commander shaped the reconstruction effort in the city and surrounding region in a manner that best supported his goal of making Memphis a depot to support future campaigning.[50] Like many of his West Point peers, Sherman was forced during this period to wrestle with all the issues of a field commander (garrisoning troops, patrols, deserters, counterguerrilla operations, and so on), all the duties of a city mayor (tax collection, civic policing, lease laws, and the like), and all the contested policies of the rebellion (runaway slaves, disenfranchisement, POW exchanges, among others).[51] However, he did not place the same emphasis on each of these diverse missions and appeared to view occupation duty as a regrettable but necessary interlude between campaigns. Therefore, while Sherman was forced to spend time dealing with occupation issues, his efforts were focused on building up supplies and training units for the next operation.[52]

For most regular army generals, the main issue when making policy decisions was military effectiveness and the impact any new policy would have on the current or next campaign. This tendency can be clearly seen in Grant's order expelling any Jews from his department, which was best for military effectiveness but was a political bombshell for the administration. Even after receiving a rebuke from Washington, Grant complained to Secretary of the Treasury Salmon Chase that his involvement in regulating the trade of cotton "is weakening us of at least 33 percent of our force."[53] His remark demonstrates the persuasiveness of calculation built on military effectiveness when considering policy issues. This military emphasis can be contrasted with Banks, who was actively campaigning at the same time against Port Hudson but had his focus set on the political goal of coaxing Louisiana back into the Union.[54] Although this divergence was only natural since Banks had a different mandate and different expectations from the Lincoln administration, the variance in focus was representative of a common disagreement between West Pointers and political generals over the relative importance of military operations and political efforts during the war.

Even when West Pointers were interested in becoming involved in local politics or reconstruction efforts, they tended to pick a politically astute military governor (or gladly accepted the one proposed by Washington) and then shifted the burden for the execution and details of any policy to this "expert." Sherman echoed the views of many regular officers when he justified his involvement in all these areas to the elected mayor of Memphis by claiming, "Unfortunately at this time civil war prevails in the land and necessarily the Military for the time being must be superior to the Civil authority but does not therefore destroy it."[55] Yet Sherman, like nearly all occupying Union commanders who lacked a background in politics, relied on local authorities to actually govern the populace.[56] Having little desire to get involved in the distasteful complexities of local governance, some West Pointers also felt that this was not their arena. Setting the tone at the top, Halleck appeared not to appreciate the various reconstruction efforts. Faced with assigning military officers as part of a regional government, he stated that he wanted to "spare commanders" from the "unimportant duties" of commanding openly loyal areas, these officers being needed in the field armies fighting the real war.[57]

In stark contrast to the public image of most politicians in uniform, many West Pointers appeared to prefer a view of warfare analogous to conducting the war "on a map." This conservative image was reinforced whenever West Pointers appeared to have problems with any policies or problems that threatened to radicalize the war. Halleck demonstrated this fear and this viewpoint with one of his first orders when he was made a department commander in November 1861. Reacting to what had happened to his predecessor John Frémont and wanting to avoid the explosive issue of runaway slaves, he issued his famed exclusion order one day after arriving in St. Louis.[58] By declaring that runaway slaves could not enter his lines, Halleck sought to divorce any political distractions from his upcoming military campaigns while removing a potential drag on military efficiency. He actually appeared to be surprised at the resulting political firestorm of complaint from the capital. When confronted with the concern that the exclusion rule could be seen as helping the South maintain slavery, Halleck defended the general order on the grounds of military efficiency, explaining afterward that "it was a *military* and not a *political* order."[59]

To many West Pointers, this rationale made perfect sense, as Halleck's exclusion order was sound military policy, even if it was also a bad political move. To their dismay, the idea of a separate "military strategy" was completely unacceptable to the administration and the public because of the intense partisan rhetoric that pervaded feelings on the sectional conflict. During 1862 and 1863, Lincoln was upset at the unwillingness of his senior officers to recognize that winning the war would require a combination of dismantling Confederate political control and hard fighting to destroy the

Southern will and means to resist. "That's the word—strategy," Lincoln complained. "General McClellan thinks he is going to whip the rebels by strategy; and the army has got the same notion."[60] To many politicians, and a growing number of soldiers, West Pointers' use of military theory and military principles seemed to be a simple pretext to excuse long periods of inactivity in camp and tentativeness while on campaign.

Becoming the lightning rod for this criticism, Halleck's rise to a prominent role in the Union army signaled the ascension of a negative generalization about the "conservative West Point school" of generalship. To many in the administration and to the radicals in Congress, Halleck was believed to advocate a limited war derived from an immersion in Jominian theory and appeared to take this isolation of military strategy to an extreme.[61] Halleck himself fueled this condemnation with his own perceived arrogance on military matters such as when he once justified a refusal to obey Lincoln's call for an offensive with a lecture to the president on military theory. "To operate on exterior lines against an enemy occupying a central position will fail, as it has always failed, in ninety-nine cases out of a hundred," the general told an exasperated Lincoln. "It is condemned by every military authority I have ever read."[62] Although not all West Pointers went to this extreme, Halleck and McClellan played such prominent roles in the earlier years of the war that they set the tone in the Union high command. Far more important, the two long-serving Union commanders established the stereotype of Military Academy–graduate generals as officers who disdained politicians, claimed an exclusive professional expertise, and sought to fight the war according to European traditions of treating enemy noncombatants with "kid gloves" and confining war-making to the battlefield.[63]

Often the pursuit of military effectiveness and the quest for order led to clashes with the administration over policies that radicalized the war. Whether Halleck's exclusion order or McClellan's Harrison's Landing letter, many West Pointers made repeated attempts to maintain restraints on the conduct of the war. Even Burnside, who was given a second chance after Fredericksburg because of his perceived support for the administration, opposed the use of Negro troops while commanding in Ohio during the summer of 1863. Though this was a political issue, Burnside believed it was a valid step on his part to interfere and cited the military necessity of opposing an administration policy that could hurt the military effort in his department.[64] Although he did not view it this way, while he was in Ohio Burnside was playing the same role as the political generals in interpreting and implementing policies; he was making a judgment of the effect of using black troops on the recruitment of white

Northerners and seeking to shape policy. But in contrast to former politicians, Burnside demonstrated a lack of political savvy and flexibility in his views.

Unlike most political generals, including Democrats like Butler and Logan, McClellan also displayed no flexibility in these views and combined this shortcoming with an ego that provided an overabundance of confidence that he was correct in his views on strategy. Worse for his longevity in the Union high command, the "Young Napoleon" was never reluctant to express his opinions and rebuff Lincoln's efforts to align their contrasting views on the war's conduct. That McClellan had a coherent, though flawed, view of the war was most clearly outlined in his famed Harrison's Landing letter. The letter was in response to the acceptance by Lincoln of the general's offer right before the Seven Days' battles to detail his views on the state of military affairs and a strategy for advancing the Union war effort.[65] The war should not be waged against the Confederate people or their property, McClellan argued in his letter, only against their armed forces, and the struggle should be conducted with the "highest principles known" to civilized people. In McClellan's view, this approach automatically excluded property confiscation, military arrests, and loyalty oaths and interference with slavery should not be contemplated even "for a moment."

For all his claims of detesting politics and politicians, McClellan was one of the most prolific officers at lodging complaints about political interference and experimenting with political involvement. His reaction to the Emancipation Proclamation was to meet with Democratic patrons and weigh his public response, very possibly already eyeing the chance to challenge the man he scorned as the "original gorilla" in a run for the White House. As was obvious to all observers, McClellan was dismayed by the turn the war was taking and viewed the initial proclamation of September 22 and the suspension of habeas corpus that was announced two days later as "accursed doctrine" that would radicalize the war and subvert the Constitution.[66] After checking with his political allies, McClellan felt he had to speak out as a military commander on his opinion about this political issue. "The remedy for political errors if any are committed," he informed his troops after the announcement of the Emancipation Proclamation, "is to be found only in the action of the people at the polls." McClellan issued this proclamation to the Army of the Potomac outlining his views on the Emancipation Proclamation, then forwarded a copy to President Lincoln on October 7, 1862.[67] He clearly opposed this policy because it conflicted with his own belief about the political goals of the war and seemed unwilling to adjust his viewpoint to match the administration's. Therefore, while

McClellan offered plans for conducting the war and executed numerous campaigns in the field, he never achieved, nor did he appear to seek, the trust of the president, the administration, or the home front in a strategic vision for winning the war.

McClellan refused to acknowledge or accept public sentiment or the changing political winds in Washington and warned that "a declaration of radical views, especially on slavery, will rapidly disintegrate our present armies."[68] For all his uniqueness, his perspective on warfare was very similar to that of Halleck and many other Union generals because it rested on a Jominian focus on operations against conventional military forces. McClellan viewed the war as one between two uniformed armies in a military contest for strategic points and operational supremacy. "The national forces should not be dispersed in expeditions, posts of occupation and numerous armies, but should be mainly collected into masses and brought to bear upon the Armies of the Confederacy," he argued, echoing Halleck's firm conviction on the war's conduct.[69] For all his disagreement with the administration over the policy, McClellan was also similar to Halleck in his reluctance to become directly involved in policy issues involving occupied regions, preferring to place the burden on local officials and the government.[70]

Though branded with similar criticism, Halleck, unlike McClellan, was adaptable in his conception of the war and was willing, contrary to historical accounts, to violate Jominian principles when conditions dictated the need to do so. An example of his growing flexibility occurred after the fall of Corinth in May 1862, when he accepted the need to forgo keeping his army concentrated in order to control occupied regions and consolidate the Union gains from recent campaigns.[71] After becoming commanding general, Halleck even began to understand and appreciate the changing political landscape of the Union war effort. "The character of the war has now very much changed within the last year," he asserted to Grant during the Vicksburg Campaign. "There is now no possible hope for reconciliation with the rebels."[72] Yet even as Halleck grew less and less attached to Jominian principles and voluntary restraint as wartime experience shaped his attitude, his philosophy continued to be shaped by a conception of warfare that discouraged mixing political and military "spheres."

The policy that regulars like Halleck complained about the most was the "wasting" of military resources on excursions and reconstruction experiments that they perceived as distractions from the main military effort against the Confederate field armies. When applied to the conduct of military operations, the Jominian view that Halleck and other Military Academy peers espoused dictated the concentration of forces into field armies, even at the cost of occupation troops and the reestablishment of Unionist control. For some generals, gathering troops into the main field armies became a mantra. As department commander, commanding general, and then as Grant's chief of staff, Halleck directed a constant quest for the concentration of Union forces. He believed this should be done even at the expense of occupation duties and certainly at the cost of reconstruction efforts, which he referred to as futile until the main rebel armies were defeated. Troops should be concentrated because, Halleck argued, "we have given too much attention to cutting the toe-nails of our enemy instead of grasping his throat."[73] In stark contrast to political generals like Butler and Banks, Halleck and other regulars focused on concentrating forces for active campaigns, as these were expected to be the decisive battlegrounds of the war.

A clear example of this divergence in views occurred between Halleck and Banks during May 1863.[74] While Grant lay siege to Vicksburg, Halleck pressed Banks to focus all his efforts on the campaign to clear the Mississippi River and ordered him to move to join Grant's army or at least attack Port Hudson to draw off potential Confederate reinforcements. After he delivered many telegraphed lectures to the amateur general concerning the principles of military operations, Halleck was shocked in late May to learn that Banks had moved up the Red River into northern Louisiana. To Banks, who believed that the Port Hudson garrison was too large to besiege, this course of action was sound, as it drew forces away from Vicksburg while advancing Union control into new areas. "Recent occupation of this country as far as Natchitoches," he wired an exasperated Halleck on May 21, "gives us reason to believe that at no distant day it can be permanently occupied and held with a small force, controlling substantially the entire northern part of the state."[75] These claims appeared in the very first sentence of Banks's report, for in the view of the ex-politician, the reestablishment of Union control into another region of the South was of vital importance and needed to be sustained.

Halleck did not share this view and may well have been puzzled at how the amateur general could fail to see what to the student of Jomini were fundamental military principles dictating the junction of Banks's army with Grant's. To Halleck, gaining and holding this newly won territory would only tie down troops desperately needed for the main military contest then occurring at Vicksburg. "Operations up the Red River, toward Texas, or toward Alabama, are only of secondary importance," he immediately replied to Banks upon learning of his plans. "If we fail to open up the river, these secondary operations will result in very little of military importance."[76] During Banks's failed Red River Campaign in 1864, Halleck's reaction to a request for more troops to occupy captured areas again revealed the divergence in outlooks. Halleck told Banks, "Your troops are too much scattered by occupying too many unimportant points before the [main] rebel force is broken."[77] Echoing this rationale, Grant pressed for the gathering of garrison troops for his 1864 campaign and took this focus on concentration to the limit that winter when he sought to abandon most of Arkansas because of supply problems and to gather yet more troops into the main field armies.[78]

This divergence in views based upon a lack of understanding and agreement on the priorities and the nature of the Union war effort furthered the friction between the two generals. Seeing the war through a Jominian lens, Halleck was consistently frustrated with the views of the political generals and stressed repeatedly to them that conventional military operations were needed to destroy the Confederate field armies. Banks agreed, but the former politician also saw the need to look at the overarching political goals of the war, not just to focus on the local Confederate army. Banks tried to convince Halleck that the combination of seeking popular consent while selectively using force would be a better approach toward the Confederates than relying on military force alone. Though Halleck did lessen his reliance on military principles as the war progressed, he fundamentally disagreed with the approach to warfare that Banks espoused. The disagreement between the two generals represented a larger divergence, a clash between regulars and political generals in the conduct of the war, a friction between reconstruction efforts and conventional campaigns.

This is not to suggest that most West Pointers or political generals did not understand the dynamic of these two simultaneous conflicts in the South, but rather that the vast majority of each type placed a fundamentally different priority on political reconstruction and military operations in the field. Even perceptive generals like Sherman and Grant early on spent the majority of their time and command focus on military operations because this was where they believed the war would be won or lost. Sherman demonstrated this priority during his occupation of Memphis when, though almost overwhelmed in political issues of civil governance, he often expressed his garrison policies in terms of preparing for the next offensive.[79] While Banks in New Orleans was developing a new labor system in Louisiana, Sherman in Memphis was echoing the priorities of his commander. During this period of the war, Grant as commander of the Department of the Tennessee was focused almost exclusively on conventional operations against the main

Confederate field army and had his commander's eye fixed on the fortress at Vicksburg.[80]

As these officers therefore spent much of the war in camps preparing for the next operation, West Pointers' public statements on how to conduct the war provided fodder for the Joint Committee on the Conduct of the War and elsewhere for a crusade against the military "do nothings" and "marionettes" produced by the U.S. Military Academy.[81] Led by the committee, some elements of the Union political body waged an open anti–West Point campaign during the first years of the war. This animosity was due to the perceived unwillingness of the Union high command to wage a total, unrelenting, and victorious form of warfare.[82] Distrusting West Pointers and their reliance on purely military principles, many members of Congress and the administration clung to a simple view of the war in which harsh war measures—including emancipation of slaves and seizure of Southern property—would motivate Union soldiers. In this opinion, the value of high morale, inspired by right-thinking military leaders, would prove to be far more valuable than drill and the detested "strategy" that was perceived to be the sole contribution that Military Academy graduates were providing.[83] When called to this environment in Washington, whether by a congressional investigation or by the administration, West Pointers were often justified in feeling they were entering a hostile arena.[84]

However, as the war progressed, many West Pointers whose views and rhetoric did not fit the stereotype of the "conservative West Point school" of generalship rose in the ranks. Ulysses S. Grant led this emergence, carrying with him a group of subordinates who shared the evolving viewpoint that the role of Civil War generals included the need to match political goals with military means. Many in this group were West Pointers such as Philip Sheridan, who observed firsthand the political impact of military actions; others were political generals such as Jacob Cox, who grew to see the interaction between military success and political progress. This evolution was the result of a military education in active campaigning that Grant, for one, claimed no other school could have given.[85] This strategic philosophy enabled these officers to understand the political radicalization of the war and the failure of the conservative limited-war approach to its conduct. Military Academy graduates like Sherman and Sheridan may have started the war with a Jominian view of the military struggle, but their evolving grasp of the interaction between politics and warfare led to a growing understanding of how to gain political success through military victories to defeat a rebellion.

In language that was a far cry from that of McClellan or Halleck (before 1863), both Grant and Sherman after the bloodbath at Shiloh described how the South would need to be conquered and that the war was rapidly becoming a struggle for survival between two distinct societies. Echoing his friend and mentor, Sherman went so far as to complain about the other generals in the high command who did not see the growing revolutionary nature of the war. "Most unfortunately, the war in which we are now engaged has been complicated with the belief on the one hand that all the others are not enemies," he wrote Secretary Chase in the fall of 1862. "It would have been better if, at the onset, this mistake had not been made, and it is wrong longer to be misled by it." Sherman went on to echo Grant's conclusion that the war had become one against Southern society and the home front that supported its war effort.[86] This view of the strategy needed to end the war was anathema to many West Pointers in 1862 and did little prior to Grant's appointment as commanding general in 1864 to silence the critics in Washington. Yet, to the president, these messages from the West were a welcome respite from the complaints and equivocation of other Union commanders, and their authors rapidly caught Lincoln's attention.

But prior to solid evidence that victory was moving closer, many politicians linked West Pointers to the apparent inability to win the war with fiery rhetoric in speeches, newspapers, and the halls of Congress. The venom that politicians in uniform and many of their allies in Congress and statehouses showered upon McClellan, Halleck, Irwin McDowell, Fitz John Porter, and Don Carlos Buell charged nearly the entire former regular officer corps with either timidity or incompetence. Making matters worse, some in Congress singled out aggressive regulars such as Joseph Hooker and John Pope as undeserving of such disparagement and pushed for their advancement, thereby helping to poison the senior ranks of Union officer corps. The numerous investigations of the Joint Committee on the Conduct of the War were the main arena for this summary judgment and public censure. On this partisan battlefield and in the press, many politicians both in and out of uniform offered up the curriculum at the Military Academy and prominent West Pointers themselves as scapegoats for the disappointments the Union suffered in the first three years of the war. The end result of such vicious slander was a great questioning of the competence of leading Military Academy graduates by both soldiers and politicians, which drove a wedge between the major field commanders and the administration.

During this period of anger and disappointment with the current Union generalship, Butler and some of his political allies made successive bids to wrestle control of the war away from West Pointers and place it in the hands of a general with "correct" views on how the war against the secessionists should be conducted. Butler continued his direct correspondence with the president and members of the cabinet as well as his criticism of senior Military Academy graduates. He reminded all of them about his seniority by date of rank and his availability for higher positions.[87] This pestering was not without result, as in early 1863 Lincoln even considered placing Butler over Grant for the Mississippi Campaign or returning the politician to the Gulf just to ensure that he had a major role in the war and continued his support for the administration.[88] Since Butler's political view of the war clashed with West Pointers' Jominian approach and mirrored the stance of radical Republicans, many of his political allies in Congress repeatedly proposed that Butler take over as secretary of war during the dark days of fall 1862 and spring 1863. Yet Lincoln dared not place control of the war in the hands of Butler or any other amateur general. The president had no evidence he could trust the military competence of political generals, rely on them to follow the administration's lead when dictating policy, or depend upon them to control their unmistakable political ambitions. Much to Lincoln's frustration, neither partisan political generals nor conservative Military Academy graduates appeared able to fill the strategic void at the top of the Union military command.

Conclusion

The consequences of this mutual exchange of recriminations were constant friction and periodic open warfare between the two types of generals that impaired the war effort by eroding the one perishable item that the Union army did not have in abundance: faith in its military leaders. These corrosive clashes, between Scott and Butler, McDowell and Banks, Grant and McClernand, or Halleck and all political generals, drew attention away from the battle against the Confederates and often prevented much-needed cooperation between various armies and departments. These fratricidal fights among commanders also proved to be a major distraction for the president. When one political general tried to involve the president in a campaign against regular officers, Lincoln complained, "I have too many *family* controversies (so to speak) already on my hands, to voluntarily, or so long as I can avoid it, take up another."[89] Exchanging broadsides of criticism only damaged the embryonic trust between the administration and its field commanders, and the resulting acrimony actually shaped military operation. An example of this animus was the early stages of the Vicksburg Campaign, when Grant and Sherman repeatedly made decisions based on foiling the plans of McClernand (and vice versa) rather than considering the best plan for striking the Confederates. As a consequence, the reputations of all the earlier leaders, whether West Pointers like McClellan and Halleck or amateurs like Butler and Banks, eroded as the war progressed by being tied to the worst aspects of their respective stereotypes.

In this manner, factional conflict within Union officer corps retarded the formulation and acceptance of a consistent strategy to win the war; each type of general officer attacked the plans of the other and introduced obstacles to their peers' achievement of their assigned mandates. This mutual distrust and acrimony was based on a pair of stereotypical views that had fed upon the infighting of the first two years of the war and solidified by 1863. Although some West Pointers appreciated the political impact of their actions, they still did not appreciate the political appointees who sought to infuse politics into Union generalship. Even though many political generals recognized their own military shortcomings, they did not agree with the conventional and limited war they perceived as the goal of their peers from the Military Academy. The end result of this divergence in perceived views of the war was a factional and dogmatic struggle for dominance of the Union high command—each side not only not appreciating the views of the other, not only decrying the other's view as dangerous and wrong, but also willing to wage a struggle for a monopoly on command and a dominance of the war effort even if the struggle was harmful to the war effort.

These distinctions between the two categories of Union generals were not always completely clear, since all Union commanders had some flexibility in their political views and all had to focus to some degree on the conventional military struggle. Although arguing with Halleck over the importance of garrison troops, Banks still conducted a formal siege of Port Hudson, leaving his duties in New Orleans to advance the military effort. On the other side of the dynamic, regulars like Halleck and Burnside were forced to set policies within their departments on issues ranging from trade in contraband items to tax collection and voting rights, though they disliked doing so. As these examples show, the main distinction between West Pointers and political generals was not necessarily in their *behavior* during the war, but rather in their perceived *outlook* of the war's fundamental character. West Point generals, and much of the public in the North, looked for battlefield results and measured the war in tactical victories and casualty figures. In sharp contrast, their amateur peers espoused an approach to war that focused on the partisan political struggle.

These views shaped the very words these men used to describe the war, the proper Union strategy to be adopted, and the faults in many of their peers.

This divergence in perspective and rhetoric, rather than famous anecdotes of characteristic behavior, was truly responsible for the negative stereotypes of the West Pointers and political generals during the Civil War. The resulting clash between the two stereotypes over a lack of understanding of the very character of the war only tended to polarize the Union high command and fuel the critics on all sides. To the detriment of every discussion of strategy in the capital, McClellan, Halleck, and Buell, not Grant or Sherman, became the stereotypical West Pointers. Similarly, Butler, Banks, and McClernand, not Logan or Jacob Cox, came to represent all amateur generals during debates on generalship and command selection. Neither of these extreme stereotypes accurately depicted even the archetype of each group, and for much of the war such generalizations of "do-nothing" West Pointers and inept political generals did not do justice to the complex group they depicted.

Both groups were, for the most part, correct about one aspect of the war but lacked an appreciation for the opposing view. This distinction in perspective led to contrasting standards for successful generalship, often dependent upon the fulfillment of their understanding of their mandate, which was why the majority of the criticism that West Pointers heaped on political generals involved perceived failures on the battlefield, while their amateur peers often complained that the former regulars were waging the war "with kid gloves on." In this struggle for a monopoly on command and in the two divergent views, both sides were accurately describing the war as they perceived it, yet both perceptions were inherently flawed because they neglected the bitter struggle their rivals claimed as the main arena of the war. An appropriate analogy would be that Union generals were acting as the fabled blindfolded men did when asked to describe the elephant: each commander described the side of the war that was closest to him—and most familiar to him based on his antebellum experiences.

Though Lincoln constantly sought professional men to command in the field, political generals with their view of the war as a partisan political struggle were easier for the administration to harness because they relied strictly on Lincoln's patronage for their military position. Because of this dependence and their political background and sensitivity, politicians in uniform were often willing to be flexible in their political leanings if this was necessary to maintain their stature in the war effort. Examples of such ideological flexibility included Butler, Banks, McClernand, Logan, and a score of others who changed their views on the contested policies of the times. As political generals were far more likely to reveal their political views in the performance of their duties, the president had a way to identify and remove those who did not mesh with the administration's policy, like Frémont who was not reinstated to command when his early efforts at emancipation clashed with Lincoln's stated stance. Although many West Pointers scorned politics and politicians, they too were subject to this standard, as McClellan and Buell discovered when relieved over their inflexible approach to conducting the war.

As the period 1861–1865 combined a civil war, counterinsurgency, and partisan struggles for power all rolled into one, politics was thoroughly woven into the very fabric of the war and therefore into nearly every aspect of Union generalship. The two concurrent struggles, political and military, could not be separated. As the conduct of the war demonstrated, the antebellum interpretation of Jomini and Napoleon's legacy that dominated military thought after the Mexican War was wrong—purely military campaigns alone could not lead to victory in the midst of a civil war. At its heart, the Civil War was also a political contest over significant ideological disagreements, and both sides had to agree on the war's outcome or the fighting would simply continue. Yet, the principal barrier to the reestablishment of federal authority remained the Confederate army, which dictated a need for conventional military operations to remove this obstacle. The integration of these political and military realities was hampered by the factional warfare between West Pointers and political generals, as the opposing views and contrasting stances on priorities and policies led to both sides deriding the other as being unwilling or unable to win the war. In this atmosphere of infighting and frustration, what type of general could gain the trust of President Lincoln and the Northern public?

CHAPTER SEVEN

"The Responsibility Will Be Yours"
Ulysses S. Grant and a New Faith in Military Expertise

On the evening of March 8, 1864, Abraham Lincoln watched as his guests at a White House reception in the East Room parted like the Red Sea to let a man in a military uniform approach the president. Lincoln beamed at his guest and grasped his hand, asking aloud, "This is General Grant, is it not?"[1] President Lincoln was extremely glad to meet Grant because he believed he had finally found a military commander who he trusted with the war effort. The very next day, Ulysses S. Grant was promoted to lieutenant general and placed in charge of all Union armies at a ceremony at the White House. Lincoln's level of trust rapidly became apparent as he delegated an unprecedented level of authority to his new commanding general. Much of this empowering had to do with selecting commanders and appointing general officers. For example, although Grant did not ask, Stanton telegraphed the new commanding general in May that there were eight unfilled commissions for brigadiers and asked for Grant's recommendations based on demonstrated gallantry in the field. Stanton informed Grant that he now had the authority to brevet brigadiers on the spot, stating that "if you deem it expedient to promote any officer on the field for gallant conduct you are authorized to do so provisionally and your appointments will be sanctioned by the president and sent to the Senate."[2]

Yet, the commanding general soon learned that there was one group of military officers who seemed immune to his new rank and authority. In his new position as the Union army chief of staff, Henry W. Halleck tried once again to remove the leading political generals using Grant's increased control over military affairs. In this effort, Halleck before long recognized the futility of asking for the firing of men like Benjamin Butler or Nathaniel

Banks given their numerous allies in the capital and the importance of the coming election. "General Banks is not competent," Halleck had complained to William T. Sherman after the Red River debacle, "and there are so many political objections to superseding him . . . that it would be useless to ask the President to do it."[3] Though Lincoln implied that the administration's relationship with Grant would be to "leave him alone to do as he pleases," the importance of the 1864 elections placed limits on the delegation of decisionmaking to the new commanding general.[4] This political oversight, and efforts to rally support for the administration at the expense of military efficiency, became all the more powerful as Lincoln's chances for reelection appeared to dim during the months before the election.

The urgency of this quest for political capital was demonstrated in the formulation of Grant's 1864 campaign when several political generals were given prominent roles even though their military record indicated the folly of such an act. The string of defeats these amateurs authored in that long summer did little to dislodge them from prominent roles in the Union high command. Yet, all this was to change by the spring of the following year when the most prominent political generals were purged from any active role in military operations. This change and its cause rest on the question of why, after frustration with all previous commanding generals, so much authority over military matters was entrusted to Grant. Union commanders had bickered, schemed, delayed, squandered advantages, and suffered defeat after defeat in the first three years of the war, and all the while resisted the administration's efforts to define what was expected of Union generalship. What did this humble and unassuming commander offer that no other general had proffered?

As the war stretched into 1864, Lincoln was plagued by the difficulty of attempting to wage the military struggle in a strategic vacuum, because neither amateur generals nor West Pointers could provide his administration with a winning strategic vision that he trusted. In the midst of a civil and political crisis fraught with the continual emergence of near-mortal threats to his government's authority, Lincoln's greatest source of frustration was the inability of his military commanders to support his policies and win the military struggle with the Confederacy. These impediments to the Union war effort were gradually overcome after the appointment of a new commanding general in the spring of 1864. The ascendancy of Ulysses S. Grant signaled the emergence of an agreed-upon standard for Union generalship, supported not only by a clear recognition of military expertise but also by the advent of the administration's complete trust in a commanding general. For President Lincoln, Grant's philosophy on the use of military force to accomplish political objectives appeared flexible enough to succeed without being any political threat to the administration; he had found the general he trusted to win the war. But empowerment of Grant's military expertise would not be complete until after the election of 1864 gave President Lincoln the political confidence to believe that victory in the conventional military contest was all that was required to set the conditions for achieving the administration's political objectives.

Grant and the Emergence of Strategic Vision and Trust

For three long years, no previous commanding general and no previous strategy for winning the war had met the political needs of the administration. The military commanders who had executed the initial campaigns envisioned a limited war to be conducted by limited means. Many conservative West Pointers had sought to prevent a radicalization of the war and refused to acknowledge the fierce passions growing among the Northern public. Some of these Union generals disagreed with Lincoln's policies for conducting the war and resisted any acclimatization. Most prominent in this group was George B. McClellan, who held to his own political views on how to wage the war while railing against those who disagreed with him for "political interference" in the military conflict—radical Republicans and especially his commander in chief. This friction with the administration and Congress did little to inspire cooperation and confidence in Washington. Yet by the summer of 1864, Grant and his protégés had succeeded in garnering the administration's trust by combining battlefield effectiveness with a willingness to adapt to the war's political realities.

Presenting the first strategy for winning the war, Winfield Scott followed conservative designs in developing his "Anaconda Plan," a long-term proposal for strangling the South by economic blockade. Instead of a war of conquest that would leave the South, in Scott's opinion, "devastated," he proposed a three-phase plan: first, a complete blockade to cut off trade; second, a drive to open the Mississippi River and split the Confederacy; finally, the wait for the secessionist governments and war effort to collapse. Scott supported this strategy for a prolonged war because it would bring the South "to terms with less bloodshed than any other plan."[5] What Scott had completely misjudged, or hoped to ignore, was the groundswell of enthusiasm for the war in the North and the pressure this popular opinion would have on a democratic government. The patience and slow pace of the Anaconda Plan led to its derision as a completely inappropriate and leisurely manner to suppress the vilest of treason.[6] Political concerns such as these inspired the administration to push for McDowell to march on Manassas Junction and to constantly press successive military commanders for tactical and operational victories. Though most of Scott's original plan would eventually be adopted, his failure to gain its immediate acceptance led to a strategic vacuum in the Union high command for nearly three years, as subsequent commanders either sought Napoleonic decisive battles or pursued operational maneuvers as the solution to the strategic stalemate.

The man who engineered Scott's retirement was the most prominent example of this failure to present a strategy for winning the war that satisfied the Lincoln administration and the Northern public. McClellan and his "clique" dominated the eastern theater from his appointment as commander of the Army of the Potomac in July 1861 until long past his relief in November 1862, and his political conception of and inflexible views on warfare set the tone for the first phase of the war. While recognizing the impact of popular opinion and political struggles over the goals of the war, McClellan hoped to discount the influence of what he derisively labeled "political considerations" when planning military operations because much of this "influence" was diametrically opposed to the type of war he planned on waging. "The military problem would be a simple one could it be entirely separated from political influence,—such is not the case," complained the general.[7] McClellan did not seek to wage military campaigns completely divorced from the politics of the war, but instead sought a Jominian relationship between himself as a military commander and the national government that would allow him to fight the strategy he envisioned would lead to the return of the Union without impacting the issue of slavery. In the end, he was relieved because he had failed to achieve the required military success before his refusal to accommodate Lincoln's views convinced the president that the "Young Napoleon" was not the general who should be entrusted to defeat the South and achieve the administration's objectives.

Halleck, McClellan's replacement at the helm of the Union war effort, avoided this friction with the administration over policy issues by espousing disdain for the entire "mess" of politics. Although he served the longest tenure of any Union commanding general, Halleck had a very limited vision of political-military strategy to win the war and sought to distance himself from policy issues in order to focus on the military aspect of the struggle. The military-theorist-turned-Union-general was the epitome of a Jominian thinker, with his appeals to the "laws of war" directly echoing the Jominian cries against waging a "people's war."[8] Halleck's approach was shaped by his conception of warfare, based on his constant study of Jomini, and he lacked the ability, and a willingness, to wrestle with the chaos of a prolonged total war that was revolutionary in nature. Required to integrate political goals and military strategy, Halleck was ill-prepared for this new role and became increasingly frustrated with his military peers and his political overseers. "There are so many cooks," he complained to his wife, "they destroy the broth."[9] With this perspective, Halleck spent his time as commanding general wrapped up in the administrative details of the war and tried to marshal support for military campaigns without providing a strategic vision that would tie these operations to accomplishing the political objectives of the government.

Though holding the title, Halleck did not really fulfill his role as commanding general. To the frustration of the administration, he repeatedly refused to overrule subordinates in the field and always judged that the field commander knew the situation better. While this may have been true of the military situation, Halleck never appeared to understand that he was supposed to be more of an expert than lower level commanders, coordinating the various Union armies and matching their efforts to a strategic plan to win the war. Tasked with interpreting the strategic situation and the political needs of the government, he refused to give orders to field generals based on these essential interests, which should have outweighed local military situations. Although disappointing to the president and increasingly derided as a military "clerk" who was the most unpopular man in Washington, Halleck retained his job, due for the most part to his ability to master the constant organizational and logistical challenges of maintaining the Union armies in the field.

After McClellan's relief, the absence of the administration's trust continued during Halleck's tour as commanding general, while a series of field commanders sought tactical victories and operational gains without the guidance of clear strategic objectives from the Union high command. During 1862 and 1863, Burnside, Hooker, Meade, Rosecrans, and their peers conducted the war as theater commanders focused on operational objectives such as Chattanooga or Richmond, while Halleck's actions as commanding general ensured that there was a vacuum in strategic planning for the war effort as a whole. The only mixture of military and political pursuits identified by these department and army commanders was the near-constant political pressure for successful offensives and endless complaints of the involvement of patrons and partisans in promotions and assignments. When Lee's army escaped after Gettysburg and Braxton Bragg's army turned the tables on Rosecrans at Chickamauga, the president desperately sought a general who could provide the strategic acumen to coordinate the war effort. This search proved frustrating prior to the fall of 1863. With the conspicuous exception of Grant's campaigns in the West, all that the Military Academy graduates in high command could offer was the continual search for an operational panacea and repeated calls for additional resources and time to conduct deliberate campaigns against the South.

Grant stood out from his peers not just by his string of impressive military victories, although these accomplishments were important to the administration. Unlike many of his fellow commanders, Grant was willing to support the political goals of the administration as they were presented to him. During the Vicksburg Campaign, he demonstrated this fidelity when his subordinates asked about his view on the divisive issue of runaway slaves. "Rebellion has assumed the shape now that it can only terminate by the complete subjugation of the South," he wrote one of his division commanders, who appeared to desire an avoidance of the administration's stated policy. Therefore, Grant believed Union officers should use every means sanctioned by the government to weaken the Confederates, including encouraging slaves to flee to the Union lines and enlisting these runaways in new black regiments.[10] On this and many other issues, he demonstrated to politicians and subordinates alike that he was unwilling to dictate policy based on his personal beliefs and had enough ideological flexibility to support the intent and letter of any policy dictated by the War Department.

Grant established to Lincoln's satisfaction that he wanted to achieve the administration's goals and expected his subordinates to echo this loyalty. Facing one of the most difficult policies for many Union soldiers to stomach, he went so far as peremptorily ordering his officers to support the policy of recruiting black regiments regardless of their personal political beliefs. Grant published orders telling officers to "exert themselves in carrying out the policies of the administration, not only in organizing colored regiments and rendering them efficient, but also in removing prejudice against them."[11] He then ordered the dismissal from service of some officers who openly opposed the stated policy. Clearly differentiating himself from the political generals and West Pointers with whom the administration was used to dealing, Grant then wrote to Halleck expressing his view of his responsibility as a general officer and the command climate that he sought to promote:

At least three of my army Corps commanders take hold of the new policy of arming the negroes and using them against the rebels with a will. . . . They at least are so much of soldiers as to feel themselves under obligation to carry out a policy (which they would not inaugurate) in the same good faith and with the same zeal as if it was of their own choosing. You may rely on my carrying out any policy ordered by the proper authority to the best of my ability.[12]

To Grant, this was the task of generalship: achieving the government's political objectives by the use of military force—a viewpoint that clashed with those of many of both his Jominian peers and prominent political generals. Frustrated with the interpretations of generalship espoused by McClellan, Butler, Halleck, and others, language of this type must have been very refreshing to the Lincoln administration.

This support from Grant for the administration's political objectives also extended into the conduct of operations and the plans of army commanders. Sensing the interaction between politics and military success, Grant recognized the need for a military victory after the congressional elections had gone against the administration in the fall of 1862. He knew that a decisive military victory would be required to raise Northern morale and ensure that volunteers continued to join the ranks because of his perceived link between recent military frustrations and the administration's declining support on the home front.[13] Grant also believed that the damage caused by another Union reversal would extend far beyond his own demise to adversely affect the entire war effort. The result was a dogged determination to take the Confederate fortress at Vicksburg and an unwillingness to take a single backward step in the eyes of the Northern public. After a brilliant operational campaign, Grant took the city and opened the Mississippi, which gave a significant boost to Union spirit and raised the political standing of the administration.

Grant saw the intrinsic linkage between political effects and battlefield results and was willing to use unconventional tactics to achieve the desired ends. This resolution was most clearly illustrated in the rapid release of the defeated defenders of Vicksburg. When faced with deciding the fate of the captured garrison, Grant broke with the military practice of holding POWs until exchanged and went against the wishes of the Confederate commanders by immediately paroling the entire garrison—less the soldiers who accepted an offer to go to POW camps to avoid any chance of returning to the ranks.[14] He correctly foresaw the demoralizing impact that the return of so many defeated Confederates would have on Southern morale, and that this course of action would further spread defeatism and distress throughout the South by providing the soldiers with the greatest opportunity to desert and return home.[15] Complementing the psychological blow, Grant immediately set out to bolster his army's strength by recruiting black regiments, fully supporting one of the president's projects that so many of his peers resisted.[16] As actions like this revealed, Grant represented the emergence of a new cadre of commanders—commanders not constrained by a Jominian outlook on the war, but who instinctively understood the political implications of military campaigns during a vicious civil war because of their wartime experience climbing the ladder of commands.[17]

This increasing willingness to view the war as a military struggle tied to a war between two societies mirrored its changing direction and attracted converts as the conflict progressed. After the hostilities escalated in totality with the issuance of the Emancipation Proclamation, even the Jominian thinkers had to adjust to the harsh reality of a war between two societies, without clear distinctions between combatants and noncombatants. When Grant proposed an exclusion order to keep his final drive on Vicksburg from becoming bogged down with contrabands, it was Halleck who told him it would be a mistake to enact such a policy.[18] Halleck had slowly come to agree with Grant's earlier breakthrough that the war must become one of conquest, a far cry from the conflict envisioned by the military theorist a year earlier, the experience of war having changed his view. Grant's raiding strategy in 1864 and Sherman's March to the Sea therefore emerge as Clausewitzian uses of force, fundamentally different in outlook from either the partisan battles of political generals or the Jominian campaigning of many of their West Point comrades.[19] During the last year of the war, Sherman accurately depicted his march through Georgia and the Carolinas not as conventional warfare, but rather as "statesmanship" that would convince Southerners that their cause was lost, the message driven home through this controlled use of military force.[20]

After the victory at Chattanooga, Grant was selected as the new Union commanding general because he combined three characteristics that Lincoln sought in a general: trustworthiness, proven military expertise, and the absence of a political threat. After years of frustration, Lincoln saw in Grant the military expertise he had searched for so long in his commanders.[21] The president's only remaining fear about trusting Grant was a concern that a general with his popularity and record could have presidential aspirations and emerge, not as a faithful subordinate, but as a political rival. Lincoln asked E. B. Washburne, a mutual friend from Grant's home district, to gauge the general's political ambitions. This inquiry resulted in a letter from Grant dispelling any talk of a presidential bid in 1864 and containing a pledge to support the administration during the elections.[22] "You will never know how gratifying it is to me," Lincoln replied upon receiving Grant's letter. "No man knows when that presidential grub gets gnawing at him, just how deep it will get until he has tried it; and I didn't know but what there was one gnawing at Grant."[23] This disclosure cleared the last obstacle to total support by the administration and its political allies for the Union army's rising star, symbolized by the congressional effort to revive the rank of lieutenant general in order to promote Grant over all the generals in the army.

Unlike their Military Academy peers, Grant and his disciples accepted the political nature of the struggle, but also unlike political generals they were equally unwilling to try to shape the political objectives for which it was being waged. To the relief of the administration, Grant viewed himself as an apolitical tool of the government and believed their common goal was a military victory on terms acceptable to the administration, regardless of personal or partisan beliefs. The result of this willingness to see the war as a whole was the ability to see beyond the immediate campaigns and beyond narrow operational parameters to view the military struggle in political terms. This gift of strategic vision enabled Grant to come up with a plan to win the war that involved far more than the defeat of the Army of Northern Virginia.[24] For the first time since Scott's Anaconda Plan, a Union commanding general presented a vision and a plan for achieving the military pressure required to make the Confederacy accept the political terms for ending the struggle in terms that Grant would receive from the administration.

In a break with his predecessors, Grant offered a blueprint for victory that the president could understand and agree with. Even before the start of the 1864 campaigns, Lincoln understood Grant's strategy for winning the war because the commanding general had explained it to him and was willing to negotiate the details, such as involving key political generals and maintaining a military force between Robert E. Lee's army and Washington. From the establishment of his field headquarters at the end of March until the launching of the spring campaigns on May 4, Grant traveled back to Washington generally once a week to confer with Secretary Stanton and President Lincoln concerning the upcoming military operations.[25] When briefed in detail concerning Grant's strategy of simultaneous operations by all the Union armies, the president was pleased at the concept and easily grasped the intent. "Oh, yes. I see that," Lincoln stated at the end of the explanation. "If a man can't skin he must hold a leg while somebody else does."[26] As a consequence of this approach to being commanding general, Grant developed a compatibility and understanding with his political bosses.[27]

This degree of understanding led to the president's trust in the plan and the man executing it. When Grant sought control over the various bureaus that supplied the army, Lincoln told him that he could not legally change the military organization but promised that "there is no one but myself that can interfere with your orders, and you can rest assured that I will not." During the same period, Grant clashed with Stanton over the number of troops left in the Washington defenses after the Army of the Potomac drove into Virginia, and Lincoln was forced to settle the dispute. The president did so in a manner that reflected the change in the control of the military. "You and I, Mr. Stanton, have been trying to boss his job, and we have not succeeded very well with it," Lincoln decided. "We have sent across the mountains for Mr. Grant, as Mrs. Grant calls him, to relieve us, and I think we had better leave him alone to do as he pleases."[28] How quickly and quietly these changes took place confirmed the difference in authority Grant achieved with his trust, for as Lincoln devolved power to him, the president changed the entire dynamic of promotion and patronage in the upper ranks of the Union army.[29]

With this level of trust in his expertise and judgment even before the 1864 campaigns commenced, Grant gained an unprecedented degree of control over general officer assignments and appointments. In his first months as commanding general, he reorganized Union commands in a manner completely different from McClellan or Halleck. The control over commands now shifted to a pyramid of internal patrons with Grant sitting at the top. Unlike his predecessors, as Grant left for Washington he was able to designate the commanders of all the departments, armies, and even corps in his old command in the western theater. Even Sherman, who had decried the role of political patrons and partisanship in assignments, felt comfortable making recommendations of experienced military officers "who seem to have no special friend to aid them to advancement," knowing that Grant's approval of the list was all that was needed to gain promotion for his own group of key subordinates.[30] Demonstrating the new dynamic at work, Sherman sent his recommendations to Grant, who forwarded them to Washington with his endorsement, then Grant promptly received word back from Halleck that Stanton and Lincoln had approved the entire list of changes.[31] With this authority, Grant even made efforts to bring back all the previously fired West Pointers, including McClellan, Ambrose Burnside, Joseph Hooker, Don Carlos Buell, and David Hunter, claiming the need for their talent and experience.[32]

Lincoln had not entrusted any previous commanding generals with such broad authority because of an absence of trust in their judgment and military expertise. Prior to the spring of 1864, the president had personally controlled the assignment of Union commanders and had dealt with Congress over promotions and appointments of general officers. This practice resulted in political patronage dominating command assignments and in the political impact of each assignment overshadowing considerations of military competence. A clear example of the president's lack of trust in his military commanders was his discretionary appointment of the Union army's first corps commanders against the wishes of his commanding general. Although McClellan even at the low point of his relationship with Lincoln had some input in designating commanders, his constant advocacy for his supporters and the bias shown against any who criticized him led the president to completely take over the management of senior officer assignments.[33] Prior to Grant's ascendancy, Lincoln used this power over general officer assignments to control the war effort, to promote winners and relieve losers, and to respond to political patrons' petitions in support of their favored commanders.[34] Grant did not face this check on his authority, however, as Lincoln openly claimed he wanted someone with the military expertise to manage the war for him and Grant responded with initiative, competence, and strategic vision.

Yet, prior to Lincoln's reelection, there was a limit to Grant's authority in that he could not remove the prominent political generals who, according to Halleck and other West Pointers, so plagued the war effort. In reorganizing the Union high command for the campaigns of 1864, Lincoln approved all of Grant's changes except one: the removal of Nathaniel Banks from the Department of the Gulf after the disastrous Red River Campaign. "I have been satisfied for the last nine months that to keep General Banks in command was to neutralize a large force and to support it most expensively," Grant complained to Halleck in April 1864, claiming that his replacement was necessary in "the best interests of service."[35] Though agreeing wholeheartedly with the move, Halleck replied that Banks would not be removed by Lincoln until the president had time to test the possible reactions to such a politically risky maneuver.[36] Both Halleck and Grant probably understood that this was Lincoln's polite way of saying no to a man who he had claimed he would deny nothing. The response demonstrates that Grant's authority, and the dominance of the Union high command by West

Pointers, was not complete at the start of the campaigns of 1864. Grant's rise to commanding general would not truly signal the triumph of the regulars' standard of generalship until the internal battle with amateurs was won and West Pointers gained a monopoly on major field commands after the election of 1864.

The Election of 1864 and the Triumph of the Regulars

The emergence of Ulysses S. Grant did little initially to stop the often bitter and acrimonious struggle between political generals and West Pointers over the nature and conduct of the war. As the conflict progressed, the deep divergence of the two contrasting views fueled a further stereotyping of both types of officers into caricatures that did much to exacerbate the differing interpretations of what was expected of Union generalship. The year 1864 marked the culmination of this infighting in the Union high command, as a formalized "team" system of command was attempted wherein a political general would retain command and deal with occupation policy while in theory entrusting field operations to an experienced and school-trained subordinate. Although conceptually sound, too much ill will had been generated and too many headstrong personalities were involved to allow the system to work. The failed attempts to force cooperation only served to move the traditional friction between the two types of officers into major field commands where the animosity poisoned some of the military operations of that critical year. The struggle over military expertise did not end until Military Academy graduates not only gained a monopoly of major commands but also imposed their viewpoint that the war would be won by West Pointers through a conventional military struggle on the battlefield. This result did not occur with Grant's promotion to commanding general, but rather after and because of Lincoln's landslide reelection in the fall of 1864.

As a department commander and then as commanding general, Halleck gladly became the point man in the drive by regulars to end the "damage" these amateurs were causing, though he could only remove politicians in uniform with Lincoln's blessing. Since the first months of the war, Halleck had felt frustrated with the "political wire-pulling in military appointments" in the capital, as he could not purge the war effort of these amateurs. He lamented that "every Governor, Senator, and Member of Congress has his pet general to be provided with separate and independent commands."[37] Since he rarely received permission to remove political generals because of the administration's need for their support, he resorted to slander and scheming against them in order to weaken their attractiveness to the administration and the legitimacy of their claim to the military competency required for command.[38] With each setback that Sigel, Banks, Butler, and other amateur generals suffered, Halleck increased his criticism in his correspondence with uniformed peers and his dealings with the cabinet. "It was foreseen from the first that you would eventually find it necessary to relieve General B[utler] on account of his total unfitness to command in the field, and his generally quarrelsome character," he complained to Grant in July 1864, frustrated at his inability to have the politician cashiered.[39] Such scurrilous attacks eroded the standing of popular amateur generals and also helped make Halleck the most despised Union general among many politicians in the capital.[40]

As Grant recognized the importance of political factors, he also seemed to understand the need for generals like Butler and Banks. Even after disparaging reports from the Red River Campaign and the Bermuda Hundred, he always tempered criticism for Banks with praise for his civil-military projects in the Gulf, and he consistently praised Butler's administrative skills as a department commander.[41] This moderation in his opinion of political generals was good for the new commanding general, as there was little he could do about their presence until after the fall elections. Though Grant sought to concentrate the Union armies for concurrent offensives in May 1864 under the best commanders, Lincoln maintained his belief in the necessity of giving popular politicians a prominent role in the war. Therefore, Butler retained command of the Army of the James because of pressure from radical Republicans, and Franz Sigel was given a field army in the Shenandoah to please the large number of German-Americans.[42] Other political generals like Alpheus Williams, Jacob Cox, and James Wadsworth commanded at corps and division levels during these campaigns, each entrusted to inspire allegiance from his supporters every day that he played a conspicuous role in the field. Despite the extremely poor tactical record of some of these generals, Grant was stuck with them.

In spite of the rise of a popular West Pointer like Grant and a long record of tactical debacles, Lincoln still needed political generals like Butler and Banks in 1864 to support his policies and his reelection. The president's support for individual political generals waxed and waned with their record of battlefield successes and failures as well as with the volume of their constituents and their political allies.[43] To retain these benefits and decrease the risk incurred by their presence, Lincoln attempted to transfer some of the political appointees who lacked national prominence to less dangerous and more suitable roles in the war effort.[44] Political generals who maintained the favor of the administration were given assignments where their political skills and followings could be harnessed to garner support to benefit the Union cause. Even generals with as poor a battlefield record as Franz Sigel were returned to field command in 1864, in his case because Lincoln yielded to the intense petitioning by Unionist members of the West Virginia legislature to appoint the popular politician to command in the Shenandoah Valley.[45] With the war dragging on and facing the prospects of a difficult reelection in the fall of 1864, the president needed all the political allies he could get, hence the continuing need for using general officer assignments as military patronage.

As Halleck and other West Pointers recognized that they could not stop the awarding of volunteer general officer rank to amateurs, they waged a fervent campaign to protect their monopoly on the awarding of general officer commissions in the regular army. This task was deemed even more important than gaining a monopoly on wartime commands, because the issue of regular army commissions to volunteer generals threatened to bring partisan influence and greater divisiveness into the peacetime officer corps. In May 1864, Halleck enlisted Grant's assistance because of the opening of two regular army major general commissions and his fear of who would get selected. Halleck told Grant that he believed that "after your splendid victories almost anything you ask for will be granted" and requested his support to secure the promotions for Meade and Sherman. "I do not wish to see these vacancies left so long unfilled, lest outside political influences may cause the President to fill them by the promotion of persons totally unworthy," Halleck warned the new commanding general. "I know that influences have been exerted in favor of a man utterly unfit to hold any commission in the army."[46] The selection of a Butler or a Banks or a Sickles for this promotion was one of Halleck's greatest fears because it could extend the services (and meddling) of political generals beyond the end of the war.[47]

As Banks and Butler experienced tactical setbacks so reminiscent of previous campaigns but still could not be removed because of their political necessity, some means had to be found to maintain their support while limiting the damage that their inexperience and lack of training all but guaranteed. In 1864, the solution was to try a team-command system in which a political general maintained his prominent role in the war but was assigned a competent and experienced tactician to command under him in the field, this being the best compromise to increase military effectiveness without removing the amateur leader at the top.[48] This notion to place all the field armies under the control of regular officers was often suggested by West Pointers like Halleck, who harbored an open animosity toward politically appointed amateurs and believed that they all were incapable of conducting the operations required to win the decisive military struggle against the Confederacy.[49] In spite of this step, both Banks's and Butler's campaigns ended in frustration for all involved, in part because the contrasting philosophies of generalship led to a natural friction between the army commanders and their key subordinates at critical times during the campaigns. The strong personalities on both sides ensured that the team-command effort would fail because the combination of personal animosity, a lack of respect between commanders, an absence of trust in the army commander, and an inability to establish a common vision resulted in a poisoned command climate.

How this mixture of problems could lead to tragedy was best seen during Butler's unsuccessful offensive with the Army of the James. In the spring of 1864, Butler was again a department commander in control of a large Union army and was expected to play a major role in Grant's 1864 campaign. During this campaign, Butler would have responsibility for thirty thousand men in two Union corps, each commanded by an experienced West Pointer handpicked by Grant in order to negate Butler's lack of training and tactical ability.[50] On the first day of April 1864, Butler met with a visiting Grant and proposed a plan to take Richmond with an offensive starting at his base at Fortress Monroe. The Massachusetts politician offered to move his Army of the James by ship up the James River to the Bermuda Hundred, an enclosed peninsula bordered by the James and Appomattox Rivers and situated a mere fourteen miles southeast of the Confederate capital.[51] This bold offensive required a clear understanding of the plan and an effective coordination of the various forces involved to ensure success before the Confederates could react.[52]

However promising the campaign seemed at its outset, the result revealed the damage that could be done when the bad blood between West Pointers and political generals in the Union high command seeped into and contaminated field operations. Given the clash of personalities between the army commander and his two key subordinates, Butler had neither firmly developed nor articulated his campaign plan prior to its execution, nor had he reached a consensus on the plan with his corps commanders. These omissions would be significant, causing vacillation over the campaign's objective and aggravating the already acrimonious relationship between Butler and the regular officers in his army. The ensuing offensive was so poorly executed as to spoil what may have been the best chance to cut off Lee's army from its supplies while generating enough blame for all the generals involved. Though Butler's generalship was plainly a major contributing factor, the failure of the campaign had other authors and signified deeper problems in the Union officer corps.

One of the main causes of the disaster was the blame and finger-pointing involving both the army commander and his key subordinates who had been intentionally assigned to their posts by Grant to ensure success. As the campaign repeatedly failed to achieve its goals, Butler blamed both of his corps commanders, Generals William F. "Baldy" Smith and Quincy A. Gillmore, accusing them of failing to follow his orders and not moving their troops vigorously in any of the attacks. Since both corps commanders were experienced West Pointers, Grant had hoped the two veterans would make up for Butler's lack of training. But, in fact, their confidence in their own expertise combined with their lack of faith in Butler's generalship only exacerbated the tensions in the leadership of the Army of the James. Neither corps commander acted with any energy or drive, and both let their dislike of Butler cloud their command relationships and actions.[53]

The two corps commanders had solid grounds for complaint because Butler repeatedly failed to communicate his plans clearly or accept any modifications recommended by the experienced veterans. This tension came to a head on May 8 when both corps commanders rejected Butler's plan for an immediate assault on a weakly defended Petersburg, soon after having given their assurances that the attack would be pressed vigorously. The army commander exploded with rage. "I shall [not] yield to . . . a change of plan made within thirty minutes after I left you," Butler immediately informed them. "Military affairs cannot be carried on, in my judgment, with this sort of vacillation." He went on to disapprove of their proposed alternative of shifting operations to City Point, stating that he had no intention of "building bridges for West Pointers to retreat over."[54] This exchange revealed the frustrations felt by both Butler and his corps commanders, neither of whom thought the other was performing his job as expected. The mutual acrimony only increased as the army became more frustrated in its failure to accomplish its goals; Butler's attempt to shift all the blame for the campaign's failure onto his subordinates only further inflamed the friction.[55] Getting "bottled up" in the Bermuda Hundred by a smaller Confederate force ruined any remaining shred of Butler's reputation as an effective field general, and even the prominent Democratic newspapers turned viciously against their former hero.[56]

Yet Butler remained in charge of his army and the Department of Virginia and North Carolina and demonstrated the sheer resiliency of political generals in the face of military disasters. With Grant's permission, Halleck had sent an investigative board to assess Butler's situation and recommend what to do with his army. Headed by the quartermaster general, Montgomery Meigs, the board suggested either removing most of Butler's troops or assigning "an officer of military experience or knowledge" to command the Army of the James.[57] Preferring the latter, Grant contemplated firing Butler or assigning him a command "where there are no great battle[s] to be fought, but a dissatisfied element to control no one could manage it better than he" at the administrative tasks of an occupied region of the South. As an alternative, Grant proposed moving Butler away from the fighting since, because he was not "a soldier by education or experience," any subordinates would be burdened with the execution of military operations.[58] Both options received encouragement from Halleck, but with the election approaching, Lincoln was cool to the idea of any command change. As a result, Grant was limited to ordering Butler to return to his headquarters at Fort Monroe, never foreseeing that the amateur general would take the field again.[59]

The fate of the generals involved in the Bermuda Hundred Campaign demonstrated that many elements of the administration's method of deciding generals' fates had not changed with the elevation of Grant, because the two types of commanders were still judged using two different standards. Lincoln had little choice but to retain Butler because firing or demoting such a popular general would threaten the president's political support and could even lead the Massachusetts politician to reenter politics. Butler was already being touted as a presidential candidate, so Lincoln retained him in spite of his lackluster operational generalship and Grant's opposition in order for him to continue marshaling political support for the administration.[60] Yet, Butler's West Point corps commanders did not meet so forgiving a fate, which aggravated the frustration many regular officers felt over Butler's retention. Both Smith and Gillmore were removed from the Army of the James, with Gillmore reassigned away from Butler and a very bitter "Baldy" Smith relieved and sent home.[61] Although the two Military Academy graduates were punished for failing to exhibit the required military expertise and aggressiveness and for being tactically unsuccessful, Butler was retained regardless of his tactical record because he was still needed to fulfill his mandate. This outcome demonstrates that the different standards that were applied to the two different types of generals were still true in the summer of 1864.

Even though Butler was safely entrenched in his position, the rise of a system of military patronage did impose a new "glass ceiling" for political generals, because Grant now had the authority from the president to designate new corps and army commanders. How this change limited the potential advancement of amateur generals can best be seen in the story of John Alexander Logan during the Atlanta Campaign. Unlike many of his peers, "Black Jack" Logan was a talented military leader whose natural ability and record of tactical accomplishment led to a corps command and earned the respect of both Sherman and Grant.[62] At the Battle of Atlanta on July 22, 1864, Logan was the senior corps commander in James B. McPherson's Army of the Tennessee, and when McPherson was killed in the fighting, Logan took over and shattered Hood's attack. Driving back the Confederates with great loss, the acting army commander was credited by Sherman with winning the day through his dynamic presence and inspirational leadership.

Yet, before a week had gone by and Logan had settled into his new job, Sherman issued orders on July 27 appointing fellow USMA alumnus Oliver O. Howard as the new commander of the Army of the Tennessee.[63] Howard had proved himself a skilled, if cautious and uninspiring, corps commander during the drive on Atlanta but had a mixed record owing to his involvement in tactical setbacks at Chancellorsville and the first day at Gettysburg. In the initial days after the death of McPherson, Sherman was leaning toward appointing Logan as the replacement but met vehement resistance from George Thomas, who wanted a West Pointer as his fellow army commander. Defending his decision to overlook a corps commander of proven talent, Sherman justified his choice of Howard on the familiar grounds of expected military effectiveness. "I wanted to succeed in taking Atlanta," Sherman argued after the war, "and needed commanders who were purely and technically soldiers, men who would execute my orders promptly and on time. . . . I believed that General Howard would do all these fairly and well."[64] Given Logan's impressive tactical record, Grant initially questioned Sherman's decision to select the unassuming Howard, but in the end he backed the promotion as a subordinate's call on the scene.[65] Observing this debate over the appointment of an army commander, President Lincoln remained passive for the first time and approved Grant's and Sherman's recommendation without question.

During this phase of the war, the definition and standards for generalship were changing, as assignments were now completely controlled by military commanders using criteria such as training and loyalty that they valued, demonstrated by Howard's selection and Logan's glass ceiling. If given the opportunity, Logan might well have been more effective than Howard or Thomas based on his previous performance, but he never received the chance because the general officer patronage system had become an internal military province dominated by Grant and Sherman. To West Pointers like Sherman, a bias against amateurs led to the recommendation for advancement only of those trusted to share the same values and priorities. In his *Memoirs*, Sherman made it very clear how Logan was different from officers like himself and Howard, claiming that "I regarded both Generals Logan and Blair as 'volunteers' that looked to personal fame and glory as auxiliary and secondary to their personal ambitions, not as professional soldiers."[66] Logan reacted furiously to this verdict and the mindset that sustained it, and he blamed Howard's appointment on scheming among the regulars.[67] Yet even Logan's direct appeals to Lincoln and an outcry among his political allies could not overturn Sherman's decision, for West Pointers had at last gained control of promotions and the standards by which candidates would be selected.

The emergence of this new dynamic of generalship, controlled by military officers and assessed according to their criteria, was complete after the 1864 elections because Lincoln had secured enough of a political mandate to finish the war on his terms. The importance of the role of political generals had begun to diminish with the introduction of the draft, which gave the federal government a tool to gather recruits that did not rely so heavily on local and regional politicians. The necessity for the support of prominent politicians in uniform may have reached a new height during Lincoln's campaign for reelection because the anticipated challenge in garnering enough votes made the appeasement of every possible political faction and ethnic group of the utmost importance. However, after the election, Lincoln emerged in his strongest political position because of a mandate from the people that clearly signaled support for his conduct of the war. The administration no longer needed such militarily inept agents to rally support among the Northern people.

Whatever the actual level of public support for the administration's policies in the fall of 1864, the common perception by those in the government was that public sentiment gave the Lincoln administration a degree of power it had lacked during the first years of the war. Therefore, Lincoln's reelection manifested itself in a Congress much more supportive of the administration's policies and in the noticeable muting of the most severe of the president's critics.[68] Asking the now-lame-duck Congress to reconsider passage of the Thirteenth Amendment, Lincoln demonstrated the newfound security of his position by arguing for enactment because "some deference shall be paid to the will of the majority, simply because it is the will of the majority."[69] This increased authority and political capital from the electorate meant a less urgent need in policy battles for the political allies who could be garnered through the use of military patronage. In the Union high command, the change in the political authority of the administration meant that a prominent political general like Butler could be purged after a tactical debacle or a clash with fellow commanders with little regard for the political consequences. This alteration was best seen during December 1864, as Halleck continued his battle to get Benjamin F. Butler removed from command because the Massachusetts politician was the epitome of all that he detested.[70]

When Grant ordered an expedition to capture Fort Fisher, which protected one of the last inlets near Wilmington for blockade runners, Butler provided another demonstration of his military amateurism and another opportunity for Halleck to attempt to engineer his demise. Because he sought to assign the mission to a trusted subordinate, Grant selected Major General Godfrey Weitzel to command the operation. But as Weitzel was assigned to the Army of the James, the orders had to go through Fort Monroe, where Butler was impatiently looking for his chance to end his exile from active operations.[71] Butler not only took charge of the expedition (never passing on the original orders to Weitzel) but also added a dose of his "natural genius" to the operation. Dismissing a conventional naval bombardment as ineffective, the political general instead based the attack on the use of a "powder boat," a steamer filled with 215 tons of gunpowder that would be exploded near the fort to make its capture an easy task. Setting the operation in motion, Butler and the naval task force reached the approaches to Fort Fisher on December 15, 1864. However, within the next two weeks, the powder boat had failed to damage the fort, the initial landing troops were withdrawn, and the fleet had put to sea to return to base. Grant was furious about the failure, writing President Lincoln that "who is to blame [for the debacle] will, I hope, be known."[72] Sensing the best opportunity yet to remove an unsuccessful commander and personal antagonist, Halleck gladly forwarded Grant's request for Butler's removal to President Lincoln and went as far as suggesting the wording of the relief order.

Yet, during the same period, Halleck fought another battle to save fellow West Pointer General George H. Thomas from getting the ax over traditional complaints of lack of aggressiveness and unnecessary delays. As John Bell Hood's army remained outside the besieged city of Nashville during December 1864, Lincoln and Stanton grew nervous about the possibility that Hood might avoid Thomas and raid further North, a fear that Grant

also shared.[73] The desire to have Thomas take the field against Hood dominated the message traffic during the first week of December as Stanton, and
then Grant, sent order after order to force Thomas to act. When the cautious commander in Nashville continued to delay, Halleck rapidly came to
his defense and acted as a buffer between him and cries for his relief. "If you
wish General Thomas relieved from [command], give the order. No one here
will, I think, interfere," Halleck informed Grant at City Point. "The responsibility, however, will be yours, as no one here [in Washington], so far as I am
informed, wishes General Thomas' removal."[74] Revealing a bias as strong,
though opposite, to that shown Butler, Halleck's last comment did not
reflect the true status in the capital.

Although Halleck claimed in his messages to Grant that there was no
pressure to replace Thomas, Stanton went as far as reminding both Halleck
and the commanding general of the administration's frustration with "slow"
generals. "This [delay] looks like the McClellan and Rosecrans strategy of do
nothing, and let the enemy raid the country," an exasperated Stanton wired
Grant during the first week of December. "The President wishes you to consider the matter."[75] Grant's sensitivity to the administration's worries had
grown considerably after his slow initial reaction to Jubal Early's raid earlier
that year, so his response this time was swift. Using Halleck as a relay, Grant
sent order after order to Thomas to attack Hood, finally in frustration ordering the removal of the cautious commander on December 9. Like many
Union generals, Thomas heard the growing calls for aggressive action coming from Washington and felt the building pressure for a military victory. But
unlike so many of his predecessors, the Union general from Virginia survived
and stayed in command thanks to a military patron bent on protecting West
Point graduates.

Unbeknownst to the commanding general, the message ordering
Thomas's relief sat in the War Department for days undelivered, as Halleck
bought time to save his West Point colleague. The secretary of war had actually issued a general order relieving Thomas, using as his justification, "In
accordance with the following dispatch from Lieutenant General Grant . . .
the President orders: That Maj. Gen. J. M. Schofield assume command."[76]
Halleck delayed sending the order to Nashville, using a barrage of telegraph
messages to convince Grant that Thomas deserved more time to start his
attack because of frozen ground and difficult weather, mitigating factors that
neither he nor the administration had ever accepted from previous generals.
Halleck quickly wore down Grant's resolve. "I am very unwilling to do injustice to an officer who has done so much good service," Grant responded to

Halleck's extenuation, "and will, therefore, suspend the order relieving [General Thomas] until it is seen whether he will do anything."[77] When Thomas reported to the commanding general that he was still not ready to attack, Halleck continued to sit on the relief orders. Grant's anger at this further deferment grew until he decided that the orders must be delivered (by one of those Civil War coincidences Grant's special messenger with the relief orders was John A. Logan). However, word of the victory at the Battle of Nashville arrived before Grant could relieve Thomas, thanks to the time bought by Halleck.

Thomas's story was similar in many ways to the clashes between the administration and its commanders over military operations, and Butler's fight to retain command echoed the numerous long-running battles between regulars and amateur generals in the Union high command. These particular conflicts were the culmination of a long campaign waged by regulars to define generalship in Jominian terms and to remove political generals in an effort to establish a monopoly on military expertise. Prior to Lincoln's reelection in 1864, these popular amateurs were still needed for gathering volunteers and harnessing political support, and any West Pointers who failed to act aggressively were quickly relieved. Yet, in the winter of 1864, the fates of Butler and Thomas took unprecedented turns when the political general was relieved and the cautious West Pointer remained in command. This situation revealed a shift in how Union generalship was judged and how generals' fates would be decided, as both their fates were left up to Grant instead of being decided by Lincoln or political partisans.

Halleck's campaign against the political generals he so detested bore fruit at the end of 1864 in Butler's removal and Banks's complete isolation from field command. Upon receiving word of the failure of Butler's expedition against Fort Fisher, Halleck warned Grant to act quickly before Lincoln was influenced by politicians to save their ally as had occurred in previous clashes. Because Butler was perceived to be responsible for the humiliating withdrawal from the beachhead, Grant felt that he had finally found the "military necessity" needed to justify his relief. "In my absence General Butler necessarily commands [in Virginia]," Grant warned Stanton in the first days of 1865, "and there is a lack of confidence in his military ability, making him an unsafe commander for a large army."[78] Grant recommended to the secretary of war that Butler could not be entrusted to command, and because he had demonstrated that he was unwilling to restrict himself to administrative duties at Fort Monroe, the popular Democrat would have to be relieved.[79] Unlike all previous appeals for Butler's ouster, this request was approved.

After Lincoln's political base was solidified in his reelection, a political general like Butler was simply not worth the military risk because the political rewards for the administration no longer outweighed the military liabilities.

Therefore, when Grant once again asked Lincoln for the authority to relieve Butler, the president consented, and the highest ranking and most prominent political general went home to Massachusetts. This dismissal signaled an end to the military career of perhaps the most controversial general to wear Union blue. After the news of Butler's demise spread, Lincoln came under familiar pressure from radical Republicans and some newspapers to reassign the popular politician to another command. Customary parties once again came by the White House on Butler's behalf. They appealed to be heard and expected accommodation.[80] But, unlike his response at any earlier period in the war, Lincoln took no action to satisfy these demands. Also unlike earlier in the war, Butler's fate and the fate of other general officers were left nearly entirely up to the commanding general. When Grant got wind in the newspapers of a political deal to make Butler the provost marshal of South Carolina, the commanding general managed to halt any talk of the assignment after writing to the secretary of war to "respectfully enter my protest."[81] Faced with Grant's criteria for assessing command potential, Butler's military career was over.

The main justification for appointing political generals may have been removed, yet some continued to serve based on their solid tactical record or the increasing need to deal with the political issues of national reconstruction. However, to remain in uniform, these officers had to conform to the standards set by West Pointers. Banks, for example, survived until May 1865, working in occupied New Orleans but responsible solely for civil projects and occupation policies. In April 1864, Grant wanted Banks completely removed from command because of the damage that the Red River Campaign had done to the strategic situation in the Gulf. But owing to the "difficulties" Halleck ran into in this effort, the isolation of Banks from field command was the best that could be accomplished because Lincoln still valued his political support.[82] At that time, Halleck told Grant that Banks's removal might still be possible, but that the commanding general would have to insist upon it as "a military necessity" because the president would be reluctant to offend Banks's allies in Congress and in the cabinet. "Moreover, what could be done with Banks?" a worried Halleck asked Grant. "He has many political friends who would probably demand for him a command equal to the one he now has."[83] Banks had survived because he had accepted his diminished role after being ordered to go to New Orleans and demonstrate the administration's plan for reconstruction. In accordance with orders from Grant, he therefore left command of his department's field forces to the consummate regular E. R. S. Canby.

How the circumstances had changed for politically appointed amateur generals after the elections was evident even in the backwater theater of Louisiana. When Banks complained to the president about Canby's interference in his reconstruction work at the end of November 1864, Lincoln's reply demonstrated the shift in influence from political to military patrons. "I entertain no abatement of confidence, or friendship for you," the president told Banks. "I have told you why I can not order Gen. Canby from the Department of the Gulf—that he whom I must hold responsible for military results, is not agreed."[84] Though this deference to Grant may simply have been the president's cover for not appeasing Banks and changing the winning team in the Gulf, it was only one of many indicators of the way the dynamic of Union generalship had changed after the fall elections. Because Banks did not air this disagreement or openly fight with Canby in the press, he remained in command of the reconstruction work in Louisiana but had no further field command.[85] Canby, who had already taken command of all other regions in Banks's Department of the Gulf, finally replaced him as commander a month after Appomattox.[86] This conflict between the politician in uniform and the West Pointer in New Orleans was simply the last small skirmish in a war whose outcome had already been decided.

Conclusion

Lincoln's search for a general to entrust with winning the war was a long and frustrating endeavor for the administration and the Union high command. One of the reasons the search may have taken so long was the lack of appreciation by senior West Pointers for the political facet of the conflict. Lincoln could not have trust in his commanding general until he had found the combination of success in battle and a willingness to embrace the administration's political viewpoints. Military effectiveness was not enough: McClellan and Buell were competent field commanders. Adoption of Lincoln's policies was also insufficient by itself: Pope was nearly a sycophant to the party line, yet he did not last long after tasting defeat at Second Bull Run. Sound decisionmaking and professional military advice were not enough: Halleck provided these attributes and articulated clear guidance to the army on policy decisions. The commander who eventually combined these facets of generalship was Grant when he offered a strategy to win the war that meshed with administration policies and embraced Lincoln's view of political reality.

By the first day of 1865, the regulars emerged triumphant in their struggle to gain a monopoly on commands. The only remaining political generals in major commands at the end of 1864 were John Dix, in charge of the Department of the East, and Butler, whose days in a uniform were numbered.[87] In combination with the impact of the president's reelection, this situation was the result of an understanding between Lincoln and Grant that recognized Grant as the military expert who could be entrusted with the military conduct of the war. In the end, he had succeeded where McClellan and Halleck had failed because the recognition of professional expertise boils down to a matter of trust.

Grant's ascendancy not only changed command at the top but also shaped how the Union war effort was conducted, because he brought a hierarchy of officers up with him, men like Sherman and Sheridan who saw the military effort against the enemy in political terms. Many of these commanders, like Sherman, had arrived independently at an understanding of the relationship between war and politics. But they had Grant's rise to commanding general to thank for their own ascendancy through the ranks. Their collective elevation signaled the emergence of an internal patronage system that would change the entire dynamic of how American generalship was judged. After 1865, generals would be evaluated more on battlefield performance and their effectiveness at military duties and less on patronage issues of political standing and support.

Yet, things were not so simple as a shift from one conception of generalship to another. In his basic understanding of warfare, Grant was intrinsically breaking the stereotype of both political generals and most of his West Point peers. Antebellum military culture inspired the regulars to regard the war as strictly a military problem requiring a focus on the battlefield. Rejecting this view, Grant and his protégés understood that military victory was not the ultimate goal of the war and that the political aims of the government must be achieved in order for the conflict to be won. The raucous nature of prewar politics led the politically adept amateur to look upon the rebellion as a partisan political struggle for power, an impression that held little appeal for commanders like Grant who believed that the main Confederate armies were the greatest obstacle to reestablishing federal authority. Grant and Sherman deduced that the war was both a political and a military struggle and that it would only end when Southern society "cried 'enough.'" This development in Union generalship during the Civil War more than justifies the claim that these two commanders deserve to be labeled as the first "modern" American generals.

The recognition of Grant's expertise and authority, however, did not translate into professional status being granted to all Military Academy graduates, even successful wartime commanders like Sherman. Many in the administration and Congress noted how Sherman resisted implementing policies he disagreed with, such as the use of black troops and reestablishment of the cotton trade, which led to the recognition that even a brilliant operational commander could be unwilling to advance the political agenda of civilian policymakers. The apex of this apprehension came when Sherman accepted the military surrender of Joseph E. Johnston's ragged army in North Carolina and proceeded to negotiate a political settlement with the Confederate general that incorporated all the contested issues of the war—but not on the terms embraced by the administration. The announcement of the treaty and its subsequent rapid repudiation by an administration reeling over the president's assassination did little to foster a mutual trust between the uniformed military leaders and politicians. Instead the result was a public quarrel between a general and the secretary of war reminiscent of McClellan's days as commanding general. As Sherman's fate at the end of the war illustrates, while Grant was entrusted with matching military means to political ends, this recognition of expertise did not extend to the entire Union high command.

The conduct of the American Civil War clearly demonstrated that an occupation cannot be recognized as a profession and its leaders cannot have their advice completely accepted unless society is willing to agree that these specialists have, and should be granted, a monopoly on expertise. This supposition was evident in the way that the very presence of amateur generals eroded the collective authority of West Pointers. The main prerequisite for the endorsement of military expertise in either type of general was *trust*, the faith that such a commander could be entrusted to use the nation's military resources effectively and to pursue the same political goals that the democratically elected administration sought. The lack of political flexibility in early commanders like McClellan delayed West Pointers' recognition as experts because they were unwilling to agree with, or at least obey, the president on the appropriate political aims and strategy for the war effort. Consequently, Lincoln did not wholly entrust the prosecution of the war to one of his generals until he developed the faith that Grant was not a political threat and would conform to the administration's vision of the proper objectives and course of the war. He had to have proof that Grant was not a presidential candidate for fear that the general might change the course of the war effort or influence ongoing operations based on his own set of political priorities. With these fears laid to rest, Lincoln was more than happy to shift the burden of managing the military conflict to an expert.[88]

Grant achieved this confidence and, far more important, established fidelity to the democratically elected political representatives of the nation as the standard for the subordinates he sponsored, thereby setting the model of expectations for West Point–educated generals that would prove one of the lasting legacies of the war. This example did not mean an apolitical disdain for partisanship that easily became antipolitical, as Halleck so often demonstrated, but was instead an expectation that commanders would understand the politics of the war and loyally support their commander in chief's position on the contested issues of objectives and strategy. "They may be relied on for an honest and faithful performance of their duties regardless of their private views of the policy pursued," Grant wrote Senator Henry Wilson when recommending the promotion of Sherman and McPherson. Summarizing this quality, which he expected in every military officer, Grant praised his protégés by declaring that "in a word they are not men to discuss policy whilst their country requires their services."[89] This simple sentiment was a strong indicator of how Grant believed military officers, including West Pointers, should be judged. By projecting this standard into American military culture, Grant helped spell the demise of the traditional American faith in amateur political generals.

In the traditional historical accounts of the Civil War, political generals were steadily relieved after their numerous battlefield disasters until the experienced professionals rose to dominate the upper ranks of both sides by the end of 1864. As with most historical caricatures, this depiction contains some truth, but it does not fully explain the decline of politically appointed generals in the Union high command. Military debacles were not the sole, or perhaps even the principal, events that heralded their demise; rather, the adoption of conscription and Lincoln's reelection may have been the real harbingers of the end. Without the need to influence Northern voters and potential volunteers into donning uniforms, the Lincoln administration lost its primary motivations to risk the military inexperience of these amateur commanders. But even the surrender of the main Confederate field armies and the triumphant parade of victorious Union troops through Washington did not end the struggle over the nature of the war and the criteria upon which to judge generalship. The final campaigns in this struggle over the definition of American generalship would only come after the war, in the guise of a fight over its true legacy.

CHAPTER EIGHT

"War as an Instrument of Policy"
Expanding the Study of Generalship

In May 1865, the victorious Union armies paraded down the streets of the capital, passing throngs of jubilant onlookers who had waited so long for this day. On May 23, the triumphant Army of the Potomac led by George Meade and his corps commanders, fresh from receiving the surrender of Lee's vaunted Army of Northern Virginia at Appomattox, marched proudly past the crowds. The following day, William T. Sherman rode down the main parade route leading the famed Western troops who had spent the last six months marching from Atlanta. For sixteen hours over two days, Ulysses S. Grant and Henry Halleck sat in the reviewing box with the new president as the principal Union armies paraded by and watched many of their West Point peers with stars on their epaulets at the heads of their commands. Marching in the Army of the Tennessee were its two corps commanders, John Logan and Francis Blair, who were among the few political generals still holding major commands at the end of the war. Benjamin Butler was at home, exhorting crowds in Massachusetts about the Union victory (and his role in it), and Nathaniel Banks was in New Orleans tending to experiments in local reconstruction. At the end of the war, the most prominent political generals already seemed relegated to the sidelines of history, while notable West Pointers received the accolades of victory.

As the triumphant parade signified to all, the Union commanding general and his subordinates had won the epic military struggle to suppress secession. The dreaded Confederate armies that had so frustrated Union commanders were all captured; the cities and regions they had so steadfastly defended were either razed or occupied. Throughout the North, crowds rallied to celebrate Lee's surrender and recount Union battlefield victories. In the nation's capital, people gathered around the commanding general whenever he appeared and fixed on him as the epitome of Union generalship. When asked what terms had been offered to the Confederate soldiers, Grant asserted, "I told them to go back to their homes and families, and they would not be molested if they did nothing more."[1] Defeated in the field and demoralized by tales from home, Confederate soldiers and their leaders were compelled to comply in the face of Union military victory. But far more was asked of former Confederate soldiers and Southern civilians than a cessation of hostilities. The turmoil and violence of Reconstruction soon demonstrated the difference between conventional military victory and successfully achieving the political objectives for which the war was waged.

The struggle over the definition of successful generalship continued long after the war, and the battle between political generals and Military Academy graduates over the legacy of the war grew anew during Reconstruction. Although the triumph of the regulars' view of the war ensured their rise in prominence in Civil War history, the acceptance of West Pointers as military professionals did not immediately follow. Society itself would have to change in some way to promote the recognition of professional occupations, including the military. As the postwar officer corps soon came to discover, the end of the Civil War marked the demise of an acceptance of military amateurism in generalship, but not the real end of political meddling or partisan scheming in their own ranks. This infusion of politics into the military affairs of both war and peace is intrinsic and unavoidable because, to paraphrase Clausewitz, generalship is inherently politics by other means. Given this combination of conventional military operations and underlying political struggle, how then should Civil War generals be judged?

Although contemporary standards and historical interpretations focus on judging the success of Civil War general officers by the criteria of character or comparative achievements on the battlefield, the best yardstick by which to measure generalship is the fulfillment of the assigned missions and overall contribution to the accomplishment of political objectives. The true "test of generalship" is not as simple as a win/loss tactical record. Instead it lies in the vision to understand the government's political goals, the ability to comprehend the general's role in this effort, and the capacity to advance the cause toward victory by fulfilling the assigned mandate, regardless of tactical prowess. Taking this approach results in a far more balanced judgment of political generals while presenting another method for unbiased criticism of truly deserving commanders. This measure of generalship links military means with the national political ends for which they were created and employed and illuminates the need to extend the study of generalship beyond the borders of the battlefield.

The Legacy of the Struggle over Expertise

The end of the Civil War did not signal the end of the clash between the amateurs and the regulars over the value of the service rendered by political generals. The struggle for Civil War history began immediately after the guns fell silent, as the two strands of the American military tradition reemerged to present two conflicting portraits of the army that won the war. Was the Union army an army of trained soldiers led by professionals in the legacy of Winfield Scott at Mexico City, or was it an enthusiastic mass of volunteers inspired by amateur generals in the tradition of Zachary Taylor and the victory at Buena Vista? As in the aftermath of previous American wars, these two sides of the nation's military heritage presented different pictures not only of the battles and leaders but also of the lessons from the war that should be used to shape the country's military institutions.

As a self-appointed spokesman for the regular army, West Pointer Emory Upton became one of the foremost advocates for the professionalization of the officer corps and an increase in the reliance on an enlarged regular army. He based this belief on a recounting of the Civil War that painted the volunteer militia as wasteful and unreliable owing to the numerous tactical debacles endured by the Union army before competent officers rose to high command. Assailing the entire concept of military amateurism, Upton concluded that the primary weakness of American defense policy was the "employment of militia and undisciplined troops commanded by generals and officers utterly ignorant of the military arts."[2] In the eyes of Upton, and of the many who agreed with him, commanders who embraced a professional approach to their duties won the Civil War by conventional operations on the battlefield. This viewpoint echoed Halleck's statement that political generals were "simply murder" and placed the blame for their poor conduct of the Union's early campaigns on their lack of education and experience.

Opposing the views of these career military officers were the military reminiscences of many prominent political generals who approached the issue of Union generalship through the lens of an officer's political impact. Representing this group of veterans, Major General Jacob Cox defended the Lincoln administration's use of "political appointments" to rally support for the war from a politically active society. He contended that the West Pointers were no better prepared for war than any other generals, that indeed they were much less professional in their training than historians have suggested. While Upton held aloft the accomplishments of Grant and Sherman and condemned the battlefield debacles of the political generals, Cox placed the initial blame for the poor tactical performance on the early retention of experienced officers concentrated in the few regular army units and praised the volunteer groups who acquired experience while they achieved battle-field victories.[3]

Other veterans carried the struggle over commands into the postwar years by writing articles and memoirs defending their reputations or attacking others'. Most were like the autobiographies of McClellan and Sherman, seeking to explain their own decisions in a favorable light to present a positive interpretation of controversial aspects of their commands. Butler, William "Baldy" Smith, and others sought redemption for their relief, Butler claiming that his repeated firings from command were the result of a "West Point clique" that conspired to take over the war effort and even posed a threat to the Constitution and the government. An even more aggressive opponent of the professional officer corps was John Logan, whose book *The Volunteer Soldier of America* recounted his Civil War experience while presenting American military history up to 1865 as proof of the superiority of a military policy based on the citizen-soldier. Attempting in vain to reverse the rising dominance of West Point graduates in military affairs, Logan became an advocate in Congress for reducing the regular officer corps in favor of state militia leaders and replacing West Point with a system of tactical schools for militia officers.[4] Though individual commanders like Grant, Sherman, and Logan had proven their expertise, the questions over the value of West Point, its graduates, and the best military policy for the United States remained subjects of intermittent debate within the military, in Congress, and in the press.

In many ways, both sides of the struggle over the military record of the war were correct. The campaign victories of Ulysses S. Grant and William T. Sherman were the products of a growing sense of professionalism in the officer corps, and their successes hastened the impending end of the Confederacy. However, the Civil War was not solely a military struggle but also, as Lincoln contended, "a people's contest," with an ongoing struggle for popular support in which the conduct and accomplishments of volunteer soldiers and amateur officers shaped popular impressions of the war. The social and political culture of the time, along with the absence of any mobilization system that was capable of producing soldiers in huge numbers, made it impossible for Secretary of War Cameron to form a national recruiting system and a unified (regular and volunteer) army. This situation, combined with a faith in "natural genius" and a lingering disdain for regular officers, led to the great need for Union political generals. These factors explain why the majority of appointments of political generals occurred during new recruiting drives and high points of public outcry against regular officers such as McClellan and Buell.[5] Consequently, the Union victory was a product of both strands of American military culture, leaving a mixed legacy in the push for a professional officer corps. Yet, in the end, it was the regulars who emerged triumphant in the Union high command, and their victory reverberated in the postwar army wrestling with Reconstruction.

As Reconstruction all too quickly demonstrated, the political victory sought by the Lincoln administration remained incomplete. Southern opposition to federal authority was halted by Lee's surrender at Appomattox, but only temporarily. Slowly, resistance to the more onerous federal policies grew, soon followed by more open hostility to occupation by the postwar U.S. Army. By September 1865, Sherman expressed a common complaint among army commanders that "no matter what change we may desire in the feelings and thoughts [of Southerners], we cannot accomplish it by force. Nor can we afford to maintain there an army large enough to hold them in subjugation."[6] What then was accomplished at Appomattox Court House? Grant and his key subordinates had interwoven the political and military struggle during the last year of the Civil War, but this web had disintegrated with the disappearance of a conventional military enemy. What followed during Reconstruction was in some ways an insurgency equally as vicious as that of the war, and the West Pointers' Jominian view of warfare provided little insight for defeating what has since been recognized as little short of unconventional warfare.

The political changes that political generals like Banks and Butler had sought to impose through occupation policies melted away all too quickly as the struggles over Unionist control, black enfranchisement, and postslavery labor policy were lost by their regular army successors. In some respects, the West Pointers who had won the conventional conflict (all the while denigrating the efforts of political generals) were being asked during the postwar occupation to perform the same form of political reconstruction that Banks, Butler, and a score of other politicians-in-uniform had attempted during the war. This was not an easy transition, and many Union generals never made it. Even Lieutenant General Grant wrestled with this new role as shown in a response to a request for guidance by the Union commander in occupied

North Carolina. "Until a uniform policy is adopted for the reestablishing civil government in the rebellious states," Grant informed a frustrated John Schofield, "the Military authorities can do nothing but keep the peace."[7] But keeping the peace proved to be both difficult and insufficient in the decade after the surrender at Appomattox. The Reconstruction-era U.S. Army, black freemen in the South, and Unionists in the deep South would in a way all pay a heavy price for the failure to support and follow through with wartime reconstruction efforts by the most prominent politicians in uniform.

Although this mission of policy interpretation and enforcement in occupied regions in the South played to the strengths and experience of ex-politicians in uniform, some regulars had always begrudged them the task and sought to gain control over all uses of military force. During the war, Halleck had believed that regular generals should control reconstruction because the involvement of political generals could justify their retention after the end of the war. Therefore, he wrote Sherman, amateurs must be purged not only from field commands but also from occupation duties, a step necessary to protect "our profession." "I have always opposed the organization of a civico-military government, under civilians," Halleck told Sherman in October 1863. "It merely embarrasses the military authorities without effecting any good."[8] He believed that reconstruction efforts should be delayed until the Confederate armies were destroyed, when West Pointers like Grant, Sherman, and himself could provide the president with the "correct opinions" on how the tasks should be conducted.[9] Halleck got his wish, because the removal of the most prominent and politically powerful political generals from major field commands, along with their harsh treatment by West Pointers, which made many long for the familiar partisan battles in Congress, ensured regulars' continued dominance over command positions in the postwar army.

Much as they had responded to the challenges of wartime occupation, West Pointers were often unable or unwilling to take up the arduous tasks of imposing contested policies, and as a group they were unprepared for the challenges of Reconstruction. As commanding general during the war, Grant had concentrated on destroying the Confederate field forces, as seen in his orders to various political generals and the removal of troops from civil-military operations whenever possible. "I look upon the conquering of the organized armies of the enemy," he telegraphed Banks during the Red River Campaign, "as being of vastly more importance than the mere acquisition of territory."[10] In the summer of 1865, the dreaded Confederate armies were destroyed, but so too were many of the embryonic Unionist political parties in the South, while many of the wartime experiments in local political reconstruction and freeman labor policies were crippled by a lack of support and protection. Yet, in the Northern capital the impression of total victory was maintained, and while partisan squabbles consumed Washington and congressmen waved the "Bloody Shirt" of Union casualties, the U.S. Army demobilized to a mere shadow of the force that had vanquished the Confederates. Although the war was supposedly over, the emergence of the Klu Klux Klan, the Knights of the White Camellia, and other terrorist groups signaled a continuation of the struggle over the very issues that the war had been waged to decide. An entire century had passed, and many of the problems of the war were still unresolved.

In spite of the political nature of postwar occupation of the South, military reconstruction commands from 1865 to 1877 were almost completely dominated by regular army generals, with all but one of the military division and department commands during this period going to regulars. The sole politician-turned-general remaining on duty was one-legged Daniel Sickles, who accepted a colonel's commission in the regular army, a brevet set of stars, and command of the Department of the Carolinas, and supported the Johnson administration strongly enough to hold off the ax until the fall of 1867.[11] Even though the Reconstruction commands were heavily involved in policy development and interpretation, without any tactical field duty, Edwin Stanton as secretary of war and Grant as commanding general together ensured the dominance of career officers in the occupation effort.

There is evidence that Stanton originally intended for volunteer general John Logan to have a major command after the war, because his name was listed in the draft order reorganizing the army for occupation duty. However, his name was scratched out and "Slocum" was handwritten above it, presumably by Grant. When the order was published, General Henry W. Slocum received the command, and Logan left the army to return to Congress.[12] This exclusion could not have been based solely on victorious wartime service, since regulars with questionable records, such as Joseph Hooker, George Stoneman, John Pope, and even Irvin McDowell, all received major Reconstruction commands, while few if any of those selected had wartime records better than John Logan's. Though the political leanings of individual generals impacted their selection and retention in Reconstruction commands by President Andrew Johnson, Grant was able to control the list of candidates to ensure its dominance by West Pointers who he trusted from wartime service.

Further evidence of this rising monopoly by career officers lies in the choice of a leader for the Freedman's Bureau, founded in March 1865 by

Congress as the Bureau of Refugees, Freedmen, and Abandoned Lands. There is evidence that Butler, German abolitionist Charles Schurz, and other volunteer generals were considered for the job of protecting the rights, interests, and safety of the former slaves.[13] However strongly these politicians desired to administer and shape this policy, President Johnson and Secretary Stanton instead turned to West Pointer Oliver O. Howard.[14] The selection of regular army officers to lead the Freedman's Bureau and regional commands during Reconstruction may well indicate the presence of a collective agenda by the regular officers to eliminate the political generals and gain a true corporate monopoly over military affairs. However, the question of whether political generals failed the challenges placed before them at the end of the Civil War, were pushed out by career officers seeking a monopoly of military expertise, or were ushered out by changes in American political culture clearly warrants further historical study.

Much to the frustration of the general officers who stayed in service after the end of the Civil War, political considerations again dominated generalship during Reconstruction as they had during the war. The president tried to pick generals based not on military effectiveness or seniority, but by their political leanings and their willingness to support the administration's goals. Yet, although the Reconstruction-era army witnessed the return of political patronage and the partisan struggles that had plagued the officer corps during the war, something fundamental had changed in American military culture during the course of the sectional crisis. While Civil War service provided a springboard for many West Pointers like Grant, Burnside, and Hancock to begin successful careers in politics, very few political generals remained in uniform for even a short period after the war. Consequently, even though the American Civil War did not signal the emergence of true military professionalism, it did mark the end of a cultural acceptance of military amateurs in command.

The Death of American Military Amateurism

The demise of political generals in the upper ranks of the Union army demonstrated the triumph of the regulars' definition of generalship, but contrary to some judgments, these West Pointers were not recognized by society as professionals during the period 1861–1865. Although the military continued the progress toward professionalization that the army officer corps had begun prior to 1860, this goal was unachievable until institutional training was elaborated and formalized with the establishment of a mature military education system long after the Civil War. The period prior to such development proved to be an era of emerging professionalism because officers were still predominantly amateurs at the "controlled application of violence for political purposes." Few officers had even attempted to master the theoretical aspects of their profession or were prepared in times of peace to conduct the practical aspects of their wartime function.

Before the advent of a general staff and an education system that focused on preparing officers for wartime positions in the upper ranks of the army, reformers in uniform were hampered by a lack of any tradition of professional behavior, a scarcity of occupational legitimacy in an often hostile political culture, and an absence of a formalized theoretical study of warfare. The very acceptance of political generals in command positions during the Civil War proves that society did not yet recognize a distinct occupational specialization in military command and still had faith that prominent men with "natural genius" could quickly master generalship. Much to the frustration of reformers like Upton, the army officer corps could not achieve professional autonomy until society acknowledged the need for military expertise and decided that regular officers possessed a monopoly on this expertise.

In some ways, the clash between political generals and West Pointers reflected a broader cultural clash in nineteenth-century America, as the old respect for "natural genius" and good character (as represented by political generals) was giving way in nearly every occupation to a quest for professionalism and the recognition of occupational expertise (as among regular officers). As the nineteenth century passed, American society's growing faith in science and education provided the necessary foundation for the medical and legal fields to refute the idea that a "gentleman of good character" could perform his functions through personal character. The growing criticism in antebellum America of uneducated doctors as "quacks" and poorly trained lawyers and engineers as menaces to society anticipated much of the public outcry over the military debacles orchestrated by amateur commanders like Butler and Banks. Therefore, the stereotypes of the Civil War generals may simply have reflected a division in public opinion over the nature of expertise, as American society wrestled with a transition from a faith in egalitarianism, the practical application of universal values, and individually based client relationships to an acceptance of emerging specialization, professional association, and occupational autonomy.[15] Yet, because of the nation's powerful heritage of amateur military leadership, the military trailed behind some other occupations in this struggle for professional recognition and the exclusion of "gifted" amateurs.

Professional recognition for any American occupation came down to a matter of trust—entrusting the occupational institution to produce specialists capable of performing in fields that the common man no longer understood. In this quest for occupational autonomy, education held the key to gaining a recognition of specialization and expertise because of the distinct role it played in designating status in American culture and the equation of higher learning and occupational proficiency. The way that this dynamic played out for graduates of West Point during the Civil War was best summed up by a volunteer officer writing in the *Atlantic Monthly*. "In our general military inexperience [at the beginning of the war], the majority were not disposed to underrate the value of specific professional training," wrote Thomas Higginson in September 1864. "Education holds in this country much of the prestige held by hereditary rank in Europe, modified only by the condition that the possessor shall take no undue airs upon himself."[16]

This simple analogy may explain why West Pointers attracted such stinging criticism for their "aristocratic bearing," "undue airs," and "swelled egos." Any confidence they displayed in the course of their duties early in the war, unwarranted to many because it did not rest on an acknowledged foundation of superior education or knowledge, fostered a natural resentment in the large segment of American society exposed to career military officers for the first time during the massive influx of volunteer regiments. Outside the engineering realm, there was little recognition of West Point as a center of higher learning in the military arts; therefore, its graduates were deemed no more prepared to command than any educated man. In the absence of a system of higher military education, West Pointers had not yet earned society's trust to wage the war.

After the war ended, the trust gained by Grant, Sherman, and a handful of other commanders proved both fleeting and nontransferable to the entire regular army officer corps because of its individual nature and the immense amount of criticism of Union generals that flowed during the war and tainted the reputation of every commander at some point. The few men entrusted to autonomously wage military operations were recognized as experts based upon demonstrated wartime performance rather than educational background or a set of occupational criteria they shared with all their peers. Although the groundwork was laid during the Civil War for professional reforms and the recognition of distinctive occupational expertise, gifted amateurs like Dan Sickles, Theodore Roosevelt, and Leonard Wood still made appearances in the U.S. Army command hierarchy after the war's end. Professional recognition would only come later after education reforms and societal experience with Progressivism made this trust in organizational expertise routine and not based on individual performance. As this generation of officers passed on, the Spanish-American War provided the next generation with stark evidence that the reformers were correct in stressing the need for occupational improvement. This realization enabled the theories of Upton, along with the impetus of the Progressive and Preparedness movements, to provide justification for both growth and reform during the years just before the First World War.

Consequently, it was actually Sherman, not Grant, who made the key contribution in the evolution of the officer corps toward gaining society's recognition of military professionalism through his efforts to reform the military schools system. During Sherman's fourteen-year tenure as commanding general (1869–1883), he laid the foundation for advanced education in the officer corps, becoming an advocate of "Schools of Application" for the combat branches. This system of higher military education, and the reforms of Sherman's successors who added the Army War College, Army Staff College, and a formal general staff, introduced career "gates" that all officers would have to pass through in order to advance to high command. These reforms provided both a mechanism to eliminate those who failed to adopt institutional norms and concrete evidence to society that the field of military endeavor required a lifelong calling and occupational specialization. With the emergence of the generation of officers who would fight the First World War, this new focus on theoretical study and institutional education would revolutionize the process of professional socialization while providing the tools required for the development of specialized occupational expertise.

The enormous strides taken during this period in the evolution of military officership were not, nor could they have been, the result solely of uniformed reformers or factors internal to the military. Prominent figures in government and business participated as civilian reformers in the process of professionalization. Some, such as President Theodore Roosevelt, played an important part by simply supporting the efforts of reformers in the service.[17] Others, like Secretary of War Elihu Root during the creation of the Army General Staff in 1903, undertook an active role in planning and nurturing institutional changes. This participation illuminates how professionalization was not the work of one or a few, but of many generations of leaders both inside and outside the military services, and was also the product of Progressivism and the Preparedness movement as well as the desires of uniformed military officers.[18] It was not enough for military officers to declare themselves professionals; society must grant professional status and autonomy to those it acknowledges as the experts in a given occupation. In spite of all the efforts of early military reformers, this acknowledgment did not happen until long after the end of the Civil War.

To achieve the corporateness required for a profession, a monopoly of expertise must be recognized and granted to the occupational group and denied to any outside individual or agency that is not sanctioned by the occupational hierarchy. Therefore, not only is professional status contingent upon the establishment of stable career patterns for practitioners, but it also relies on society's willingness to exclude unsanctioned individuals. From this reasoning, two conclusions can be drawn concerning additional prerequisites for military professionalization. The first is that military professionalism is incomplete until the demise of "political generals" and the practice of lateral entry into the officer corps. The second is that the client society must have established the differentiation of political leadership from military management to produce a body of practitioners whose occupational efforts are specialized in a single field and do not involve partisan political agencies in their own advancement.

This example of human dynamics inside military officership illuminates a potential problem with Huntington's trinity of criteria for determining professional status.[19] When objectively applied to individuals or institutions, no pure combination of expertise, social responsibility, and corporateness can be found owing to the constant presence of personal ambition, political lobbying, service and branch parochialism, and tradition-bound conservatism. If a perfect record of behavior is upheld as the standard, then no occupation or individual can be proven to have achieved professionalization. Therefore, a degree of subjective interpretation must be used to differentiate between the real and very human officers being examined and the ideal standards established by social scientists. Perhaps a concept of "real" versus "ideal" officer professionalism could be used to judge adherence to professional standards. As in Clausewitz's theory of the impossibility of absolute warfare, perfect adherence to objective criteria of professionalism may not be possible, and an occupation should be judged instead in relative terms, on its intent and relative success in meeting these ideals. Otherwise, the inherent problem with the conflict between any objective standard and the human dimension, as in the constant tension between corporateness and social responsibility in the military, will invalidate any theory of professionalization.

Though the regular officers who waged the Civil War failed to be recognized as professionals by society, the legacy of conspicuously poor generals and tactical debacles authored by the more prominent political generals was enough to end the cultural acceptance of military amateurs and create support for a professional officer corps. The contrast in histories of the war between heroic soldiers and the officers who often appeared to lack any knowledge of their occupation drew attention to how unprepared all of the military commanders were. Historian Allan R. Millett argues that the war dispelled the tendency in American culture to trust "natural genius" or the "inspired amateur" to lead troops in wartime because of the infamous cases when the lack of education and experience among prominent political generals appeared to directly cause staggering casualties.[20] Therefore, the rising dominance of West Pointers during the war signaled not only a growing faith in the competence of regular officers by the administration but also a growing disdain for the military amateurism of political generals by the public. The final blow to amateurism was administered by the new military education system, which provided a powerful impetus to refrain from turning to any but its products and ensured the presence of a pool of trained specialists in the use of military force.

American participation in the First World War was the last step necessary for military professionalization, because by the end of the war, with general staffs and advanced educational institutions established and the importance of the theoretical study of warfare recognized by all, public legitimacy was unequivocally granted to the military profession. But the death of amateurism, and even the recognition of professional expertise in military officership, did not signal the emergence of an apolitical "hired gun," a military tool isolated from politics and divorced from partisan influence. As the sometimes bitter partisan and ideological infighting of the Civil War demonstrated, such a separation of warfare and politics is inherently impossible; the significant impact of political generals during the Civil War shows the timeless impact of political culture and civil-military sponsorship on military commands. Lost in Jominian recollections of a conventional military contest, one of the more powerful lessons to be learned by studying the conduct of the Civil War is that Clausewitz was correct: war is a continuation of politics by other means—and so is its conduct by military commanders.

Conclusion: Generalship as "a Continuation of Politics by Other Means"

Historians, military officers, and doctrinal manuals often describe generalship as the "art of command," the combination of strategic vision, operational art, and tactical prowess that produces military victories in the field. Revealing the subconscious lens that many have adopted to view warfare, generalship is equated with military effectiveness, customarily measured in either select leadership characteristics or by tactical accomplishments. Yet, in actuality, military victories on the campaign trail and on the battlefield are simply the tools that military commanders use to support or achieve a greater political objective for which the conflict is being fought. Far from seeking barren and fleeting military victories, generals are tasked to use military force or the threat of force to accomplish political goals, only being able to justify the prodigious costs of tactical combat when an armed opponent tries to impede the achievement of those goals. In this manner, politics and military effort are inherently intertwined and inseparable in a manner most accurately described by Clausewitz's most famous dictum. Any refusal to acknowledge or failure to understand this relationship gives a distorted picture of warfare.

During the American Civil War, Union generals were tasked to advance the national policy objectives of the government, and the defeat of the Confederate armies was a means to secure those objectives, not an end in itself. Operational commanders who failed to see or accept this distinction frequently got into trouble when they planned and executed campaigns that did not advance the Union cause toward victory or, more often, delayed taking the field in order to prepare, which had a disastrous effect on the strategic situation or home front morale. In addition, West Pointers who adopted a strictly Jominian view of the war that focused narrowly on the military struggle often failed to understand, or perhaps refused to accept, the goals of the national government. These generals repeatedly refused to support the occupation policies and local Unionist factions vital to the achievement of political changes that would actually signal significant and lasting victories for the Union. Yet, regardless of each general's view of the nature of the war, his effectiveness as a "military" commander was ultimately judged by the administration through a political and sometimes partisan lens. As this study's litany of the political influences on general officer selections, assignments, missions, and fates has revealed, generalship cannot be fully understood as anything but "a continuation of politics by other means."

Far from being an apolitical instrument of the government, every facet of a military commander's conduct has political roots and political impact. How a general comes to perceive policy, how he interprets war aims, and the path he feels best supports their accomplishment shapes his conduct and performance. This conduct reflects human nature, whether the general is an army commander wrestling with weighty issues of emancipation or a brigadier explaining to his subordinates how enemy noncombatants and their property should be treated. Far more is expected of senior military officers than to echo directives and follow orders like a puppet; they are instead expected, and actually appointed, to interpret instructions and policies, which can never cover all possible contingencies, necessarily bringing into play their own political views. The actions that the commander then takes, the orders he issues, and even the tone he uses when discussing the nation's war aims send ripples into the conduct of the war through the behavior of his troops. Subsequently, his tactical success and his troops' morale affect the home front and thereby may impact the very course of the war. The troops, the home front, the government, and the military commanders are thus linked together in a web that binds the military conflict to the political issues that caused it and the society that supports it.

Explaining this trinity of dominant tendencies of violence, the play of chance, and subordination to policy in warfare, the famed military theorist Carl von Clausewitz revealed the shaping influence of politics that linked the behavior of the public, the army, and the government. This interrelatedness inspired Clausewitz to caution that "a theory that ignores any one of them or seeks to fix an arbitrary relationship between them would conflict with reality to such an extent that for this reason alone it would be totally worthless."[21] His counsel should be heeded, for to attempt to isolate the study of the army from either the people or the government, or to dissociate military operations from politics, would misinterpret the nature of the American Civil War and indeed of American society during the conflict. In a manner unique to the United States during that era, the American people *were* the mass volunteer army, the military leadership, and the elected government, with a political culture of democracy and liberalism that ensured their kindled passions were heard and released. The three components were acutely, and inextricably, intertwined.

Indeed, the vast majority of soldiers on both sides were citizen-volunteers, numerous enough to drown much of the institutional influence of the antebellum regular army and recruited in a manner that guaranteed that the majority would maintain contact and political involvement with their parent communities. The resulting mass of volunteers was not simply a tool in the hands of the government, but an outgrowth of the populace, endowed with political and cultural beliefs that would influence how and how well government policies would be carried out. Many of the volunteers and some of their more politically astute commanders understood that they were the military representatives in a larger conflict over the future course of the nation. "We constitute the military arm of the Government," Logan explained to his soldiers concerning their responsibility to society. "That the Civil power is threatened . . . is the reason for resort to military power."[22] The character of Civil War armies produced an interdependence between politics and military operations that cannot be neglected.

An officer corps led this mass army with powerful links both to citizens in and out of uniform and to the policymakers within the government. Far from a politically neutral "drawn gun" of the government, Civil War officers maintained contact with public officials, read partisan newspapers, and corresponded with political patrons. In the conduct of the war, both regular and volunteer officers often interpreted their instructions in order to advance the aims of their own political beliefs. This interchange between the people, the army, military leaders, and the government spread the connection between politics and warfare throughout all levels of the military contest and signaled the need for military leaders with political, not just military, skills. In the midst of a vicious civil war, the government required not only generals who could gain battlefield victories but also generals who could mobilize public support and who openly endorsed the administration's war aims. Political generals could better be counted on to make these contributions than career regulars because of their reliance on patronage for their own retention as well as their political ambition.

Were the appointments of political generals "simply murder" as Halleck claimed? In a strict military sense the answer would be in the affirmative, yet the history of their political accomplishments highlighted in this book surely indicates that it was not. Nor, judging by the number of politically influenced military appointments, did Lincoln believe it was equivalent to murder. However, in one respect, Halleck was right: it would have been impossible to prevent the appointment of popular politicians to military commands during a civil war in nineteenth-century America. The antielitism and patronage of contemporary political culture united with the populist heritage in American military culture to make the use of political generals not only inevitable but also a necessity to rally the support of the American people.[23]

With all the historical evidence of the vital contributions made by politically appointed amateur generals during the Civil War, what then is the reason for the rise of the conventional caricature of political generals as inept wartime leaders? The cause for this unattractive generalization may well be an approach to Civil War military history that neglects examining the *war* ("a state or period of open and declared conflict between states or nations; a struggle between opposing forces for a particular end") in order to isolate and concentrate on the *warfare* ("military operations between enemies; armed conflict").[24] The studies that depict political generals negatively also tend to present the opposing armies as apolitical tools of the governments, deciding the issues of war by tactical contest regardless of the social, political, and cultural context. This is the very approach that the famous Prussian theorist of war warned against. Only by seeking a balance between political ends and military means as Clausewitz suggests can generals determine how they can best support or advance their government's war aims.

In a fascinating blend of politics and war, the Civil War encompassed both a massive conventional military conflict and a "people's contest" over radical political and social change for the entire nation. Although an undercurrent of politics and partisan warfare influenced every aspect of the war, an acceptance of West Pointers' strictly military view on warfare has emerged in the historiography of the leading commanders of the Union army. Consequently, a major effect of the triumph of the regulars in their struggle against the political generals was the shaping of a new standard used to measure generalship, because once the regulars could claim to have won the war, they could effectively dictate how that victory would be judged. This was not simply a victory of sound generals over poor generals, but the harbinger of a major change in American military culture and popular opinion, because one of the profound impacts of the Civil War would be an end to the popular acceptance of amateur generals.

However limited in perspective, this Jominian view of generalship is in some ways justified because tactical success was still the fundamental means for advancing the Union cause during the war, and military victories were needed to enable and sustain political achievements. Therefore, the historians who focused solely on the military aspect of the war were in one manner correct. The fate of the Lincoln administration and its occupation and reconstruction policies was directly tied to the battlefield; without military victories, all policy initiatives to reestablish the Union in the South were doomed to failure because of the military shield that the Confederate armies provided to secession. Lincoln clearly understood this relationship between the battlefield and political fortunes, once remarking on the importance of military operations on morale and political success to a group of abolitionists who came to the White House complaining that the field generals and soldiers were not vigorously enforcing the Emancipation Proclamation. "My own impression," the president answered, "is that the masses of the country generally are only dissatisfied at our lack of military successes. Defeat and failure in the field make everything seem wrong."[25] Tactical success or failure was the main indicator to the home front, both North and South, of the status of each side's war effort—impacting not only morale and support for the war but also behavior. The very impression of military success had value for Lincoln.

Given the popular acceptance of a tactical win-loss standard as a political barometer, the president was forced to echo impatience with and criticism for generals who failed this test. The administration's lead provided essential support for criticism of political generals by West Pointers, the public, and historians, for the best efforts of amateurs like Butler and Banks in this arena could not mask their inability to effectively command large bodies of troops in combat. Owing to their almost complete lack of military training and experience, which was a by-product of joining the army directly as senior commanders and major generals, many of these politicians-in-uniform amassed a dismal record using strictly military criteria for effective generalship. In the eyes of their contemporaries and the pens of historians, these amateur generals were failures based on their long and infamous record of tactical debacles.

Yet, it remains biased to use this Jominian standard on the political generals, because they were expected to perform a different, yet still vital, task in winning the war. In the political arena of the conflict, these experienced and popular politicians performed services for the administration that no West Point graduate was capable of: marshaling popular support for the president in the states and regions from which they came, working with Unionist parties in the South, gathering recruits, and helping the Lincoln administration to form and hold together a diverse political coalition behind the war effort.[26] With both military and political dimensions of generalship vital to Union victory, Lincoln valued the services of political generals like Banks and Butler because they were continually successful in their mandate to rally support for the administration. Instead of a tactical scorecard, the judgment of these amateurs' value rested on a scale of support gained versus battles lost, which was the true criterion of the generalship of such commanders for those who appointed them. By this standard, they were truly a necessity in a democracy fighting a civil war. What is therefore needed is a method to measure generalship that encompasses both the military and political aspects of warfare in order to assess accurately the performance of military commanders of all types and positions.

Current Civil War historiography appears to suggest several models for the evaluation of generalship. Many historians judge commanders simply on quantitative military results, and this focus has dominated the historiography on the military commanders of the Civil War. The attractiveness of this method is its simplicity, since it turns a subjective issue like generalship into an objective measurement of ground gained or lost, casualties inflicted or taken, and an assessment of victories and defeats at the tactical and operational levels. Another common approach to Civil War generalship is a relative-scale method that compares the performance and traits of one commander to another, most often that general's opponent on a given field. This method often produces widely varying results because it can be very biased predicated solely on the peer group selected or who is being compared to whom. A third method often seen in Civil War literature is an assessment based on an examination of the character of the commander, which assumes that effective generals share intrinsic traits separating them from their less proficient peers. Yet, all these approaches tend to be dominated by military factors, and many, indeed most, neglect political contexts for military campaigns and battles. Given the use of these standards and numerous attempts to consider warfare in isolation from its political master in popular military studies of the Civil War, the source of the conventional caricature of the political generals becomes all too apparent.

This study of the contrasts and similarities between the two different types of Civil War generals reveals the need for a method of evaluating generalship that reconciles military fortunes with political gains. The inseparable nature of politics and warfare during the Civil War highlights the need to expand any military study far beyond the boundaries of the battlefield. "The political objective is the goal, war is the means of reaching it, and means can never be considered in isolation from their purpose," Clausewitz so astutely warns in his classic *On War*. "Therefore, it is clear that war should never be thought of as *something autonomous* but always as an instrument of policy; otherwise the entire history of war would contradict us. Only this approach will enable us to penetrate the problem intelligently."[27] Therefore, military historians must resist the tendency to reduce war to the movement of symbols on a map or to judge generalship and military effectiveness without leaving the parameters of the battlefield.

As the Lincoln administration had different expectations of general officers, each given their command with a form of mandate to accomplish a task that would make Union victory closer or more certain, success in fulfilling this mandate became the most important contemporary standard for the president for judging a commander's effectiveness: was the general moving the

Union war effort closer to eventual political and military victory? Since this was Lincoln's standard, it is the appropriate criterion to judge Union generals, regardless of their source and background. Accordingly, the most valid test of generalship is a commander's *overall* impact on the war effort—a balanced assessment of the consequences of his service, command decisions, and leadership on the achievement of the nation's war aims. Only by attending to the political context of military operations and seeking a balance between the three tendencies of war as Clausewitz suggests can the true criterion for evaluating the contributions of the political generals be determined: how well they supported or advanced the national objectives—ultimately, inherently, and inescapably political ones—for which the war was being waged. This measure of generalship links political ends with military means and reveals the need to extend the study of generalship beyond the borders of the battlefield to the life of the society for which those battles are fought.

NOTES

Introduction

1. Halleck to W. T. Sherman, April 29, 1864, from *War of the Rebellion: A Compilation of the Official Records of the Union and Confederate Armies*, 128 vols. (Washington, D.C.: Government Printing Office, 1880–1901), series 1, vol. 34, part 3, 332–333. All further references to the *Official Records of the Union and Confederate Armies* will appear as OR.

2. An up-to-date synopsis of the debate over military professionalism in America is Matthew Moten, *The Delafield Commission and the American Military Profession* (College Station: Texas A&M University Press, 2000), 3–24. William B. Skelton, *An American Profession of Arms: The Army Officer Corps, 1775–1861* (Lawrence: University Press of Kansas, 1992), remains one of the most comprehensive studies of the professionalization of the U.S. Army officer corps. Historian Marcus Cunliffe, *Soldiers and Civilians: The Martial Spirit in America, 1775–1865* (Boston: Little, Brown, 1968), has done the most comprehensive study available on the history of American military heritage, and he gave three strands: professional, antiprofessional, and antimilitaristic. Although the author agrees with Cunliffe's interpretation, the antimilitaristic aspect will not be addressed, as it has little effect on this topic. Richard B. Winders, *Mr. Polk's Army: The American Military Experience in the Mexican War* (College Station: Texas A&M University Press, 1997), does examine the phenomenon of "political generals" during the Mexican War.

3. Illustrating this sentiment, Archer Jones, *Civil War Command and Strategy: The Process of Victory and Defeat* (New York: Free Press, 1992), 18, 64, described Frémont as a general with "all the qualities of genius except ability" and concluded that Banks's performance "deprived the Union of an adequate general on a number of important occasions."

4. Figures are from Ezra J. Warner, *Generals in Blue* (Baton Rouge: Louisiana State University Press, 1964), xv.

5. Though a few memoirs, such as Jacob D. Cox, *Military Reminiscences of the Civil War* (New York: Charles Scribner's Sons, 1900), and Lew Wallace, *Lew Wallace: An*

Autobiography, 2 vols. (New York: Harper and Brothers, 1906), were generally balanced and accurate historical narratives, many others, such as Benjamin Butler, *Butler's Book* (Boston: A. M. Thayer, 1892), were viewed as political narcissism and a tool for personal attacks against old adversaries. Because of the reservoir of spite over their loss of military status, some of these works, such as John Logan, *The Volunteer Soldier of America* (New York: R. S. Peale, 1887), were diatribes against West Pointers or the Lincoln administration. Though filled with fascinating insight into the character of these amateur commanders and their view of the war, these early autobiographies and tirades did little to redeem their reputations. Their lack of widespread availability and the powerful perception that many of these men had been unsuccessful commanders in the war, with little to tell about Union victory and battlefield glory, limited their impact.

6. For example, T. Harry Williams, *Lincoln and His Generals* (New York: Random House, 1952), 3–11, praised Grant and Sherman as great commanders but denigrated the rest of the Union generals as being unable and unwilling to break out of a Jominian mindset; a similar opinion is offered in Williams, "Military Leadership of North and South," in *Why the North Won the Civil War*, ed. David H. Donald (New York: Collier Books, 1960), 35–37. In his five-volume work, Kenneth P. Williams, *Lincoln Finds a General: A Military Study of the Civil War* (Bloomington: Indiana University Press, 1949–1959), 1:ix–x, stated that "Lincoln's chief military problem was to find a general equal to the hard task the North faced," and political generals seemed impediments to Union success in this search because of their inability to master the complexity of large-scale military operations.

7. Thomas Buell, *The Warrior Generals: Combat Leadership in the Civil War* (New York: Random House, 1998). Books like W. J. Wood's recent *Civil War Generalship: The Art of Command* (Westport, Conn.: Praeger Publishing, 1997), equate the art of command with operational and tactical skill and devote attention to campaigns and battles where famous commanders confronted each other, but they provide little insight on the larger issues of strategy and its political impact.

8. The use of the terms "Jominian approach" or "Jominian view" throughout this work does not mean to imply that many Civil War generals, even West Point graduates, had ever read one of the few books by Jomini that had been translated into English. Officers like Halleck and McClellan who have left evidence of study in military theory are actually the exception rather than the rule when considering Civil War generals. Far from implying an embracing of strategy or tactics from the famed Swiss military theorist, the phrase "Jominian view" in this book describes belief in the separation of military and political "spheres" and an adoption of the philosophy that equates war solely with military matters at the operational and tactical level.

9. James M. McPherson, *Battle Cry of Freedom: The Civil War Era* (New York: Ballantine Books, 1988), and Bruce Catton, *America Goes to War* (Middletown, Conn.: Wesleyan University Press, 1958). This aspect of Civil War historiography, the interaction between politics and the military conflict, is continuing to attract well-needed attention in recent studies such as Bruce Tap, *Over Lincoln's Shoulder: The Committee on the Conduct of the War* (Lawrence: University Press of Kansas, 1998), which examines the impact of congressional scrutiny and hearings on the war effort.

10. Catton asked the simple but revealing question of whether the Union government would have reached victory quicker by stressing the military effectiveness of West

Pointers at the cost of the political support and recruiting efforts of these prominent politicians-in-uniform (*America Goes to War*, 40).

11. This tendency is most readily apparent in the recent outpouring of books on the strategy, generalship, and military conduct of the war. Examples of this group include Archer Jones, *Civil War Command and Strategy*, Herman Hattaway and Archer Jones, *How the North Won: A Military History of the Civil War* (Champaign: University of Illinois Press, 1991), and Richard E. Beringer, Herman Hattaway, Archer Jones, and William N. Still Jr., *Why the South Lost the Civil War* (Athens: University of Georgia Press, 1986), all of which are highly critical of individual political generals and amateur commanders as a group on the grounds of military effectiveness.

12. Beringer et al., *Why the South Lost the Civil War*, 44. T. Harry Williams was critical of Lincoln's appointment of Banks as the new commander of the Department of the Gulf: "Why he thought that Banks could command it is a mystery. Banks was no better than Butler. He was another Massachusetts politician turned warrior . . . he had not demonstrated that he possessed the ability to manage a large department. The appointment of Banks was a case of Lincoln misreading his man" (*Lincoln and his Generals*, 188).

13. Bruce Catton, *Mr. Lincoln's Army* (Garden City, N.Y.: Doubleday, 1962), 29.

14. Examples include Thomas J. Rowland, *George B. McClellan and Civil War History: In the Shadow of Grant and Sherman* (Kent, Ohio: Kent State University Press, 1998), and Stanley P. Hirshson, *The White Tecumseh: A Biography of General William T. Sherman* (New York: John Wiley and Sons, 1997).

15. Although prominent political generals have received their own attention from biographers, most of these authors viewed their topics through the lens of prewar and postwar politics or attempted to explain away tactical defeats through their subjects' lack of military training or individual character flaws. Indeed, these biographies are surprisingly few and far between, usually written not by prominent military historians but by historians of the American political system. These writers naturally devote extensive attention to political infighting and partisan ties at the expense of critical analysis of military operations, though they often present a more balanced judgment of their subjects' command ability and tactical prowess. Recent examples include James P. Jones, *Black Jack: John A. Logan and Southern Illinois in the Civil War Era* (Carbondale: Southern Illinois University Press, 1995), and James G. Hollandsworth Jr., *Pretense of Glory: The Life of General Nathaniel P. Banks* (Baton Rouge: Louisiana State University Press, 1998).

16. Prussian theorist Carl von Clausewitz, *On War*, ed. Michael Howard and Peter Paret (Princeton: Princeton University Press, 1976), 88, warned against this concept by stressing that "war should never be thought of as *something autonomous* but always as an *instrument of policy*." One of his main themes is the danger in attempting to isolate military and political aspects of war because of the infusion of political factors into every aspect of a conflict, including both a nation's military policy and its expectations of general officers. The central insight of *On War* is, of course, that war is "not a mere act of policy but a true political instrument, a continuation of political activity by other means" (87).

17. The landmark of military professional reform appeared during the American mobilization for the First World War when, though desperately short of experienced officers to head the vast new army, there was no use of anything resembling political generals.

The West Point domination of the U.S. Army high command reached the point that even a pair of combat veteran volunteers, former president Theodore Roosevelt and the ranking major general in the army, Leonard Wood, would both be denied an opportunity to command in France. As U.S. Army historian Russell F. Weigley concludes, "The same modern social disciplines that permitted the Selective Service Act also permitted this apolitical war making in a fashion not possible in early wars" (*History of the United States Army* [New York: Macmillan, 1967], 373–374).

18. Many historians who actually present a definition of political generals mostly list subjective criteria for the reader to apply without clearly designating their view on the parameters of this group. An example of such subjective criteria is James M. McPherson's definition of political generals: "Powerful political figures, several of them prewar Democrats, they were appointed in order to attract various Northern constituencies to support of the war. Some received their commissions as rewards for raising large numbers of volunteers. Others obtained appointment because of sponsorship by important governors or congressmen. Some were leaders of ethnic groups" (*Ordeal by Fire: The Civil War and Reconstruction* [New York: Alfred A. Knopf, 1982], 172).

19. The question of military professionalism must be considered separately from the evolution of professionalism in America owing to the unique nature of military trade. Although the societal need for security is as constant and as pressing as its need for justice or medicine, the functional differentiation of officership has always introduced political and cultural influences on military policy that determined the status of military officers in society. The evolution of military professionalism therefore involves broad functions of officership well beyond technical skills.

20. In the study of military professionalism, Samuel P. Huntington, *The Soldier and the State: The Theory and Politics of Civil-Military Relations* (Cambridge: Harvard University Press, 1957), 8–18, has helped to establish the terms of the debate. In this book, Huntington's criteria of expertise, social responsibility, and corporateness will be accepted as the distinguishing characteristics of a profession and will provide the criteria to determine when the professionalism threshold had been crossed. The Lasswell quote is on page 11.

Chapter 1. The Legacy of a Dual Military Tradition

1. Lincoln had a seemingly instinctive understanding of the political and military challenge he faced. The president expressed this understanding to fellow Republican Carl Schurz in the same letter when he observed: "The war came. The administration could not even start in this, without assistance outside its party. It was mere nonsense to suppose a minority could put down a majority in rebellion" (Lincoln to Schurz [marked "Private and Confidential"], November 10, 1862, Schurz, *Speeches, Correspondences and Political Papers of Carl Schurz*, ed. F. Bancroft [Philadelphia: Lippincott, 1865], 1:212–213).

2. Political culture is a historical classification with multiple and often confusing definitions. American historian George C. Rable's is perhaps the most straightforward and workable. He defines political culture as "beliefs, attitudes, and values expressed through political statements and behavior." His definition goes on to state that "some

aspects of political culture can be implicit and unspoken, and . . . the rational, emotional, and symbolic dimensions of political culture appear often in speeches, editorials, sermons, pamphlets, textbooks, and even in private documents. This rich body of evidence reveals common assumptions about the legitimacy of the political process in general and about the role of government in particular" (*The Confederate Republic: A Revolution against Politics* [Chapel Hill: University of North Carolina Press, 1995], 3). Rable based his definition on Lynn Hunt's construction detailed in *Politics, Culture, and Class in the French Revolution* (Berkeley: University of California Press, 1984).

3. An informative survey about the effects that the Jacksonian era had on these characteristics is Harry Watson, *Liberty and Power: The Politics of Jacksonian America* (New York: Hill and Wang, 1990).

4. Voting statistics are from Philip Paludan, *A People's Contest: The Union and the Civil War* (New York: Harper and Row, 1988), 11.

5. Ibid., 11–12.

6. The changes in political culture in nineteenth-century America are explored in Michael F. Holt, *Political Parties and American Political Development: From the Age of Jackson to the Age of Lincoln* (Baton Rouge: Louisiana State University Press, 1992).

7. This cultural influence occurred despite Jackson's open support of West Point as "the best school in the world" and his faith in the discipline of the regular army officer corps. J. S. Bassett, ed. *Correspondence of Andrew Jackson* (Washington, D.C.: Carnegie Institution, 1926–1935), 3:190.

8. The growing use of political patronage provided the second party system with the ability to penetrate down to state and local levels. Abraham Lincoln became involved with this system during his service as a congressman long before the Civil War. Lincoln's immersion into party patronage is evident in a letter sent to the secretary of state in March 1849 from this junior Whig representative from Illinois. Lincoln requested that "[Baker] and myself are the only Whig members of congress from Illinois. . . . We have reason to think the whigs of that state hold us responsible, to some extent, for the appointments which may be made for our citizens. . . . I therefore hope . . . that when a citizen from Illinois is to be appointed in your Department to an office either in or out of the state, we respectfully asked to be heard" (*The Collected Works of Abraham Lincoln*, ed. Roy P. Basler [New Brunswick, N.J.: Rutgers University Press, 1953], 2:32). As historian Philip Paludan concludes, "The spoils system gave structural sinews to the political ideologies of parties" (*A People's Contest*, 14).

9. With faith placed in the heritage and legacy of the virtuous citizen-soldier, many early Republican state governments had this right of officer election written into their state constitutions. Lawrence Cress, *Citizens in Arms: The Army and the Militia in American Society to the War of 1812* (Chapel Hill: University of North Carolina Press, 1982), 61–62. By exploring political expressions such as these, the influence of a society's political culture upon its military institutions can be inferred. In a similar vein, military culture can be defined as the heritage, beliefs, judgments, and expectations internal to a nation's armed forces regarding its use of socially sanctioned organized violence and its place inside the greater society. This aspect of American culture is most easily detected in the government's military policy, the level of institutional support in the military for these policies, the level of corporate professionalization of the officer corps, and the atmosphere of tolerance and acceptance for the nation's officers and soldiers. Taken together, the two

elements of political and military culture in a society combine to determine the military institutions, strategies, and policies adopted to provide for the common defense.

10. The antiprofessionalism battle included numerous attempts by several congressmen to pass legislation to limit the percentage of new commissions or new commands given to career officers to allow for the maintenance of direct civilian appointments. Even the bastion of the professional army came under repeated attack in the form of an anti–West Point crusade waged in Congress and in the newspapers to close the Military Academy or transform it into a training school for militia officers and soldiers. Resolutions were passed by the state legislatures from Tennessee (1833), Ohio (1834), Connecticut (1842), Maine (1843), and New Hampshire (1844) calling for the abolition of West Point as aristocratic, unnecessary, and expensive. See Cunliffe, *Soldiers and Civilians*, 106–111, 152–155. The history of the crusade against the Military Academy is recounted in James L. Morrison Jr., *"The Best School in the World": West Point, the Pre–Civil War Years, 1833–1866* (Kent, Ohio: Kent State University Press, 1986), 132–133.

11. Donald R. Hickey, *The War of 1812: A Short History* (Champaign: University of Illinois Press, 1995), 108.

12. Richard B. Winders, "Mr. Polk's Army: Politics, Patronage, and the American Military in the Mexican War" (Ph.D. diss., Texas Christian University, 1994), 137.

13. These selected thirteen included future Civil War generals Robert Patterson, Gideon Pillow, Joseph Lane, James Shields, Sterling Price, and future U.S. president Franklin Pierce.

14. Nor did their military service completely separate them from politics while they were in uniform. One appointed Democrat resigned his seat in Congress to go to Mexico, and two of the volunteer generals even ran for political office while serving in Mexico. See Winders, "Mr. Polk's Army: Politics, Patronage, and the American Military in the Mexican War," 137–139.

15. Cunliffe, *Soldiers and Civilians*, 307.

16. Polk's appointment of prominent Democrats to the general officer ranks in examined at length in Winders, "Mr. Polk's Army: Politics, Patronage, and the American Military in the Mexican War," 139–162.

17. Philip Paludan makes this point a central thesis of his seminal work *A People's Contest*, arguing that Northern society played a pivotal role in the Union victory through their continued support for the war effort.

18. The major exception to Military Academy dominance of the officer corps was the continuing service of old regular officers like John Wool and Winfield Scott, who stayed on active duty into their seventies owing to the absence of any retirement system. See Morrison, *Best School in the World*, 15; Skelton, *An American Profession of Arms*, 138–139.

19. Samuel P. Huntington, *The Soldier and the State*, 8–18, defines the distinguishing characteristics of a profession as threefold: expertise, social responsibility, and corporateness. Expertise is the specialized knowledge and skill in a distinct field gained through prolonged education and experience. Responsibility is defined as the performance of a service that is essential to the functioning of a society and the recognition that the responsibility to serve society provides the primary professional motivation. Corporateness is the recognition that the occupation's members share a sense of unity and a formalization of occupational standards and codes of behavior.

20. Huntington goes as far as setting August 6, 1808, as the precise origin of military professionalism, which was the day the Prussian government first set forth a decree on the appointment of officers that stressed duty, merit, and education as requirements for a commission. Ibid., 30.

21. The curriculum there included not only the military engineering and tactical drill common in other nation's military academies, but also an in-depth study of military history, practical exercises in tactics and operations, instruction in staff operations, and even seminars on the study of strategy. Ibid., 48–49.

22. In the 1830s, as evidence of the Prussian growth in professionalism, the general staff and the *Kreigsakademie* began systematic study of the military uses for railroads. This foresightedness would be rewarded in the 1860s. Gordon A. Craig, *The Politics of the Prussian Army, 1640–1945* (New York: Oxford University Press, 1956), 77–78, 193–194.

23. Ibid., 79–81.

24. Huntington, *The Soldier and the State*, 36.

25. In the revised constitution of 1850, the army was completely divorced from legislative control and subject only to the authority of the Kaiser. See Craig, *Prussian Army*, 122–123.

26. During this period, "The wine-red trouser stripe of the General Staff officers became the symbol of a new elite within the officer corps, the cream of the profession, signifying the highest standards of knowledge, competence, and devotion to duty" (Huntington, *The Soldier and the State*, 51).

27. According to Gordon Craig, this was an intentional attempt to limit "political meddling" (*Prussian Army*, 204–205).

28. The French military school system provided the model for West Point, and its influence was one of the causes for the persistent focus at the Military Academy on engineering, artillery, and fortifications. See Skelton, *An American Profession of Arms*, 168.

29. These exercises became formalized and were extensive enough that the use of tactical "umpires" became standard, and a complete mock fortress was built to train on siege warfare. Paddy Griffith, *Military Thought and the French Army, 1815–51* (Manchester, England: Manchester University Press, 1989), 74–76.

30. Ibid., 164–165.

31. Craig, *Prussian Army*, 82–83.

32. Prince Frederick Charles of Prussia openly complained about the political involvement of the officer corps in an essay published in 1860, a concern echoed by the Bavarian minister of war in 1859. Both reports are reprinted in Karl Demeter, *The German Officer-Corps in Society and State, 1650–1945* (New York: Frederick A. Praeger, 1965), 260–266.

33. Paddy Griffith, *Military Thought and the French Army*, 3–4, 9–10, 43, challenges the idea that the French officer corps of 1815–1851 was a "blind and silent" apolitical institution.

34. The French army in particular provided the model for the American officer corps, starting even before a young Captain Sylvanus Thayer visited French military schools and brought back their textbooks for use at West Point. Many American regulars envied the European officers because of their recognized expertise and occupational autonomy and viewed exposure to the rich French military heritage as fuel for professional growth. See Skelton, *An American Profession of Arms*, 115.

35. Thomas Everett Griess, "Dennis Hart Mahan: West Point Professor and Advocate of Military Professionalism" (Ph.D. diss., Duke University, 1968), 289.

36. Samuel J. Watson, "Professionalism, Social Attitudes, and Civil-Military Accountability in the United States Army Officer Corps, 1815–1846" (Ph.D. diss., Rice University, 1996), 225–226.

37. Samuel Huntington, *The Soldier and the State*, 195–203, goes so far as to label this trend in West Point's focus a form of "technicism" that divided the officer corps into subgroups based on technical specialties having little to do with military skills. He argues that this principle of specialization, while popular with government and businesses who profited from the practical engineering skills, delayed officer professionalization by degrading corporateness and ignoring the necessary focus on distinctly military skills. Skelton, *An American Profession of Arms*, 168–169, places much of the responsibility for this engineering focus on French influence and on the domination of the Military Academy by the Corps of Engineers.

38. The frontier experiences of the 1850s, with regiments scattered between various posts and no units established larger than regiments, did not provide any training for the officers in organizing and controlling even regiment-sized formations. Of the 198 company-sized units in the regular army in January 1861, 183 were distributed piecemeal to 79 frontier posts in the West, and the other 15 companies manned defensive posts along the Atlantic coast, the Canadian border, and garrisoned the 23 arsenals scattered among the states. Even a crisis as desperate as the Civil War would not allow these frontier posts to be abandoned so that the army could concentrate for battle. Marvin A. Kreidberg and Merton G. Henry, *History of Military Mobilization in the United States Army, 1775–1945*, pamphlet no. 20-212 (Washington, D.C.: Department of the Army, 1955), 88.

39. Morrison, *Best School in the World*, 94–96.

40. The full title of Mahan's book was *An Elementary Treatise on Advanced-Guard, Outpost, and Detachment Service of Troops, With the Essential Principles of Strategy and Grand Tactics* (New York: John Wiley and Son, 1870). First published in 1847, this text would serve as one of the few available manuals for army officers during both the Mexican War and the Civil War.

41. Visits to Europe and contact with European officers fueled much of the professional literature written by American army officers during the antebellum era. See Skelton, *An American Profession of Arms*, 241.

42. After listing the various types of wars, one of which was labeled *civil wars*, Halleck concluded, "It is not the present intention to enter into any discussion of these different kinds of war, but rather to consider the general subject, and to discuss such general principles and rules as may be applicable to all wars" (*Elements of Military Art and Science* [New York: D. Appleton, 1846], 35–36). Halleck was very open about limiting his analysis of strategy to a Jominian focus on military operations and "war on a map" that similarly limited the utility of Jomini's *Summary of the Art of War* to generals about to fight a vast and fierce civil war over political and cultural differences.

43. The most recent synopsis of antebellum military thought can be found in Moten, *The Delafield Commission and the American Military Profession*, 54–71.

44. This well-known argument is explained most clearly in Hattaway and Jones, *How the North Won*, 11–16, and in Russell F. Weigley, *The American Way of War: A History of the United States Military Strategy and Policy* (Bloomington: Indiana University

Press, 1973), 72–82, 92–127. A countervailing view expresses that the supposed obsession with Napoleonic decisive battle inherently conflicted with Jomini's focus on the occupation of territory and resulted in Civil War officers relying solely on strategic concepts gleaned through experience. This interpretation can be found in Azar Gat, *The Development of Military Thought: The Nineteenth Century* (Oxford: Clarendon Press, 1992), 22–24.

45. Although evaluating the influence of Jomini and Napoleon is the staple for many Civil War military historians, others who study the evolution of military theory downplay the effect of the small amount of military theory taught at West Point. John I. Alger summed up this school of thought when he concluded: "The American Civil War was fought by practical men with practical means. A comprehensive theory of war was unknown to its generals, untested in its conduct, and uninfluenced by its results" (*The Quest for Victory: The History of the Principles of War* [Westport, Conn.: Greenwood Press, 1982], 54–55). The same conclusion is depicted in Gat, *The Development of Military Thought*, 22–24.

46. James Lunsford Morrison, "The United States Military Academy, 1833–1866: Years of Progress and Turmoil" (Ph.D. diss., Columbia University, 1970), 163.

47. An officer went so far as to complain in an article published in *Army and Navy Chronicle* that *"practical strategy* is *totally* neglected at West Point." Mahan's class on the "art of war" may have been popular with some cadets, but it did little to build a foundation of military theory and strategic thought. See *Army and Navy Chronicle* 8 (January 24, 1839): 50, and (February 21, 1839): 123, and Morrison, *Best School in the World*, 94–97.

48. Ulysses S. Grant, *Personal Memoirs of Ulysses S. Grant* (New York: Da Capo Press, 1982), 128–129.

49. Sherman's General Order No. 62 to his officers, July 24, 1862, printed in OR, series 1, vol. 17, part 2, 118–119.

50. Morrison, *Best School in the World*, 96–99, and Gat, *The Development of Military Thought*, 20–25.

51. Huntington, *The Soldier and the State*, 35.

52. Ibid., 10, 16–18.

53. Sherman, *Memoirs of General William T. Sherman* (New York: Da Capo Press, 1984), 1:74–80; Johann Sutter to William T. Sherman, June 28, 1849, Sherman Papers, Library of Congress.

54. Ben Perley Poore, *The Life and Public Service of Ambrose E. Burnside: Soldier–Citizen–Statesman* (Providence, R.I.: J. A. and R. A. Reid, Publishers, 1882), 77–82.

55. Watson, "Professionalism, Social Attitudes, and Civil-Military Accountability in the United States Army Officer Corps, 1815–1846." 727–729.

56. The article goes on to stress the importance of experience by stating: "Test it by shifting the positions. No lawyer would trust his case to a West Point graduate, without evidence of thorough preparation. Yet he himself [as a volunteer officer] enters on a career equally new to him, where his clients may be counted by thousands, and every case is capital" (Thomas Wentworth Higginson, "Regular and Volunteer Officers," *Atlantic Monthly* 14 [September 1864]: 351).

57. The leadership of the army was just as unprepared. The four serving general officers in March 1861 were General in Chief Winfield Scott (age 74), Brevet Major General John Wool (77), Brevet Major General David E. Twiggs (71), and Brigadier General

William S. Harney (60), none of whom were graduates of the Military Academy. The advanced age of these officers was a product of the seniority system and the lack of a retirement system; together these two factors encouraged officers to remain on active duty awaiting advancement to the next rank (sometimes for decades). Men of such age were ill-prepared to raise and lead mass armies during a time of national emergency, thus requiring the mobilization of the volunteer militia and the appointment of volunteer officers. See Kreidberg and Henry, *History of Military Mobilization*, 88.

58. OR, series 3, vol. 1, 67–68.

59. Paludan, *A People's Contest*, 61–63.

60. OR, series 3, vol. 1, 309.

61. Enlisted soldiers could not resign, only desert, which was a punishable military offense. Abraham Lincoln, *Complete Works of Abraham Lincoln*, ed. John G. Nicolay and John Hay (New York: Francis D. Tandy, 1905): 320.

62. The list of names of the congressmen appeared in the *New York Herald*, October 20, 1861, page 1.

63. Kreidberg and Henry, *History of Military Mobilization*, 97.

64. Jacob Cox, a prominent politician from Ohio and a successful corps commander during the war, also warned that if a disciplined and regimented army had been raised by regulars, they would not have been as popular and perhaps would not have blended back into society so readily at the end of the struggle. "War Preparations in the North," *Battles and Leaders of the Civil War* (New York: Thomas Yoseloff, 1956), 1:94.

65. Harry J. Carmen and Reinhard Luthin, *Lincoln and the Patronage* (New York: Columbia University Press, 1943), 154–155.

66. These sentiments about the value and pitfalls of relying on West Pointers for high command were not monopolized by serving officers or the press. As early as June 1861, Montgomery Blair revealed that a similar view existed in Lincoln's cabinet. Concerned about the negative influence that he thought regulars had on the army's patriotism and aggressiveness, Blair wrote to Butler about a recent meeting in Washington with the general's brother. He warned Butler that he feared that the "army spirit" had crept over his brother and that this new officer was hurting the Union cause by "imitating some of the little fellows who have graduated at West Point, and suppose because they know the Manual better than a citizen they are therefore better qualified to command an army than any Citizen General." But, later in the same letter, Blair warned that "you cannot dispense with the regular officers, and you may rest assured that if you do not use their practiced eye and skill . . . you will be exposed to great danger of miscarriage from trivial causes which they alone could guard against." This was advice that the amateur general would have been smart to heed. Letter from Blair to Butler, June 25, 1861, from Butler, *Private and Official Correspondence of General Benjamin F. Butler during the Period of the Civil War* (Norwood, Mass: Plimpton Press, 1917), 1:159–160.

67. On May 4, Lincoln had called for ten new regiments of about 22,700 men for increasing the size of the regular army. On July 29, Congress further supported Lincoln's efforts by authorizing an increase in the regular army to provide for 42,000 regular soldiers. But the federal recruiting efforts were so inefficient and haphazard that by December 1861, barely two new regiments of regulars had been recruited. By December, the troop strength of the regular army scarcely exceeded 20,000 soldiers at a time when 640,000 volunteers had already been accepted into service from the state governors. See

OR, series 3, vol. 1, 383–384. Nor, despite all the federal efforts at recruitment, were the regular army goals of May and July 1861 ever reached before the surrender at Appomattox. See Fred Albert Shannon, *The Organization and Administration of the Union Army, 1861–1865* (Gloucester, Mass.: Peter Smith Publishing, 1965), 46–47.

68. During the initial mobilization drives, little planning or scrutiny by the War Department had gone into the commissioning of the vast new volunteer officer corps. Cameron gave simple criteria to the Northern governors: "To commission no one of Doubtful Morals or Patriotism and not of Sound Health . . . that the higher the moral character and general intelligence of the officers . . . the greater the efficiency of the troops and the resulting glory of their respective states." It was in this area of volunteer officer commissions that Scott's decision to maintain the regular army together did the most harm to the Union army. The governors rapidly ran out of men with military experience and turned toward local politicians and prominent citizens, who were conducting the recruiting drives, to provide the leadership for the constantly forming new regiments. Without any candidacy examination or training requirements handed down from the War Department, these volunteer officers would be left to learn their duties in the field and their tactics on the battlefield. Cameron to each Northern governor, May 22, 1861, OR, series 3, vol. 1, 227–228.

69. Hattaway and Jones, *How the North Won*, 29. To show an indication of exact numbers, the adjutant general reported that by January 14, 1862, the number of brigadier generals nominated to the Senate from the regular army was fifty-one, while the number nominated from civilian life was sixty-five. OR, series 3, vol. 1, 908.

70. Warner, *Generals in Blue*, xx.

71. General Order No. 49 (announcing an act of Congress), August 3, 1861, OR, series 3, vol. 1, 380–383.

72. Secretary Cameron's struggle with various state governors over general officer appointments is detailed in A. Howard Meneely, *The War Department 1861: A Study in Mobilization and Administration* (New York: Columbia University Press, 1928), 155–156.

73. Ibid., 169.

74. Morgan to Cameron, June 4, 1861, OR, series 3, vol. 1, 249–254.

75. An example of the president's direct intervention in military appointments can be seen in his June 17, 1861, letter to Secretary Cameron, Lincoln, *Complete Works*, 4:409.

76. Cameron to Lincoln, October 18, 1861, RG 107, NARA. Cameron used very similar language in the War Department annual report dated December 1, 1861, reprinted in OR, series 3, vol. 1, 698–708.

77. From Cameron's annual report to the president, December 1, 1861, OR, series 3, vol. 1, 698–708.

78. Cox, *Military Reminiscences*, 171.

79. As Cunliffe accurately concluded, regular officers were "not a caste apart, absorbed in craft and unaware of politics" (*Soldiers and Civilians*, 295–304, 333); Huntington, *The Soldier and the State*, 207–208. Skelton, *An American Profession of Arms*, 282–290, formed an opposing interpretation, though even he admits to antebellum officers becoming involved in politics for service or branch parochialism and for the advancement of their own careers.

Chapter 2. The Need for Political Generals

1. *New York Herald*, May 17, 1861, page 1.

2. Front-page coverage of a very flattering nature is given to the general in the *New York Herald*, May 15 and 16, 1861, and *Boston Evening Transcript*, May 17, 1861. *Harper's Weekly*, May 25 and June 1, 1861, also gave flowing praise to the new major-general. The June 1 edition of *Harper's Weekly* dedicated the entire front page to a sketch and biography of him under the headline, "The First Hero of the War."

3. The arrival in Washington of the general who had squashed the secessionist crowds in Baltimore and opened the roads to the capital caused the *New York Herald* to declare, "He has conquered a peace, and is deserving the new honors conferred upon him" (May 17, 1861, page 1).

4. Cox, *Military Reminiscences*, 171.

5. As a New England Democrat, Butler did rally a significant amount of support for the new Republican administration. Secretary of War Simon Cameron justified the appointment of Butler to the governor of Rhode Island by simply claiming that "the President and his official advisors have deemed the interest of the public service to demand the promotion of General Benjamin F. Butler, and he has accordingly been appointed a major general" (Cameron to Governor William Sprague, May 15, 1861, OR, series 3, vol. 1, 207).

6. Butler opened the road to Washington in May 1861, and the throngs of well-wishers called for speeches that the politician-turned-general never failed to deliver. These eloquent orations consistently called for support for the war effort and always inspired the crowd. For an example of Butler's public reception and a sample of his standard early war oratory, see *The Rebellion Record: A Diary of American Events*, ed. Frank Moore (New York: G. P. Putnam, 1861–1865), vol. 1, doc. 171.

7. Butler was a proud descendant of a military family and tried to continue this heritage of military service. He believed his grandfather had fought with British General James Wolfe at Quebec, and his father, John Butler, a captain in the regular army, had fought in the War of 1812; see *Butler's Book*, 80. Prior to the war, he had yearned to go to West Point and repeatedly defended the value of a military education during the antebellum period. In June 1839, Butler, already a prominent New England political figure, had been invited to speak at West Point and chose as his topic the important role the Military Academy played in developing leaders. The challenges of military service, he asserted, "embrace a large amount of professional science, which is only to be acquired by careful and laborious study, and by diligent attendance on the appropriate exercises" (Butler, *The Military Profession of the United States and the Means of Promoting Its Usefulness and Honor* [New York: Samuel Colman, 1839], 22–23).

8. Cunliffe, *Soldiers and Civilians*, 247–254. The year 1839 also marked Butler's introduction to the duties of a soldier. The prominent Lowell attorney became involved with a volunteer militia unit, joining the newly formed "Lowell City Guard" as a private. After his Civil War service, Butler remarked with some pride, "I carried my musket in that company for three years. . . . I did this to learn the duties of a soldier, for I believed then that in the course of my life I should be called upon sometime to perform those duties as a soldier in an actual war" (*Butler's Book*, 123). A similar sentiment can be found in Wallace, *Lew Wallace: An Autobiography*, 1:93–95, 244–246.

9. Butler also described the advantage of service in the junior officer ranks to pre-

pare future commanders for the challenges of wartime service. During this eloquent defense of West Point, the future Union general had outlined the very argument against military amateurism that would be used against him during the war. Ironically, both of these methods of developing commanders—formal military education and experience as a junior officer—would be missing from Butler's own qualifications to be a general officer. Butler, *The Military Profession of the United States*, 28.

10. Butler, *Butler's Book*, 127.

11. Ibid., 124–125.

12. As a way to strike back at Butler, Governor Gardner reorganized the militia and put Lowell, Butler's hometown, in a different regimental area. Deeming this an "injustice" and a "trick," Butler gained revenge, claiming, "I said nothing, but waited for a vacancy in the office of brigadier-general of the brigade.... Under our Constitution the field officers of the brigade elected their brigadier, and if there was no objection, they usually elected the senior colonel. My fellow-officers were kind enough to treat me as if I had not been turned out, and elected me brigadier-general. I had the pleasure of receiving from Governor Gardner a commission as brigadier-general, signed by himself as chief executive of the commonwealth [of Massachusetts]" (ibid., 126).

13. Unlike during or after his wartime service, before the war Butler respected West Point, its mission, and its graduates as being the best prepared for the challenges of wartime command. Ironically, he had been on the Military Academy's prestigious Board of Visitors in February 1857, appointed by then secretary of war Jefferson Davis. For this visit to West Point, Butler donned his new militia uniform and as "the youngest general in the United States," as he bragged, enjoyed a handshake with the oldest general, Winfield Scott. See Richard S. West, *Lincoln's Scapegoat General: A Life of Benjamin F. Butler, 1818–1893* (Boston: Houghton Mifflin, 1965), 42.

14. Prior to Fort Sumter, Butler had the reputation as a very moderate Democrat who had lost the governorship of his home state to Nathaniel Banks in part because of his conservative views on slavery. During the explosive Democratic convention in 1860, he reinforced this image by voting for Jefferson Davis on fifty-seven ballots for the presidential nomination. The suddenness of his political transformation can be seen in the fact that, by the end of 1860, Butler had informed one group of Southerners that if war came, Massachusetts would hunt down and hang every "traitor." This dialogue and political sentiment were prominently reported in the *New York Times*, January 2, 1861; see *The Rebellion Record*, 1:1 9.

15. February 15, 1861, letter to Massachusetts regiment, and March 9, 1861, letter from Adjutant General of Rhode Island, Butler Papers, Library of Congress.

16. Butler, *Butler's Book*, 170, recounted with great drama his departure from the court after being handed a note ordering him as the brigade commander to mobilize the 6th Massachusetts, claiming the trial was so disrupted that the case was never completed.

17. See the April 16, 1861, *Boston Post*, for an example of the reaction to Butler's announcement on mobilizing to defend the Union.

18. Butler's quest to get an appointment as a commander and get in the war is recounted in *Butler's Book*, 169–172.

19. Ibid., 170–171.

20. John G. Nicolay and John Hay, *Abraham Lincoln: A History* (New York: Century, 1886), 4:133.

21. "The President and his official advisors have deemed the interest of the public service to demand the promotion of General Benjamin F. Butler, and he has accordingly been appointed a major-general" (Secretary of War Simon Cameron to Governor William Sprague of Rhode Island, May 15, 1861, OR, series 3, vol. 1, 207).

22. In 1859, Banks on the Republican ticket soundly defeated his Democratic opponent Ben Butler for governor—another of those Civil War coincidences.

23. The ex-governor had expected a cabinet appointment from the new president, believing he was the natural choice to represent the interests of New England. But he was passed over in favor of Gideon Welles's selection as secretary of the navy and the voice of New England on the cabinet. Banks remained nationally known and respected in 1861, and his moderate leanings could influence others, be they ex-Whigs, Know-Nothings, War Democrats, or moderate Republicans, because he had allied himself at different times with each of these groups. Lincoln claimed to need "a man of Democratic antecedents from New England." Banks's prominence in the House made his name certain to be on this short list. Lincoln's December 1860 letters to Hannibal Hamlin on the subject are in Lincoln, *Collected Works*, 4:147 and 161. Why Banks did not get selected is covered in Hollandsworth, *Pretense of Glory*, 43–44.

24. Ibid., 45.

25. Accounts of the "martial splendor" of the annual Massachusetts militia encampment appeared in the September 11 and 12, 1859, *New York Herald*, but described pomp and ceremony, not training for war.

26. From a letter from William Schouler to Banks, May 6, 1845, Banks Papers, Library of Congress.

27. The editor went as far as claiming that General Scott admired Banks's "prestige" and labeled him as "the Napoleonic representative to our army" (*New York Herald*, June 2, 1861).

28. Banks's appointment received widespread newspaper coverage, yet the tone of most of the coverage given to political generals was often shaped by the political affiliation of the newspaper. This particular flattering quote is from an openly Republican newspaper; see *The Rebellion Record*, vol. 1, D85.

29. Banks's stand with the administration attracted attention even outside his home state and beyond the shadow of the capital, an example of which is the positive coverage both he and Butler received in the *New York Herald*, June 2, 1861.

30. Letter from Samuel Hooper to Banks, dated May 30, 1862, Banks Papers, Library of Congress. Unlike many of his peers, Banks actually spent little of his political exertions on his own advancement and recognition. "Detail me where you please," he was claimed by a newspaper to have said, "it is my duty to obey" (*New York Herald*, June 2, 1861).

31. Banks asked for and received Jomini's *Summary of the Art of War* and *The Seven Years' War of Frederick the Great*, along with some German military books as well as books on military court-martials and the law of war; in a December 31, 1861, letter from J. M. C. Armbruster, Banks Papers, American Antiquarian Society.

32. From a July 29, 1862, letter from Banks to Mary Banks, Banks Papers, Library of Congress.

33. Banks offered his wife these assurances in letters dated October 21, 1861, and September 4, 1862, during two points in his military career when he felt he needed support to maintain his position as a senior commander; Banks Papers, Library of Congress.

34. There is evidence that many of the Logan stories from Manassas are wrong and that he was actually in Washington when the battle was fought at Bull Run on July 21. His exploits during the Bull Run Campaign are detailed in Jones, *Black Jack*, 94–97.

35. Logan wrote to his wife on July 20, declaring, "I feel very much inclined to go into the Army, not for the heart of the contest, but that if the Government is to be preserved to help do it" (Logan to Mary Logan, Logan Papers, Library of Congress).

36. Jones, *Black Jack*, xvi.

37. Ibid., 102.

38. Grant, *Memoirs*, 124–125.

39. An example of these appeals was a March 20, 1863, letter from Yates to the president, in Logan Papers, Library of Congress.

40. John Shy, *A People Numerous and Armed: Reflections on the Military Struggle for American Independence* (Ann Arbor: University of Michigan Press, 1990), 218.

41. Lincoln to Cameron, August 17, 1861, *Complete Works*, 4:489.

42. Senator Lane was very open about offering to resign his political seat if he could wear the two stars of a major general. Lane to Lincoln, October 9, 1861, OR, series 1, vol. 3, 529–530.

43. The emergence of the War Democrats is detailed in Joel Silbey, *A Respectable Minority* (New York: W. W. Norton, 1977).

44. About the attempts to form a Union Party, see Holt, *Political Parties and American Political Development*, 338–342.

45. The political campaign waged to influence the Lincoln administration to vigorously prosecute the war is the subject of Hans L. Trefousse, *The Radical Republicans* (New York: Alfred A. Knopf, 1969).

46. The effect of the Joint Committee on the Conduct of the War is examined in Tap, *Over Lincoln's Shoulder*, and T. Harry Williams, "The Committee on the Conduct of the War: An Experiment in Civilian Control," in *The Selected Essays of T. Harry Williams* (Baton Rouge: Louisiana State University Press, 1983), 15–30.

47. Butler's version of the capture of Baltimore, reflecting his disdain for Scott's caution, is detailed in *Butler's Book*, 227–235.

48. Butler's drive to determine the political reasons for and ramifications of this command change can be seen in his letter to Secretary of War Cameron, May 18, 1861, *Private and Official Correspondence*, 1:95–96.

49. The first steps included the formation of "Competency Boards" to test volunteer officers and the release of all volunteer generals who held commissions in state militias but were not selected by the president and confirmed by the Senate. On August 15, 1861, the War Department issued General Order No. 57, repealing the commissions of all officers who entered service as three-month volunteer officers without being formally mustered in. OR, series 3, vol. 1, 411.

50. General Order No. 12 from Adjutant General Lorenzo Thomas, February 6, 1862, OR, series 3, vol. 1, 882–883.

51. General Order No. 111 was published on August 18, 1862, OR, series 3, vol. 2, 401–402.

52. This quote became a staple of Butler's recounting of his wartime exploits. See T. A. Bland, *Life of Benjamin F. Butler* (Boston: Lee and Shepard, 1879), 199.

53. Examples of this positive coverage can be seen in the *Chicago Tribune*, Septem-

ber 27, 1862, page 1, and the *Chicago Times*, September 2, 1862. These bipartisan efforts eventually faded away as the Democratic Party returned as an opposition party later in the war. This resurgence is depicted in Silbey, *A Respectable Minority*.

54. W. H. Terrell, *Indiana in the War of the Rebellion: Report of the Adjutant General* (Bloomington: Indiana Historical Bureau, 1960), 19–20.

55. Wallace, *Lew Wallace: An Autobiography*, 1:264–266.

56. For examples, see Benjamin F. Cook, *History of the Twelfth Massachusetts Volunteers* (Boston: Twelfth Regimental Association, 1882), and W. S. Morris, L. D. Hartwell, and J. B. Kuykendall, *History of the 31st Regiment Illinois Volunteers: Organized by John A. Logan* (Carbondale: Southern Illinois University Press, 1902).

57. For a description of a typical recruiting meeting, see Bell Irvin Wiley, *The Life of Billy Yank: The Common Soldier of the Union* (Baton Rouge: Louisiana State University Press, 1952), 20–21.

58. How this process was started in Ohio is recalled in Jacob Cox, "War Preparations in the North," in *Battles and Leaders of the Civil War*, 1:84–90.

59. Lincoln to Cameron, June 20, 1861, OR, series 3, vol. 1, 280–281.

60. *Butler's Book*, 297–298.

61. Butler himself warned of this problem early in the war. "As the war has gone on, recruiting is getting very difficult," he cautioned the administration, "and unless pretty extraordinary measures are taken it will be impossible to get men" (Butler to Montgomery Blair, August 19, 1861, *Correspondence*, 1:219–220).

62. However, Butler's return to his home state raised a potentially embarrassing problem for the administration, as he quarreled with Massachusetts governor John Andrews throughout the fall of 1861. This disagreement was over Butler's authority to raise regiments independently in the state and over who had the authority to appoint officers to the new regiments. See Hans L. Trefousse, *Ben Butler: The South Called Him Beast* (New York: Twayne, 1957), 90.

63. Butler to Adjutant General Lorenzo Thomas, November 18, 1861, OR, series 3, vol. 1, 652–655.

64. During Butler's recruiting drive in New England, he was repeatedly writing to Lincoln with requests for promotion and posting to field command. The extent of his ambition and confidence stands out in his November 9, 1861, letter to the president: "Gen. Wool has resigned. Gen. Frèmont must. Gen. Scott had retired. I have an ambition, and I trust a laudable one, to be Major General of the United States Army. Has anyone done more to deserve it? No one will do more. May I rely upon you as you have confidence in me to take this matter into consideration? . . . I have made the same suggestion to other of my friends" (*Correspondence*, 1:253). These are not the words of a man who considers himself an amateur in a professional's job.

65. Victor Hicken, "From Vandalia to Vicksburg: The Political and Military Career of John A. McClernand" (Ph.D. diss., University of Illinois, 1955), 147–148.

66. Ibid., 152.

67. Victor Hicken, *Illinois in the Civil War* (Champaign: University of Illinois Press, 1966), 12–13.

68. Grant, *Memoirs*, 124–126.

69. *Chicago Tribune*, September 16, 1861, page 2.

70. Halleck's orders simply read, "General J. A. McClernand will repair to Spring-

field, Ill., and assist the Governor in organizing volunteers" (Halleck to Grant, August 25, 1862, OR, series 1, vol. 17, part 2, 187).

71. Neither McClernand nor his biographers explain his selection of the usurper tyrants Julius Caesar and Oliver Cromwell as non–West Pointers instead of more popular and relevant examples of American citizen-soldier war heroes like Andrew Jackson, Zachary Taylor, or George Washington. One disturbing possibility is that these figures sprang into McClernand's mind as he basked in the crowd's enthusiasm and considered his own future. The entire speech was reprinted in the *Chicago Tribune*, September 8, 1862, page 2.

72. The bad relationship between McClernand and his superiors eventually found its way into the newspapers, often with a significant bias shown toward the popular politician. An example of such favoritism can be seen in the article crying out against the "intriguing and maneuvering" among West Pointers against McClernand; *Chicago Tribune*, December 27, 1861, page 2.

73. The "secret" part of this plan was lost almost immediately, as the newspapers reported on McClernand's recruiting drive and his "Mississippi expedition" almost daily during September and October 1862. See the *Chicago Tribune*, September 8, October 28, November 4, 1862, and the *Chicago Times*, September 2, 1862.

74. McClernand aggressively pushed Lincoln on the need for a new campaign to open the Mississippi, culminating in a personal letter on November 10, 1862, which warned of the possible secession of the old Northwest states if the Mississippi was not opened soon; doc. no. 19478-8, Robert Todd Lincoln Collection of the Papers of Abraham Lincoln, Library of Congress.

75. Stanton to McClernand, October 21 and 29, 1862, OR, series 1, vol. 17, part 2, 282, 302.

76. Stanton to McClernand, October 30, 1862, ibid., 308.

77. Richard L. Kiper, *Major General John Alexander McClernand: Politician in Uniform* (Kent, Ohio: Kent State University Press, 1999), 133–153.

78. Although the majority of these new regiments were formed without direct appeals from McClernand himself, his name and prestige were used prominently during recruiting drives throughout the region. However, Lincoln proved to be a better politician than McClernand and inserted a clause in their bargain that would eventually be invoked to deny him any position higher than that of corps commander under Grant. The orders that McClernand believed agreed to his terms actually read that his command could only be independent if the troops were "not required by the operations of General Grant's command" (McClernand to Grant, December 28, 1862, OR, series 1, vol. 17, part 2, 502).

79. McClernand to Halleck, December 15, 1862, ibid., 415.

80. McClernand to Stanton, November 10, 1862, ibid., 332–334. McClernand's personal contribution to this recruiting drive receives a strong endorsement in Kiper, *McClernand*, 151–153.

81. Newspaper coverage like this was partly responsible for making these men national, and not just local, figures. See *Boston Evening Transcript*, October 12, 1861, page 1, and *Chicago Tribune*, September 23, 1862, page 2.

82. "The Germans are entering fully into the spirit of the war. . . . Scarcely a vessel arrives from Hamburg or Bremen without recruits for Sigel from the 'radicals' of Germany, who sympathize with him in exile" (*Chicago Tribune*, September 23, 1862, page 2).

83. "Irishmen of Massachusetts. . . . We have known you of Old. . . . Fight for the Green Isle Astore! For Hibernia Aroom!" (*Boston Evening Transcript*, October 12, 1861, page 1). "All patriotic young Irishmen who desire to defend the flag of their adopted country . . . are requested to meet at Hibernian Hall" (from the New Haven *Palladium*, in Thomas H. Murray, *History of the Ninth Regiment, Connecticut Volunteer Infantry* [New Haven, Conn: Price, Lee, and Adkins, 1903], 27).

84. John Hay, *Lincoln and the Civil War in the Diaries and Letters of John Hay*, ed. Tyler Dennett (New York: Dodd, Mead, 1939), 13.

85. Even politicians with clouded reputations and limited contacts sought to use the war to advance their ambitions. The best example may be the incredible military career of New York Democrat and congressman Daniel Sickles. At the start of the Civil War, Sickles's political career was on the ropes after he publicly gunned down his wife's lover across the street from the White House in February 1859. In April 1861, with his congressional term ended and the Republicans in control of the New York governorship, he was at the apparent end of his political life. Yet the firing at Sumter offered the wily politician a bold opportunity. Sickles saw his chance for redemption and set out to recruit a regiment, later expanded to a full brigade, from among his political contacts in New York City. He raised the needed troops in the chaos of early wartime New York City but ran into problems with the Republican governor, who attempted to cut the largely Democratic brigade to a single regiment. Sickles, displaying the political boldness for which he was famous, rode a train to Washington to appeal directly to President Lincoln. Meeting Lincoln for the first time, he suggested that his brigade be accepted as "U.S. Volunteers," therefore technically outside the control of the politically hostile state authorities. Seeing another opportunity to gain Democratic political support, the president agreed. Sickles, reborn, then went on to notoriety at the Battle of Gettysburg and to a lengthy second political career that lasted until 1895. See W. A. Swanberg, *Sickles the Incredible* (New York: Charles Scribner's Sons, 1956).

86. Lincoln to Halleck, January 15, 1862, *Collected Works*, 5:100. Halleck responded to the president on January 21 that he had already made Governor Koerner colonel of his staff. Halleck seemed very resistant to the idea of giving generals' stars to yet another politician so unprepared to command troops. If the president wanted him made a brigadier, Halleck promised to "give him such employment as may best suit him" (OR, series 1, vol. 18, 826).

87. Stephen D. Engle, *Yankee Dutchman: The Life of Franz Sigel* (Fayetteville: University of Arkansas Press, 1993), 52.

88. Lincoln was peppered with letters from German organizations concerning Sigel's fate and acknowledgment of the contributions of the German community to the cause. An example of their impact can be seen in a letter from the president to the German Committee of New York, in which he promises to give Sigel command of a new division; January 22, 1862, *Collected Works*, 5:106.

89. Accounts of Butler's speeches are recounted in the *New York Weekly Tribune*, January 10 and 17, 1863.

90. Butler's defense of the administration was reported in the *New York Times*, April 28, 1863. How this presentation played with the radicals is told in Trefousse, *Ben Butler*, 137.

91. Lincoln's reason was best expressed in a letter he was forwarded from a local

politician explaining Logan's impact. "[Logan] is doing much good for our cause here in Ill.," William P. Dole stated in August 1863, asking for an extension to one of Logan's military leaves. "Logan calls things by their right names and his speeches will do a world of good in this state as showing the spirit and temperament of the army" (Lincoln, *Collected Works*, 6:382–383).

92. Front page of the September 24, 1862, *Chicago Tribune*. While it is problematic to rely on newspaper accounts to judge the effect of these speeches, the fact that prominent newspapers continually refer to "war speeches" and "Union meetings" during the war shows their prevalence and prominence.

93. All direct quotations are from a July 31, 1863, speech by John Logan, *Speech of Major-General John A. Logan on Return to Illinois after the Capture of Vicksburg* (Cincinnati: Cabel Clark, 1863).

94. *Chicago Tribune*, September 16, 1861, page 2.

95. John Logan, *Letters of Loyal Soldiers: How Douglas Democrats Will Vote* (New York: Loyal Publication Society, 1864).

96. For examples of this coverage, see *Chicago Tribune*, September 10, 1861 (McClernand), October 26, 1862 (Sigel), September 24, 1862 (Logan); *Chicago Times*, September 1, 1862 (Frèmont), September 2, 1862 (McClernand); and *New York Herald*, May 17, 1861 (Butler).

97. Butler, *Butler's Book*, 1034–1035.

98. Cox, *Military Reminiscences*, 170–171.

99. Lincoln was constantly badgered by the supporters and opponents of the various political generals. His exasperation at their fickleness is readily apparent in his January 1865 reply to a delegation of Kentuckians who were asking for Butler to be placed in command of their state's military department: "You howled when Butler went to New Orleans. Others howled when he was removed from that command. Somebody has been howling ever since at his assignment to military command. How long will it be before you, who are howling for his assignment to rule Kentucky, will be howling to me to remove him?" Lincoln's question went unanswered, as the delegation continued their demand for Butler. Lincoln to "Delegation of Kentuckians," January 2, 1865, *Collected Works*, 8:195.

100. Early in the war, the administration drew lessons from the struggles in Missouri, Kentucky, and western Virginia, where the return of loyal governments rested on the forced removal of any rebel troops. Secretary Cameron's report to the president on the War Department, December 1, 1861, OR, series 3, vol. 1, 701.

101. This hope was also echoed in his 1861 annual War Department report to Congress; letter from Cameron to Lincoln, October 18, 1861, RG 107, NARA.

Chapter 3. The Need for Regular Officers

1. McClellan gave these instructions to General Halleck on November 11, 1861, as Halleck was about to leave for Missouri to take command of that department. OR, series 1, vol. 5, 37.

2. Halleck to Sigel, December 25, 1861, and Halleck to McClellan, December 26, 1861, OR, series 1, vol. 8, 461–463.

3. Many West Pointers during the antebellum period used these words and synonyms to describe their Military Academy experience. See Watson, "Professionalism, Social Attitudes, and Civil-Military Accountability in the United States Army Officer Corps, 1815–1846," 250–262, for an assessment of these experiences and their effects on the initial training that antebellum officers received at West Point.

4. Williams, *Lincoln and His Generals*, 18–19.

5. Lincoln, *Collected Works*, 4:327.

6. Historian William Skelton, *An American Profession of Arms*, 287–297, referred to such activity as regulars viewing politics from a professional perspective. Besides branch and service parochialism, officers sought to influence their careers using political lobbying and the mobilization of powerful friends, a common activity in the antebellum officer corps and an accepted practice.

7. Lincoln, *Collected Works*, 4:344–345.

8. Both Governor Richard Yates and Congressman William Butler of Illinois petitioned the president to award a major generalship on Pope. When the newly minted brigadier had taken Island Number 10 on the Mississippi, Pope's patrons from his home state of Illinois sought to have him promoted to major general as a reward. "I fully appreciate General Pope's splendid accomplishments," Lincoln replied, "but you must know that major-generalships in the regular army are not as plenty as blackberries" (*Collected Works*, 7:145).

9. This letter included a list of names about whom the president believed he had already made promises to patrons. The list included Butler, Banks, Pope, McClellan, "Rosecrantz," and others. Lincoln to Cameron, July 29, 1861, *Collected Works*, 4:463.

10. Examples were letters from Fitz John Porter to McClellan, and William F. Smith to McClellan, both dated April 15, 1861, McClellan Papers, Library of Congress.

11. Letter from Militia headquarters to General Scott over McClellan's appointment, April 21, 1861, OR, series 3, vol. 1, 97–98. McClellan's depiction of the events is recounted in a letter to his wife, dated April 21, 1861, McClellan Papers, Library of Congress. Nicolay and Hay, *Abraham Lincoln*, 4:281–283. George B. McClellan, *McClellan's Own Story* (New York: Charles L. Webster, 1887), 40–44.

12. Warner, *Generals in Blue*, 291.

13. McClellan, *McClellan's Own Story*, 157, 159–161; Stephen W. Sears, *George B. McClellan: The Young Napoleon* (New York: Ticknor and Fields, 1988), 72.

14. Scott to Cameron, October 4, 1861, OR, series 1, vol. 2, part 1, 491–493. Although evidence exists that Lincoln read Halleck's book, there is little support for the idea that many other generals were influenced by it, though many copies circulated in their ranks. David H. Donald, *Lincoln* (London: Random House, 1995), 329.

15. On August 17, 1861, Lincoln wrote to the Secretary of War, asking, "Let Henry Wager Halleck, of California, be appointed a Major General in the *Regular Army*. I make this appointment on Gen. Scott's recommendation" (*Collected Works*, 4:498).

16. Burnside served for a time as both unit quartermaster and post commissary at the desolate post known as Las Vegas. Burnside to F. Burt, October 3, 1853, Burnside's Papers, "Generals' Papers," RG 94, National Archives.

17. The original state commission for Burnside is in Burnside Papers, Rhode Island Historical Society.

18. The prominent role Burnside played in the formation of the first volunteer unit

from his home state can be seen in Augustus Woodbury, *A Narrative of the Campaign of the First Rhode Island in the Spring and Summer of 1861* (Providence, R.I.: Sidney S. Rider, 1862), 20–26, 50–53.

19. Burnside, *Battles and Leaders of the Civil War,* 1:660.

20. A foundation for future military patronage was built during these vital organizational efforts, because West Pointers selected key subordinates based on shared antebellum experiences and personal contacts from both cadet life and service in the regular army. Burnside, like other USMA graduates, selected classmates and peers from the academy whenever the opportunity presented itself. When he recruited his amphibious division in the fall of 1861, he selected as his brigade commanders John G. Foster (USMA 1846), Jesse Reno (USMA 1846), and John Parke (USMA 1849), friends from his days as a cadet. All three of these officers would rise to general officer rank in the Ninth Corps, each riding the coattails of his military patron, each initially recommended for promotion by Burnside. He also handpicked young regulars to be his key staff officers, offering each a higher volunteer rank to join his new unit. This pattern of internal military patronage was significant because it offered an alternative to political sponsorship and could advance individuals higher in the chain of command as their patrons were promoted. Ambrose Burnside, "The Burnside Expedition," in *Personal Narratives of the Events of the War of the Rebellion,* 2d series (Providence, R.I.: N. B. Williams, 1882), 5–9.

21. Even at the onset of the war, Sherman did not mince words concerning his disdain for the volunteer militia and "Home Guards" that were mustering all across the Union: "I will not volunteer among the irregular militia, for I like not the class from which they are exclusively drawn" (William T. Sherman to John Sherman, April 18 and 22, 1861, in *Sherman's Civil War: Selected Correspondence of William T. Sherman, 1860–1865,* ed. Brook D. Simpson and Jean V. Berlin [Chapel Hill: University of North Carolina Press, 1999], 75–76).

22. Ibid., 69–72.

23. Thomas Ewing to W. T. Sherman, May 6, 1861, Sherman Papers, Library of Congress.

24. When the thirty-year-old lieutenant was married in May 1850, his wedding was a major political event in the capital. Senators Daniel Webster, Henry Clay, and T. H. Benton attended, along with President Zachary Taylor and his entire cabinet. Sherman also returned to Washington to attend President Taylor's funeral as a temporary aide-de-camp to the adjutant general of the army; *Memoirs,* 1:84–85.

25. William T. Sherman, *The Sherman Letters: Correspondence between General and Senator Sherman from 1837 to 1891,* ed. Rachel Sherman Thorndike (New York: Scribner's, 1894), 110.

26. Sherman recounts several frank and informal meetings with the president in *Memoirs,* 1:167, 175, 192.

27. Senator Ewing had gone so far as asking Secretary of the Interior Caleb Smith of Indiana to support Sherman's appointment. Secretary Smith said he would support Ewing if Sherman's name was mentioned again in cabinet meetings. Thomas Ewing to W. T. Sherman, May 8, 1861, and W. T. Sherman to Thomas Ewing, May 23, 1861, William T. Sherman Papers, Library of Congress.

28. Thomas Ewing to W. T. Sherman, May 31, 1861, reel 1, William T. Sherman Family Papers (microfilm).

29. W. T. Sherman to Thomas Ewing, May 27, 1861, ibid.

30. Sherman, *Sherman's Civil War*, 80.

31. W. T. Sherman to John Sherman, May 22, 1861, ibid., 90.

32. However, Sherman was no more ready for the challenges of being a general officer in 1861 than many of his fellow West Point graduates, as his military experience was confined to small units and irregular conflicts. After graduating sixth in his class in 1840, the young artillery lieutenant had served in the Seminole War and in California with Halleck. During this time, he garnered no experience with units above company level or even with the role of his own artillery branch in combat. Sherman understood his limitations as he contemplated a position in the high command of the growing Union army; he regretted "missing" the Mexican War, as it would have provided what he described as "schooling" with large masses of troops in the field; W. T. Sherman to John Sherman, May 24, 1861, *Sherman's Civil War*, 92. What his background provided was the characteristics Sherman shared with most Military Academy graduates: exposure to army organization and discipline and the appearance of being ready to fulfill the mandate of preparing and leading new volunteers into battle.

33. Grant's request for appointment back into the army is in a May 24, 1861, letter to the adjutant general of the U.S. Army, for which no reply was ever received; OR, series 3, vol. 1, 234.

34. Jacob Cox, "War Preparations in the North," in *Battles and Leaders of the Civil War*, 1:89–90.

35. Ibid., 90–93. Governor Dennison and Secretary Cameron exchanged hopes for what these organizational skills would produce; see OR, series 3, vol. 1, 68–69, 101, 148–149.

36. Watson, "Professionalism, Social Attitudes, and Civil-Military Accountability in the United States Army Officer Corps, 1815–1846," 593–594.

37. As Historian Kenneth Williams observed, "Few American officers had ever seen such an army; none had ever commanded one" (*Lincoln Finds a General*, 66).

38. This sentiment was repeatedly offered as the main cause for the defeat by the senior officers present on the field. See OR, series 1, vol. 2, 350–354, 483, 497, 524–525, 532–533, 535–536.

39. This tirade against the poor discipline of the volunteers filled Sherman's correspondence for a full two months after the battle and for a month after Shiloh. On August 3, he would explain the debacle at First Bull Run by concluding, "Oh—but we had a few regulars." These specific quotes are from letters to his wife dated July 19 and July 24, 1861. William T. Sherman, *Home Letters of General Sherman*, ed. M. A. DeWolfe Howe (New York: Scribner's, 1909), 201, 203, 210–214, 224–225.

40. Burnside's account of this meeting is in *Battles and Leaders*, 1:660–661.

41. Adjutant General S. Williams to Burnside, September 12, 1861, OR, series 3, vol. 1, 500.

42. Burnside to Adjutant General S. Williams, September 24, 1861, ibid., 534–536.

43. Burnside's reports of his success with the state governors is in various September 1861 reports to the War Department, ibid., 534–536, 551, 562.

44. The difference in recruiting methods between West Pointers and political generals narrowed as the war progressed because the states and local communities themselves had increasing difficulty meeting War Department quotas. When Burnside returned to

New England in the spring of 1864 for a second recruiting drive to fill out the ranks of his Ninth Corps, his approach was more like his amateur general contemporaries. A year and a half after his first drive, Burnside relied much more on patronage from political allies to fill the officer ranks in the new units and changed his methods to emphasize personal appeals for patriotic service rather than acting merely as an agent of the government. He addressed both recruiting rallies and state legislatures in an effort to spur volunteers, often using the same appeals and phrases that politicians like Butler had employed in 1861. He described this new experience in a series of letters to friends and family dated from February 17 through 23, in Burnside's Papers, "Generals' Papers," RG 94, National Archives. An example of the positive press coverage that Burnside's public appearances gathered can be seen in *Boston Evening Transcript*, February 2 and 4, page 1.

45. Burnside did not raise the numbers necessary to fill out his depleted Ninth Corps and again mustered mostly existing regimental formations. He reported in his April 1864 returns only 27,487 men—far fewer than the 50,000 sought by Secretary Stanton for his corps; OR, series 1, vol. 33, 803, 807, 1045. Burnside repeatedly expressed frustration in correspondence to the War Department about the difficulty in gathering new recruits during the first two months of 1864; ibid., 373, 427, 542.

46. W. T. Sherman to Ellen Sherman, July 6 and 15, 1861, reel 1, Sherman Family Papers (microfilm).

47. Sherman, *Memoirs*, 1:192.

48. W. T. Sherman made strong complaints to his wife on July 6 and to his sister on July 14, 1861, about the low training level of the green volunteers and how personally tasking it was to organize and prepare first his regular regiment, then his entire brigade; *Sherman's Civil War*, 107–111.

49. Hirshson, *The White Tecumseh*, 92.

50. W. T. Sherman to Ellen Sherman, August 17 and 19, 1861, *Home Letters of General Sherman*, 215–216.

51. Sherman, *Memoirs*, 1:210–211; William T. Sherman to John Sherman, August 19, 1861, Sherman Papers, Library of Congress.

52. Sherman to his wife, August 17, 1861, *Sherman's Civil War*, 130–131.

53. Sherman had little faith in the support he would receive from the states of the Old Northwest and lamented their disorganized and fluctuating support for the Union cause, telling his brother at one point, "If they [the Confederates] are united and we disunited or indifferent, they will succeed" (Sherman to John Sherman, September 9, 1861, William T. Sherman Papers, Library of Congress). He paints a similarly pessimistic picture in his *Memoirs*, 1:198–199.

54. Ibid., 1:201–204.

55. Rapidly, the story of this meeting was leaked, and Sherman was deemed mad by many in Washington and the press. General Lorenzo Thomas's account of the meeting was reprinted in nearly every newspaper in the country. The original exchange between Secretary Cameron and General Thomas is in OR, series 1, vol. 3, 548–549, and vol. 4, 316.

56. Though he seemed destined to sit out the war, Sherman's career was salvaged by military patrons. He showed visible signs of stress, and Halleck intervened with the War Department to get the exhausted general twenty days' leave to recover. While Halleck did his best to reassure Sherman that his problem was solely exhaustion, he warned the Union commanding generals that "in his present condition it would be dangerous to give

[Sherman] a command here" (Halleck to McClellan, December 2, 1861, OR, series 1, vol. 52, part 1, 198). Once granted a rest, Sherman's fate became linked to a new mentor and patron when he was assigned under the new department commander of West Tennessee, Ulysses S. Grant. Halleck thus saved the future commanding general of the U.S. Army and gave him a chance in the West to redeem his reputation and career, based on a bond from their days at the Military Academy and their experiences in California.

57. Frémont's Proclamation, August 30, 1861, OR, series 1, vol. 3, 466–467. Lincoln's reaction to Frémont's antislavery proclamation is in Lincoln to Frémont, September 2, 1861, OR, series 1, vol. 3, 469–470. The political damage it caused is recounted in Donald, *Lincoln*, 314–317, 363, 479.

58. Letter from Halleck to McClellan, December 10, 1861, Halleck Papers, "Generals' Papers," RG 94, National Archives.

59. Even Confederate president Jefferson Davis, no fan of any Union officer, remarked on Halleck's arrival in St. Louis and warned the Southern commander in Missouri that a professional military officer had arrived to oppose their efforts. Because of the replacement by Lincoln of the political general John C. Frémont with the career soldier Henry Halleck, Davis cautioned General Price, "The federal forces are not hereafter, as heretofore, to be commanded by 'path-finders' and holiday soldiers, but by men of military education and experience in war: the contest [in the West] is therefore to be on a scale of very different proportions than that of the partisan warfare witnessed during the past summer and fall." Davis feared that Halleck's presence signaled a change in the nature of the struggle into a more conventional military contest, because with his assignment would come military order, troop discipline, and the formation of a victorious Union army in the West. Jefferson Davis, *The Papers of Jefferson Davis*, vol. 7, *1861*, ed. Lynda Crist and Mary Dix (Baton Rouge: Louisiana State University Press, 1992), 433–434.

60. Letter from Halleck to Frémont, November 23, 1861, Halleck's Papers, entry 2571, RG 393, National Archives.

61. *The Rebellion Record*, vol. 3, doc. 430–431.

62. Examples of the long series of these messages can be seen in OR, series 1, vol. 8, 378 (militia organization); 379–380 (railroad protection); 382–383 (paymaster system); 389, 394 (militia command); 380–381, 382, 389, 402–403 (supply problems); 401–402 (board to coordinate defense of St. Louis); and 405–407 (military law and order).

63. Halleck to McClellan, November 28, 1861, ibid., 389–391.

64. Evidence of this trend in communication fills Halleck's reports for November 1861 through February 1862; Halleck's Papers, "Generals' Papers," RG 94, National Archives. When Halleck came across subordinates who demonstrated talent in these endeavors, he was quick to commend them. An example was a former quartermaster by the name of Philip Sheridan who Halleck enthusiastically recommended for a jump to brigadier general; Halleck to Stanton, July 1, 1862, OR, series 1, vol. 17, part 2, 76.

65. Halleck to Lincoln, January 1, 1862, OR, series 1, vol. 7, 526.

66. Halleck to Lincoln, January 6, 1862, ibid., 532–533.

67. Halleck to McClellan, December 6, 1861, Halleck's Papers, "Generals' Papers," RG 94, National Archives.

68. Halleck to McClellan, January 8, 1862, OR, series 1, vol. 8, 389–391. McClellan shared this opinion of the value of West Pointers to be trained staff officers, even to

the point of suggesting that the Corps of Cadets be enlarged. This measure was very quickly defeated by Congress in January 1862. See George B. McClellan, *The Civil War Papers of George B. McClellan: Selected Correspondence, 1860–1865*, ed. Stephen W. Sears (New York: Ticknor and Friends, 1989), 133–134.

69. Sherman to William Dennison, November 6, 1861, *Sherman's Civil War*, 156–157.

70. Telegram from Stanton to Halleck, February 21, 1862, OR, series 1, vol. 7, 648. To some of the citizens of St. Louis who had bridled at Frémont's command, this result occurred because Halleck was "free from political favoritism," which allowed him to consolidate volunteers into an army ready for active campaigning after only a handful of months; from a letter from the "prominent citizens of St. Louis," February 28, 1862, Halleck Papers, USMA Archives.

71. Halleck's new Department of the Mississippi was ordered in a War Department message, March 7, 1862, OR, series 1, vol. 8, 605. See also Lincoln's "President's War Order No. 3," dated March 11, 1862. *Collected Works*, 5:155.

72. Lincoln himself had selected Meigs as the quartermaster general after meeting the colonel, even over the objections of Secretary Cameron who supported Colonel Charles Thomas, the senior officer in the Quartermaster Corps, for the position; see *Collected Works*, 4:394–395.

73. The sheer scale of Meigs's contribution to the Union war effort is the topic of Russell Weigley, *Quartermaster General of the Union Army: A Biography of Montgomery C. Meigs* (New York: Alfred A. Knopf, 1969).

74. Thomas Wentworth Higginson, "Regular and Volunteer Officers," *Atlantic Monthly* 14 (September 1864): 348.

75. Morris, Hartwell, and Kuykendall, *History of the 31st Regiment Illinois Volunteers*, 19.

76. Both of these friends and future corps commanders in McClellan's army wrote the promising military star at the outbreak of the war about his plans and their availability; Fitz John Porter to McClellan, and William F. Smith to McClellan, both dated April 15, 1861, McClellan Papers, Library of Congress.

77. New Jersey governor Charles Olden wrote an example of such a request in August 1861; OR, series 3, vol. 1, 451.

78. John M. Schofield, *Forty-Six Years in the Army* (New York: Century, 1897), 34–35.

79. Scott to McClellan, May 3, 1861, OR, series 1, vol. 51, part 1, 370.

Chapter 4. Union Generals and the Test of Battle

1. Lincoln was reported to have made these comments by John Hay, *Inside Lincoln's White House: The Complete Civil War Diary of John Hay*, ed. Michael Burlington and John R. Turner Ettlinger (Carbondale: Southern Illinois University Press, 1997), 45–46.

2. In the spring of 1862, President Lincoln's confidence in his military commanders reached its nadir. He had written General Halleck and General Buell and ordered a coordinated offensive that would gain control of the Unionist areas of eastern Tennessee, a region that seemed like a military backwater to the generals but was considered vital by

the commander in chief. After he received a long reply from Halleck about how an offensive could not be waged anywhere in the near term, the president grew increasingly frustrated with his senior commanders. "It is exceedingly discouraging," Lincoln complained to Secretary of War Simon Cameron. "As everywhere else, nothing can be done" (*Collected Works*, 5:94–95).

3. Halleck issued this astute warning while informing Wright of the precarious state of Buell's assignment in Kentucky and Tennessee; Halleck to Wright, August 25, 1862, OR, series 1, vol. 16, part 2, 421.

4. Halleck to W. T. Sherman, April 29, 1864, OR, series 1, vol. 34, part 3, 332–333.

5. Fred H. Harrington, *Fighting Politician: Major General N. P. Banks* (Philadelphia: University of Pennsylvania Press, 1948), 63.

6. Evidence of this mandate was West Pointers being repeatedly called in to replace political generals when they had problems organizing their forces or when a major battle was expected: John Wool for Ben Butler at Fort Monroe, Henry Halleck for John Frémont in St. Louis, and John Pope over Nathaniel Banks, Frémont, and James Shields in the Shenandoah Valley, among other instances.

7. Butler claimed "longer and as successful service as any other major general in this war" in a letter to the secretary of war over his held-up staff appointments; Butler to Stanton, July 3, 1862, *Private and Official Correspondence*, 2:42. Not all the political generals were that confident in their inherent leadership ability; for a strong contrast, see Lew Wallace's autobiography, wherein he attempts to turn down an appointment to brigadier general, claiming, "I don't know anything about the duties of a brigadier-general." Yet it did not take more than two minutes for the governor to convince Wallace that he was as prepared as any man "who is willing to admit that he don't know it all" (*Lew Wallace: An Autobiography*, 1:342–344).

8. Butler, *Butler's Book*, 1034–1036. Early in the war, Halleck's ambition and confidence were rivaled only by that of Butler and other ex-politicians. In February 1862, Halleck was bold enough to repeatedly ask for command of all the West, presenting the justification that "I ask this in return for Forts Henry and Donelson" (Halleck to McClellan, February 17 and 20, 1862, OR, series 1, vol. 7, 628, 641).

9. Butler himself hinted at this reasoning in his postwar memoir; *Butler's Book*, 267–269.

10. Montgomery Blair, who was Lincoln's postmaster general and Butler's staunchest ally on the president's cabinet, warned Butler against a premature offensive before his manpower was increased and his green regiments trained. He warned Butler not to risk a battle, because Butler's political enemies and General Scott would use any defeat as an excuse to remove the popular general; Blair to Butler, June 1, 1861, Butler, *Private and Official Correspondence*, 1:125–130. Rejecting the advice, Butler, feeling pressure from the cries of "On to Richmond" that were prevalent in the press and the capital, decided to attack on June 10; *Butler's Book*, 267.

11. Butler's formal report to Scott on the battle is reprinted in *The Rebellion Record*, vol. 1, doc. 244. His much more biased account is recalled in *Butler's Book*, 267–275.

12. Butler's orders for the attack on Big Bethel are reprinted in *Private and Official Correspondence*, 1:132–133.

13. This practice culminated in the spring of 1864 in Butler's Army of the James, which was to a large extent an "army of amateurs." While almost 80 percent of the gen-

erals in Meade's Army of the Potomac during the 1864 campaigns were either West Pointers or former regular army officers, a full 70 percent of Butler's subordinate generals were former civilians with neither of these qualifications for command. This concept is the premise of Edward G. Longacre, *Army of Amateurs: General Benjamin F. Butler and the Army of the James, 1863–1865* (Mechanicsburg, Pa.: Stackpole Books, 1997), xi.

14. Lincoln received a letter from Governor Edwin Morgan, who stated that "the duty of disciplining undrilled troops could be most safely committed to an experienced army officer" and proposed that Butler be replaced by War of 1812 veteran General John E. Wool; Morgan to Lincoln, August 5, 1861, Lincoln, *Collected Works*, 4:478. Under this pressure, supplemented by the strong advice of General Scott, Lincoln authorized Butler's replacement, and the commanding general wasted no time in assigning Wool to train and organize the inexperienced troops at Fortress Monroe; Scott to Wool, August 8, 1861, and General Order No. 1, Department of Southeast Virginia, August 17, 1861, OR, series 1, vol. 4, 600–601.

15. But as with nearly all aspects of the ongoing military struggle against the Confederacy, the tone and slant of the newspaper reporting were directly related to the political affiliations of the editorial staff. An example of prominent negative coverage can be seen in the *New York Times*, June 12, 1861, page 1. Butler was also excused by some in the press for Big Bethel, even while they decried any delay in further attacks in order to better prepare. One newspaper concluded early in the war that "it is only by great battles . . . that this rebellion will be extinguished. So much for the lesson of Big Bethel" (*New York Daily Tribune*, June 12, 1861, page 4).

16. Banks's defeat at Cedar Mountain was especially embarrassing for the administration, as it was one of a series of losses that plagued the Union effort for the entire spring and summer of 1862, OR, series 1, vol. 12, part 2, 136–139, 145–149, 179–185.

17. David H. Strother, *A Virginia Yankee in the Civil War: The Diary of David Hunter Strother*, ed. Cecil Eby Jr. (Chapel Hill: University of North Carolina Press, 1961), 42–43.

18. Banks's reports on his actions at Winchester and Cedar Mountain can be found in OR, series 1, vol. 12, part 2, 147–149, 153–157, 179. Critical contemporary analysis of the battles appeared in the August 11 and 19, 1862, issues of the *New York Tribune*. The news reporters (or their more partisan editors) appeared to share the frustration of the Lincoln administration with the outcome of Banks's fights in the Shenandoah Valley. His questionable command decisions at Port Hudson are clear from his subordinates' reports on the failed assault in OR, series 1, vol. 26, part 1, 501–507, 511–512, 526–528.

19. Pope's report, August 13, 1862, OR, series 1, vol. 12, part 2, 134.

20. Strother did not detect any inherent character flaw or lack of motivation in the amateur general. It was not an absence of personal courage, according to Strother, or any lack of coolness under fire that led to Banks's inability to gain success (*A Virginia Yankee*, 57–58).

21. Banks to his wife, May 28, 1862, Banks Papers, Library of Congress.

22. Halleck to Banks, January 12, 1864, OR, series 1, vol. 34, part 2, 61; Hollandsworth, *The Life of General Nathaniel P. Banks*, 51–52.

23. George L. Andrews to his wife, August 12, 1863, Andrews Papers, Military History Institute.

24. Strother, *A Virginia Yankee*, 158. Hollandsworth, *The Life of General Nathaniel P. Banks*, 50–51.

25. McClernand's report described Logan's conduct during the attack, November 8, 1861, OR, series 1, vol. 3, 277.

26. Logan received praise and thanks from not only his commander, General McClernand, but also from Grant himself; Grant's report, November 12, 1861, ibid., 278–282. The fight at Belmont is explored in Nathaniel C. Hughes Jr., *The Battle of Belmont: Grant Strikes South* (Chapel Hill: University of North Carolina Press, 1991), and Logan's role is highlighted in Jones, *Black Jack*, 109–117.

27. A sample of the positive depiction of Logan and the fighting at Belmont can be seen in *The Rebellion Record*, vol. 3, doc. 68–69.

28. Grant's report to Secretary of War Edwin Stanton, March 14, 1862, OR, series 1, vol. 10, part 2, 35.

29. Grant's impression of Logan's ability is in Grant, *Memoirs*, 487, and an example of the opinion held of Logan by regimental soldiers can be seen in R. L. Howard, *History of the 124th Regiment Illinois Infantry Volunteers* (Springfield, Ill.: H. W. Rokker, 1880), 159.

30. Logan's account of the January 1862 meeting with Lincoln is told in a letter from Logan to his wife, January 12, 1862, Logan Papers, Library of Congress.

31. Grant, *Memoirs*, 300. The view was no different from the White House. "Logan exhibited every day," President Lincoln's personal secretaries observed during the siege of Vicksburg, "a constantly increasing aptitude for military command and the highest soldierly qualities, not only of courage and subordination" (Nicolay and Hay, *Abraham Lincoln*, 7:136).

32. A list of the fifty major battles of the Civil War is in the table in chapter 4. Although any measure of battlefield "wins" and "losses" is, in the end, subjective in nature, a quantitative analysis of casualties and operational results does show some trends worthy of citing as evidence in arguments over the comparative effectiveness of West Pointers and amateur generals. Numbers in this analysis are originally from Thomas L. Livermore, *Numbers and Losses in the Civil War in America, 1861–1865* (Boston: Houghton, Mifflin, 1901).

33. A major problem during the war was the absence of a commonly understood doctrinal language. During the campaign leading to Second Bull Run, Irwin McDowell directed Brigadier George Bayard, the brigade commander of the cavalry screening his corps, to establish pickets to search for Stonewall Jackson. Although a West Point graduate and a veteran of frontier warfare, Bayard was puzzled at his orders from McDowell. "I have received your order to establish *estafettes* along the road," the old cavalryman replied. "That means couriers, does it not?" The puzzled brigadier highlighted this command problem when he added, "Excuse my ignorance, but I have no dictionary to see what it is" (Bayard to Colonel E. Schriver, August 7, 1862, OR, series 1, vol. 12, part 3, 541, 544–545).

34. So much of Civil War history is dominated by the powerful personalities of the famous commanders to the neglect of those who were in the background. Many military studies of the war start with the image of Irwin McDowell conducting a personal reconnaissance before First Bull Run and dwell on such famous scenes as Ulysses S. Grant and Robert E. Lee squaring off in the Wilderness. Yet, these men did not command by force of will; their staffs enabled the dissemination and execution of their orders. Staff officers played a key role in determining a commander's ability to command, and poor staff work

could cripple the most hardened and experienced army. Because of an absence of standardization and guidance on staff compositions and duties, the personal staffs of Civil War generals directly reflected the personality of their commander and were only as independent and effective as they were allowed to be. As each staff was bonded to its commander by friendship and loyalty, the personalities involved determined their effectiveness. This is the main conclusion of R. Steven Jones, *The Right Hand of Command: Use and Disuse of Personal Staffs in the Civil War* (Mechanicsburg, Pa.: Stackpole Books, 2000).

35. Grant's orders, which led to the gathering of forces, a quick victory, and a disorganized withdrawal from Belmont, are condensed in his own report from the battle, November 17, 1862, OR, series 1, vol. 3, 267–273. The most recent scholarly study of his first action is Hughes, *The Battle of Belmont*. Grant also saw little need to inform his subordinate commanders when he fundamentally changed their mission from a demonstration on Columbus to a raid on the Confederate camp at Belmont. His aggressive and almost reckless planning and conduct of the raid are detailed in his own words in *The Papers of Ulysses S. Grant*, ed. John Y. Simon, 15 vols. (Carbondale: Southern Illinois University Press, 1982), 3:114, 143–152, 271. Also see Hughes, *The Battle of Belmont*, 50–55.

36. Grant openly admitted this behavior in his subordinates but blamed it solely on their lack of tactical experience; *Memoirs*, 139–141.

37. The twenty thousand killed and wounded at Shiloh were five times the casualties of First Bull Run that had so shocked the nation.

38. OR, series 1, vol. 10, part 1, 108–111 (Grant's report, April 9, 1862), 248–254 (Sherman's report, April 10, 1862), 277–280 (Prentiss's report, November 17, 1862).

39. Grant, *Memoirs*, 185.

40. Although some generals displayed flashes of superb skill and leadership, there was little correlation between the source of a commander's appointment and his performance. Two of the anchors of this defensive line were Generals Sherman and McClernand, as each directed, inspired, rallied, and cajoled his troops to punish the Confederates for every yard the Union line was pushed back. In sharp contrast to Buell's slow movement and Wallace's amateur performance, General Benjamin Prentiss heroically followed Grant's orders to hold at all costs, and his division's determined resistance gave Grant the time to organize a coherent defense. For an analysis of the performance of Grant's subordinates, see *Memoirs*, 186–191, and James L. McDonough, *Shiloh—In Hell before Night* (Knoxville: University of Tennessee Press, 1997), 170–175.

41. Grant piled criticism on Lew Wallace; Grant to Assistant Adjutant General J. C. Kelton, April 13, 1863, and W. R. Rowley to John Rawlins, April 4, 1863, OR, series 1, vol. 10, part 1, 178–180.

42. Grant's efforts to summon reinforcements from across the river were numerous; Grant to Buell (two messages) and to Buell's division commanders, T. J. Wood (two), William Nelson (three), and George Thomas (three), all April 6, 1862, OR, series 1, vol. 10, part 2, 94–96.

43. Halleck also stated that his presence would help remedy these problems; letter of April 14, 1862, in James G. Wilson, "Types and Traditions of the Old Army II: General Halleck—A Memoir," *Journal of the Military Service Institution of the United States* 36 (1905): 556.

44. Grant, *Memoirs*, 185–191, Sherman, *Memoirs*, 1:244–247.

45. Grant, *Memoirs*, 191. Though cognizant of the mixed performance of his generals at Shiloh, President Lincoln was satisfied with the leadership, determination, and aggressiveness shown there. In the capital, Shiloh inspired a firestorm of criticism from newspapers and politicians over Grant's failure to entrench, his initial surprise, and the heavy casualties that resulted. But when combined with the capture of Fort Donelson, Island Number 10, Memphis, and Nashville and the fall of Corinth the following month, Lincoln was pleased with the results of Shiloh, which led to promotions for both the West Pointers and the political generals who tasted victory there.

46. Burnside's report of the Fredericksburg Campaign is in OR, series 1, vol. 21, 78–97.

47. Burnside to W. Cullums, December 19, 1862, Burnside Papers, Rhode Island Historical Society.

48. Burnside was actually one of the youngest men in the upper ranks of the Army of the Potomac: all three grand division commanders were his seniors (Sumner, in fact, was an officer long before Burnside was born), four of six corps commanders had preceded him at West Point, one corps commander was a classmate with higher class rank, and two-thirds of his division commanders had also graduated before him. These generals, many veterans of the Mexican War and long stints in the regular army, were being asked to follow a younger man who had a grand total of five years of regular army service. See William Marvel, *Burnside* (Chapel Hill: University of North Carolina Press, 1991), 171. Before the battle, Burnside had held a conference on December 9 with his wing and corps commanders, and they all agreed to the plan for the battle, though some argued afterward that they had done so reluctantly. None had stepped forward to call the plan doomed, as many would later claim. Within a week of the defeat, General Edwin Sumner, commanding Burnside's right grand division, told an investigating congressional committee that supporting his commander's plan was the correct thing to do, since even after the repulse he believed the Confederate works could be taken. William Marvel, "Ambrose Burnside," in *The Fredericksburg Campaign: Decision on the Rappahannock*, ed. Gary W. Gallagher (Chapel Hill: University of North Carolina Press, 1995), 6.

49. Many of the tactical problems of the Union assault at Fredericksburg, along with the mishap with the late pontoons, revealed the absence of the trained staff officers and doctrine necessary for coordinating such a vast undertaking. The Union effort at Fredericksburg was in many ways unprecedented, an opposed river crossing followed by military operations in urban terrain, with little for commanders to draw on. Burnside only had his attack across the Rohrbach Bridge at Antietam to look back upon, and the lessons from that success, of assaulting the enemy head-on and feeding units into the fight, proved more harmful than helpful in this larger operation. An interpretation that goes to great lengths to shift the blame from Burnside's shoulders can be found in Marvel, *Burnside*, 176–183.

50. Burnside announced his intent to meet the enemy once more, claiming "the auspicious moment seems to have arrived to strike a great and mortal blow to the rebellion, and gain that decisive victory which is due to the country" (General Order No. 7, January 20, 1862, OR, series 1, vol. 21, 127). Burnside's report from January 21, 1862, on the "Mud March" is in ibid., 752.

51. That means West Pointers commanded the Union side in 88 percent of the

major battles, while political generals held the command position in only 12 percent. The major battles are determined as the fifty American Civil War battles with over ten thousand troops engaged on both sides; Livermore, *Numbers and Losses in the Civil War in America*, 140–141. A list of these major battles is in the table in chapter 4.

52. This record can be compared to two wins (33%) and four losses (66%) for the six battles commanded by political generals. An analysis of the fifty major battles of the Civil War is in the table in chapter 4.

53. The comparison of battlefield results and experience level of the Union commanders shows a clear trend:

	West Point generals		Political generals
Results	*Average no. of previous battles*	*Results*	*Average no. of previous battles*
Win	5.1	Win	2.0
Draw	4.7	Draw	N/A
Loss	4.1	Loss	1.0

A detailed analysis of the experience level of Civil War commanders is in the table in chapter 4.

54. The average number of previous battles for West Point graduates was 4.7 versus only 1.3 for amateur commanders. See the detailed analysis in the table in chapter 4.

55. The best explanation may be the idea of military "expertise" from Samuel Huntington, *The Soldier and the State*, 8–9, 11–12, who considered this attribute one of the requirements defining a military professional. He proposed that a distinct sphere of military competence exists for army officers, its purpose to be successful in maintaining an army in the field and in combat. Focusing on the military aspect of an armed struggle, Huntington defined the duties of military commanders as using this ability to organize, equip, and train military forces, plan military operations, and direct operations in and out of combat.

56. The letter was written on March 3, on the heels of the victories at Henry-Donelson. All the appointments were made and approved by the Senate. Lincoln, *Collected Works*, 5:142.

57. The formation of the prominent interpretation of the defeat at Second Bull Run and McDowell's fate reveals the impact that the Joint Committee on the Conduct of the War could have on an individual general's career. The record of McDowell's Court of Inquiry is in OR, series 1, vol. 15, 36–332.

58. Lincoln may have taken a shine to the boastful young general, not only for his bold talk and aggressiveness but also for Pope's antislavery Republican background and the influence of his patron on the cabinet, Secretary Chase. After winning at Island Number 10 on the Mississippi, Pope came east right before the Seven Days' Battles and had served as a military aide and confidant to the president during this frustrating period. An interpretation of these events that is very favorable to Pope can be found in Wallace J. Schutz and Walter Trenerry, *Abandoned by Lincoln: A Military Biography of General John Pope* (Champaign: University of Illinois Press, 1990).

59. Pope magnified his troubles by attempting to shift the responsibility for his own errors of judgment onto others, who naturally fought back with countercharges and insinuations. His first reaction to the defeat at Second Bull Run was to blame McClellan

and his "clique" and urge an immediate court-martial for Porter and William Franklin for failing to obey orders to assist the hard-pressed Army of Virginia. Yet, Pope accurately foresaw the fate of his supposed nemesis when he prophesied to Halleck on September 30, "McClellan will inevitably be set aside. I know of nothing conceivable that can prevent it before many months go by" (OR, series 1, vol. 12, 820–824).

60. Halleck and Pope exchanged correspondence concerning Pope's fate and the return of McClellan to field command. Pope to Halleck, September 3, 1862; Halleck to Pope, September 3, 1862; Pope to Halleck (two letters), September 5, 1862; Halleck to Pope, September 5, 1862, all in OR, series 1, vol. 12, part 3, 808–809, 811–813.

61. In a moment of extreme frustration over the situation, Halleck complained to Pope that "the differences and ill-feeling among the [Union] generals are very embarrassing to the administration, and unless checked will ruin the country. It must cease. . . . We must all act together or we shall accomplish nothing, but be utterly disgraced" (Halleck to Pope, September 5, 1862, OR, series 1, vol. 12, 812–813). Regardless of efforts to stop this clash of personalities and ambitions, the infighting would continue, damaging the war effort as well as the administration's faith in its military commanders.

62. Looking at the quantitative relationship between battlefield results and the fate of the commander (an admittedly objective use of subjective data), a clear link appears. For the forty-four major battles of the Civil War commanded on the Union side by West Pointers, the following table depicts the operational results of the battle and the administration's action taken against the commander:

	Battlefield result		
Union commander's fate	Win	Draw	Loss
Commander promoted	8	0	0
No change for commander	17	3	10
Commander relieved	0	0	6

These results strongly indicate a direct linkage between wins and promotions and defeats and reliefs. A complete listing of battles, results, and commanders' fates is in the table in chapter 4.

63. Grant, *Memoirs*, 231, 301.

64. Even Sherman, who originally opposed Grant's refusal to fall back and start again from supply bases in Memphis, admitted that many were "raising a clamor" for Grant's relief based on the apparent stalemate of the drive on Vicksburg; *Memoirs*, 1:314–315. Though there is no direct evidence that this conservative operational strategy would have immediately resulted in Grant's firing, the fate of various unsuccessful Union commanders during 1862 makes it a strong possibility.

65. The quote is from Brooks D. Simpson, *Ulysses S. Grant: Triumph over Adversity, 1822–1865* (New York: Houghton Mifflin, 2000), 215. Lincoln also heaped praise on Grant even before the surrender of the Vicksburg garrison, calling Grant's campaign "one of the most brilliant in the world" (Lincoln to N. Isaac, marked "private and Confidential," May 26, 1863, *Collected Works*, 6:230).

66. Lincoln to Gamble, May 14, 1863, *Collected Works*, 6:218, 234.

67. Lincoln sent this justification in a letter to John Schofield, telling the newly appointed Department of Missouri commander that he did not need to follow the poli-

cies of either Gamble or Curtis and warning him to "exercise your own judgment, and do *right* for the public interest" (Lincoln to Schofield, May 27, 1863, *Collected Works*, 6:234).

68. Banks received this attention from the *Chicago Tribune* as late as November 4, 1862. McClernand, with just as weak a tactical record, would be depicted as a great field commander right up until his relief by General Grant. Examples appear on the second page of the November 4 and December 27, 1862, editions of the *Chicago Tribune*, which also praised McClernand for the "steady and unswerving support he has given to the administration and to the war."

69. Pope's report on Cedar Mountain, August 13, 1862, OR, series 1, vol. 12, part 2, 133–135; Halleck to Pope, August 14, 1862, ibid., 135.

70. After being beaten in the Shenandoah Valley and seeing the constant friction and infighting among the Union generals, Banks complained to his wife, "I have no doubt that I am the only officer who has not bothered [the President and Secretary of War] with complaints—There are very few of our people who know how to do their duty without grumbling—I am very glad I did mine—no withstanding the constant advice given me to resign and to make a row, and that given by the regular army officers" (letters to his wife, June 7 and 22, 1862, Banks Papers, Library of Congress).

71. Banks recounted this harrowing experience to his wife in a letter dated August 16, 1862, Banks Papers, Library of Congress.

72. Ben Butler was also judged by a standard that did not stress his tactical record, as his performance showed the dangers of military amateurism in a way very similar to Banks's. Even when political pressure forced Lincoln to remove Butler from command of the Department of the Gulf, the Massachusetts volunteer major general continued to receive commands based on his political mandate and the benefits the administration obtained from his support. After he was relieved from his command in Louisiana, Lincoln informed Stanton that the popular politician needed to be returned to department command, warning that "we can no longer dispense with General Butler's services" (Lincoln to Stanton, written in the White House on January 23, 1863, OR, series 1, vol. 53, 547). That Butler had demonstrated little ability to command troops in the field had no bearing on the president's continued dependence on the Massachusetts general. Butler bounced between his home state and the capital supporting the administration with his political skills until November 1863, when he returned to Fort Monroe as the commander of the Department of Virginia and North Carolina.

73. In sharp contrast to the seemingly direct link between operational results and the administration's action against West Point commanders, there is no apparent connection for the six major battles commanded on the Union side by amateur generals:

Battlefield result

Political general's fate	Win	Draw	Loss
Commander promoted	0	0	0
No change for commander	2	0	3
Commander relieved	0	0	1

A complete listing of the battles, results, and commander's fates is in the table in chapter 4.

74. The only other former regular on the list was Charles F. Smith, and his career was also cut short in 1862, but not by the Lincoln administration. During the drive on Corinth after Shiloh, Smith developed an infection and died at Grant's headquarters in late April 1862.

75. Sherman, *Memoirs*, 1:182.

76. Halleck to Wright, August 25, 1862, OR, series 1, vol. 16, part 2, 421.

77. January 20, 1862, letter from Halleck, then department commander in St. Louis, to McClellan, commanding general in Washington, complaining about political guidance from the capital; OR, series 1, vol. 8, 508–511.

Chapter 5. The Politics of Generalship

1. Halleck to Rosecrans, December 4, 1862, OR, series 1, vol. 20, part 2, 117–118.

2. Rosecrans to Halleck, December 4, 1862, ibid., 118.

3. If General McClellan had no offensive plans for the Army of the Potomac, the president informed the gathered division commanders, he would like to "borrow it" and employ it against the Confederates. This story and Lincoln's growing frustration with McClellan are recounted in Donald, *Lincoln*, 329–331.

4. When Secretary of War Stanton returned with the president from meeting with McClellan and his senior commanders on the issue of how to conduct the campaign, the secretary of war blasted the state of Union generalship in the Army of the Potomac with the comment, "We saw ten generals afraid to fight." This report on the meeting was given by Stanton to Lincoln's secretary, John Hay; see Hay, *Inside Lincoln's White House*, 35.

5. Lincoln, *Collected Works*, 5:149–150.

6. The generals selected were not the most senior, nor were they McClellan's choices—he would have preferred his confidants William Franklin and Fitz John Porter—nor were they based completely on advice from Winfield Scott, as the commanding general would have opposed the appointment of the amateur Banks.

7. Hay, *Inside Lincoln's White House*, 35. Three days later, Lincoln indicated his distress over the continued lack of action from the Army of the Potomac. He relieved McClellan from duties as commanding general so he could concentrate on the planned offensive campaign. The actual orders just specified that McClellan was relieved as commanding general but remained commander of the Department (and Army) of the Potomac. In an early draft of "President's War Order No. 3," Stanton was even more open in giving the reason for McClellan's demotion: he was to "devote his attention exclusively to the operations of the Army of the Potomac" in hopes that such activity would encourage a more aggressive campaign in Virginia. "President's War Order No. 3," March 11, 1862, Lincoln, *Collected Works*, 5:155–158.

8. Mark Grimsley, *The Hard Hand of War: Union Military Policy toward Southern Civilians, 1861–1865* (Cambridge: Cambridge University Press, 1995), 67–68, details both the inherent conservatism in early Union strategy and the reaction to it from the government and the public.

9. T. Harry Williams, "The Attack upon West Point during the Civil War," *Mississippi Valley Historical Review* 25 (March 1939): 503.

10. Halleck repeatedly communicated warnings of Confederate strengths and claims

of his progress; Halleck to Stanton, almost daily from April 29 to June 9, 1862, OR, series 1, vol. 10, part 1, 664–671.

11. Quote is from a letter from Halleck to his wife, in Wilson, "General Halleck— A Memoir," 549. See also Stephen E. Ambrose, *Halleck: Lincoln's Chief of Staff* (Baton Rouge: Louisiana State University Press, 1990), 46–48.

12. Gathered at Pittsburg Landing were four future generals in chief of the U.S. Army: Halleck, Grant, Sherman, and a young captain named Philip Sheridan; added to this group were five other present or future army commanders: Buell, Pope, Rosecrans, George H. Thomas, and James B. McPherson. McPherson, *Battle Cry of Freedom*, 416.

13. Each of his talented and aggressive subordinates was told by Halleck to avoid bringing on an engagement and, "in so many words," that it would be better to retreat than to risk battle. Grant, *Memoirs*, 194–196.

14. By May 18, Halleck reported to Stanton that his forces were deployed within two miles of the Confederate trenches, and that "the enemy is apparently waiting our attack upon his works" (Halleck to Stanton, May 18, 1862, reproduced in the Robert Todd Lincoln Collection of the Papers of Abraham Lincoln).

15. Halleck proudly reported that the enemy had fled and had abandoned arms and destroyed stores in his haste to escape; Halleck to Stanton, May 30, 1862, OR, series 1, vol. 10, part 1, 668.

16. Logan, *The Volunteer Soldier of America*, 662.

17. *Chicago Tribune*, June 2, 1862.

18. Stanton to Halleck, July 11, 1862, Lincoln to Halleck, July 14, 1862, OR, series 1, vol. 11, part 3, 314, 321. With his demonstrated organizational skills and background of military study, Halleck appeared the obvious choice to conduct war on so massive a scale, so on July 11 Lincoln appointed him to take over the military direction of the war. Indeed, from a long-range perspective, Halleck had great success in the spring of 1862, cracked the Confederate defensive line in Tennessee, and pushed the war all the way to Mississippi. Lincoln turned to him because of the advice of retired General Winfield Scott, though Lincoln denied the obvious linkage between his visit to Scott at West Point and his immediate command changes during remarks to a Jersey City rally on June 24, 1862; *Collected Works*, 5:284.

19. Halleck to Buell, October 23, 1862, OR, series 1, vol. 16, part 2, 421, 638.

20. Halleck was also fearful that a politically appointed amateur might be named to replace Buell. Warning of "outside applicants for command who are now urging their claims," he worried that "not one of these applicants, so far as I have learned their names, is competent to command a single division, much less a geographical department" (Halleck to Buell, August 12, 1862, OR, series 1, vol. 16, part 2, 314–315).

21. Lincoln to Buell, January 6, 1862, *Collected Works*, 5:90–91.

22. The governor of Indiana telegraphed the president, claiming that Buell's failure to act raised the twin political poisons of distrust for the administration and despair for military success that could ruin the party's chances in the upcoming election; O. P. Morton to Lincoln, October 21, 1862, OR, series 1, vol. 16, part 2, 634. The governor of Ohio was even more blunt, claiming that "with one voice the army from Ohio demands the removal of General Buell" (David Todd to Stanton, October 30, 1862, OR, series 1, vol. 16, part 2, 652).

23. Buell to Halleck, October 22, 1862, OR, series 1, vol. 16, part 2, 636–642.

24. Halleck to Horatio Wright, August 25, 1862, ibid., 421.

25. McClellan even bragged of this trait to General Scott's adjutant very early in the war by writing, "Say to the General too that I am trying to follow a lesson long ago learned from him—i.e.—not to move until I know that everything is ready and then to move with the utmost promptness" (July 5, 1861, *The Civil War Papers of George B. McClellan,* 44–45). Yet, for McClellan, everything was never completely ready.

26. Initially appointed as Scott's replacement as general in chief with the full confidence of the administration, McClellan formed the Army of the Potomac and deserves some of the credit for its later accomplishments. After Pope's disaster at Second Bull Run, Lincoln went against the wishes of his cabinet and many influential Republicans and reluctantly reinstated McClellan as field commander. "I must have McClellan to reorganize the army and bring it out of chaos," the president told his inner circle. "McClellan has the army with him." Lincoln's motives for the reappointment of McClellan and the resistance to this move, especially from Secretary Stanton, are detailed in Donald, *Lincoln,* 370–373.

27. Lincoln to McClellan, October 13, 1862, OR, series 1, vol. 21, 97–99.

28. McClellan may not have realized it, but during the month of October he was undergoing a test of his resolve and aggressiveness. Lincoln actually had hopes for an offensive by the Army of the Potomac before the weather turned poor but soon began receiving all too familiar messages from its commander. The president could not stomach the ensuing delay, and when he received a letter from the general complaining of insufficient cavalry, he signaled back his disgust. "I have just read your dispatches about sore-tongued and fatigued horses," Lincoln replied tersely. "Will you pardon me for asking what the horses of your army have done since the battle of Antietam that fatigue anything" (Lincoln to McClellan, October 24, 1862, *Collected Works,* 5:474).

29. According to *McClellan's Own Story,* 654–655, Lincoln was very happy with his generalship, with the only complaint being that the general insisted on having everything prepared before he proceeded and the president constantly wanting an immediate movement.

30. As these factors reveal, a professional officer corps divorced from partisan politics simply did not exist during the Civil War. The view that a professional officer corps emerged only after the Civil War, espoused by Allan R. Millett and Samuel Huntington, has been challenged by William Skelton, *An American Profession of Arms,* 282–290, who sees the emergence of professional military officers prior to the Civil War. But even Skelton, while presenting his belief that antebellum officers shunned politicians, acknowledges their partisan involvement in politics and agrees that they were not an apolitical tool of the policymakers.

31. Halleck to Rosecrans, December 5, 1862, OR, series 1, vol. 20, part 2, 123–124.

32. Ibid.

33. Rosecrans's sense of frustration comes through clearly in his closing comment: "I have but one word to add, which is, that I need no other stimulus to make me do my duty than the knowledge of what it is. To threats of removal or the like I must be permitted to say that I am insensible" (Rosecrans to Halleck, December 4, 1862, ibid., 118).

34. Prior to First Bull Run, Lincoln told an apprehensive General McDowell not to be concerned about the untrained and undisciplined nature of his troops. "You are green, it is true, but they are green also; you are all green alike," said the president, unconvinced

of the difficulty in waging an offensive campaign with new troops and inexperienced officers. Williams, *Lincoln and His Generals*, 21.

35. Halleck to Lincoln, January 6, 1862, OR, series 1, vol. 7, 532–533.

36. Lincoln to McClellan, October 13, 1862, OR, series 1, vol. 21, 97.

37. Halleck to Buell, October 19, 1862, OR, series 1, vol. 16, part 2, 421, 626.

38. Donald, *Lincoln*, 429.

39. In March 1862, McClellan went on to tell the president that, although cautious and unready to actively campaign, "no one is more anxious to terminate speedily this fratricidal war than I am" (*The Civil War Papers of George B. McClellan*, 133–134).

40. William E. Smith, *The Francis Preston Blair Family in Politics* (New York: Macmillan, 1922), 2:144–145.

41. Further evidence of this connectedness was the selection of their replacements, West Pointers William Rosecrans and Ambrose Burnside. Lincoln believed that these two Union generals were good choices as field commanders, as they both fit two important political criteria: each had demonstrated that he was generally in favor of the president's policies, and both were believed to be politically neutral. Donald, *Lincoln*, 390.

42. Williams, "The Attack upon West Point during the Civil War," 499.

43. Ibid., 503. A more reasoned and balanced challenge to the value of West Point was made by Ohio politician and volunteer major general Jacob Cox; see his *Military Reminiscences*, 178–191.

44. Halleck constantly blamed the lack of success in the war on political interference and grew more charged in his discourse that political generals were to blame. A notable example of this rhetoric can be seen in a letter from Halleck to McClellan, January 20, 1862, OR, series 1, vol. 8, 508–511.

45. Letter from Butler to Sarah Butler, August 11, 1861, *Private and Official Correspondence*, 1:208–209. Butler wrote three days later that "I think there will be a fight in Washington" that would determine his fate. He in no way referred to a military battle with the Confederates; ibid., 215.

46. Letter from Butler to Wade, February 13, 1862, ibid., 353–354.

47. How much his former political opponent Simon Chase approved of Butler's political flexibility and support are apparent in a June 1862 letter from him to Butler. Chase ends his letter filled with political calculations and conniving with the praise, "Meanwhile, my dear general, I trust you will so proceed as you [have] begun" (OR, series 3, vol. 2, 173–174).

48. Butler concluded his November 12, 1862, letter with the statement, "Although we differ in politics, we are both bent upon doing the best for the country, and I have no hesitation therefore in asking your aid" (*Private and Official Correspondence*, 2:465–466).

49. Blair went on to claim, "This war will last forever if something does not happen to unseat old [General Winfield] Scott" (letter from Blair to Butler, June 8, 1861, in ibid., 1:116–117).

50. Butler to Lincoln, November 29, 1862, ibid., 2:512–514.

51. The reaction of the secretary of war is recounted in Benjamin P. Thomas and Harold Hyman, *Stanton: The Life and Times of Lincoln's Secretary of War* (New York: Alfred A. Knopf, 1962), 242–243.

52. Letter from Butler to Cameron, July 30, 1861, *Private and Official Correspondence*, 1:185–188.

53. In this instance he was addressing Simon Cameron's "namby pamby" reply on the issue of runaway slaves; letter from Butler to Sarah Butler, August 14, 1861, ibid., 1:185–188.

54. Political generals, with their background in the dynamics of political support and changing coalitions, were willing to cultivate patrons in the administration and work to make them happy. Butler would even enlist the aid of a political rival, and, at times, bitter opponent, if it would advance his policies or his military stature. He even appealed to Secretary of State William Seward, who he would later hold responsible for his relief at New Orleans, to intervene in a long-running battle with Massachusetts governor Andrew, asking, "Shall I rely upon your friendly intervention if necessary to prevent any orders which shall embarrass me?" Secretary Seward replied three days later, informing Butler that "your wishes . . . will be attended to with the utmost care" (letters from October 15 and October 18, 1861, ibid., 1:253–254). Butler was confident that in Secretary of War Edwin Stanton, a fellow Democrat turned radical, he had "an old political and personal friend of mine." Less than a week later, he was citing the importance of this friendship, when Stanton "had done all and more than I could ask of him" in supporting Butler's planned expedition against New Orleans against "Intrigues, petty malice, and a jealousy" from a group of regular officers led by McClellan. Butler claimed in January 1862, "Were it not for the Sec. of War I should have gone to the dogs" (letters from Butler to Sarah Butler, January 21 and January 26, 1862, ibid., 1:323, 330–331).

55. Butler was very confident about his own political skills, regardless of his absence of military experience or formal training, claiming after the war, "There was but one ear in Washington that was always open to me, the President's" (*Butler's Book*, 325).

56. Letter from Lincoln to Orville H. Browning, September 22, 1862, *Collected Works*, 4:531.

57. Butler even went as far as publishing his views on military operations while the war was ongoing in a pamphlet, *Character and Results of the War: How to Prosecute It and How to End It—A Thrilling and Eloquent Speech* (New York: W. C. Bryant, 1863).

58. On June 26, Grant complained to Lorenzo Thomas, the adjutant general of the Union army, that the president asked him to tolerate McClernand long after he thought his removal was justified. "It was only when almost the entire army under my command seemed to demand it was [McClernand] relieved," Grant stated; OR, series 1, vol. 24, part 1, 158–159. See also Lincoln, *Collected Works*, 6:380.

59. As this clash demonstrated, Grant had little tolerance for personal ambition or disruptive behavior in his subordinates, or for any conduct that retarded the war effort; Lincoln to McClernand, August 12, 1863, *Collected Works*, 6:383.

60. Letter from Butler to Phelps, August 5, 1862, *Private and Official Correspondence*, 2:154–155. Ironically, it was Butler who recruited Phelps and who recommended the West Pointer for his stars. Butler's recommendation argued that Phelps should not be held back by his regular army peers based solely on his "deep religious enthusiasm upon the subject of slavery" (letter from Butler to Blair, July 23, 1861, ibid., 1:177).

61. Butler to Chase, November 14, 1862, ibid., 2:423–426.

62. This affair is recounted in ibid., 2:142–154.

63. Sears, *George B. McClellan*, 349.

64. Regardless of Burnside's original intent for the campaign, the desire to drive on Richmond and the willingness to fight the main Confederate army were conveyed in his

orders. Evidence of this intent was John Gibbon's description of a "Plan for a winter campaign" written on November 30, 1862, which was found among Burnside's papers after the war; Burnside's Papers, RG 94, National Archives. This strategy, focused on geographic objectives as opposed to the enemy army, was a common precept springing from a West Point education, shared by the majority of Burnside's regular army peers. General Montgomery Meigs told Burnside as late as December 30 to seek victory in another "great battle," claiming that "such a victory would be of incalculable value. It would place on your head the wreath of immortal glory" (OR, series 1, vol. 21, 917). Another example of this viewpoint was General E. D. Keyes's appeal in a personal letter to Senator Ira Harris that McClellan's object on the peninsula in April 1862 was the "great battle of the war," to seize Richmond. This is also an example of the political actions of many regular officers, as Keyes's intent from his language was obviously to try to influence the command arrangements in Virginia. See OR, series 1, vol. 11, part 1, 13–15.

65. Burnside's plan was approved on November 14, but the president warned his new commander that he believed success depended on moving rapidly. The warning was conveyed in a letter from Halleck to Burnside, November 14, 1862, OR, series 1, vol. 21, 84.

66. Burnside repeatedly used the need to get to Richmond to explain his intent in his orders during the Fredericksburg Campaign; see ibid., 79–101. He learned the lesson that justified the attack at Fredericksburg, as he sought to make the crossing "decisive" by driving the Army of Northern Virginia from the heights beyond the town. Burnside explained his plan to General Halleck in a December 17 letter in ibid., 66–67. He used the idea of the "shortest road to Richmond" to explain his selection of Fredericksburg as a crossing site; Burnside to Halleck, November 9, 1862, ibid., 99.

67. Only ten days after approving the campaign plan, President Lincoln was already privately complaining that his new commander of the Army of the Potomac seemed no faster than his old one; Lincoln to Carl Schurz, November 24, 1862, *Collected Works*, 5:509–510.

68. The prominent editor of the Democratic-leaning *Chicago Tribune* went as far as claiming in the December 20 edition that the defeat at Fredericksburg proved "the war is drawing toward a disastrous and disgraceful termination."

69. The somewhat biased conclusions of the Joint Committee on the Conduct of the War investigation are in U.S. Congress, *Report of the Joint Committee on the Conduct of the War*, Senate Report 108 (Washington, D.C.: Government Printing Office, 1863), 2:56–57.

70. "For the failure in the attack, I am responsible," Burnside informed Halleck in a letter a week after the battle. "That you left the whole movement in my hands, without giving me orders, makes me responsible" (Burnside's report to Halleck, December 17, 1862, OR, series 1, vol. 21, 67). This confession of responsibility was made public on December 23 when the *New York Times* published a letter from Burnside to Halleck that expressed the same theme.

71. Donald, *Lincoln*, 410–411.

72. Lincoln praised Burnside's skill and determination even after the disaster at Fredericksburg in "Congratulations to the Army of the Potomac," December 22, 1862, *Collected Works*, 6:13.

73. As an example of the harsh criticism by newspapers, the editor of the *Chicago Tribune* wrote that "the war is drawing toward a disastrous and disgraceful termination" (Donald, *Lincoln*, 399).

74. The most detailed and balanced account of the scheming involved in Burnside's command is A. Wilson Greene, "Morale, Maneuver, and Mud," in Gallagher, *The Fredericksburg Campaign*, 170–191.

75. Although Burnside was thought to dislike few people, he detested Joseph Hooker immensely by the start of the Fredericksburg Campaign. The falling out most likely started with what Burnside judged as Hooker's insubordinate behavior at South Mountain and Antietam. There also may have been an element of jealousy for the popular man dubbed "Fighting Joe" by the press. Burnside is known to have only accepted command of the Army of the Potomac after being warned that Hooker was the next in line if he refused; Marvel, *Burnside*, 111, 159–160.

76. Many on General Burnside's staff blamed a combination of general officer scheming and unfriendly news reports for the outcry in Washington for his resignation and its acceptance by Lincoln; Daniel Larned to his wife, December 16, 1862, Daniel Larned Papers, Library of Congress.

77. The brash center wing commander, stationed on the Union side of the river and denied permission to cross, had both his corps committed out from under him to the other wings of the army. Even though Hooker would soon demonstrate his own flaws all too well, he may have been a much better choice to command one of the wings that assaulted the Confederates. Although there is no direct evidence that this decision was based solely on dislike for a rival, the contemporary perception that these two commanders would strike at each other's reputations even at risks to their mission demonstrates the cancerous effect of petty jealousy and animosity between Union generals. Burnside downplayed Hooker's role in a December 17 letter to General Halleck, OR, series 1, vol. 21, 66–67.

78. Burnside to Lincoln, Burnside to Halleck, both January 5, 1863, ibid., 944–945.

79. Burnside to Lincoln, January 1, 1863, ibid., 941–942.

80. Franklin and Smith were openly critical of Burnside's leadership in this lengthy letter and went on to propose an alternate campaign strategy, presumably under a new commander. The letter is reprinted in ibid., 868–870. The reaction of the president was quick and scathing in a letter to the pair on the same day he issued an official "congratulations" to the Army of the Potomac and its commander; Lincoln to William B. Franklin and William F. Smith, December 22, 1862, *Collected Works*, 6:15.

81. Burnside's General Order No. 8 and the list of officers and charges are reprinted in OR, series 1, vol. 21, 998–999, and Lincoln, *Collected Works*, 6:74–75.

82. Burnside's report, November 13, 1865, OR, series 1, vol. 21, 96.

83. Burnside's relief order is reprinted in ibid., 1004–1005.

84. Tap, *Over Lincoln's Shoulder*, 149–166. The competing versions of the Fredericksburg Campaign and the charges being leveled against peers can be seen in the Joint Committee on the Conduct of the War testimony reprinted in OR, series 1, vol. 51, part 1, 1019–1030.

85. After being relieved of his corps command after Fredericksburg, General William Franklin went as far as having his version of the events published in a pamphlet that was very critical of both Halleck and Burnside. This public airing of the dissension over Fredericksburg continued the feuding between many of the general officers over the responsibility for the Union defeat. Halleck and Burnside's reactions can be seen in May 1863 letters between Franklin, Halleck, and Burnside, OR, series 1, vol. 21, 1006–1009.

86. Halleck's initial period as general in chief demonstrated how unprepared the Union command system was to handle warfare of this scale. Halleck was expected to direct the armies of the United States, which numbered nearly a million soldiers in over ten field armies. His task also included controlling the various military departments and bureaus that mustered in, administered, and supplied the growing Union armies. This duty demanded a flood of incoming and outgoing messages, hundreds of telegrams a week, all managed with a staff at Army Headquarters of only seven officers and sixteen enlisted men. As a result, Halleck became overwhelmed with his responsibilities during the chaotic period from Second Bull Run to Antietam. He complained in a letter to his wife dated September 2, 1862, that he was "almost worn out" from just answering all the message traffic. See Wilson, "General Halleck—A Memoir," 558.

87. Halleck's November 15, 1863, report from the Fredericksburg Campaign is in OR, series 1, vol. 21, 46–49.

88. After Burnside had met with defeat in December 1862, he requested permission to recross the river and risk another battle with the entrenched Confederates. President Lincoln received disturbing reports from some of Burnside's subordinates about the chances for success and wanted an expert's opinion on the plan. Turning to Halleck, who as a recognized theorist on warfare was expected not only to be experienced but also to have expertise, the president asked the commanding general to examine Burnside's plan and form a judgment on its chances. "Tell Gen. Burnside that you do approve, or that you do not approve his plan," Lincoln asked on the first day of 1863, warning "Old Brains" that "your military skill is useless to me if you do not do this." Halleck's reaction was frustrating to the president, as he wrote to Stanton the same day requesting to resign as general in chief because of "very important differences in opinion" with generals in the field. In frustration, Lincoln withdrew the request and refused to accept the resignation, instead smoothing Halleck's ruffled feathers by saying how much he was still needed in uniform. See Lincoln, *Collected Works*, 6:31; OR, series 1, vol. 21, 940–941.

89. This was the famous letter in which the president addressed Hooker's claim that the country needed a dictator; Lincoln to Hooker, January 23, 1863, *Collected Works*, 6:78–79.

90. Lincoln to Hooker, May 14, 1863, ibid., 217.

91. Lincoln to Burnside, January 8, 1863, OR, series 1, vol. 21, 954, and *Collected Works*, 6:46–48.

92. The president would use any method to try to get commanders to act aggressively. During the long strategic stalemate in Virginia after the Gettysburg Campaign, Lincoln tried to get General George Meade to advance and engage Lee's army in battle. If Meade would only attack Lee, the president wrote Halleck, "the honor will be his if he succeeds, and the blame may be mine if he fails." Yet, even this prodding could not get Meade to risk battle with the Army of Northern Virginia. So while Meade's job was secure in the fall of 1863 owing to the legacy of Gettysburg that gave the impression of a great victory, Lincoln still sought an aggressive commander to bring East. Lincoln to Halleck, October 16, 1863, *Collected Works*, 6:518–519.

93. This example comes from the November 10, 1862, *Chicago Tribune* editorial page under the heading "Action Is the Word."

Chapter 6. Diverging Views on Generalship

1. After taking command in the Gulf, Banks's initial communications to Halleck stressed these reconstruction tasks and revealed a higher priority on spreading political control than on conventional military operations in the field; Banks's Proclamation, December 26, 1862, OR, series 1, vol. 15, 624.

2. In sharp contrast to the bleak military situation that Halleck portrayed at the capital, Banks was optimistic about his situation and his progress in the Gulf. He assessed the political atmosphere and judged there to be no "permanent and irreconcilable elements of hostility" that would stand in the way of reconstruction and the return of federal control. To the Massachusetts politician, this estimation more than justified his prioritization of occupation efforts over active campaigning. Banks to Halleck, January 7, 1863, OR, series 1, vol. 15, 639–641.

3. Halleck to Banks, April 9, 1863, ibid., 700–701.

4. Facing a civil war over issues as explosive as secession, slavery, black enfranchisement and military service, reconstruction conditions, and occupation policies, nearly all Union generals were involved in these political issues owing to the very nature of the Union command arrangement. As an example of this diverse challenge, a survey of the nearly one hundred general orders issued by General Butler during the short time he was a department commander in New Orleans reveals the scope of his responsibilities (and power). He controlled all military matters, dictated civil policies by fiat, and acted as the regional military commander, field army commander, state governor, and city mayor all rolled into one. A box with all the original publications of Butler's general orders are in the Butler Papers, Library of Congress.

5. The exceptions to this dual command arrangement were department commanders of purely Northern regions such as John Dix, who served in New York in 1863 and 1864 as the commander of the Department of the East. The diverse challenges faced by Dix reveal how the generals in these roles had to deal with civil-military issues just as contentious, such as suspending habeas corpus, enforcing the draft, and gathering needed recruits and supplies from local and state politicians.

6. Secretary of the Navy Gideon Welles wrote in his diary after a meeting with the president and General Banks in December 1862, "Banks has some ready qualities for civil administration and if not employed in the field or active military operations will be likely to acquit himself respectively as a provisional or military governor" (*Diary of Gideon Welles: Secretary of the Navy under Lincoln and Johnson*, ed. Howard K. Beale [New York: Norton, 1960] 1:210).

7. Logan to Rawlins, July 7, 1863; Logan was officially appointed occupational commander in Special Order No. 135, July 11, 1863, OR, series 1, vol. 24, part 3, 483, 501–502.

8. Jones, *Black Jack*, 178–179.

9. Because not all the slaves had performed service that directly supported the war, Butler suggested, perhaps not all of them fully qualified to be freed as contrabands of war. However, he argued, after their owners fled and abandoned them, the slaves were legally comparable to items found after a shipwreck: property legally salvageable by the finder. Therefore, Butler contended, all proprietary relationships had ceased and the slaves were legally emancipated. His legal argument is detailed in his lengthy letter to Secretary Cameron, *Private and Official Correspondence*, 1:185–188.

10. Letter from Cameron to Butler, May 30, 1861, OR, series 3, vol. 1, 243.

11. Butler's accomplishments in the Department of the Gulf are the subject of James Parton, *General Butler in New Orleans* (Boston: Ticknor and Fields, 1866).

12. Although Sherman may have felt he was in a policy void, Congress had already forbidden army commanders to return runaway slaves—he had that much guidance. Yet, no guidance had been provided as to how to execute this policy and what to do with the deluge of "contrabands" entering Union camps near Memphis; letter from Sherman to Major John Rawlings, August 14, 1862, *Sherman's Civil War*, 275–277.

13. Stanton to Butler, June 23, 1862, in Butler, *Private and Official Correspondence*, 1:627.

14. Cameron to Butler, May 30, 1861, ibid., 1:119.

15. Letter from Blair to Butler, May 29, 1861, ibid., 1:116–117.

16. Stanton's very vague expectations of Butler in Louisiana are in a June 1862 letter in ibid., 1:185–188.

17. Senator Sumner hoped that Butler "will appreciate the sympathy and friendly interests" that were behind the letter; letter from Sumner to Butler, January 8, 1863, in Butler, *Private and Official Correspondence*, 2:570–571. President Lincoln wrote the secretary of war on January 23 stating his desire to return Butler to New Orleans. This move was never accomplished, as the administration could ill afford to please Butler at Banks's expense. The support of both was sought, and Butler was offered other commands to keep him in uniform; ibid., 587.

18. The best comprehensive study of Banks's involvement in the complex and sometime baffling political struggle in wartime Louisiana is Peyton McCrary, *Abraham Lincoln and Reconstruction: The Louisiana Experiment* (Princeton, N.J.: Princeton University Press, 1978).

19. Abraham Lincoln, *Abraham Lincoln: His Speeches and Writings*, ed. Roy P. Basler (New York: World Publishing, 1946), 714–716.

20. Banks to Halleck, January 15, 1863, OR, series 1, vol. 15, 639.

21. The political skills and allies developed by the amateur generals before the war were also harnessed to the administration because of this use of military patronage. A clear example was Banks's lobbying Congress for support for the reconstruction efforts in Louisiana while serving as commander of the Department of the Gulf. Banks became the point man for both the enactment of these policies and their defense, going as far as writing and publishing a pamphlet called *Emancipated Labor in Louisiana*. Suffering attacks from both ends of the political spectrum, Lincoln was repeatedly forced to ask Banks to come to the capital and join in the political struggle over Reconstruction. See letter from publisher J. W. Harper, February 27, 1865, Banks Papers, American Antiquarian Society.

22. How Banks's labor system worked can be seen in a typical contract printed in the *New York Herald*, February 21, 1863. The details and reasoning behind his plan for labor are explained in a February 1, 1865, report from Thomas Conway (head of the Gulf's Freeman Labor Bureau) to Major General Stephen Hurlbut (Banks's replacement as commander, Department of the Gulf); see OR, series 1, vol. 47, part 1, 703–710. Criticism of Banks's labor arrangement from the view of the regulars can be best seen in a scathing letter between two of his subordinate officers; see R. A. Cameron to Oliver Matthews, August 13, 1864, OR, series 1, vol. 41, part 2, 683–684.

23. After Butler's heavy-handed occupation, Banks attempted a policy of concilia-

tion more in line with Lincoln's hopes for eventual reconstruction. His conciliatory policy with former secessionists and foreign consuls pleased the moderates in Washington, while many of his reconstruction programs, including the establishment of an education system for the freed slaves, satisfied the radicals. See Harrington, *Fighting Politician*, 92–195.

24. Banks's running fight over Louisiana with both the radicals and the Democrats in Congress is detailed in Hollandsworth, *The Life of General Nathaniel P. Banks*, 215–228, and William C. Harris, *With Charity for All: Lincoln and the Restoration of the Union* (Louisville: University Press of Kentucky, 1997), 92–95, 112–125.

25. Lincoln to Banks, December 2, 1864, Banks Papers, Library of Congress. Banks demonstrated in Louisiana how vital the task of reconstructing occupied areas was to the administration and how it was a true test of generalship. "Your confidence in the practicability of constructing a free state-government, speedily, for Louisiana, and your zeal to accomplish it, are very gratifying. It is a connection, than in which, the words '*can*' and '*will*' were never more precious" (Lincoln to General Banks, January 13, 1864, *Collected Works*, 7:123–124).

26. "The armies of the United States came here not to destroy, but to make good," Butler assured them, "to restore order . . . and the government of laws in place of the passions of men" (General Order No. 7, April 1862, Butler Papers, Library of Congress).

27. For examples of Butler's repeated complaints concerning a lack of troops for occupation duty, see Butler to Stanton, June 1 and 17, 1862, *Private and Official Correspondence*, 1:535–539, 595–596.

28. Butler claimed to need the new troops to combat local guerrillas who were "doing infinite mischief" (Butler to Halleck, July 26, 1862, ibid., 2:111).

29. Letter from Banks to Seward, May 4, 1863, OR, series 3, vol. 3, 187–190.

30. Butler, for example, always complained about having too few troops for both garrison and field operations, a common complaint from department commanders. However, when the requested troops could not be provided, he demonstrated his view of the focus of the Union military effort by expressing a willingness to reduce his field army to support political programs and counterguerrilla efforts. An example of this predisposition is a letter from Butler to Stanton, June 10, 1862, *Private and Official Correspondence*, 1:568–570. Butler expressed this view in his memoirs, marshaling an argument for the focus on the political aspects of military occupation in terms that West Pointers like Halleck would have found detestable; *Butler's Book*, 463. Even a field commander such as Logan, while focused on tactical struggle as a corps commander, agreed with his fellow political generals that the goal must be to spread Union control; see a proclamation from Logan to his division, February 12, 1863, Logan Papers, Library of Congress.

31. McClernand spent late January 1863 attempting to convince Grant and Halleck of the importance of driving into Arkansas, a peripheral operation that promised no results other than expanding Union control. Before this matter could come to a head and bring on the by then inevitable clash between Grant and McClernand, Admiral Porter rendered the plan academic by judging the Arkansas River too shallow for Union gunboats. OR, series 1, vol. 17, part 2, 562–564, and vol. 22, part 2, 41.

32. At times, these commanders went too far even for the administration in using patronage and electoral mischief in occupied areas. While doing reconstruction work that the president sought, the politically appointed generals often used their military

powers to enforce partisan policies on the occupied populace and to create dictatorial fiefdoms ruled by patronage and control of contraband trade, especially the lucrative cotton trade. Agreeing often with the aims but not the disreputable methods, Lincoln saw both sides of the issue of "military necessity," as he demonstrated in responding to one of Butler's attempts to pass laws by proposition and bypass the existing political system in New Orleans. "Nothing justifies the suspending of the civil by the military authority, but military necessity," the president informed the general, "and of the existence of that necessity the military commander, and not the popular vote, is to decide" (letter from Lincoln to Butler, August 9, 1864, *Collected Works*, 7:487–489).

33. McClellan to Lincoln, at Harrison's Landing, July 7, 1862, *The Civil War Papers of George B. McClellan*, 344–345.

34. At the same time McClellan appeared to be seeking to restrain Union war aims and means, orders from Butler to one of his division commanders included a far different choice. Answering the question of what should be done with captured guerrillas, Butler directed, "They should be captured, tried at the drum head by Military Commission, and shot, every man; their houses burnt . . . and every means taken to show them that they are enemies of the human race." Butler offered this opinion to Brigadier T. Williams, commander at the often attacked Baton Rouge depot, in a letter dated June 12, 1862, *Private and Official Correspondence*, 1:585–586. This harsh language resembled William T. Sherman's famed tirades but predated his call for a "hard hand of war." Sherman warned Halleck late in the war that "we are not only fighting hostile armies, but a hostile people, and must make the old and young, rich and poor, feel the hard hand of war" (Sherman to Halleck, December 24, 1864, OR, series 1, vol. 54, 798–800).

35. Lincoln issued this prophetic warning in his annual message to Congress on December 3, 1861, *Collected Works*, 5:48–49.

36. See Banks's General Order No. 26, dated March 13, 1862, OR, series 1, vol. 5, 513.

37. Grimsley, *The Hard Hand of War*, 53–54.

38. This disdain was evident when Halleck was forced to address the poor discipline of Kansas state militia troops. "It appears, however, that there are some political influences connected with this matter," he complained to the secretary of war. "Not being a politician, this did not occur to me." Halleck went on to complain, "I am a little surprised, however, that politicians in Congress should be permitted to dictate the selection of officers for particular duties in this department. Under such circumstances I cannot be responsible for the results" (Halleck to Stanton, March 28, 1862, OR, series 1, vol. 8, 647–648).

39. Burnside to Halleck, May 7, 1863, Burnside Papers, Rhode Island Historical Society. The political intensity of the Vallandigham trial, and Burnside's involvement, can be best appreciated through reading one of the first published accounts from the event, a pamphlet called *The Trial of Hon. Clement L. Vallandigham by a Military Commission* (Cincinnati: Rickey and Carroll, 1863).

40. Burnside to Halleck, May 11, 1863, RG 393, National Archives. Burnside also reacted to the criticism in the press by suppressing the publication and distribution of the *Chicago Times* and the *New York World* within his department, papers that had both spoken out against Burnside for the arrest. Lincoln, *Collected Works*, 6:248, and OR, series 3, vol. 3, 252.

41. Burnside to Stanton, May 20, 1863, Burnside Papers, Rhode Island Historical Society.

42. Lincoln to Burnside, May 29, 1863, *Collected Works*, 6:237. Gideon Welles bluntly summed up his opinion by recording in his personal diary that "it was an error on the part of Burnside" (*Diary of Gideon Welles*, 1:306).

43. Lincoln to Schofield, July 13, 1863, *Collected Works*, 6:326–327.

44. General Order No. 64 (speculation in cotton), July 25, 1862; General Order No. 65 (commerce across the lines), July 28, 1862; Sherman to Rawlins (complaining of commerce distractions), July 30, 1862; General Order No. 69 (trade and coinage in Grant's department), August 6, 1862; General Order No. 68 (Grant's trade restrictions), August 11, 1862, all in OR, series 1, vol. 17, part 2, 123, 130, 141, 155.

45. General Order No. 11, December 17, 1862, ibid., 123.

46. Ulysses S. Grant, *The Papers of Ulysses S. Grant*, ed. John Y. Simon, 15 vols. (Carbondale: Southern Illinois University Press, 1989), 7:50–56.

47. Almost every correspondence during December 1861 and January 1862 addressed the issue of organizational problems and the shortage of regular officers to help the commanding general deal with them. Halleck Papers, "Generals' Papers," RG 94, National Archives.

48. A clear example was Sherman's occupation of Memphis from July through December 1862, when the corps commander found himself assigned a duty for which he had little preparation or guidance; Sherman, *Memoirs*, 1:265–266.

49. Sherman repeatedly ruled against the wishes of local politicians of all stripes; see *Memoirs*, 1:265–275, and *Sherman's Civil War*, 275–288.

50. Sherman, *Sherman's Civil War*, 258–259.

51. All of the issues that Sherman wrestled with are represented in his correspondence from this period; *Sherman's Civil War*, 255–288. The overwhelming nature of these occupation assignments was summed up in his complaint to Major John Rawlins on August 14. "It has been physically impossible to me personally to give attention to the thousands of things which had to be done here since my arrival," Sherman lamented, "and at the same time keep you fully advised of their progress" (ibid., 275). These duties could be just as challenging for those assigned in Northern states, as Burnside demonstrated in nine months during 1863 by sending over two hundred general orders from his headquarters, dealing with issues from recruiting volunteers from Kentucky to furloughs for enlisted men currently in the hospital. Burnside Papers, "Generals' Papers," RG 94, National Archives.

52. Sherman, *Memoirs*, 1:278–280.

53. Grant to Chase, July 31, 1863, OR, series 1, vol. 24, part 3, 538.

54. For Banks's priorities during the spring of 1863, see OR, series 1, vol. 15, 615, 619–621, 640, and OR, series 3, vol. 3, 187–190.

55. Letter from Sherman to John Park, the mayor of Memphis, July 27, 1862, *Sherman's Civil War*, 258–259.

56. For Burnside on the North Carolina coast in the spring of 1862, this arrangement meant that the reconstruction effort in his department would be influenced much more by the military governor, Edward Stanly, than by the commanding general. Evidence of the relationship can be seen in letters from Secretary Stanton to both Stanly and Burnside in late May 1862, OR, series 1, vol. 9, 391, 396–397. An analysis of the situation in reconstructed North Carolina is in Harris, *With Charity for All*, 59–69.

57. This issue came to a head over Burnside's appointment of "district commanders"

in Ohio and Indiana in June 1863; Halleck to Burnside, June 13, 1863, OR, series 3, vol. 3, 385.

58. The heart of Halleck's exclusion order, officially published as General Order No. 3 in St. Louis on November 20, 1861, read: "It is directed that no such persons [fugitive slaves] be hereafter permitted to enter the lines of any camp or of any force on the march, and that any now within such lines be immediately excluded therefrom" (OR, series 1, vol. 8, 370).

59. Halleck used this defense to Frank Blair, in a letter on December 8, 1861, in ibid., 248.

60. Donald, *Lincoln*, 388–389.

61. Halleck also struggled to have the war fit his understanding of the law of war, on one occasion going so far as to address his Confederate counterpart on their mutual duties "under the Laws and usages of war." An example can be seen in Halleck's letter to Major General Sterling Price in January 1862, in which he informed the Confederate commander concerning the rules of flags of truce and acts of pillaging, thievery, marauding, and other wanton destruction he deemed in violation of the laws of war; see OR, series 1, vol. 8, 529.

62. Halleck to Lincoln, January 6, 1862, OR, series 1, vol. 7, 532–533.

63. The historical precedents for such a conciliatory policy toward Southern civilians is described in Grimsley, *The Hard Hand of War*, 7–21.

64. When reminded of the administration's policy regarding colored troops, Burnside immediately wrote Lincoln. "I am satisfied from my knowledge of Kentucky that it would be very unwise to enroll free negroes of that state," the general from Rhode Island told the president. "It would not add materially to our strength, and I assure you it would cause much trouble. I sincerely hope this embarrassment to the interests of the public service will not be placed in our way" (letter from Burnside to Lincoln, June 26, 1863, OR, series 3, vol. 3, 418). With this logic, Burnside demonstrated his lack of flexibility on policy issues and his confidence in lecturing the president on political matters. Ironically, he followed this call against enlisting colored troops with a letter to the state governor the very next day pleading that more troops be recruited to repel a "threatening danger" of invasion; ibid., 420.

65. Harrison Landings letter, McClellan to Lincoln, July 7, 1862, *The Civil War Papers of George B. McClellan*, 344–345. A balanced account of the circumstances behind the letter and the reaction to it can be found in Sears, *George B. McClellan*, 226–232.

66. McClellan to his wife, September 25, 1862, McClellan Papers, Library of Congress; McClellan to William H. Aspenwall, September 26, 1862, *The Civil War Papers of George B. McClellan*, 482.

67. OR, series 1, vol. 19, part 2, 395; McClellan, *The Civil War Papers of George B. McClellan*, 493–494.

68. McClellan to Lincoln, at Harrison's Landing, July 7, 1862, *The Civil War Papers of George B. McClellan*, 344–345. McClellan's desire to avoid divisive political issues such as slavery was not new in 1862. From the start of the Civil War, his political views impacted his military outlook; in November 1861, the commanding general asked his political allies to help him limit war aims, keeping the slavery issue "incidental and subsidiary" to the Union war effort. "Help me dodge the nigger—we want nothing to do with him," he asked his friend Samuel Barlow. "I am fighting to preserve the integrity of the

Union and the power of the govt—on no other issue" (McClellan to Barlow, November 8, 1861, ibid., 127–128).

69. McClellan to Lincoln, at Harrison's Landing, July 7, 1862, ibid., 344–345.

70. Sears, *George B. McClellan*, 80–83.

71. Halleck to Stanton, June 9, 1862, OR, series 1, vol. 10, part 1, 671, and Halleck to Stanton, June 25, 1862, vol. 16, part 2, 62–63.

72. Halleck to Grant, March 31, 1863, OR, series 1, vol. 24, part 1, 18.

73. Halleck made this argument in a February 17, 1864, letter to Grant marked "confidential," dealing with various expeditions in the Gulf and on the Atlantic Coast; Halleck Papers, USMA Archives.

74. The best source on this friction between Halleck and Banks over the Vicksburg and Port Hudson Campaigns is Curt Anders, *Henry Halleck's War: A Fresh Look at Lincoln's Controversial General-in-Chief* (Carmel, Ind.: Guild Press of Indiana, 1999), 426–430.

75. Banks to Halleck, May 21, 1863, OR, series 1, vol. 24, part 1, 498–499.

76. Halleck to Banks, May 23, 1862, ibid., 500–501. Earlier in the war, Halleck had clearly expressed his opinion on the value of secondary operations in a letter to McClellan. "The division of our force upon so many lines and points seems to me a fatal policy," argued Halleck in January 1862, "these movements having been governed by political expediency and in many cases directed by politicians in order to subserve particular interests" (OR, series 1, vol. 8, 508–511).

77. Halleck to Banks, March 15, 1864, OR, series 1, vol. 34, 610. Halleck at times also offered an argument defending the need for occupation troops, but only when trying to give reasons why he could spare no troops from his department to reinforce another commander. For an example of this somewhat disingenuous logic, see his letter to Stanton on July 1, 1862, in ibid., vol. 17, part 2, 59.

78. Grant, *Memoirs*, 365–369. Willingness to abandon Arkansas was discussed in a letter from Grant to Halleck, January 1, 1865, Grant Papers, University of Arkansas Libraries.

79. Sherman, *Memoirs*, 1:265–279, and Sherman, *Sherman's Civil War*, 254–255, 275–280, 311–314.

80. Grant, *Memoirs*, 219–225.

81. When Buell and McClellan were both relieved in November 1862 and replaced by radical favorites Burnside and William Rosecrans, the time of the "kid gloves" approach to the sectional struggle seemed to be ending. The radicals in Congress hoped that this was a sign that the president intended to purge the Union high command of Democrats and problematic West Pointers. See Tap, *Over Lincoln's Shoulder*, 45–48, and Carmen and Luthin, *Lincoln and the Patronage*, 162–163. "Be patient a very little while," predicted an excited Horace Greeley in an editorial, "and all the 'augers that won't bore' will be served as Buell has been" (*New York Daily Tribune*, October 25, 1862).

82. What was welcome by politicians in Washington was the remorseless effort promised by some generals, both regular and volunteer. Yet, military leaders did not always equate such endeavors with speed and make their political allies happy. Scott's attempts to organize the army before any offensive in 1861 started the "On to Richmond" pressure, and many commanders such as Halleck and even Butler later echoed the cry. Soldiers could also be influenced by the temper of Congress and the people, decrying the

slow and methodical preparation deemed necessary by many commanders. See Butler, *Butler's Book*, 289; Sherman, *Memoirs*, 1:179.

83. An in-depth analysis of the Joint Committee's anti–West Point crusade can be found in Tap, *Over Lincoln's Shoulder*, 45–48, 60–64, and 120–128.

84. In this atmosphere, many politicians and their peers in uniform saw malevolent intent behind the military influence that West Pointers had on policy without the counterbalance of the traditional political process to vet their proposals. Although taking this belief to the extreme, Butler reflected the rhetoric of many politicians when he painted McClellan and his fellow West Pointers as agents of tyranny, a potential threat to overthrow the government. Butler was even willing to say openly that McClellan's objective in the war was to set himself up as a tyrant, a dictator placed in power by copperhead allies; see *Butler's Book*, 570–576.

85. Grant, *Memoirs*, 300.

86. Sherman wrote a long letter to Secretary Chase on August 11, 1862, describing all the policy dilemmas he faced in occupied Memphis; see *Memoirs*, 1:179.

87. Even after Grant's promotion to three stars, Butler repeatedly stressed his seniority to Lincoln and openly campaigned for the regular army major general rank available by the promotion; Butler to Lincoln, May 17, 1864, and reply dated May 18, in Lincoln, *Collected Works*, 7:346–347.

88. Lincoln to Stanton, January 23, and to Butler, January 28, *Collected Works*, 6:100. Stanton drafted an order dated February 27, 1863, placing Butler in charge of all forces in both the Departments of the Gulf and of Mississippi. The order was never issued.

89. When McClernand tried to pull the president into his clash with Halleck and Grant over control of the campaign to open the Mississippi River, Lincoln told the political general to focus on fighting the war against the Confederates. "You are now doing well—well for your country, and well for yourself," Lincoln pleaded, "much better than you could possibly be, if engaged in open war with Gen. Halleck." This sound advice went unheeded; Lincoln to McClernand, January 22, 1863, *Collected Works*, 6:70.

Chapter 7. Ulysses S. Grant and a New Faith in Military Expertise

1. Simpson, *Ulysses S. Grant*, 259–260.

2. Stanton to Grant, May 15, 1864, *The Papers of Ulysses S. Grant*, 10:436; see also OR, series 1, vol. 31, part 2, 781. Similar sentiments can be found in Stanton to Grant, July 24, 1864, OR, series 1, vol. 40, part 3, 421.

3. Halleck to Sherman, April 8, 1864, OR, series 1, vol. 32, part 3, 289. Halleck also, with apparent regret, informed Grant of the strength of Banks's political support with the administration and Congress and warned that the press in Louisiana and the East was already coming to the defense of the Massachusetts politician in reaction to rumors he would be relieved; Halleck to Grant, May 3, 1864, OR, series 1, vol. 34, part 3, 409–410.

4. Donald, *Lincoln*, 497.

5. Scott proposed this plan in June 1861; OR, series 1, vol. 51, part 1, 369–370.

6. How poorly Scott had misjudged public opinion could be seen in the immediacy and volume of cries in the capital and in newspapers for a decisive "On to Richmond"

drive. Although public sentiment appeared split in this demand for action, Lincoln himself insisted on an immediate advance to encourage Unionists in the South and the administration's supporters in the North. Grimsley, *The Hard Hand of War*, 29–31; McPherson, *Battle Cry of Freedom*, 334–336.

7. McClellan made his views clear in a letter to Buell on November 7, 1861, concerning his guidance on operations in Buell's department; *The Civil War Papers of George B. McClellan*, 125–126.

8. In early 1863, while the Union lacked a strategy for winning the war, Halleck appointed a commission that studied the legal ramifications and rules of both a conventional conflict and a civil war. The result was General Order No. 100, a lengthy document containing 157 paragraphs written by Francis Lieber that covered every conceivable legal issue of the war from prisoner paroles to the status of partisans. Though a fascinating legal document that influenced many later attempts to codify the conduct of war, it is very easy to conclude that the commanding general's time and energy could have been better spent. General Order No. 100 is reprinted in OR, series 2, vol. 5, 671–682. A far more favorable interpretation of Halleck's efforts can be found in Anders, *Henry Halleck's War*, 383–389.

9. Halleck expressed this complaint in a letter to his wife dated September 9, 1862; see Wilson, "General Halleck—A Memoir," 556.

10. Grant to Major General Frederick Steele, April 11, 1863, *The Papers of Ulysses S. Grant*, 8:49.

11. Department of the Tennessee General Order No. 25, April 22, 1863, in ibid., 3:94.

12. Grant to Halleck, April 19, 1863, ibid., 8:91–92.

13. Grant, *Memoirs*, 231, 301.

14. Over twenty-nine thousand prisoners were taken when Vicksburg fell; OR, series 1, vol. 24, part 1, 62.

15. Grant described his decisionmaking process for this unconventional tactic in *Memoirs*, 297–300. He also details the impact that he hoped the immediate paroles would have in two letters to James McPherson on July 5 and July 7, 1863, in *The Papers of Ulysses S. Grant*, 8:483 and 9:3.

16. Grant's evolution of thought and opinion on the subject can be seen in a series of personal letters in ibid., 9:23–25, 39, 110.

17. Sherman, like Grant, integrated political calculations as well as operational art into his planning. An example of this mindset was Sherman's letter to Grant dated November 2, 1864, in which he described the hoped-for effect of his March to the Sea. "I think Jeff Davis will change his tune when he finds me advancing into the heart of Georgia instead of retreating," he told Grant; OR, series 1, vol. 39, part 3, 594–595. Taking this political focus one step further, Sherman advocated targeting the Southern will to continue resistance to federal authority. Though the conduct of many of his campaigns was in ways similar to his predecessors, Sherman's operations differed in their purpose and their intended target. Rather than a military struggle to subdue armies, he saw the need to impose pressure on Southern society to make them cry "enough" (Sherman to Grant, October 4, 1862, OR, series 1, vol. 17, part 2, 261).

18. Halleck to Grant, March 31, 1863, OR, series 1, vol. 24, part 1, 18.

19. Like military amateurs such as Butler, Sherman recognized no "law of war" that

would prohibit his actions and—unlike his friend Halleck—saw war as revolutionary struggle. "I attach more importance to these deep incursions into the enemy's country, because our war differs from European wars," he realized, drawing a strong distinction from Halleck's beliefs. "We are not only fighting hostile armies, but a hostile people, and must make the old and young, rich and poor, feel the hard hand of war" (Sherman to Halleck, December 24, 1864, OR, series 1, vol. 44, 798–800).

20. Sherman to Halleck, November 6, 1864, OR, series 1, vol. 39, part 3, 658–661. Sherman had a flair for expressing this sentiment in poetic style. "War is cruelty," he warned, "and you cannot refine it" (W. T. Sherman to E. E. Rawson, September 1864, Sherman Papers, Military History Institute).

21. Long before selecting Grant as commanding general and promoting him to lieutenant general, Lincoln had identified the general as a commander who delivered victories and fought the war as he wanted it fought. This was part of a letter marked "private and confidential" to Isaac Arnold on May 26, 1863, in which Lincoln defended his selection of commanders and justified his retention of Halleck and other detested West Pointers; Lincoln, *Collected Works*, 6:230–231.

22. Grant's letters on the topic are in *The Papers of Ulysses S. Grant*, 9:124–126.

23. Grant's thoughts on the nomination can be clearly determined in his personal letters responding to questions about his willingness to run for president; see *The Papers of Ulysses S. Grant*, 9:541–544.

24. Grant, *Memoirs*, 365–370. The most recent interpretation on how Grant formed and presented his strategy for the 1864 campaigns can be seen in Simpson, *Ulysses S. Grant*, 266–270.

25. Grant, *Memoirs*, 372.

26. The level of understanding between the commanding general and the president is depicted in Hay, *Lincoln and the Civil War in the Diaries and Letters of John Hay*, 178. Grant's opinion on Lincoln's comprehension of his plans is depicted in *Memoirs*, 372–373.

27. Also in a sharp break, Grant openly accepted responsibility for the outcome. Prior to the start of the May 1864 campaigns, Grant wrote the president in thanks for the administration's political support. He also freed Lincoln from worry over the responsibility for the result by ending the letter with the written pledge, "Should my success be less than I desire, and expect, the least I can say is, the fault is not with you." These words must have been very reassuring to a president used to McClellan's complaints and Halleck's evasions. See Grant to Lincoln, May 1, 1864, *The Papers of Ulysses S. Grant*, 10:380.

28. Donald, *Lincoln*, 497.

29. Stanton repeatedly explained to the new commanding general that his powers were extensive enough to make changes in the high command. See Stanton to Grant, May 15, 1864, *The Papers of Ulysses S. Grant*, 10:436; also see OR, series 1, vol. 31, part 2, 781. Stanton reiterated that Grant had new authority to fill command vacancies in a July 24 letter, OR, series 1, vol. 40, part 3, 421.

30. Sherman offered his lengthy list of recommendations for promotion "so as to save the President the invidious task of judging so many worthy men" (Sherman to Halleck, October 24, 1864, OR, series 1, vol. 39, part 3, 412–413).

31. Sherman to Grant, April 2, 1864, and Grant to Adjutant General Lorenzo

Thomas, April 4, 1864, *The Papers of Ulysses S. Grant*, 10:250–251. The actual orders making the command changes are in OR, series 1, vol. 32, part 3, 246–247.

32. Halleck completely supported this effort except for the mention of McClellan, for whom he still bore ill will, and Hunter, who he claimed would be "worse than McClernand in creating difficulties" (OR, series 1, vol. 32, part 3, 322–323). Although Hooker and Burnside were both given corps commands and a role to play in the 1864 campaigns, Buell refused to serve under his "junior" Canby and was not returned to active field duty.

33. Clear evidence of this situation occurred in May 1862 when Lincoln received a petition from twenty-three senators and eighty-four representatives to restore to division command a brigadier who McClellan had relieved. Under this political pressure, the president wrote McClellan that "I wish to do this, and yet I do not wish to be understood as rebuking you." Though the general's reply was clear and quick, stating that "the discipline of the army will not permit the restoration of General Hamilton to his Division," Lincoln satisfied Hamilton's patrons (and McClellan's enemies) by reassigning the brigadier to Banks's command. Both letters between Lincoln and McClellan on May 21 and 22, 1862, are in Lincoln, *Collected Works*, 5:227. Hamilton's reassignment orders from Stanton on May 25 are in OR, series 1, vol. 12, part 1, 630.

34. Halleck had little input into general officer changes after McClellan's demise because of the president's rapid loss of trust in his abilities as commanding general. When Lincoln decided to relieve Burnside after the Mud March, Halleck complained to Major General William Franklin, "He asked no opinion or advice either from the Secretary [of War] or myself." Though Halleck was not happy with this relationship with the president, there was nothing he could do to increase his influence, as he was unwilling to take control of the war effort and demonstrate his expertise by authoring military success. See Halleck to William B. Franklin, May 29, 1863, OR, series 1, vol. 21, 1008–1009.

35. Grant to Halleck, April 22, 1864, *The Papers of Ulysses S. Grant*, 10:340–341.

36. In a characteristic display, Halleck used this reply to again berate Banks's generalship and state the further damage that could result if the amateur was left in command; Halleck to Grant, April 26, 1864, OR, series 1, vol. 34, part 3, 293.

37. Halleck made this characteristic complaint in a November 28, 1862, letter to John M. Schofield concerning "too many political axes to grind" in the Department of Missouri; OR, series 1, vol. 22, part 1, 793–794.

38. Examples of the vicious language Halleck used to describe the amateurs he so despised can be seen in two letters to Grant right before the start of the 1864 summer campaigns. The overly harsh words may have been in reaction to the fact that Halleck could not stop these politicians in uniform, in whom he had no faith, from gaining major roles in Grant's strategy of simultaneous offensives; OR, series 1, vol. 31, part 2, 840–841 (attacks on Sigel and Butler), and vol. 34, part 3, 278–279 (attacks on Banks).

39. In the same letter, Halleck concluded that Butler would pose a problem regardless of where he was sent as long as he held such a high rank; Halleck to Grant, July 3, 1864, OR, series 1, vol. 40, part 2, 598.

40. How this could happen can be seen in Halleck's opposition to Frémont's return to the active ranks in March 1863. When Frémont traveled to the capital seeking to go back to the field, Lincoln, who most likely opposed restoring this political rival and loose cannon to a prominent place in the war effort, avoided granting his request on the

grounds of Halleck's hostility to the idea. After Frémont, upset at his treatment, left the capital on March 17, the *New York Tribune* immediately ran a scathing article blaming Halleck for the failure to return such a popular and promising general to command. See Lincoln to Stanton, March 7, 1863, *Collected Works*, 6:127.

41. Grant was also astute enough to understand that the friction between amateurs such as Butler and his fellow West Pointers was destructive and dangerous. "Whilest I have no diff[i]culty with Gen. Butler, finding him always clear in his conception of orders and prompt to obey," he explained to Halleck after the start of the 1864 campaigns, "yet there is a want of knowledge how to execute, and particularly a prejudice against him, as a commander, that operates against his usefulness." When thinking of amateur generals as a group, Grant would be prone as commanding general to picture effective field commanders like Logan and Blair, adding these generals to stereotypical ex-politicians like Butler and Banks who he had rarely clashed with in person. See Grant to Halleck, July 1, 1864, *The Papers of Ulysses S. Grant*, 11:155–156.

42. Donald, *Lincoln*, 498.

43. For example, as the prospects of the 1864 elections grew closer, Butler's importance to the administration increased because of the threat that the Massachusetts politician would run against Lincoln. This possibility led to the president supporting Butler's military career to keep him in uniform and ensure his loyalty. An example of this support was a memorandum issued after an open question about Lincoln's confidence in Butler as a military general. "Genl Butler has my confidence in his ability and fidelity to the country *and to me*," Lincoln wrote for public notice, "and I wish him sustained in all his efforts in our common cause" (Memorandum Concerning Benjamin F. Butler, February 26, 1864, *Collected Works*, 7:207).

44. This was the reason why former senator and superannuated veteran John Dix was assigned to recruit and enforce the draft in New England, former senator James Cooper became the commander of various POW camps in Ohio, and former chairman of the Republican National Committee and governor of New York Edwin Morgan mustered, armed, and forwarded no less than 223,000 from his home state. See Warner, *Generals in Blue*, 90–91, 125–126, 332–333.

45. General Order No. 80 from the Union adjutant general assigned Sigel to command the Department of West Virginia on February 29, 1864. For the impact of the petitioning for this appointment, see Lincoln to Stanton, January 14, 1864, *Collected Works*, 7:129.

46. Halleck asked Grant to push his recommendations, as "I think you would fully appreciate the importance of doing so, if I were at liberty to tell you who is a candidate for one of those vacancies." Judging by his later correspondence with Sherman, Halleck was most fearful of Butler receiving a regular army commission as a major general; OR, series 1, vol. 31, part 2, 810–811. He may not have known that Grant had already written Secretary Stanton on May 13, asking for the two promotions and stating that he "would be personally gratified" if Sherman and Meade received the promotions; Grant, *The Papers of Ulysses S. Grant*, 10:434.

47. When Grant's reply contained only agreement as to the best candidates, without any plan or ammunition that Halleck could use in his fight, the chief of staff wrote again a week later using even stronger language about the "threat." Advising that there were obstacles to selecting Meade and Sherman for the positions, Halleck wrote: "Perhaps you will be enlightened a little by knowing what are some of the outside influences. I understand the

names of Butler and Sickles have been strongly urged by politicians, in order they say to break down 'West Point influences.' It will not be difficult to draw conclusions. This is *entre nous* [between us]" (Halleck to Grant, May 23, 1864; OR, series 1, vol. 31, part 2, 810–811).

48. This informal command system had first been tried in the fall of 1861 when David Hunter, a West Point graduate and the fourth highest-ranking major general in the Union army, was sent out to assist the struggling John Frémont. Winfield Scott had suggested to Lincoln that many of Frémont's problems stemmed from a lack of experience, arguing that if Hunter were serving by his side "some rash measures might be staved off & good ones accepted by insinuation." Seeing the need for a trained military officer to turn Frémont's vague plans into effective operations, Lincoln personally asked Hunter to go to St. Louis to assist him; Scott to Lincoln, September 5, 1861, OR, series 1, vol. 3, 553. The result in this case was a complete failure, as both Frèmont and Hunter got into trouble for partisan political activities and for failing to sustain effective field operations; see Lincoln to Hunter, September 9, 1861, *Collected Works*, 4:513. After gaining a command of his own in the West, Hunter was eventually relieved for issuing an "Order of Military Emancipation" freeing the slaves in his area. Lincoln quickly repudiated the order, informing the former regular that "no commanding general shall do such a thing upon my responsibility without consulting me" (*Complete Works*, 6:167).

49. Grant was very open about efforts to limit the authority of political generals as seen by his orders to Franz Sigel for the May 1864 campaign in the Shenandoah Valley. The commanding general directed Sigel where to send his units and under which hand-picked regular they should be controlled. In this way, when combat erupted, Grant hoped that either regulars George Crook or E. O. C. Ord would be in direct command; Grant to Sigel, March 29, 1864, *The Papers of Ulysses S. Grant*, 10:236–237.

50. The best recent scholarship on this campaign is William Glenn Robertson, *Back Door to Richmond: The Bermuda Hundred Campaign, April—June 1864* (Baton Rouge: Louisiana State University Press, 1987); Grant's plan for Butler's assault is described on pages 13–24.

51. Butler's account of this meeting is recalled in *Butler's Book*, 627–629.

52. Timed to coincide with the May offensive of the larger Army of the Potomac, Butler's troops would rapidly drive on Richmond before Robert E. Lee or coastal forces from the south could reinforce the capital's defenses. The main physical obstacle would be a fort near Drewry's Bluff just south of Richmond (also called Drury's Bluff). The best recent scholarship on why these plans were not successful is Longacre, *Army of Amateurs*, which dedicates four chapters to Butler's problems and defeats during the 1864 campaign against Richmond and Petersburg.

53. Most historians place much of the blame for Butler's ultimate failure to take Petersburg square on Smith's shoulders for not pressing home the assault ordered on June 15. For example, see Trefousse, *Ben Butler*, 147–155. Butler expressed his view of the campaign in *Butler's Book*, 655–719, which naturally placed all of the blame on the West Pointers, especially "Baldy" Smith. General Smith expressed a far different recounting in his autobiography, in which he severely criticizes Butler and equates his appointment to army command (and his own relief from command) with a criminal act; see William Farrar Smith, *From Chattanooga to Petersburg under Generals Grant and Butler* (Boston: Houghton, Mifflin, 1893), 84–110.

54. OR, series 1, vol. 34, part 2, 593–594. Smith's response to Butler's criticism about

his slow battlefield movements did little to cure the ill will between them, as he became increasingly caustic and overbearing as the campaign progressed. Smith went as far as writing Butler that "you will pardon me for observing that I have some years been engaged in marching troops, and I think in experience of that kind, at least, I am your superior" (Smith to Butler, June 21, 1864, OR, series 1, vol. 40, part 2, 300).

55. Arguing about the merits of entrenching to consolidate gains during the advance on Richmond, Butler and Gillmore exchanged acrimonious messages, with the army commander ordering a continuance of the attack as the troops halted to dig in. This failure to collaborate during the drive on Drewry's Bluff reflected, according to Gillmore's signal officer, "the usual hard feelings natural between a technically instructed officer . . . [and] a civilian political general" (Longacre, *Army of Amateurs*, 91). "Baldy" Smith was much more blunt, writing Grant in June 1864 to ask, "How can you place a man [like Butler] in command of two army corps, who is helpless as a child on the field of battle, and as visionary as an opium eater in council[?]" (Grant, *The Papers of Ulysses S. Grant*, 11:163).

56. Newspapers that had hailed Butler a month before as the soon-to-be conqueror of Richmond now began labeling him as a blunderer who lacked the military skills to command an army in battle. As quickly as May 22, prominent newspapers were already describing him as a leader with "high administrative abilities" who sadly lacked the same ability "for field operations" (*New York Herald*, May 22, 1864, page 2). Questioning Butler's right to be in charge of soldiers' lives, one reporter concluded, "I suppose that nobody will pretend that General Butler was educated a soldier. And it seems tolerably clear that he was not born one" (*New York Times*, May 24, 1864, page 1).

57. "General Butler is a man of rare and great ability, but he has not experience and training to enable him to direct and control movements in battle," the quartermaster general concluded, suggesting that Smith serve as Butler's field commander because "success would be more certain [given the mutual bad blood between commanders] were Smith in command untrammeled, and General Butler remanded to the administrative duties of the department in which he has shown such rare and great ability" (Meigs and Brigadier General J. G. Barnard to Halleck, May 24, 1864, OR, series 1, vol. 36, part 3, 177–178). Butler's view of the commission was expressed in a letter to his wife, dated May 25, 1864, *Private and Official Correspondence*, 3:262–263.

58. Grant to Halleck, July 1, 1864, OR, series 1, vol. 40, part 2, 558–559.

59. To negate Butler's poor generalship, Grant also had all of the field troops in the Army of the James assigned to "Baldy" Smith, along with the order telling Butler to move back to Fort Monroe; Grant to Halleck, July 6, 1864, OR, series 1, vol. 40, part 3, 31.

60. For a full year prior to the 1864 election, Lincoln's political standing was deemed weak enough to attract attention from many would-be candidates, including from within the president's own party. Both Butler's and Banks's names were prominent in many of these discussions, as was Grant's. For an example of these predictions, the secretary of the treasury often judged his own candidacy against that of named rivals; Salmon P. Chase to George Harrington, November 19, 1863, *The Salmon P. Chase Papers*, ed. John Niven (Kent, Ohio: Kent State University Press, 1993–1997), 4:195–196.

61. For Gillmore's fate, see OR, series 1, vol. 36, part 2, 282–292; for Smith's, vol. 40, part 2, 301, 458–460, 489–491.

62. Logan's impressive list of military accomplishments is summarized in a lengthy memorandum labeled "Extracts from official reports and official correspondence in which

mention is made of the distinguished services of the late Major General John A. Logan," *Records of the Office of the Secretary of War, 1800–1942*, RG 107, National Archives.

63. Sherman, *Memoirs*, 2:85; Sherman, *Home Letters*, 303.

64. Sherman, *Memoirs*, 2:86.

65. Grant, *Memoirs*, 487.

66. Sherman, *Memoirs*, 2:86.

67. Logan would take his complaint directly to the president after a monthlong visit to Illinois campaigning for the administration, but he did not base his support on any promotion or assignment, which is perhaps why Grant's support for Howard was upheld by Lincoln. Lincoln may have instinctively known the reason for the visit, as he replied to the request by stating that "if, in view of maintaining your good relations with Gen. Sherman . . . you can safely come here, I shall be very glad to see you" (Lincoln to Logan, November 12, 1864, *Collected Works*, 8:105). As a result of Howard's selection, Logan's spite for West Pointers would continue to slowly grow and develop into an attack on the entire concept of a "privileged class" of officers from the academy. His distaste for Military Academy graduates and his fiery rhetoric concerning their collective sins and faults only increased in intensity after the war; Logan, *The Volunteer Soldier of America*, 583.

68. Donald, *Lincoln*, 552–554.

69. From the president's annual message to Congress, December 6, 1864, *Collected Works*, 8:149.

70. Halleck had been frustrated since Butler had survived an attempt to remove him after the Army of the James failed to take either Richmond or Petersburg and got "bottled up" in the Bermuda Hundred in July 1864. Urged on and supported by Halleck, Ulysses S. Grant had gone so far as ordering Butler relieved of field command, only to recant the order when confronted by the wily politician and the absence of support from the administration. In frustration, Halleck continued to slander Butler at every opportunity, blaming his continued presence on the amateur general's "talent at political intrigue and his facilities for newspaper abuse." In a partial victory for Halleck, Grant ordered Butler to his headquarters at Fort Monroe and had his field troops shifted out from under his direct control; Halleck to Grant, June 1864, OR, series 1, vol. 40, part 2, 598.

71. Grant's version of the events, and his frustration at their unfolding, can be seen in his *Memoirs*, 506–510.

72. Grant to Lincoln, December 28, 1864, *The Papers of Ulysses S. Grant*, 13:177–178. Halleck's reaction to the Fort Fisher fiasco was unabashed glee at Butler's failure, writing his friend Sherman that "thank God, I had nothing to do with it" (OR, series 1, vol. 47, part 2, 3). Butler was more than willing to reciprocate this animosity, as demonstrated in his farewell address to the Army of the James on January 8, 1865. "I have refused to order the useless sacrifice of the lives of such soldiers, and I am relieved from your command," he told his troops, openly slandering Grant and other West Pointers. "The wasted blood of my men does not stain my garments" (OR, series 1, vol. 46, part 2, 71).

73. Seen in a series of letters from Stanton to Grant and Grant to Thomas, often with Halleck acting as a relay, December 7–8, 1864, OR, series 1, vol. 45, part 2, 84–96.

74. Halleck to Grant, December 8, 1864, ibid., 96.

75. Anders, *Henry Halleck's War*, 632–633. Stanton followed up this message with another appeal to the commanding general on December 7. "Thomas seems unwilling to attack because it is hazardous, as if all war was anything but hazardous," he complained

to Grant. "If [Thomas] waits for Wilson to get ready, Gabriel will be blowing his last horn" (Stanton to Grant, December 7, 1864, OR, series 1, vol. 45, part 2, 84).

76. Issued on December 9 by order of Stanton, these orders were never put into effect; OR, series 1, vol. 45, part 2, 114.

77. Grant to Halleck, December 9, 1864, ibid., 116.

78. Grant to Stanton, January 4, 1865, OR, series 1, vol. 46, part 2, 29.

79. When Butler returned to Hampton Roads and heard of the uproar over the expedition's lack of success, the wily amateur again blamed a key subordinate, General Weitzel, for the failure to take the fortress. Describing the apparent strength of the Confederate defense, Butler claimed that the troops were withdrawn from the beachhead solely because of Weitzel's recommendation that it would be folly to assault so strong a fortification. But neither this traditional defense nor any political allies in the cabinet and in Congress could save Butler this time from the taint of yet one more tactical defeat. How much the environment in Washington had changed and how weak his position had become were quickly apparent as, in spite of threats of an inquiry by the Joint Committee on the Conduct of the War, Weitzel remained in command of a corps for the Petersburg and Appomattox Campaigns. Meanwhile, Butler was stuck in Washington arguing to a rapidly diminishing audience about his qualifications to return to the field. Grant's official report about Butler's Fort Fisher along with copies of his orders are in OR, series 1, vol. 36, part 1, 40–45.

80. "You howled when Butler went to New Orleans. Others howled when he was removed from that command," the president replied to a delegation from Kentucky. "Somebody has been howling ever since his assignment to military command. How long will it be before you, who are howling for his assignment to rule Kentucky, will be howling for me to remove him?" Even this retort failed to stop the cries for Butler's return to command. See *New York Tribune*, January 4, 1865, and Lincoln, *Collected Works*, 8:195.

81. Grant to Stanton, February 23, 1865, OR, series 1, vol. 47, part 2, 537.

82. Grant even suggested that Halleck temporarily go himself to the Gulf, as his seniority might have made Banks's replacement more palatable to the politician's supporters. Keeping in character, Halleck refused to go; Halleck to Grant, and Grant's reply, both April 29, 1864, OR, series 1, vol. 34, part 3, 331.

83. Halleck to Grant, April 29, 1864, ibid., 331–332.

84. Banks answered Lincoln on the same day, demonstrating his willingness to do his small part for the war effort. "You are under some misapprehension as to my views of the command assigned to me in New Orleans," he informed Lincoln. "I am not at all dissatisfied. It is my wish on the contrary to do every thing within my power to aid you and your administration, whether or not it comports with my wishes or interest." (Lincoln to Banks, December 2, 1864, *Collected Works*, 8:131).

85. Writing Canby that he would take over as field commander in Louisiana, Halleck did little to help establish any team effort between the two commanders in the Gulf. Grant had no confidence in Banks's military capacity, Halleck warned Canby, and Banks's record of scattering his troops and focusing on civilian projects had ruined the promising military fortunes in the Department of the Gulf. In this poisoned atmosphere, Banks continued to work on reconstruction projects, doing valuable work for the administration, while keeping his quarrels with Canby as local affairs. See Halleck to Canby, May 7, 1864, OR, series 1, vol. 34, part 3, 491–492.

86. Banks's relief order was published as General Order No. 95, May 17, 1865, OR, series 1, vol. 48, part 2, 475.

87. Consolidated abstract of returns from the U.S. Army for December 31, 1864, OR, series 3, vol. 4, 1034.

88. By the spring of 1865, Grant's control of the military aspect of the war effort would therefore become nearly total because the administration's trust in him reached an unprecedented pinnacle of confidence based on the perception that he was winning the war. Stanton ensured that Grant understood this change by telling him explicitly, "There is no occasion to expect the President will make any order against your wishes" (Stanton to Grant, February 25, 1865, OR, series 1, vol. 47, part 2, 562).

89. As a means of additional praise, Grant also told Senator Wilson of Massachusetts that "neither of these officers are aware that a word is being said in their favor and I know them well enough to assert that they would not ask the intervention of any one even if they knew, without it, they would be defeated in their confirmation" (letter, February 8, 1864, The Papers of Ulysses S. Grant, 10:35–37).

Chapter 8. Expanding the Study of Generalship

1. Welles, Diary of Gideon Welles, 2:282.

2. Emory Upton, The Military Policy of the United States (Washington, D.C.: Government Printing Office, 1917), xiii.

3. Cox, Military Reminiscences, 179–191.

4. Logan, The Volunteer Soldier of America.

5. One of the keys to McClernand's success in influencing Lincoln and the public in the fall of 1862 was the tremendous popular outcry against West Pointers, specifically McClellan and Buell. For an example, see the Chicago Tribune, November 10, 1862, page 2, and December 27, 1862, page 2.

6. William T. Sherman to John Sherman, September 21, 1865, The Sherman Letters, 256.

7. This brief reply was to a lengthy letter from Schofield outlining in detail the complex political problems he faced in North Carolina; Grant to Schofield, May 18, 1865, The Papers of Ulysses S. Grant, 15:64–65.

8. Halleck thought all reconstruction efforts should be controlled by the Union military high command because he felt that "the advice of politicians generally on this question [of Reconstruction] I regard as utterly worthless—mere Utopian theories" (Sherman to Halleck, October 1, 1863, OR, series 1, vol. 52, part 1, 717–718).

9. Sherman to Halleck, April 16, 1864, OR, series 1, vol. 32, part 3, 375–376.

10. Grant to Banks, March 15, 1864, The Papers of Ulysses S. Grant, 10:200–201.

11. Sickles's ability not only to gain a Reconstruction command but also to gain a regular army commission as a major general speaks volumes about his political skills and President Andrew Johnson's willingness to use political factors in determining his key commanders. For the story of Sickles's second military career during Reconstruction, see James E. Sefton, The United States Army and Reconstruction, 1865–1877 (Baton Rouge: Louisiana State University Press, 1967), 117–188, and Swanberg, Sickles the Incredible, 275–293.

12. Stanton to President Johnson, June 3, 1865, Andrew Johnson Papers (entry 4164), Library of Congress. The selection of Reconstruction commanders is covered in Sefton, *The United States Army and Reconstruction*, 16–24, 255–259.

13. Chase to Butler, May 2, 1865, Butler, *Private and Official Correspondence*, 5: 610–611.

14. This outcome is examined in William S. McFeely, *Yankee Stepfather: General O. O. Howard and the Freedmen* (New Haven: Yale University Press, 1968), 10–19, 57–63.

15. Allan R. Millett, *Military Professionalism and Officership in America* (Columbus: The Mershon Center, Ohio State University, 1977), 11–13.

16. Higginson, *Atlantic Monthly* 14 (September 1864): 348.

17. Jack C. Lane, *Armed Progressive: General Leonard Wood* (San Rafael, Calif.: Presidio Press, 1978), 49, 178–179.

18. Social forces played an enormous role in this drive for professionalism among many occupations. Progressivism and its emphasis on rationality and professional expertise encouraged the adoption of a promotion system based on merit rather than seniority, the development of effective staff operations, and the support for a continuing system of officer education, while the preparedness movement inspired enough support to ensure that the military was ready for the trials of World War I; ibid., 94.

19. Huntington's trinity of expertise, social responsibility, and corporateness provide the terms for the discussion and a good starting point for any debate on military professionalism; see *The Soldier and the State*, 8–18.

20. Millett concludes, "The Civil War killed some six hundred thousand American amateurs and the concept of amateurism" (*Military Professionalism and Officership in America*, 17–18).

21. Clausewitz, *On War*, 88–89.

22. From a proclamation Logan issued to his division, February 12, 1863, Logan Papers, Library of Congress.

23. That these ambitious and often patriotic politicians were justified to seek military service during the Civil War to further their careers there can be little doubt; from the inauguration of Ulysses Grant to the end of William McKinley's administration in 1900, every president except Grover Cleveland had been a former Union army officer in the Civil War.

24. The definitions for war and warfare are paraphrased from *Webster's New Ideal Dictionary*, 3d ed., 1978, 605–606.

25. Donald, *Lincoln*, 429.

26. After the debacle at Petersburg, even General Grant was inspired to write, "General Butler certainly gave his very earnest support to the war; and he gave his own best efforts personally to the suppression of the rebellion." Grant prefaced this comment on Butler with what might have been an offhand apology to all the volunteer officers who were relieved after he took over as commanding general in the spring of 1864: "I make this statement here because, although I have often made it before, it has never been in my power until now to place it where it will correct history; and I desire to rectify all injustice that I may have done to individuals, particularly to officers who were gallantly serving their country during the trying period of the war for the preservation of the Union" (*Memoirs*, 377).

27. Clausewitz, *On War*, 87–88.

WORKS CITED

Manuscript Collections

Library of Congress, Washington, D.C.

Nathaniel P. Banks Papers
Benjamin F. Butler Papers
Simon Cameron Papers
Andrew Johnson Papers, 55 volumes (microfilm)
Daniel R. Larned Papers
Robert Todd Lincoln Collection of the Papers of Abraham Lincoln, 194 volumes
   (microfilm)
John A. Logan Papers
George B. McClellan Papers
William T. Sherman Papers

National Archives, Washington, D.C.

Record Group 94: Special Civil War Collection, "Generals' Papers and Books"
Record Group 107: Records of the Office of the Secretary of War, 1800–1942
Record Group 108: Records of the Commanding Generals of the Army
Record Group 393: Records of the Headquarters of the Army

U.S. Army Military History Institute, Carlisle Barracks, Pennsylvania

George L. Andrews Papers
William T. Sherman Papers

U.S. Military Academy, West Point, New York

Henry Wager Halleck Papers
William T. Sherman Papers and Manuscripts (microfilm)
William T. Sherman Family Papers (microfilm)

University of Arkansas, Fayetteville, Arkansas

Ulysses S. Grant Papers

Yale University, New Haven, Connecticut

John Alexander Logan Correspondence

Rhode Island Historical Society, Providence, Rhode Island

Ambrose Burnside Papers

American Antiquarian Society, Worcester, Massachusetts

Nathaniel P. Banks Papers
Benjamin F. Butler Papers

Newspapers and Periodicals

Army and Navy Chronicle
Atlantic Monthly (Boston)
Boston Evening Transcript
Boston Post
Chicago Times
Chicago Tribune
Harper's Weekly (New York)
New York Daily Tribune
New York Herald
New York Times
New York Tribune
New York Weekly Tribune
Vanity Fair (New York)

Theses, Dissertations, and Unpublished Papers

Griess, Thomas Everett. "Dennis Hart Mahan: West Point Professor and Advocate of Military Professionalism." Ph.D. diss., Duke University, 1968.

Hicken, Victor. "From Vandalia to Vicksburg: The Political and Military Career of John A. McClernand." Ph.D. diss., University of Illinois, 1955.

Morrison, James Lunsford. "The United States Military Academy, 1833–1866: Years of Progress and Turmoil." Ph.D. diss., Columbia University, 1970.

Morton, Julia J. "Trusting to Luck: Ambrose E. Burnside and the American Civil War." Ph.D. diss., Kent State University, 1993.

Patrick, LaVone. "A Comparative Study of Methods for Raising Volunteers during the Civil War." Ph.D. diss., University of Wisconsin, 1930.

Schmiel, Eugene D. "The Career of Jacob Dolson Cox, 1828–1900: Soldier, Scholar, Statesman." Ph.D. diss., Ohio State University, 1969.

Watson, Samuel J. "Professionalism, Social Attitudes, and Civil-Military Accountability in the United States Army Officer Corps, 1815–1846." Ph.D. diss., Rice University, 1996.

Winders, Richard B. "Mr. Polk's Army: Politics, Patronage, and the American Military in the Mexican War." Ph.D. diss., Texas Christian University, 1994.

Published Sources

Alger, John I. *The Quest for Victory: The History of the Principles of War.* Westport, Conn.: Greenwood Press, 1982.

Ambrose, Stephen E. *Halleck: Lincoln's Chief of Staff.* Baton Rouge: Louisiana State University Press, 1990.

Anders, Curt. *Henry Halleck's War: A Fresh Look at Lincoln's Controversial General-in-Chief.* Carmel, Ind.: Guild Press of Indiana, 1999.

Bassett, J. S., ed. *Correspondence of Andrew Jackson.* 7 vols. Washington, D.C.: Carnegie Institution, 1926–1935.

Battles and Leaders of the Civil War. 5 vols. New York: Thomas Yoseloff, 1956.

Beringer, Richard E., Herman Hattaway, Archer Jones, and William N. Still Jr. *Why the South Lost the Civil War.* Athens: University of Georgia Press, 1986.

Bland, T. A. *Life of Benjamin F. Butler.* Boston: Lee and Shepard, 1879.

Buell, Thomas. *The Warrior Generals: Combat Leadership in the Civil War.* New York: Random House, 1998.

Burnside, Ambrose. "The Burnside Expedition." *Personal Narratives of the Events of the War of the Rebellion.* 2d series. Providence, R.I.: N. B. Williams, 1882.

Butler, Benjamin F. *Butler's Book.* Boston: A. M. Thayer, 1892.

———. *Character and Results of the War: How to Prosecute It and How to End It—A Thrilling and Eloquent Speech.* New York: W. C. Bryant, 1863.

———. *The Military Profession of the United States and the Means of Promoting Its Usefulness and Honor.* New York: Samuel Colman, 1839.

———. *Private and Official Correspondence of General Benjamin F. Butler during the Period of the Civil War.* 5 vols. Norwood, Mass.: Plimpton Press, 1917.

Carmen, Harry J., and Reinhard Luthin. *Lincoln and the Patronage*. New York: Columbia University Press, 1943.

Catton, Bruce. *America Goes to War*. Middletown, Conn.: Wesleyan University Press, 1958.

———. *Mr. Lincoln's Army*. Garden City, N.Y.: Doubleday, 1962.

Chase, Salmon P. *The Salmon P. Chase Papers*. 4 vols. Edited by John Niven. Kent, Ohio: Kent State University Press, 1993–1997.

Clausewitz, Carl von. *On War*. Edited by Michael Howard and Peter Paret. Princeton, N.J.: Princeton University Press, 1976.

Cook, Benjamin F. *History of the Twelfth Massachusetts Volunteers*. Boston: Twelfth Regimental Association, 1882.

Cox, Jacob D. *Military Reminiscences of the Civil War*. New York: Charles Scribner's Sons, 1900.

Craig, Gordon A. *The Politics of the Prussian Army, 1640–1945*. New York: Oxford University Press, 1956.

Cress, Lawrence. *Citizens in Arms: The Army and the Militia in American Society to the War of 1812*. Chapel Hill: University of North Carolina Press, 1982.

Cunliffe, Marcus. *Soldiers and Civilians: The Martial Spirit in America, 1775–1865*. Boston: Little, Brown, 1968.

Davis, Jefferson. *The Papers of Jefferson Davis*. Vol. 7, *1861*, edited by Lynda Crist and Mary Dix. Baton Rouge: Louisiana State University Press, 1992.

Dawson, Joseph G. *Army Generals and Reconstruction: Louisiana, 1862–1877*. Baton Rouge: Louisiana State University Press, 1982.

Demeter, Karl. *The German Officer-Corps in Society and State, 1650–1945*. New York: Frederick A. Praeger, 1965.

Donald, David H. *Liberty and Union*. Boston: Little, Brown, 1978.

———. *Lincoln*. London: Random House, 1995.

Engle, Stephen D. *Yankee Dutchman: The Life of Franz Sigel*. Fayetteville: University of Arkansas Press, 1993.

Gallagher, Gary W., ed. *The Fredericksburg Campaign: Decision on the Rappahannock*. Chapel Hill: University of North Carolina Press, 1995.

Gat, Azar. *The Development of Military Thought: The Nineteenth Century*. Oxford: Clarendon Press, 1992.

Grant, Ulysses S. *The Papers of Ulysses S. Grant*. Edited by John Y. Simon. 15 vols. Carbondale: Southern Illinois University Press, 1982.

———. *Personal Memoirs of Ulysses S. Grant*. New York: Da Capo Press, 1982.

Griffith, Paddy. *Military Thought in the French Army, 1815–51*. Manchester, England: Manchester University Press, 1989.

Grimsley, Mark. *The Hard Hand of War: Union Military Policy toward Southern Civilians, 1861–1865*. Cambridge: Cambridge University Press, 1995.

Halleck, Henry Wager. *Elements of Military Art and Science*. New York: D. Appleton, 1846.

———. *The Mexican War in Baja California: The Memorandum of Captain Henry W. Halleck*. Edited by Doyce B. Nunis. Los Angeles: Dawson's Book Shop, 1977.

Harrington, Fred H. *Fighting Politician: Major General N. P. Banks*. Philadelphia: University of Pennsylvania Press, 1948.

Harris, William C. *With Charity for All: Lincoln and the Restoration of the Union.* Louisville: University Press of Kentucky, 1997.

Hattaway, Herman, and Archer Jones. *How the North Won: A Military History of the Civil War.* Champaign: University of Illinois Press, 1991.

Hay, John. *Inside Lincoln's White House: The Complete Civil War Diary of John Hay.* Edited by Michael Burlington and John R. Turner Ettlinger. Carbondale: Southern Illinois University Press, 1997.

———. *Lincoln and the Civil War in the Diaries and Letters of John Hay.* Edited by Tyler Dennett. New York: Dodd, Mead, 1939.

Heitman, Francis B. *Historical Register and Dictionary of the United States Army from Its Organization, September 29, 1789, to March 2, 1903.* 2 vols. Washington, D.C.: Government Printing Office, 1903.

Hesseltine, William B. *Lincoln and the War Governors.* Gloucester, Mass.: Peter Smith Publishing, 1972.

Hicken, Victor. *Illinois in the Civil War.* Champaign: University of Illinois Press, 1966.

Hickey, Donald R. *The War of 1812: A Short History.* Champaign: University of Illinois Press, 1995.

Hirshson, Stanley P. *The White Tecumseh: A Biography of General William T. Sherman.* New York: John Wiley and Sons, 1997.

Hollandsworth, James G., Jr. *Pretense of Glory: The Life of General Nathaniel P. Banks.* Baton Rouge: Louisiana State University Press, 1998.

Holt, Michael F. *Political Parties and American Political Development: From the Age of Jackson to the Age of Lincoln.* Baton Rouge: Louisiana State University Press, 1992.

Holzman, Robert S. *Stormy Ben Butler.* New York: Macmillan, 1954.

Howard, R. L. *History of the 124th Regiment Illinois Infantry Volunteers.* Springfield, Ill.: H. W. Rokker, 1880.

Hughes, Nathaniel C., Jr. *The Battle of Belmont: Grant Strikes South.* Chapel Hill: University of North Carolina Press, 1991.

Hunt, Lynn. *Politics, Culture, and Class in the French Revolution.* Berkeley: University of California Press, 1984.

Huntington, Samuel P. *The Soldier and the State: The Theory and Politics of Civil-Military Relations.* Cambridge: Harvard University Press, 1957.

Jomini, Henri. *The Art of War.* Westport, Conn.: Greenwood Press, 1862.

Jones, Archer. *Civil War Command and Strategy: The Process of Victory and Defeat.* New York: Free Press, 1992.

Jones, James Pickett. *Black Jack: John A. Logan and Southern Illinois in the Civil War Era.* Carbondale: Southern Illinois University Press, 1995.

Jones, R. Steven. *The Right Hand of Command: Use and Disuse of Personal Staffs in the Civil War.* Mechanicsburg, Pa.: Stackpole Books, 2000.

Kiper, Richard L. *Major General John Alexander McClernand: Politician in Uniform.* Kent, Ohio: Kent State University Press, 1999.

Kreidberg, Marvin A., and Merton G. Henry. *History of Military Mobilization in the United States Army, 1775–1945.* Pamphlet no. 20-212. Washington, D.C.: Department of the Army, 1955.

Lane, Jack C. *Armed Progressive: General Leonard Wood.* San Rafael, Calif.: Presidio Press, 1978.

Lincoln, Abraham. *Abraham Lincoln: His Speeches and Writings.* Edited by Roy P. Basler. New York: World Publishing, 1946.

———. *The Collected Works of Abraham Lincoln.* Edited by Roy P. Basler. 8 vols. New Brunswick, N.J.: Rutgers University Press, 1953.

———. *Complete Works of Abraham Lincoln.* Edited by John G. Nicolay and John Hay. 10 vols. New York: Francis D. Tandy, 1905.

Livermore, Thomas L. *Numbers and Losses in the Civil War in America, 1861–1865.* Boston: Houghton, Mifflin, 1901.

Logan, John A. *Letters of Loyal Soldiers: How Douglas Democrats Will Vote.* New York: Loyal Publication Society, 1864.

———. *Speech of Major-General John A. Logan on Return to Illinois after the Capture of Vicksburg.* Cincinnati: Cabel Clark, 1863.

———. *The Volunteer Soldier of America.* New York: R. S. Peale, 1887.

Longacre, Edward G. *Army of Amateurs: General Benjamin F. Butler and the Army of the James, 1863–1865.* Mechanicsburg, Pa.: Stackpole Books, 1997.

Mahan, Dennis Hart. *An Elementary Treatise on Advanced-Guard, Outpost, and Detachment Service of Troops, With the Essential Principles of Strategy and Grand Tactics.* New York: John Wiley and Son, 1870.

Marszalek, John F. *Sherman: A Soldier's Passion for Order.* New York: Free Press, 1993.

Marvel, William. *Burnside.* Chapel Hill: University of North Carolina Press, 1991.

McClellan, George B. *The Civil War Papers of George B. McClellan: Selected Correspondence, 1860–1865.* Edited by Stephen W. Sears. New York: Ticknor and Friends, 1989.

———. *McClellan's Own Story.* New York: Charles L. Webster, 1887.

McClure, A. K. *Abraham Lincoln and the Men of War-Times: Some Personal Recollections of War and Politics during the Lincoln Administration.* Philadelphia: Times Publishing, 1892.

McCrary, Peyton. *Abraham Lincoln and Reconstruction: The Louisiana Experiment.* Princeton, N.J.: Princeton University Press, 1978.

McDonough, James L. *Shiloh—In Hell before Night.* Knoxville: University of Tennessee Press, 1997.

McFeely, William S. *Yankee Stepfather: General O. O. Howard and the Freedmen.* New Haven: Yale University Press, 1968.

McPherson, James M. *Battle Cry of Freedom: The Civil War Era.* New York: Ballantine Books, 1988.

———. *Ordeal by Fire: The Civil War and Reconstruction.* New York: Alfred A. Knopf, 1982.

Meneely, A. Howard. *The War Department, 1861: A Study in Mobilization and Administration.* New York: Columbia University Press, 1928.

Millett, Allan R. *Military Professionalism and Officership in America.* Columbus: The Mershon Center, Ohio State University, 1977.

Morris, W. S., L. D. Hartwell, and J. B. Kuykendall. *History of the 31st Regiment Illinois Volunteers: Organized by John A. Logan.* Carbondale: Southern Illinois University Press, 1902.

Morrison, James L., Jr. *"The Best School in the World": West Point, the Pre–Civil War Years, 1833–1866.* Kent, Ohio: Kent State University Press, 1986.

Moten, Matthew. *The Delafield Commission and the American Military Profession.* College Station: Texas A&M University Press, 2000.

Murray, Thomas H. *History of the Ninth Regiment, Connecticut Volunteer Infantry.* New Haven, Conn.: Price, Lee, and Adkins, 1903.

Nicolay, John G., and John Hay. *Abraham Lincoln: A History.* 10 vols. New York: Century, 1886.

Paludan, Philip. *A People's Contest: The Union and the Civil War.* New York: Harper and Row, 1988.

Parton, James. *General Butler in New Orleans.* Boston: Ticknor and Fields, 1866.

Pierpont, Francis H. *Letter of Governor Pierpont to His Excellency the President of the United States on the Subject of Abuse of Military Power in the Command of General Butler in Virginia and North Carolina.* Washington, D.C.: McGill and Witherow, 1864.

Polk, James K. *The Diary of James K. Polk during his Presidency, 1845 to 1849.* Edited by Milo M. Quaife. 4 vols. Chicago: A. C. McClurg, 1910.

Poore, Ben Perley. *The Life and Public Service of Ambrose E. Burnside: Soldier–Citizen–Statesman.* Providence, R.I.: J. A. and R. A. Reid, 1882.

Rable, George C. *The Confederate Republic: A Revolution against Politics.* Chapel Hill: University of North Carolina Press, 1995.

The Rebellion Record: A Diary of American Events. Edited by Frank Moore. 11 vols. New York: G. P. Putnam, 1861–1865.

Robertson, William Glenn. *Back Door to Richmond: The Bermuda Hundred Campaign, April–June 1864.* Baton Rouge: Louisiana State University Press, 1987.

Rowland, Thomas J. *George B. McClellan and Civil War History: In the Shadow of Grant and Sherman.* Kent, Ohio: Kent State University Press, 1998.

Schofield, John M. *Forty-Six Years in the Army.* New York: Century, 1897.

Schurz, Carl. *Speeches, Correspondences, and Political Papers of Carl Schurz.* Edited by F. Bancroft. 2 vols. Philadelphia: Lippincott, 1865.

Schutz, Wallace J., and Walter Trenerry. *Abandoned by Lincoln: A Military Biography of General John Pope.* Champaign: University of Illinois Press, 1990.

Sears, Stephen W. *George B. McClellan: The Young Napoleon.* New York: Ticknor and Fields, 1988.

Sefton, James E. *The United States Army and Reconstruction, 1865–1877.* Baton Rouge: Louisiana State University Press, 1967.

Shannon, Fred Albert. *The Organization and Administration of the Union Army, 1861–1865.* Gloucester, Mass.: Peter Smith Publishing, 1965.

Sherman, William T. *Home Letters of General Sherman.* Edited by M. A. DeWolfe Howe. New York: Scribner's, 1909.

———. *Memoirs of General William T. Sherman.* 2 vols. New York: Da Capo Press, 1984.

———. *Sherman's Civil War: Selected Correspondence of William T. Sherman, 1860–1865.* Edited by Brook D. Simpson and Jean V. Berlin. Chapel Hill: University of North Carolina Press, 1999.

———. *The Sherman Letters: Correspondence between General and Senator Sherman from 1837 to 1891.* Edited by Rachel Sherman Thorndike. New York: Scribner's, 1894.

Shy, John. *A People Numerous and Armed: Reflections on the Military Struggle for American Independence.* Ann Arbor: University of Michigan Press, 1990.

Silbey, Joel H. *A Respectable Minority.* New York: W. W. Norton, 1977.

Simpson, Brooks D. *Ulysses S. Grant: Triumph over Adversity, 1822–1865.* New York: Houghton Mifflin, 2000.

Skelton, William B. *An American Profession of Arms: The Army Officer Corps, 1775–1861*. Lawrence: University Press of Kansas, 1992.

Smith, William E. *The Francis Preston Blair Family in Politics*. 2 vols. New York: Macmillan, 1922.

Smith, William Farrar. *From Chattanooga to Petersburg under Generals Grant and Butler*. Boston: Houghton, Mifflin, 1893.

Stackpole, Edward J. *Drama on the Rappahannock: The Fredericksburg Campaign*. Harrisburg, Pa.: Military Service Publishing, 1957.

Strother, David H. *A Virginia Yankee in the Civil War: The Diary of David Hunter Strother*. Edited by Cecil Eby Jr. Chapel Hill: University of North Carolina Press, 1961.

Swanberg, W. A. *Sickles the Incredible*. New York: Charles Scribner's Sons, 1956.

Tap, Bruce. *Over Lincoln's Shoulder: The Committee on the Conduct of the War*. Lawrence: University Press of Kansas, 1998.

Terrell, W. H. *Indiana in the War of the Rebellion: Report of the Adjutant General*. Bloomington: Indiana Historical Bureau, 1960.

Thomas, Benjamin P., and Harold Hyman. *Stanton: The Life and Times of Lincoln's Secretary of War*. New York: Alfred A. Knopf, 1962.

Trefousse, Hans L. *Ben Butler: The South Called Him Beast*. New York: Twayne, 1957.

———. *The Radical Republicans*. New York: Alfred A. Knopf, 1969.

The Trial of Hon. Clement L. Vallandigham by a Military Commission. Cincinnati: Rickey and Carroll, 1863.

Upton, Emory. *The Military Policy of the United States*. Washington, D.C.: Government Printing Office, 1917.

U.S. Congress. *Report of the Joint Committee on the Conduct of the War*. 3 vols. 37th Congress, 3d session. Senate Report 108. Washington, D.C.: Government Printing Office, 1865.

Wallace, Lew. *Lew Wallace: An Autobiography*. 2 vols. New York: Harper and Brothers, 1906.

Warner, Ezra J. *Generals in Blue*. Baton Rouge: Louisiana State University Press, 1964.

War of the Rebellion: A Compilation of the Official Records of the Union and Confederate Armies. 128 vols. Washington, D.C.: Government Printing Office, 1880–1901.

Watson, Harry L. *Liberty and Power: The Politics of Jacksonian America*. New York: Hill and Wang, 1990.

Weigley, Russell F. *The American Way of War: A History of the United States Military Strategy and Policy*. Bloomington: Indiana University Press, 1977.

———. *History of the United States Army*. New York: Macmillan, 1967.

———. *Quartermaster General of the Union Army: A Biography of Montgomery C. Meigs*. New York: Alfred A. Knopf, 1969.

Welles, Gideon. *Diary of Gideon Welles: Secretary of the Navy under Lincoln and Johnson*. Edited by Howard K. Beale. 3 vols. New York: Norton, 1960.

West, Richard S. *Lincoln's Scapegoat General: A Life of Benjamin F. Butler, 1818–1893*. Boston: Houghton Mifflin, 1965.

Wiley, Bell Irvin. *The Life of Billy Yank: The Common Soldier of the Union*. Baton Rouge: Louisiana State University Press, 1952.

Williams, Kenneth P. *Lincoln Finds a General: A Military Study of the Civil War*. 5 vols. Bloomington: Indiana University Press, 1949–1959.

Williams, T. Harry. "The Attack upon West Point during the Civil War." *Mississippi Valley Historical Review* 25 (March 1939): 491–504.

———. *Lincoln and His Generals*. New York: Random House, 1952.

———. *McClellan, Sherman, and Grant*. Chicago: Elephant Paperbacks, 1991.

———. "Military Leadership of North and South." In *Why the North Won the Civil War*, edited by David H. Donald, 33–54. New York: Collier Books, 1960.

———. *The Selected Essays of T. Harry Williams*. Baton Rouge: Louisiana State University Press, 1983.

Wilson, James G. "Types and Traditions of the Old Army II: General Halleck—A Memoir." *Journal of the Military Service Institution of the United States* 36 (1905): 537–558; 37 (1905): 333–356.

Winders, Richard B. *Mr. Polk's Army: The American Military Experience in the Mexican War*. College Station: Texas A&M University Press, 1997.

Wood, W. J. *Civil War Generalship: The Art of Command*. Westport, Conn.: Praeger, 1997.

Woodbury, Augustus. *A Narrative of the Campaign of the First Rhode Island in the Spring and Summer of 1861*. Providence, R.I.: Sidney S. Rider, 1862.

Wright, Marcus J. *Memorandum Relative to the General Officers in the Armies of the United States during the Civil War, 1861–1865*. Washington, D.C.: War Department, 1906.

INDEX

283